# BLOODFEUD IN SCOTLAND

'You have heard that it was said, "Love your neighbour and hate your enemy." But I tell you, Love your enemies and pray for those who persecute you, that you may be sons of your Father in heaven.'

(Mathew 5, v43, N.I.V.)

# BLOODFEUD IN SCOTLAND
## 1573–1625

Violence, Justice and Politics
in an Early Modern Society

### KEITH M BROWN
Glenfiddich Fellow
at the University of St Andrews

JOHN DONALD PUBLISHERS LTD
EDINBURGH

ISBN 0 85976 134 7

Exclusive distribution in the United States of America and Canada by Humanities Press Inc., Atlantic Highlands, NJ 07716, USA.

Phototypeset by Quorn Selective Repro, Loughborough.
Printed in Great Britain by Bell & Bain Ltd., Glasgow.

# Acknowledgements

All the research and writing of this book was made possible by the financial assistance of the Carnegie Trust and of Messrs. William Grant and Sons, patrons of the Glenfiddich Fellowship, for which I am grateful. I received a great deal of help in the way of advice and suggestions from Professor Geoffrey Parker, Professor John Bossy, Dr. Alan Smith, Dr. Norman Macdougall, and Dr. Roger Mason who each read all or part of the typescript of this book, or the thesis which preceded it. To all of them I am greatly indebted, especially to Roger who also proof-read the entire text. That debt is an even deeper one in the case of Dr. Jenny Wormald who has given generous and unqualified help since I first began my research in 1979. For practical assistance I am also grateful to Professor Archie Duncan and Professor Chris Smout. Thank you too to Mrs Mary Manchester for her useful co-operation in the former, and much missed, Baillie's Library in Glasgow. There are, of course, many others, family, friends, members of staff and fellow researchers, who are unnamed here, but who have all helped in one way or another. Thanks to you all. Finally, a special thanks to my parents who never ceased to encourage, and to my wife Janice whose timely Henry Ford-like jibes at history kept all in perspective.

# Contents

# List of Abbreviations

| | |
|---|---|
| A.P.S. | The Acts of the Parliaments of Scotland |
| Balfour, 'Annales' | Balfour, Sir James, 'Annales of Scotland' |
| Basilikon Doron | McIlwaine, C. H. (ed.), The Political Works of James I |
| Birrel, 'Diary' | Birrel, Robert, 'The Diary of Robert Birrel' |
| B.U.K. | The Booke of the Universall Kirk of Scotland |
| Bruce, Sermons | Sermons by the Rev. Robert Bruce |
| Brunton, Senators | Brunton, G., An Historical Account of the Senators of the College of Justice from its Institution in MDXXXII |
| Calderwood, History | Calderwood, D., The History of the Kirk of Scotland |
| C.B.P. | Calendar of Letters and Papers relating to the Affairs of the Borders of England and Scotland |
| C.S.P., Scot. | Calendar of the State Papers relating to Scotland and Mary, Queen of Scots, 1547–1603 |
| C.S.P., Span. | Calendar of Letters and State Papers, Spanish, Elizabeth |
| Chambers, Domestic Annals | Chambers, R., Domestic Annals of Scotland |
| Estimate | Estimate of the Scottish Nobility During the Minority of James the Sixth |
| Fowler, Works | The Works of William Fowler |
| Fraser, Annandale | Fraser, W., The Annandale Family Book of the Johnstones |
| Fraser, Colquhoun | Fraser, W., The Chiefs of Colquhoun and their Country |
| Fraser, Douglas | Fraser, W., The Douglas Book : Memoirs of the House of Douglas and Angus |
| Fraser, Eglinton | Fraser, W., Memorials of the Montgomeries Earls of Eglinton |
| Fraser, Elphinstone | Fraser, W., The Elphinstone Family Book |
| Fraser, Grant | Fraser, W., The Chiefs of Grant |
| Fraser, Pollok | Fraser, W., Memoirs of the Maxwells of Pollok |
| Gordon, Sutherland | Gordon, Sir Robert, A Genealogical History of the Earldom of Sutherland |
| H.M.C. | Report of the Royal Commission on Historical Manuscripts |
| H.M.C., Various | Report of the Historical Manuscripts Commission, Various Collections |
| H.M.C., Mar and Kellie | Report of the Historical Manuscripts Commission on the Earls of Mar and Kellie |
| H.M.C., Laing | Report of the Historical Manuscripts Commission on the Laing Manuscripts preserved in Edinburgh University |
| Historie | The Historie and Life of King James the Sext |
| Hume, History | Hume, D., A General History of Scotland from the year 767 to the Death of King James |
| Hume, Poems | The Poems of Alexander Hume |
| Leslie, Historie | Leslie, J., The Historie of Scotland |
| Maitland Quarto | The Maitland Quarto Manuscript |
| Melrose | State Papers and Miscellaneous Correspondence of Thomas, Earl of Melrose |

| | |
|---|---|
| Melville, *Diary* | Melville, J., *Autobiography and Diary* |
| Melville, *Memoirs* | Melville, Sir James of Halhill, *Memoirs of His Own Life, 1549–93* |
| Montgomerie, *Poems* | *The Poems of Alexander Montgomerie* |
| Moysie, *Memoirs* | Moysie, D., *Memoirs of the Affairs of Scotland from 1577 to 1603* |
| Napier, *A Plaine Discovery* | Napier, J., *A Plaine Discovery of the Whole Revelation* |
| Pitcairn, *Criminal Trials* | *Criminal Trials in Scotland from 1488 to 1624*, (ed.) R. Pitcairn |
| Pitcairn, *Kennedy* | *Historical Account of the Principal Families of the Name of Kennedy*, (ed.) R. Pitcairn |
| *Reg. Mag. Sig.* | *Registrum Magni Sigilii Regum Scotorum* |
| *R.P.C.* | *The Register of the Privy Council of Scotland* |
| *Reg. Sec. Sig.* | *Registrum Secreti Sigilli Regum Scotorum* |
| Rollok, *Works* | Rollok, R., *Select Works* |
| *Scots Peerage* | Balfour Paul, Sir James, *The Scots Peerage* |
| *S.H.R.* | *The Scottish Historical Review* |
| S.H.S. | The Scottish History Society |
| S.R.O., G.D. | Scottish Record Office, General Deposit |
| S.R.O., R.D. | Scottish Record Office, Register of Deeds |
| *Spalding Miscellany* | *Miscellany of the Spalding Club* |
| Spottiswoode, *History* | Spottiswoode, John, *History of the Church of Scotland* |
| Stewart, *Poems* | *Poems of Sir John Stewart of Baldynneis* |
| Waus, *Correspondence* | *Correspondence of Sir Patrick Waus* |

# Introduction

In that famous book on kingcraft, *Basilikon Doron,* James VI wrote of his subjects:

> and for anie displeasure, that they apprehend to be done unto them by their neighbours, [they] tak up a plaine feid against him, and (without respect to God, King or commonweale) bang it out bravely, hee and all his kinne, against him and all his.[1]

Feud was a subject on which James considered himself to be something of an expert, and his expert definition is as good a place as any to begin an analysis of the Scottish feud during his reign. Today the word 'feud' is liberally used to describe rivalries in sport, in politics, in academic competition, and in any area of human activity where confrontation can be identified. Such a wide application is not only a modern phenomenon; in the sixteenth century one also finds it in unexpected contexts. Yet it was not just a heightened sense of rivalry James had in mind when he wrote his book in 1599, but a relationship which had deeper and more complex implications than any of our modern usages of the word. As to what it did mean, the king remained uncertain, in spite of all his linguistic skills. He excused himself by writing that 'if this Treatise were written in French or Latin, I could not get them named unto you but by circomlocution' because 'their barbarous name is unknawen in anie other nation'.[2] However, only a few years before, an Elizabethan border official had suggested of the etymology of the word that 'I knowe not where better to fetch then from Spiegelius in his *Lexicon, Juris, in verbo* 'feydam': he saith it is an old Teutch word whereof is derived by Hermanus Nironanus, *faydosum, Hostis publicus*: 'foed' *enim, Bellum significat*'.[3] 'Feud', therefore, has an etymological history of some antiquity, there being variants of the spelling in late Latin 'faida', old French 'faide', old High German 'fechida', Middle English 'fede', and a number of Scottish spellings, one of which provides us with its modern English spelling.[4]

That feud, or bloodfeud, was written about in Scotland when it was still a contemporary issue is of enormous importance. Scotland is not unique in this, but the late survival of the feud there has ensured that it is better documented than in many other European societies where it disappeared at an earlier stage in the development of literacy.[5] Partly because of this, and because it has never been a very fashionable topic, the bloodfeud has been subject to more research from anthropologists than historians, and consequently more is known about feuding among the tribes of twentieth-century Sudan than about feuding in pre-modern Europe. Of course for the historian there is a value in such work which ought not to be overlooked, and it was Max Gluckman who, when writing about the feud, advised historians to turn to the social sciences in order to better understand the historical European feud.[6] A great deal of current thinking about feud has been shaped by the conclusion of E. E. Evans-Pritchard and Gluckman about its place

1

in the society of the Nuer people of southern Sudan.[7] Perhaps the most influential view has been what Gluckman called the 'Peace in the feud'. In essence what Gluckman and Evans-Pritchard have said is that feud is a legal sanction, recognised as such by the community, and is thus a means of enforcing justice and minimising any violence which might follow the committing of a crime, particularly a violent crime. Customary principles defining who has the right to vengeance, and on whom it should be inflicted, clearly recognised procedures for pacifying the parties involved, and the multiplicity of relationships within the community inhabited by these parties all operate in such a way as to generate pressures for peace and not war. This is not to say that violence never occurs, and as Evans-Pritchard argued, 'The larger the segment involved the greater anarchy that prevails'.[8] Thus violent feuds between tribes are more likely than feuds within a tribe. Furthermore, even within fairly intimate corporate groups the acceptance of compensation, and agreement on a settlement, does not guarantee an enduring peace since the dead man's kin never cease 'to have war in their hearts'.[9] In practice, however, peace within the feud is established and, according to Gluckman, custom triumphs over conflict.

Gluckman's challenge to historians has been a useful catalyst, but in spite of efforts to accommodate his model to specific historical periods, his sanitised bloodfeud sits uncomfortably amidst our perceptions of the past. One obvious explanation for this is that Nuer society at the time when Evans-Pritchard investigated it was not the same as Jacobean Scotland. Nor was it the same as the Balkans and North Africa in the mid-twentieth century, research on which has produced a variety of interpretations of bloodfeud.[10] Jacob Black-Michaud is less dismissive of the violence of the feud, and while recognising the place of peace amidst it, he believes that 'each episode of violence in feud and raiding perpetuates the relationship through time'. Thus, feuds are interminable, and 'by definition eternal'.[11] Yet in contrast to this James VI claimed that 'the matter of feadis is not eternal',[12] and he went out of his way to prove the point. Here one is encountering the kind of problem which plagues the building of universal models, or the construction of a typology for bloodfeuds which will satisfy everyone. E. L. Peters' definition of feud as a relationship between corporate groups who are unable to compromise is vague enough to fulfil that need, but it is also fairly meaningless, and when he fills it in with a list of indices appropriate enough to the bedouin of Cyrenaica, he immediately puts it beyond general use. The bedouin are no more useful than the Nuer in model building. For the feud to exist, he writes, economic conditions of 'total scarcity', must prevail, as should an egalitarian social structure in which leaders spontaneously emerge.[13] That may be true for Nuer society, but neither of these conditions is relevant to an understanding of why feud was found in early modern Scotland. This is not to argue that there is no value in comparative evidence. Both the Balkan and North African examples of feud show characteristics which have parallels in the Scottish evidence. Similarly, the Jibaro and Yanomamo tribes of South America and the Tausug of the Philippines may be separated from sixteenth-century Scotland by an even greater cultural gap, but there too one can find some common ground.[14] In a quite different social context the American experience of bloodfeud has been in two forms: that of the nineteenth-century settlers in Kentucky and other southern states which probably has its roots in Scottish and Irish immigrants, and the urban vendettas of the twentieth century which are associated with the Mafia.[15] Outside the Mafia and its various Italian manifestations, feud has survived in a number of forms, both in more remote and primitive societies, and in the politics of states like the Lebanon. Edmund Leach has even suggested that there is a significant similarity between feuding and modern terrorism, a phenomenon which is often associated with what are still, or were relatively recently, feuding societies, such as in the Middle East, North Africa and Northern Ireland.[16]

While evidence drawn from such diverse cultures is useful, especially in helping to conceptualise feud, the Scottish example was very much the product of a shared European experience which has to be viewed historically. Feud was not introduced into Europe by the barbarians who ended the Western Roman Empire, having had an important place in ancient Greece until it was largely outlawed and undermined by the classical city states.[17] Even then the politics of late Republican Rome were deeply influenced by family feuds, and it is doubtful just how far Roman justice displaced the bloodfeud in many of the territories embraced within the empire.[18] The removal of Rome's authority did not mean a complete loss of Roman law, and medieval society evolved a system of justice which mixed law, Christian beliefs, tribal culture, and the chivalric code of the warrior. Within this the bloodfeud survived or flourished in varying degrees, but in one form or another it has a place of enormous importance in the history of medieval Europe.[19] Yet while the idea of Europe as a feudal society, or a chivalrous society, is common and widely accepted, in spite of the different emphasis which one finds throughout the continent, there has been little willingness to see Europe as a feuding society, and feuds largely appear as an obstruction to the development of institutions. That may only reflect historians' interest in other questions, or perhaps differentiation took place too early and too sharply for it to be a useful concept. Certainly in Britain that may have been the case, but even in England, where the feud went into decline relatively early, aspects of it survived into the early modern period.[20] The history of the European bloodfeud remains to be written, but while Scotland may arguably be a peripheral and atypical example of sixteenth-century society, one suspects it was less so than has often been imagined. What the Scottish evidence has to say about feud should have a relevance to the wider European community to which Scots belonged, and will, one hopes, reveal a little about the nature of bloodfeud in general in that community, and about the changes which brought about its suppression.

Almost any attempt to quantify from Scottish records of this period immediately confronts a whole range of often insurmountable problems. In the case of feuds these are compounded by the lack of clarity in defining what one is looking for in the first place. To James VI feuding meant 'to bang it out bravely'. To a Tudor border official 'Deadly foed' was 'the word of enmitye in the Borders, implacable without the blood and whole family distroied'.[21] John Leslie, the former bishop of Ross, wrote that those with a 'deidlie fade, ... persekuted and persuet the hail stok and familie ... sa this deidlie faid was nevir put in the buke of oblivione'.[22] The Spanish diplomat, Don Alvaro de Mendoza, commented on 'mortal feud' in Scotland when men 'entertain terrible bands and refuse all quarter to each other'.[23] The privy council itself wrote of

> the deidlie feidis and contraverseis standing amangis his Hienes subjectis of all degreis, and thairwithall calling to mynd quhat unnaturall slauchtaris, bludeshed, barbarous cruelteis and inconvenientis hes occurrit and is liklie to occur and fall oute, to the forder trouble and inquietatioun ... gif the same feidis sall not be removit.[24]

Yet a modern historian of the feud has also written that

> Bloodfeud is a misleading word. The point of course, was not that the feud was bloody, but that the escalation of bloodfeud was halted by settlement and compensation.[25]

This may be an overstatement, but feud was not simply about violence, and feuds were not necessarily violent, which makes a definition, and, therefore, identification virtually impossible. In 1598 parliament declared that 'all feidis ar ane of thir thrie natures namelie that thair is ather na slauchter upoun nather syde or slauchter upoun ane syde onlie or ells slauchter upoun bath sydis'.[26] Feuding, therefore, included a whole range of relationships of conflict, from bloody genocide to simply avoiding social contact or taking up aggressive postures.

Such a wide-ranging definition creates great difficulties in identifying feuds. However, one can begin to quantify by collecting cases in which primary sources describe a relationship as one of feud. This occurs, to date, in 137 cases. In all of these feud is used by an official or private contemporary source at least once, and often more than once. Analysis of these reveals a great variety of conflicts and confrontations from regional wars which lasted for years to ill feeling between individuals who were quickly pacified, thus confirming the 1598 parliament's interpretation of feud. Obviously contemporaries might have been wrong in particular instances, but the general principle of accepting contemporary perceptions as the basis for identification seems to be the most useful one. These records, however, tend to discriminate in favour of the long and more violent feuds between great noblemen and their families, while most of the cases receive no more than a passing comment in the records. Thus in 1584 the privy council ordered William Burnett to find caution for 'sic deidlie feidis as he hes interesse in',[27] but about which one can find no further evidence. Certain regions and families are also better documented than others due to their accessibility to the crown, or to the particular interests of the author of a narrative source. Given this relatively random survival of evidence, one has to assume that there were many more feuds than those which have left written evidence, while others may survive in contemporary documents, but may not actually be called feuds by the authors. However, from the 137 cases one does have, some sort of picture can be put together of what a feud was like, and one can then use this as a norm against which other possible feuds can be measured. Thus there are a further seventy-nine cases in which the participants in a dispute acted in much the same way as in the above in their use of violence, their language, and in the observance of ritual behaviour.[28] A second category can be identified by the way in which the participants and any interested outsiders tried to bring peace to the dispute in the form of mediation, arbitration, mutual assurances or acts of caution, and these account for a further sixty-two cases.[29] With both these groups one either knows how the feud was conducted, or how it was settled, but never both, which makes analysis of other features of feuding very difficult, as there are so many unknowns. Where both can be observed, a third category can be established, and of these there are eighty-seven cases. In all 228 feuds have been identified to add to the 137 which contemporary accounts name, and with a total of 365 one has what is probably a minimum figure for the amount of feuding in Scotland between 1573 and 1625, with most of it being concentrated in the period before 1610.

Measuring the incidence of feuding is fraught with other problems. Given the high reliance on crown records, especially the privy council, one may in fact be measuring government interest rather than real levels (see graph on p. 276). This is certainly the case from the mid-1590s when the crown does begin to make the pacification of feuds a major policy in its efforts to reduce private violence. The earlier period, particularly the 1570s, appears artificially low given that a civil war had just ended in 1573, that royal power had been in decline for three decades since James V's death in 1542, that the kingdom was in the midst of religious upheaval, and that the socio-economic context was also highly unstable, especially for the landed community. Certainly the roots of the bloodfeud were deeply planted in Scottish society, but the especially stressful conditions of the mid and late sixteenth century do appear to have intensified the amount of violent feuding. During the civil war when larger issues came to the fore, private feuds were often indistinguishable from the main conflict,[30] hence Alexander Hay's observation in 1573 that there were then only a few minor feuds in the whole of Scotland.[31] However, Henry Killigrew's expectations were that 'This peace has renewed certain old private debates'.[32] In other words he was guessing, rightly, that as the issues of the war retreated from the centre of political life, private feuding would re-assume its prominence. At the same time the continuing instability in politics and religion, and the unfavourable economic context all increased the likelihood of a rise in feuding. That instability was to some extent held in check by the Regent Morton's political dominance until 1578, although Morton's style of government, and his attitude to the localities where he exercised only very superficial control, both ensured that the underlying instability was not dealt with. This does not mean that the level of feuding was a simple reflection of government effectiveness. The intense factionalism which characterised politics after 1578 certainly exacerbated feuding at the court, and made the connection between court feuds and local ones more pronounced, but the vast majority of feuds were local, and were only very indirectly affected by government. The increased feuding of the period was caused by a number of complex and interwoven factors, but the general political instability provides the most useful context in which to understand it. Faced with crisis on almost every level, the feuding society found that its own checks and balances were insufficient to maintain peace, and feuding escalated to the point of becoming uncontrollable. At its high point there were at least fifty feuds going on simultaneously in any one year from around the mid-1580s to the first decade of the seventeenth century. However, because of the inbuilt distortion in the evidence it seems more reasonable that the peak began earlier, towards the end of the 1570s, and remained high for twenty years, after which many of the feuds which continued were latent until their pacification. The entire question of the upwards and downwards trend must, however, be approached fairly tentatively, while estimates of the real volume of feuding are impossible to arrive at satisfactorily.

In working out the duration of feuds one finds that the nature of the sources, the relatively short time under examination, and the particular circumstances at the end of the period are all unhelpful (see Table 1 on page 277). Many feuds are only ever mentioned once. Does one conclude that the feud only lasted for a year or less, or that the rest of it was never documented? Almost all those feuds identified by the processing of peace fall into this category. Other feuds may receive a mention in the sources, and then appear fifteen years later. Has the feud lasted throughout that period, or is this a new feud between the same families? The assumption here — and it is a fairly arbitrary one — is that if the instances are more than ten years apart, then they are not the same feud unless internal evidence can prove they were. By beginning this analysis in 1573 one is also discriminating against long feuds which may have their origins in a period before the war. Where possible that has been taken into account, but one has to start somewhere, and to keep chasing feuds back through time would require that a quite different book be written. Future research on the feud in medieval Scotland may force reinterpretation of this, but it can be fairly confidently said that the feuds between the Lindsays and the Lyons in the 1370s, the Lindsays and the Ogilvies in the 1440s, and the Cunninghams and the Montgomeries in the 1520s were not directly linked by an unbroken chain of events with the feuds among these families in the later sixteenth century. The last of these is dealt with in detail in a later chapter, and in that case there is a fifty-year peace between the feud in the 1520s and what occurs in north Ayrshire in this period. The participants in such feuds may have liked to connect such events in their minds, but it was more probable that families living next to one another were likely to find a new issue to quarrel over which gives the appearance of long feuds. Finally, this period saw a concerted attack on feuding by the crown at a time when its ideological foundation was being undermined by the Renaissance and the Reformation, and this brought many feuds to a premature end. Thus the very short length of most feuds discovered in this period is probably inaccurate, but only thirty can be shown to have lasted for longer than twenty years, and many more than this are known to have been settled fairly quickly. Again one will need to work in a longer time span to be more authoritative about the duration of feuds, but one can at least be sceptical of Leslie's observation that 'Gret families they feid, and that perpetuallie'.[33]

Expectations of the geographic spread of feuding would probably rate the highland and border regions as much worse than elsewhere. However, when the geographic distribution of feuding is analysed, the picture appears to be much more even (see Table 2 on page 277). Once again the documentation is better for lowland and border regions than for the highlands, and one simply does not believe the relatively low level of feuding discovered in the highlands. Basic arithmetic like this also fails to show a qualitative picture, so that a feud between two Fife lairds which lasted three years and in which the most serious injury was a bodily assault is equated with the long, wide-ranging and highly destructive feud between the MacDonald and MacLean clans. Lowland regions also had more independent lairds who conducted their own feuds, while in the highlands noblemen and clan chiefs were more dominant. Consequently there may have been more feuds in the lowlands, but they were likely to be less violent, and to involve fewer people than highland feuds. Yet whatever qualifications one employs cannot detract from the basic point these figures make, which is that feuding was a Scottish experience, and not one which was a product of highland tribalism, or border lawlessness. Lowland society inhabited the same social and mental environment as these other regions, and the feud was understood throughout the kingdom. For that reason the highlands and borders have not been treated independently, and while some specific distinctions are pointed out, the general approach has been to interpret the feud in a context which is Scottish rather than regional. Some regions or localities may have been more or less prone to feuding than others, but the lowland localities of Ayrshire, Angus and Aberdeenshire were riven with feuds, and were more like border Annandale or highland Argyll than the more peaceful Lothian-Fife crescent. In fact a noticeable divergence of attitudes to the bloodfeud by highland and lowland societies did not take place until the mid-seventeenth century.

The locality was the physical environment within which most feuds were conducted, and it was in the locality that most feuds began (see Table 3 on page 277).[34] A very small number of feuds acquired a relevance beyond their immediate localities, and were of regional importance. Among these one would include the Maxwell-Johnstone feud in the south-west, the MacDonald-MacLean feud in the western isles, and the Caithness-Sutherland feud in the far north. Furthermore, because of the relationships which bound court and country together the majority of feuds were at some time or another of interest to politicians at the court. There local issues were grafted onto larger power struggles, affecting the distribution of patronage, the alignment of faction, and the measurement of power. However, a smaller percentage of feuds, less than ten per cent, had a direct bearing on the course of court politics, either originating there, or involving principals who were court figures. These feuds were among the most important in the kingdom, shaping the conduct of politics, and defining many of the issues. Among these were the feuds between Chancellor Maitland and the earl of Bothwell, Treasurer Glamis and the earl of Crawford, the Regent Morton and Captain James Stewart, and of course the great feud between the earl of Huntly and his many enemies. Feud also found its way into burghs. One finds burghs feuding with rural neighbours, being fought over by them, having feuds brought into their streets by the visiting landed classes, and feuding within the burgh communities themselves. Again there is not a large number of these, or at least not many have been identified, but they do underline the presence of feuding throughout Scottish society. Lastly, while most feuds were corporate affairs, some were personal, being conducted by individuals. Many of these appear to be closer to duels, or other forms of personal dispute, and it is doubtful if they ought to be classified as feuds at all. However, contemporary documents do, and on that basis they have been included. Most feuds were local, rural and corporate, but these refinements ought to be borne in mind.

In the medieval and early modern periods the bloodfeud has most commonly been associated with an unruly nobility. Peers and their followers account for many of the feuds of this period, especially the more important ones, but not the majority (see Table 4 on page 278). Less than fifty feuds were between peers, and only a third involved peers at all, a figure which probably represents a maximum since this status group is the most easily identified. At the other end of the social scale are a small percentage of feuds in which at least one party was below the status of a laird or a burgess. However, here one is dealing with the least identifiable cases, and one expects that their numbers are disproportionately small. It is among a class of men who are composed of more than one status layer, the barons, clan chiefs, and lairds, that one finds most feuding. More than half of the feuding took place within this group, and that proportion increases when one includes their feuds with the peerage, and with their social inferiors. This does not make them the most prone to feuding — obviously there were more of them — but it ought to dispel any idea that they disapproved of aristocratic violence and the feud. Together with the peerage they made up the landed elite, and it was that elite which made most use of the feud. As for those who actually participated in it, the social base was much wider, including servants and tenants who usually acted under orders, but who were also capable of showing an enthusiasm for their lord's feuds which outstripped those orders. To what extent a feud mentality was shared by those members of the lower class is virtually impossible to say, and one can only suggest that it seems likely they would have identified with the vertical power structure of which they were a part. Responsibility for conducting feuds, however, lay largely in the hands of the men who controlled those structures.

If a clear definition of feud is still not really possible, can one at least describe a typical feud? One might suggest that it involved a neighbouring nobleman and laird, that it had little direct significance outside their locality, and that it lasted for around five to ten years. That, however, would only be the external outline of a feud. For its substance one has to look more at the social and ideological environment which generated its violence, at the obstacles and routes to peace, at the issues which sparked it into life, and at the political role it had to play both in local communities and in government and the court. One has, in other words, to look at the fabric and the values of the feuding society.

NOTES

1. *Basilikon Doron*, in *The Political Works of James I*, (ed.) C. H. McIlwain, New York, 1965, p. 24.

2. *Ibid.,* p. 25.

3. *Calendar of Letters and Papers Relating to the Affairs of the Borders of England and Scotland,* (ed.) J. Bain, Edinburgh, 1894–96, ii, p. 163.

4. See *A New English Dictionary,* (ed.) J. A. H. Murray, London, 1901, for more details.

5. An excellent survey of the sources available for the Scottish feud throughout the middle ages and early modern period can be found in J. M. Wormald, 'Bloodfeud, Kindred and Government in Early Modern Scotland', in *Past and Present,* No. 87, May, 1980.

6. For Gluckman's essay, see M. Gluckman, 'The Peace in the Feud', in *Custom and Conflict in Africa,* Oxford, 1982. For a discussion of the usefulness of such an approach, see I. M. Lewis (ed.), *History and Social Anthropology,* A.S.A. Monographs, London, 1968; E. E. Evans-Pritchard, *Anthropology and History,* Manchester, 1971; K. Thomas, 'History and Anthropology', in *Past and Present,* 24, 1963, pp. 3–24; and the articles and comments by B. S. Cohen, J. W. Adams, C. Ginzburg and N. Z. Davis, in 'Anthropology and History in the 1980s', in *Journal of Interdisciplinary History,* xii: 2, Autumn 1981, pp. 227–275.

7. Gluckman, 'The Peace in the Feud'; and E. E. Evans-Pritchard, *The Nuer,* Oxford, 1979.

8. Evans-Pritchard, *The Nuer,* p. 157.

9. *Ibid.,* p. 154.

10. J. Black-Michaud, *Cohesive Force; Feud in the Mediterranean and the Middle East,* Oxford, 1975, is the best general discussion of the feud in these regions. For Albania, see M. Hasluck, *The Unwritten Law in Albania,* Cambridge, 1954, and I. Whitaker, 'Tribal Structure and National Politics in Albania, 1910-1950', in Lewis (ed.), *History and Social Anthropology.* For Greece, see J. K. Campbell, *Honour, Family and Patronage: A Study of Institutions and Moral Values in a Greek Mountain Community,* Oxford, 1979. Also on the Middle East is M. J. L. Hardy, *Blood Feuds and the Payment of Blood Money in the Middle East,* Leiden, 1963, and E. L. Peters, 'Some structural aspects of feud among the camel-herding Bedouin of Cyrenaica', in *Africa,* xxxvii, No. 3, 1967.

11. Black-Michaud, *Cohesive Force,* pp. 16 and 29–30.

12. *The Register of the Privy Council of Scotland,* (ed.) J. H. Burton and others, Edinburgh, 1877–98, xiii, p. 261.

13. E. L. Peters, 'Foreword', in Black-Michaud, *Cohesive Force.*

14. R. Karsten, 'Blood, Revenge and War among the Jibaro Indians', in P. Bohannan (ed.), *Law and Warfare,* New York, 1967; N. A. Chagnon, 'Yanomamo: The Fierce People', in J. P. Spradley and D. W. McCurdy (eds.), *Conformity and Conflict,* Boston, 1980; T. M. Kieffer, *The Tausug: Violence and Law in a Philippine Moslem Society,* New York, 1972.

15. Though somewhat basic, B. C. Caudill, *Pioneers of Eastern Kentucky, their Feuds and Settlements,* Cincinnati, 1969, is useful. For the American Mafia there is an extensive literature which ranges from the scholarly and critical to the anecdotal and sensational.

16. E. Leach, *Custom, Law and Terrorist Violence,* Edinburgh, 1977.

17. H. G. Treston, *Poine: A Study in Ancient Greek Blood-Vengeance,* London, 1923.

18. It is R. Syme, *The Roman Revolution,* Oxford, 1974, p. 157, who makes this point about the Republic.

19. The best survey is unquestionably B. S. Philpotts, *Kindred and Clan in the Middle Ages and After,* Cambridge, 1974, which is mostly medieval, but contains some early modern material, particularly on Denmark, Schleswig-Holstein and parts of north Germany. Also J. M. Wallace-Hadrill, 'The Bloodfeud of the Franks', in *The Long-Haired Kings and Other Studies in Frankish History,* Oxford, 1971, and F. R. H. Du Boulay, 'Law Enforcement in

Medieval Germany', in *History,* 63, 1978, pp. 343–355. For some useful and entertaining narratives *Njal's Saga,* Penguin, 1980 is most revealing; also *Eigil's Saga,* Penguin, 1980; *Beowulf,* Penguin, 1979; and *The Nibelungenlied,* Penguin, 1979.

20. For Scotland, Wormald, 'Bloodfeud, Kindred and Government in Early Modern Scotland'. For Wales, R. R. Davies, 'The Survival of the Bloodfeud in Medieval Wales', in *History,* liv, 1969, and R. R. Davies, 'The Law of the March', in *Welsh Historical Review,* 5, 1970–71, pp. 1–30. In England the feud survived in some localities, like parts of Northumberland, but some aspects associated with it did endure into late Tudor England on a wider scale; see R. Broude, 'Revenge and Revenge Tragedy in Renaissance England', *Renaissance Quarterly,* 28, 1975, pp. 38–58.

21. *C.B.P.,* ii, p. 163.

22. J. Leslie, *The Historie of Scotland,* (ed.) E. J. Cody, Scottish Text Society, Edinburgh, 1884–95, i, pp. 92–93.

23. *Calendar of Letters and State Papers, Spanish, Elizabeth,* (ed.) M. A. S. Hume, London, 1892–99, iii, p. 95.

24. *R.P.C.,* v, p. 248.

25. J. M. Brown, 'The Exercise of Power', in J. M. Brown (ed.), *Scottish Society in the Fifteenth Century,* London, 1977, p. 62. See also 'Bloodfeud, Kindred and Government in Early Modern Scotland', p. 55.

26. *Acts of the Parliaments of Scotland,* (ed.) T. Thomson and C. Innes, Edinburgh, 1814–75, iv, p. 158.

27. *R.P.C.,* iv, p. 704.

28. See Chapter 1 below.

29. See Chapter 2 below.

30. See G. Donaldson, *All the Queen's Men, Power and Politics in Mary Stewart's Scotland,* London, 1983, where the relationship between the major issues of the civil war and those narrower interests of individual lords and their kindreds is discussed.

31. *Calendar of State Papers relating to Scotland and Mary Queen of Scots,* (ed.) J. Bain and others, Edinburgh, 1898–1967, iv, p. 610.

32. *Ibid.,* p. 564.

33. Leslie, *Historie,* i, p. 103.

34. See Chapter 3 below.

*Part One: A Feuding Society*

# 1

# *The Roots of Violence*

An increasing recognition of the fact that violence is a very sophisticated tool, and a critical discussion about violence in the pre-modern period, have made it much less easy to talk about medieval or early modern Europe as violent societies. Lawrence Stone has largely reinforced existing ideas about the all-pervading and casual presence of violence in early modern England where 'tempers were short and weapons to hand'.[1] J. R. Hale has also highlighted the temperamental aspect of violence, and described how contemporaries understood the medical, psychological and sociological roots of the problem. His consensus explanation was one in which 'imagination sensed a potential injury to self-respect or self-interest, the blood began to heat up in the heart and when some of this heated blood ascended to the brain violent behaviour followed unless the individual was on his guard'.[2] In contrast to this, Keith Wrightson, Alan Macfarlane and Jim Sharpe have all argued with varying degrees of intensity for a more refined view of the problem in which violence is less prevalent. Thus Wrightson thinks that violence in England 'was to a considerable degree constrained by law', and like Macfarlane is fairly dismissive of casual or common violence.[3] Sharpe is less so, but does draw attention to the low numbers of homicides and executions in a society in which both are traditionally assumed to have been high.[4] More recently Stone has returned to the debate with further evidence that early modern England was five times more violent than contemporary England is, while others, like Louis Knafla, have shown that the traditional picture, though modified, has by no means been exploded.[5] The question of violence is clearly not a simple one, and it has to be handled with greater sensitivity than has often been the case when discussing Scotland's violent record.

There was certainly little doubt among contemporaries that late sixteenth-century Scotland was a violent place. In 1582 the privy council announced that

> his Majesties peciable gude subectis ower all his realme hes bene troublit havelie with bludescheid, stowth, reiff, masterfull oppressionis, convocationis and utheris enormiteis, to thair great hurt and skaith, without redres or puneisment of the offendouris.[6]

Is this an accurate assessment of a real problem, or the panic response of an insecure government whose outlook was anything but objective? Such sentiments were repeated elsewhere at different times, until the first decade of the seventeenth century when they alter to descriptions of an earlier anarchy which is contrasted favourably with the new peace and stability the king had brought to Scotland. Much of this was clearly myth-making in practice and with intent. This was propaganda designed to persuade men that the crown, and in particular the king himself, was doing a good job. The former king's advocate, Lord Binning, was eloquent on this subject when trying to squeeze money out of the 1617 convention of the nobility to pay for the king's visit:

> I schaw that the blessingis of justice and peace and fruttis arysing thairof, did so obleis euerie one of us, as no thing in owre power could equall it, desyring that it might be remembered, that whairas the Islander oppressed the Hielandmen, the Hielander tirrannised ouer thair Lowland nighbours; the powerfull and violent in the in-cuntrie domineered ouer the lyues and goodes of thair weak nighbours; the bordouraris triumphed in the impunitie of thair violences to the pairtis of Edinburgh; that treasons, murthours, burningis, thriftis, reiffis, hearschippis, hocking of oxin, distroyeing of growand cornis, and barbaraties of all sortis, wer exerced in all pairtis of the cuntrie, no place nor person being exemed or inviolable, Edinburgh being the ordinarie place of butcherlie revenge and daylie fightis; the paroche churches and churche-yairdis being more frequented upon the Sonday for advancement of nighbourlie malice and mischeif, nor for God's service; nobilmen, barronis, gentilmen, and people of all sortis, being slaughtered, as it wer, in publict and uncontrollable hostilities; merchandes robbed, and left for dead on day light, going on thair mercats and faires of Montrois, Wigton and Berwick; ministers being dirked in Stirling, buried quick in Cliddisdaill, and murthoured in Galloway; merchandis of Edinburgh being waited in their passage to Leith to be maid prisoners and ransoumed, and all uther abominations which setled be inveterat custame and impunitie appeired to be of desperat remeid, had bene so repressed, puniessed, and aboleissed be your maistes wisdome, caire, power, and expensis, as no nation on earth could now compaire with our prosperities; whairby we wer band to retribute to your maiestie, if it wer the verie half of oure hairt bloud.[7]

Flattery and propaganda this may have been, but was it all just a product of Binning's imagination? Historians living close to the times they narrated shared these attitudes whether they were men who had done well from crown service, like Archbishop Spottiswoode who wrote of 'bloods and slaughters daily falling out in every place',[8] or men who had been more critical of the crown, like David Calderwood who also wrote of 'muche blood shed, and manie horrible murthers committed'.[9] Of course, the church had itself been directly involved in the attack on feud and other forms of violence, and such attitudes could perhaps be expected from ministers, but why then was there such criticism from the likes of Robert Bruce and Robert Rollock in the first place?[10] English observers also expressed shock at the bloody environment in which they found themselves,[11] but if this was little more than typical English smugness about foreigners, the Scots' bloody reputation had spread as far as Spain.[12]

Examples of casual violence are certainly easy to find. The Edinburgh diarist, Robert Birrel, conveys this in his almost incidental references to events like 'Robert Cathcart slaine pisching at the wall in Peiblis wynd heid be William Stewart, sone to Sir William Stewart'.[13] Yet a source like this is obviously suspect if one's intention is to measure violence in Scottish society. A more objective picture might be forthcoming were one to adopt a quantitative approach, but as Bruce Lenman and Geoffrey Parker have pointed out, criminal statistics do not guarantee clarity and often obscure what one wants to know.[14] Certainly any quantification of criminal violence in Jacobean Scotland would encounter almost insurmountable difficulties in the nature of the sources, and in the working of criminal justice which left so much business in local courts and in private hands.[15] Whether or not the apparent rise in feuding between the 1570s and 1590s was accompanied by a rise in criminal violence cannot be answered here, and is probably unanswerable. The very substantial rise in acts of caution registered with the privy council from around 20 per annum in the 1570s to 100 by 1588, and over 300 three years later might just as easily be an indicator of confidence in the crown's ability to control violence as it is a measure of its prevalence.[16] Nor was the privy council overwhelmed with complaints from people who had suffered violent attacks. There were 20 of these in 1580, 17 in 1585, 23 in 1590, 21 in 1595, 56 in 1600 and 42 in 1605.[17] Once again the rising trend may reflect control rather than any breakdown in law and order, and this looks especially likely as the increase takes place after 1600. Whatever the trend was, the actual numbers were fairly low, and the violence itself was fairly low-key. Most of it concerned spuilyie, house-breaking, intimidation, and assault, and none of the cases reported in 1595 involved slaughter.[18] This does not, of course, mean that there was little criminal violence. The point is simply that one has to have reservations about the extent of criminal violence until more work has been specifically carried out on it. One would also need to know a great deal more about the level of state and domestic violence before one could say with any degree of authority that Scottish society was especially violent. The violence of the feud was only one form of violent behaviour, and to say that Scotland experienced a great deal of it does not necessarily imply that these other forms of violence were equally common. The fact that feuding to some extent depended on a decentralised state, strong family bonds and powerful lordship may even have reduced state, domestic and criminal violence. The very particular violence of the feud should not, therefore, be the only yardstick by which one measures violence in Scotland at this time, and its explanations are not in themselves sufficient evidence of a violent society with casual attitudes to that violence.

Debate about the effective authority of Scottish kings is likely to remain unresolved for some time, but it is perhaps less controversial to argue that the control exercised by the crown over Scottish society was minimal. Power in the Scottish state lay mostly in the localities and in the hands of the nobility who dominated those localities. The idea that the crown was constantly being overawed by the nobility has to some extent been displaced by a scenario in which strong kings held sway over a largely cooperative nobility.[19] The greater understanding one now has of the role of the nobility in enforcing justice[20] has also made it much less convincing to argue that the roots of what was wrong with criminal justice in Scotland lay in the nobility's 'basic contempt for law'.[21] Were that true, then anarchy would have prevailed since the entire policing, and most of the judicial system, would have been on the side of the criminals, and clearly that was not the case. Yet at the same time the enormous power of private men in relation to the crown cannot be discounted when looking for the socio-political context of private violence. Whatever fifteenth-century kings may have been, the Stewart monarchy had fallen a long way since 1542. When a crown official submitted a report on the Brig O' Dee rebellion in 1589, he commented that the barons of the north-east were so dependent on the earl of Huntly that they 'hes forget their dewtie to thair naturale Prince'.[22] Men throughout Scotland could be forgiven that, for it had been decades since the prince had exerted effective rule over them. A courtier blamed 'the sleuth and cairlesnes of princes', and the 'unrewlyness and sturdynes of the subiectis'. Melville also drew attention to 'the great rentes of the nobilitie and ther gret nomber', with their

> many gret cumbersom clannes sa reddy to concur togither, and to rebell for the defence of any of ther name, or to avenge the just execusion of some of them, for mowther, thift, or sic uther crymes.[23]

The English treasurer, Lord Burghley, came to the conclusion from the reports he received that 'the nobellitie ther ar not acqueynted with absolut government of ther King but rather ar them selves in a sort absolut'.[24] That is both an exaggeration and a misunderstanding of royal power in Scotland, but one can appreciate how it would have appeared to an outsider. The nobility did appear to be 'too hard for the prince', their followers did appear to lack 'regard of the prince, law or equity',[25] and there was no doubt that whole regions, like much of the highlands, 'care not much for the King, and obey him at their pleasure'.[26] While the Stewart dynasty may never have been threatened by the nobility — and why should they when it interfered so little in their lives? — the Scottish crown was unable to exert the kind of power it might often have wanted to. A nobility with great power in the localities, and 'linked and bound to one another by kindred and alliance',[27] may not have been a threat to the crown, but it could significantly curb its authority, and the enforcement of royal justice. The very fact that this was a feuding society also made it difficult to reverse the balance, since as James VI found in 1589, his supporters would only go so far, being 'afraid of a feud hereafter if they touch any great man'.[28] Feuds, however, also divided the great men, and that was the point at which the crown might attain control through manipulation. There was, therefore, some justification in Melville of Halhill's doubts about a political system which was 'mair nor a monarque', but 'les than electywe'.[29] The idea of the monarchy may have been very strong in Scotland, thus guaranteeing its political role, but its institutions were weak, and its oversight of justice was very superficial.

Scottish kinship, however, was not weak. Early modern kinship has been subjected to a great deal of critical analysis, especially in England where the nuclear family appears to have been well established by the end of the sixteenth century.[30] However, even in England there is no unanimity on that, and there were certainly regional variations,[31] while in France there has also been criticism of too early a dismissal of the kindred by largely Parisian historians.[32] In Scotland there is less need for such debate, at least about the families of the landed elite and their dependants, but in explaining Scottish kinship Jenny Wormald makes the cautionary point that 'The "whole kindred" was something of a myth',[33] and that ought to be borne in mind. Yet that kinship was still remarkably powerful. Sir Robert Gordon wrote of the feud between the MacDonald and MacLean clans:

'This warr, whilk fell furth at this tyme between those *two races of people* . . . was prosecuted to the destruction almost of both their families'.[34] Such language betrayed a very profound sense of the distinctiveness a lineage and its surname bestowed on people. In Napier's *A Plaine Discovery of the Whole Revelation* he paraphrases 'peoples' of the earth with 'kindreds',[35] so Scotsmen of one kindred would look on those of another as virtual foreigners. The importance of the surname to the identity of these kindreds was demonstrated when they did fall foul of the law. In 1600 the name of Ruthven was proscribed after the infamous Gowrie Conspiracy, as was the MacGregor name, the mere ownership of which was a death sentence commutable only if the members of the clan appeared penitent before the privy council 'to ressave a new name'.[36] The kindred was sustained both by the idea of its necessity, and by its identity with a locality, so that even a relatively minor family like the Leslies of Aberdeenshire had it said of them that the 'haill cuntrey is of thair surname, kin, freindis or assistaris'.[37] Sir James MacDonald clearly thought that locality and kindred were intimately tied up with one another when he said of his lands, 'this is certane, I will die befoir I see a Campbell possess it'.[38] Men without kinsmen were weak preys to the 'clannit' families, and two Pope brothers had to give up their businesses and offices in Sutherland where they had lived for twenty years after they quarrelled with a local family who killed a third brother. Without kinsmen in the locality they could not demand justice by the threat of revenge.[39] When Robert Rollock admitted that ministers were despised as men who were 'but kinless bodies',[40] he was implying that in popular opinion strong kinship was thought to be the best protection a man could have.

One very real weakness of kindreds elsewhere in Europe was the marriage bond. Bertha Philpotts pointed out at the beginning of this century that 'A clan system . . . is impossible where kinship is reckoned through both parents',[41] and Gluckman argued that marriage 'strikes into the unity of each vengeance group'.[42] Hence, argued Marc Bloch, feudalism evolved to fill the vacuum left by the breakdown of kindreds in early medieval Europe.[43] Scotland was, along with other countries, excepted from those which did conform to this pattern, because there kinship continued to be strongly agnatic, thus preserving the vengeance group, as also occurred in Albania where the feud survived even longer.[44] In arguing this already, Wormald has shown that marriage 'brought two kindreds into juxtaposition', but 'did not impose mutual obligations of kinship on the husband and the male relatives of the wife'.[45] Kinsmen by marriage might lend a hand in a feud, and they were less likely to be one's enemies, but their response was a free one, and the interests of their own kindred always came first. As Lindsay of Dunrod said in his letter to Maxwell of Pollok, 'consangnite of bloud is nar and kyndlear nor affinite'.[46]

One common understanding of family life in the past has been to see it as a brutalising experience in which wives, children and servants were beaten almost daily. It follows, therefore, that society at large was violent as it reflected the violence of the home. Now that picture is being seriously challenged, and a picture of domestic violence is appearing which does not differ greatly from the modern family's experience, although that is still a subject of debate.[47] In Scotland very little is known about violence in the home during the early modern period, and one is largely dependent on the argument elsewhere as a guide to what life may have been like. Church court records show very little interest in domestic violence in comparison to sexual offences, but the incidence there may be a reflection of priority rather than reality.[48] The privy council did occasionally have to discipline men who beat their wives, but the cases were rare and extreme, which was why they reached the council's attention at all.[49] Disputes within a family were sometimes dealt with by the privy council, but these cases of violence arose out of quarrels about something like land or documents, and the violence was clearly not taking place in the context of daily living.[50] Feuds did break out within kindreds, sometimes within families, but more often between cadet houses and the kindred chief.[51] Here, though, one is moving away from the idea of conditioned violence in the home to the socio-political violence of the kindred. Here was where the impetus towards violence lay, for as Bloch wrote, 'the primary duty of the kinsman was vengeance'.[52] Sir Robert Gordon told Lord Berridale after they had ended long years of feuding between their families that it was little wonder that they had been enemies since 'from their infancies they had been bred in jarrs and contentions, the one against the other'.[53] In this society it was friendship which had to be written down in bonds: competition and conflict flowed naturally from the structure and mentality of the kindreds.

Scottish lordship has been rescued from the rather unsophisticated image it was so long tarnished with, that of the 'robber barons' or 'aristocratic brigands'.[54] Here again Wormald has cut a convincing path through layers of misunderstanding which have built up over the last three centuries to conceal how that lordship functioned, and how it was understood. Thus the networks of power which these lords controlled were not simply manipulated in the cause of self-interest, but 'show a strong awareness of their responsibility, not to keep their men free from the consequences of their crimes, but to involve themselves personally in, and provide a solution to, disputes between their followers'.[55] There is no doubt that this was a major ingredient of lordship. In 1574 the 6th earl of Argyll travelled around his vast domains pacifying feuds, 'not omitting to "sedat" and mitigate the privy grudges and "particularis" among his own friends in the inner part of Argyll'.[56] This was the good lordship expected of a nobleman, and it contrasted sharply with the weak earl of Atholl in whose affairs the privy council had to intervene by 1607, because 'what the want of such a man dois, the misreable estate of the cuntrey of Athoill and all the bordouring bounds to it, dois declair'.[57] Atholl's problems stemmed both from his personality, and from the fact that he was not the native earl, but had inherited the title in 1595 when the original Stewart line had died out. He had then written to the dependants of the former earl promising 'that we ar alse willing and reddie to plesour you and to do for you and youris aganis quhatsumevir ye haif adoo wyth, as the Erlis of Athole hes done of befoir, and bettir gif we may'.[58] Unfortunately he proved unable to satisfy his dependants, or to control them, and the estates and surrounding area drifted into increasing lawlessness.

The loyalty which existed between lord and man in Scotland is, of course, legendary, and Sir George Hume of Wedderburn's reply to the Regent Morton is unmatched anywhere as an example of the strength of the bond between a man and his lord.[59] Less well known is Sir Henry Lee's rhetorical question: 'In what place in the world will kin, friends and servants adventure more for their lords?'[60] Clearly the Englishman had been puzzled with what he had seen which contrasted so sharply with the looser bonds in English lord-man relations.[61] Even the Scots themselves could be amazed by men who were 'by nature, most bent and prone to adventure themselves, their lyffs, and all they have, for their masters and lords, yea beyond all other people'.[62] The lawyer, Sir Thomas Craig, whose *Jus Feudale* was published in 1603, believed that a vassal 'by his every word and deed . . . must shew to his lord, as to a father, all reverence and fidelity'.[63] The lawyer's preference for tidy thinking which Craig espoused here described a world in which the clear obligations and demarcation of loyalty effectively excluded conflict, since the king held ultimate lordship over all men. In that context the connection between loyalty to lords and to country made by A. H. Williamson is a valid one,[64] but Scottish lordship was not simply feudal, it was also based on kinship. The earl of Bothwell wrote to the king as 'my soverane and cheif',[65] he being the king's cousin, and if Bothwell drew some satisfaction from that bond, lesser men were even more forward in holding onto the kinship which bound them to a lord. The obligations that imposed on both, in concert with those of lordship and manrent themselves, often overrode any other responsibilities. Hence the many instances of lords and their kinsmen aligning with French, Spanish and English interests throughout the sixteenth century, and, towards the end of the century, the severe criticism of unquestioning lordship by the church which quite clearly saw the relationship between that and private violence.[66]

A great deal of lordship had nothing at all to do with violence. The written bonds of friendship between noblemen were not only concerned with destabilising Scottish politics,[67] though some clearly did, and one signed by a number of nobles was an agreement not to wear clothes inlaid with fake gold, silver and jewellery as it was 'unmanly and unhonest'. Whoever broke the bond was to take the others out to dinner, and forfeit the offending clothing to the first fiddler they met.[68] Nor was the service that men did for their lords only likely to involve them in wielding the sword, and a lord's responsibilities to his man did not always involve protecting him from the law. A Glasgow bailie, George Elphinstone, wrote in his will, counselling his sons to serve their lord 'as I wes ay reddie during my tyme to serve thame treulie to my lyffis end as become me of my dewtie'.[69] That duty may never have involved Elphinstone in the riskier side of service, and was more likely to involve the mundane duty to attend on a lord when he went on journeys, when he attended court, or at days of law. Such attendance, wrote the earl of Crawford, had 'ever beine the custome of this cuntry'.[70] In return lords would accompany their dependants, lending their power to their man's cause. The earl of Mar wrote telling the laird of Abercairny that 'I man prepair me to keip the same [day of law] to assist my servand and dependar in his defens, as the custom is'.[71] Often these relationships were much more than responses to duty, and the bond could be a close, personal one, as in the case of the earl of Huntly and the laird of Gight who 'knowes most of the earles mynd of any man livinge'.[72] Good counsel was as valuable to a lord as good swordmanship. Nor was the point of all this mutual assistance simply to pervert the law. Lord Hamilton asked the session judge, Vaus of Barnbarroch, to show some favour to a servant of his who was due to face trial, but only 'as ye may of law',[73] while the laird of Pollok asked a nobleman to 'continew guid lord and maister to me and my servandis, according to the equitie of the caus, as zour Lordschippis honour and conscience will permit'.[74] Another form of service required by a lord was service in his household, and even lairds like Kennedy of Bargany 'had evir in his houshald xxiiij galland gentilmenne, doubill horsitt, and gallantly clad'.[75] Here the reward came in the form of food, clothing and horses. Leslie commented that the nobility

> With glade wil and frilie thay use to ludge kin, freind and acquaintance, ye and strangers that turnes in to thame. A sclandirous thing they esteime it to be, to deny this, and a poynt of smal or na liberalitie.[76]

Mutuality was essential to such lordship, and where it was lacking, men would look for better lords, while the latter would have approved of Morton's advice to Menzies of that Ilk to get rid of the MacGregors on his land 'because ye ressave nether proffite nor obedience of thame'.[77]

There was, however, a darker side to such relationships which should not be dismissed. One observer commented that in Scotland 'Many offenders are countenanced by noblemen, with great contempt of law and justice',[78] and he was right. A 'peculiar and proper vice' existed among men who served lords which was that 'naturallie thay are bent mair willinglie and vehementlie, gif thair maiser commande thame, to seditione and stryfe'.[79] Lordship was also about providing the lord with a private army, and his followers with protection from the law and the bloodfeud in a manner which could be very indiscriminate. Feudal law, according to Craig of Riccarton, obliged lord and man to defend one another in righteous causes,[80] but 'righteous' was too easily given subjective interpretations by men with the power to equate it with might. James Conheith was coming up against these values when he was unable to get justice in Dumfries because the man who had assaulted him was a 'household man and servand' of Lord Herries, the provost.[81] Kinship, of course, reinforced such protection, and the king was recognising that when, in discussing Huntly's sheltering of one of his men from the law, he commented that the earl 'must be a Gordon when it comes to the worst'.[82] The Kennedy historian recognised the same thinking in the earl of Cassillis, and wrote that when one of his servants suffered any loss, 'my lord thocht the samin done to him'.[83]

There was nothing inherently sinister in the fact that the earl of Sutherland 'did alwayes manteyn a cursarie and runing guard', for both his security and his honour demanded it.[84] However, as was the case elsewhere in Europe, such as in Tuscany or northern England, noblemen maintained close links with the rural underworld of bandits, or bandit-like groups and individuals.[85] Violence of this sort very easily creates its own mythology,[86] but some Scottish noblemen, especially in the highland and border regions, presided over extensive criminal networks involving protection, blackmail, terrorisation, raiding and murder. In return for immunity from the law, and protection from their enemies, these men carried out the dirty work of their lords, as well as providing them with the usual military support when required. Such relationships existed between the earl of Argyll and the MacGregors, the earl of Caithness and the clan Gunn, the earl of Huntly and the Lochaber MacDonalds, Lord Maxwell and the Armstrongs, and the earl of Bothwell and a number of border families, one of whom were the Wauchopes of Niddrie.

How far back the careers of Bothwell and Archibald Wauchope of Niddrie stretched is unknown. The laird certainly had Bothwell's protection after he slew the laird of Sheriffhall in a feud of his own, and in 1589 Bothwell was strongly suspected of having engineered Niddrie's escape from the courtroom of the justice depute in Edinburgh when he was brought for trial. The king grumbled that he was unable to 'minister justice against him that the world abhored for his vicious and bloody life', but Bothwell was too powerful a patron for anything to be done. Later that year Bothwell was given a large part of the responsibility for governing the kingdom during the king's absence in Denmark, and Niddrie joined him in Edinburgh, in spite of his outlawry, where he killed a gentleman of the court after the man had offended him. For the next two years he lived in Bothwell's shadow, and when he was named in a divorce case as an adulterer, the earl marched into the session house and arrested the cuckold husband on some other charge. Niddrie also enhanced his reputation at this time, and the fear in which Bothwell was held, by killing the laird of Edmonstone in a duel. However, with the earl's fall in 1591 Niddrie and the rest of his family had to begin paying their dues. He accompanied Bothwell on the ill-fated Holyrood raid in December of that year and was seriously wounded, but had recovered by June when he was present at the Falkland raid which was even more of a disaster. He was in fact captured by Lord Hamilton on the following day, but was freed by him for reasons which Hamilton kept to himself. As far as one knows, Niddrie remained with Bothwell until he fled the country in 1595, though he may have deserted him before then, but the Wauchope family continued with their criminal activities, killing Edmonstone of Wowmet in 1597 and a royal messenger in 1599, and indulging in other activities on the borders. Justice appears to have caught up with some of them, one being slain along with Wowmet, Niddrie's brother being brought to trial in 1598, a cousin being executed in 1602, and another brother being banished for life; the laird himself was thought to have met a sorry end.[87]

Not all dependants or servants were like Niddrie, but many were, and much the same can be said of young men who had a far higher profile than they do in modern society. When the king attained his twenty-first birthday in 1587, the average age of the higher nobility — the duke of Lennox, Lord Hamilton, and twenty-two earls — was around twenty-seven. Seven of these were children, two were elderly men in their late fifties, three might be described as middle-aged, and the remaining twelve were in their twenties and early thirties, and it was these men — Glencairn, Marischal, Sutherland, Crawford, and the younger Atholl, Bothwell,

Caithness, Erroll, Huntly, Mar and Moray — who were to be at the centre of so much of the violence of the next few years.[88] Georges Duby wrote of youth as 'the spearhead of feudal aggression', and though the feudal age may have passed, many of its values, particularly those associated with manliness and prowess, continued to dominate the attitudes of young men.[89] In the north-east 'The Society and Company of Boys', or 'The Knights of the Mortar', existed as a mixture of the medieval knightly society, of male clubbishness, and as an outlet for the more violent tendencies of John Gordon of Gight and his young friends: its suppression was eventually ordered by the privy council.[90]

More commonly young men acted on impulse, and with a bravado which was extremely dangerous in this kind of society. No doubt many fathers winked at their sons' adventures, or even encouraged them to maintain the family honour, while the privy council itself could be understanding towards actions committed 'upoun some foolische and young consait'.[91] Other fathers tried hard to curb such high spirits. In November 1591 Lord Ogilvy wrote to the earl of Crawford asking him to intervene in a quarrel between the young laird of Vane and his own son 'because itt is the thing in the warld I wald mais fainest to be tane away'. With a history of feud between the two kindreds Ogilvy desperately wanted to avoid further bloodshed, and asked the earl to investigate the dispute, while assuring him that

> ... giff my sone beis fund in the wrang ... as he hes attemptit this aganis my hairt by my knawleg and to my gret anger he sall repair itt to your Lordshipis honour and contentment or ellis as god judge me I sall become as greitt ane unfriend to him as I was and ame ane lufing father.

Crawford replied, promising that he would try to ensure that 'na youthfull thingis fall furth'.[92] Here was good lordship and good fatherhood in action, but even the best advice, cajoling and threatening could be ignored with dire consequences. The session judge and privy councillor, Sir David Lindsay of Edzell, had the last years of a very successful career marred by the actions of his son who in 1605 participated in a street fight in Edinburgh, and then a few years later killed Lord Spynie, thus infuriating the king, and intensifying his family's feud with their chief, the earl of Crawford.[93] Equally tragic was the case of the laird of Cultmalundy whose son slew Toshack of Monivaird in 1618. The laird saved his son from criminal prosecution by agreeing expensive compensation with the Toshack kin, but the privy council later wrote to the king telling him that

> this ffeade has altogidder undone Auld Cultmalundie; for his estait is exhaustit and wrackit, and he is become verie waik of his judgement and understanding, by the greif that thir troubles hes brought upoun him; whilkis wer the occassioun of his wyffis death, and of the exyle and banishment of goode rank and qualitie hes sones and freindis, now be the space of foure yoiris; in the quhilk time tua of his freindis of goode rank and qualitie has depairtit this lyffe.[94]

It was a high price to pay for delinquency.

Violence was more likely in an armed and militarised society. Scotland may not have been at war after 1573, but she had experienced almost three decades of intermittent fighting with foreign enemies and over domestic issues. The effect of that is unknown, although in France the relationship between private violence and warfare has been commented on during this period.[95] Whether Scotland was at war or not, much of the rest of Europe was, and thousands of Scots continued to make military careers on the continent. Henry of Navarre contracted fifteen hundred men for his service in 1589,[96] and employers could be found in the Netherlands, in Scandinavia and Spain. Captain James Stewart and Colonel William Stewart, who both acquired political notoriety in the 1580s, had served on the continent, the earl of Argyll entered Spanish service in 1617, and at least a tenth of the sons of the nobility followed military careers.[97] Castles and tower houses still dominated the architectural landscape, and defensive requirements remained important to their design well into the seventeenth century. Arms were owned and carried by most men, and even minor arguments, like that between the Kennedies and Crawfords at a horse race in Ayr which left one man shot in the leg and another in the groin, could assume very dangerous proportions.[98] The development of the rapier with its lethal thrust, and the enormous popularity of handguns — particularly useful in a feuding society which was not concerned with how a man was killed — made these clashes much more dangerous than they had been in the past. By the end of the sixteenth century there were thirty gun craftsmen in Edinburgh, fifteen more in the Canongate, and another eighteen in Dundee all working to supply a market supplemented by imports.[99] Thus when the laird of Johnstone clashed with the lairds of Cessford and Drumlanrig in Edinburgh, their parties were reputed to have exchanged some twenty-five shots at one another, and when Lord Oliphant and Lord Ruthven faced one another in the open field a number of men were killed and wounded as scores of shots were fired.[100] Even in his home a man was not guaranteed safety, and Campbell of Cawdor was shot dead through a window, MacAulay of Ardincaple's assassin narrowly missed him, and Lord Spynie was lucky not to be at home when the Ogilvies blew in his windows and gates with a petard.[101] There was some justification then in Edward Wotton's comment in 1585 that 'When every man carries a pistol at his girdle, as they do in Scotland, it is an easy matter to kill a man through a window or door, and not be able to discover who did it'.[102] In 1595 a revolt by the schoolboys of Edinburgh Grammar School ended when one of the boys shot dead a town bailie who was trying to remonstrate with him and his companions.[103] There can be little doubt that such universal carrying of weapons made every confrontation a potential manslaughter.

The violence in Scottish society was neither anarchic nor without restraints. Fear of punishment by the state, the even greater fear of incurring a bloodfeud, the agreements among lords to reduce tensions, the threat of eternal damnation, and enough common sense to know that society could not exist if violence was uncontrolled, all kept it within relatively acceptable and tolerable limits. Of course, like every society this one had within it those men who went beyond the generally recognised norms of behaviour. Killing a man in his home — hamesucken — was thought of as in this category, hence one explanation for the level of outrage at Huntly's murder of the earl of Moray at Donibristle,[104] and so was murder under trust which became treasonable in 1587 and was committed by the 9th Lord Maxwell on the laird of Johnstone in 1608.[105] Tormenting a victim was also seen as excessive. Men like the Drummonds who took Andrew Lawson, cut off his nose and pulled out his teeth for no apparent reason,[106] or the 'cruel man hangit for setting on ane woman's bare [arse] on ane girdill quhen it was red hot',[107] were acting in a manner which was considered abnormal. When a father caught one of his servants fornicating with his daughter, tied the man up, broke his leg with an axe, and 'with ane scharpe knyff or durk, cuttit away his secreit memberis fra him, and put in het assis and emmeris in the bag of his secreit memberis, quhilk restit uncuttit',[108] he aroused the same kind of condemnation one would expect from the courts today. The court which tried his case, which was for murder as his victim had died after five days of agony, commented that 'the lyke of the quhilk crewaltie and tyrannie was never hard to be committed within this cuntrey, nather in hieland nor lawland'.[109] That was probably untrue, but the outrage was real enough, violence had its limits, and violence like this was uncommon. However, other forms of violence were regarded as legitimate, and that of the bloodfeud had an ideology to sustain that legitimacy.

John Erskine, earl of Mar and the king's life-long friend, was described as a man who in 'honour, honesty and wisdom may well be accounted with the first courtiers of all', a man who was 'so far interested in honour as he will put all in peril rather than be 'set' with the shame he has gotten'.[110] What is meant by honour is, of course, something which varies from society to society. In early twentieth-century Greece, J. K. Campbell identified honour as 'the manliness of the man and the shame of the women', arguing that its main concern was 'strength or prepotency rather than justice'.[111] Among the Jibaro Indians, and among most of the Mediterranean societies surveyed by Black-Michaud, there was a similar exaggerated sensitivity to acts which were construed as bringing one's own honour into disrepute.[112] These themes are fairly universal to what are known as honour and shame societies, although exact definitions vary. Lawrence Stone and Mervyn James both drew attention to what the latter called 'a stress on competitive awareness' in which violence was both justifiable and necessary when discussing the English version of honour in the sixteenth century.[113] Other European countries had their own variations of such values,[114] although their roots in the chivalric honour of medieval Europe were common to most.[115]

In 1600 the newly promoted marquis of Huntly appeared at parliament demanding precedence over the earl of Angus who had previously ranked at the head of the earls in order of precedence.[116] A row broke out, but Angus was 'in the facillitie of his owne nature, and by the king's authoritie' willing to give way, thus preventing further quarrelling. However, his Douglas kinsmen then approached him, and 'protested never to acknowledge him herefter, gif he did yeild that honor which was purchased by the blood and burialls of their ancestors', and forced him to stand up to Huntly and the king.[117] Here Angus was taught a lesson in honour by his kinsmen and dependants for whom the issue was partly one of what Maurice Keen has called 'reflective honour', encapsulated in Milo von Sevilingen's phrase 'the worth of the worthy makes me worthy'.[118] Yet it was more than that, and they were also reminding him that the issue was not one of personal self-respect, but one of power, involving the reputation of the kindred, the dependency, and the lineage which Angus represented. To have given in to Huntly would have been to signal to other interested groups that the Douglases were easy game, and that Angus was a weak lord, unable to protect his family and friends. Loss of honour meant loss of real power, measured in support, and seen at this level such disputes over matters like precedence seem less peculiar than they at first appear.

Francis Stewart, earl of Bothwell, needed no such lectures from his supporters. After capturing Lord Maxwell in 1587, Sir William Stewart found himself in great favour with the king which 'made the man so swell' that he began to throw his weight about at court. One day he quarrelled with Bothwell in front of the king, and

> bad the Earll kis his . . . ; the Earll heiring that base and despytful ansuer, ther made a voue to God, that he should kis his . . . to his grete pleasour: sua therafter rancountering the said Sir William in the Black Friar vynde by chance, told he vold now kis his . . . and with that drew his sword; Sir William standing at his defence, and having his back at the wall, the Earll made a thruste at him with his rapier, and strake him in at the back and out at the belley, and killed him.[119]

Bothwell was undoubtedly a wild and violent character, and his own brother-in-law complained of 'what trouble have I still to keep him in order',[120] but in this case it was Sir William who was clearly in the wrong. The violence of Bothwell's response was 'rule governed', it was expected if he was to retain the respect necessary for his lordship to be effective. It was the challenge to it, in the form of a personal insult, which was anarchic.[121] As in the medieval *chansons,* the obligations of honour were very alike to those of law,[122] and behavioural patterns like this are not peculiar to sixteenth-century Scotland. The same thinking is found in the modern Italian Mafia where 'A man who is feared will not receive challenges to his honor, and this shield of fear will reach out to cover all those who are close to him'.[123] Sentiments like these have a timeless quality for honour societies, and Sir Robert Kerr of Cessford said much the same when he boasted that 'my fame will give any man feare to accuse mee'.[124] In killing Sir William, Bothwell simply ensured that the shield of fear remained firmly in its place.

In this context the highly sensitive behaviour of the men who inhabited this world of honour begins to make sense. When the earl of Caithness captured two servants of the earl of Orkney's, he had them sent home, but only after they had had half their hair and beards shaved off. In doing this Caithness conveyed his contempt for Orkney, and he did it in a very public manner.[125] It was 'a custome among the Scots (more than any other nation) to contend for the hight of the street',[126] because it was thought dishonourable to give way to another. Lord Sanquhar was so enraged by Louis XIII's taunt about an eye he had lost while fencing — 'Vit-il encore? Is the man still alive that did it?' — that he returned to London and had the fencing master who did it murdered, an action which cost him his own life.[127] The society of the male elite was therefore extremely tense, and 'unreverent and undeutiful' words could arouse the concern of the privy council.[128] While the discharging of kindness could occasionally be intimated formally, there was in Scotland no real equivalent of the Polish *opdowiedz* by which private war was declared.[129] Consequently, where ill feeling was expressed more privately and was allowed to spread by rumour, the social norm was destabilised without rivals knowing what their response should be. Thus the laird of Buccleuch wrote to the laird of Cessford asking him to clarify their relationship, so that 'I may the better know how to accompt of you for the time past, and how to behave my self with you in the time to come'. Cessford replied in vague terms that 'my doinges is honourable and to the good customes of the countrey', prompting a second letter from Buccleuch threatening to 'make a lyer in your absolute profession of honor' should his suspicions be justified. The letters were signed in ways which clearly documented the deteriorating relationship. Buccleuch firstly signed himself 'Your brother in law Buclugh', Cessford replied as 'Your brother in your owne termes Robert Kerre', and Buccleuch concluded the correspondence as 'Your brother in na termes, Buchlugh'.[130]

Occasionally these affairs of honour would lead to duelling, although in Scotland the duel never had anything like the popularity it had in Italy or France,[131] and the feud was usually the more conventional means of dealing with attacks on one's honour. Cartels were sometimes sent challenging rivals to single combat. Buccleuch and Cessford arranged a combat — the word duel was rarely used — and the former promised 'upon my faithe honour and aithe' not to harm Cessford before the event, or to bring to the field weapons other than those agreed upon.[132] The laird of Bargany wrote to the laird of Culzean that 'ye diretit your selff for feir, and borrowit ane sark or ye mycht cum amangis menne'. This prompted Culzean to continue the exchange of insults in his own cartel where he told Bargany that 'as for your filthie sklander, I cair nocht', and he poured scorn on Bargany's threats. He concluded, 'I dreid ye will tyne sum uther joynt, of the glengoir, as ye did the brig of your neise, the last time ye was thair', a reference to an accident Bargany had when a golf ball struck his nose on his previous visit to the place chosen for the combat.[133] Duelling was unlawful throughout this period, but even the privy council recognised some legitimacy in the sending of cartels, and in 1613 it agreed that Lord Scone was right to send one to Lord Burleigh who had slandered him.[134] Thirty years earlier the young earl of Bothwell and the master of Marischal challenged one another after an incident during a game of football in which one kicked the other.[135] Yet the majority of these combats never took place, particularly those which were arranged in the Italian manner. A combat between champions did take place in 1578 between the opposing armies of Morton and the Atholl-Argyll faction, and one man was killed.[136] Another arose when Bothwell and his servant met Cessford and his man outside Edinburgh, 'queare meiting two for two, thay focht allong tyme on horseback' until Cessford retired.[137] Spontaneous clashes like these were more common, and the judicial duel continued to be fought under royal licence until the end of the century,[138] but the duel as it was understood in most of western Europe was never very popular, and certainly failed to make the impact it did in France during this same period.

Honour forced men to make what look like surprising ethical choices. At his trial

Lord Sanquhar defended himself by saying that 'I considered not my wrongs upon terms of Christianity . . . but being trained up in the courts of princes and in arms, I stood upon the terms of honour'.[139] When John Muir of Auchindrain and his son wanted to avoid criminal investigation for murder, they thought it would be dishonourable to pass to the horn on such grounds, and so they caused a tuilyie in Ayr for which they were outlawed without loss of honour.[140] MacGregor of Glenstray surrendered to the earl of Argyll, believing that he would be conveyed into safe exile, but Argyll had him sent to Berwick 'for he promes to put him out of Scottis grund. Sus he keipit ane Hielandman's promes, in respect he sent the gaird to convoy him out of Scottis grund; bot thai wer not directit to pairt with him bot to fetche him back againe'. MacGregor was brought to Edinburgh and executed, and in spite of the fact that one commentator thought that this was 'to the gritt discredit of the Erll of Argyll', the earl himself was satisfied that his honour was intact.[141] Such thinking seems a perverse interpretation of Bishop Leslie's observation that the borderers thought nothing 'more heinous than violated fidelity',[142] but when the 5th earl of Huntly wrote to Menzies of that Ilk that 'mony falsattis and desuitis [are] now usit in this warld',[143] he was already idealising the past. Gordon was being more realistic when he commented that 'promises . . . are commonlie troden under foote, when they ly in the way either to honor or revenge'.[144] Honour was too closely associated with power for there to be any room for moralising about it. It propelled men into feuds and intensified existing ones because it was imperative that honour, and hence power, be defended, and it ensured that feud be prosecuted without restraint because it was a code of behaviour which recognised none.

Scotsmen would not really have understood the need for Vincentio Saviolo's stricture that 'the revenge ought to be done honourably',[145] for in their society revenge was itself honourable. In 1593 the duke of Lennox and Lord Spynie quarrelled, and as a consequence the duke lost some face at court, prompting him to write to Spynie telling him that he had 'so far wronged him that he could not with any honour abide the sight of him without revenge'.[146] Here Lennox was talking about shame, the shame he would have to live with if he did not wipe it away in vengeance. The Tausug of the Philippines explain this when they say that 'The thing which kills a man is embarrassment', unless he can first kill the man who caused it, or at least cause him equal embarrassment,[147] while the Jibaro Indians of Ecuador reply to an accusation of having slain an enemy, 'He has killed himself',[148] and Bothwell could easily have said this of Sir William Stewart. Among the Yanomamo people a graded system of violence is recognised within which they can express their *waiteri* or fierceness, and thus remove their shame.[149] In Scotland vengeance was less consciously structured in its execution, but the underlying reasons for executing it were much the same. As in Tudor England, the word itself had more than one meaning, and Ronald Broude has identified at least three definitions in use at the time. Revenge was used to mean punishment or retribution, and was associated with the law and the state; it could also be applied to divine justice, a form used by the king when speaking of the need to 'revenge God's cause' on the catholic earls in 1594;[150] and it was popularly understood to mean what Francis Bacon called 'a sort of wild justice', a subjective, private justice.[151]

This last form is the revenge of the bloodfeud. Unlike the Balkan feuds or other Mediterranean vendettas, the Scottish feud displayed little sign of having strict rules of conduct.[152] There is some evidence to suggest that in the sixteenth century the Mediterranean feud was closer to that in Scotland, and catholic missionaries in Corsica described something very similar to what was found in the highlands in particular.[153] Of the highlanders it was said that they

> wer bent and eager in taking revenge, that neither have they regaird to persone, tyme, aige, nor course: and ar generallie so addicted that way (as lykewise are the most pairt of all the Highlanders) that therein they surpass all people whatsoever

and 'ar so crewell in taking of revenge'.[154] Similar comments were made of the borderers:

> Bot gif thay commit ony voluntarie slauchtir, to be maist in revenge of sum iniurie; and cheiflie for the slauchtir of sum cosing or freind to sum man. Fra quhilke thay wil nocht absteine, thoch the lawes of the Realme commandit: quhairof ryses deidlie feid, nocht of ane in ane, or few in few bot of thame ilk ane and als, quha ar of that familie stock or tribe how ignorant sa evir thay be of the iniurie.[155]

Thus the complaint by the Veitches that the Tweedies had 'evir socht and seikis thair utter wrak and exterminatioun'.[156] One might prefer to define this as war,[157] and in a sense it was local warfare, but indiscriminate vengeance was common to a large number of Scottish feuds, and such a refinement is unnecessary and unhistorical. When the earl of Cassillis judiciously murdered the young laird of Stair, his kinsmen rode down into Galloway and slaughtered David Girvan for no other reason than that he was the earl's master of works.[158] Other feuds did restrict vengeance to a narrower circle of people, to the killers themselves, or their immediate kinsmen, and this was the more common pattern in the lowlands. In another feud involving the Kennedy family, Cassillis contracted his brother to slay or capture the man who had murdered their uncle, the laird of Culzean, and as a price offered him 1200 merks annually, enough corn to feed six horses, and the maintenance of two servants.[159]

Revenge had a long memory. Melville wrote that

> the way taking of the lyf of a nobleman or barroun, bredis ane hundreth enemys ma or les, according to the gretnes of the clan or surname of the quhilk number some will ly at the wait to be revengit, albeit lang efter, when they se ther turn.[160]

Even if feuds themselves were rarely very long, long past incidents could be revived to fire more immediate conflicts. When the earl of Caithness was instrumental in having the earl of Orkney sent to the block in 1613, he was said to have seen this as vengeance for the defeat of his ancestors by the Orkney men in 1529.[161] History was used to give additional meaning to new quarrels, but the 'deidlie hatrent and malice of the feud'[162] did take a long time to dissipate. In 1621 Captain Henry Bruce returned to Scotland from years in foreign service to find himself being pursued by a kinsman of a Captain John Hamilton whom he had killed in a duel in Flanders seventeen years before.[163] In many of these cases, however, the family of the dead person wanted compensation, not blood vengeance. Others would accept no such compromise, and in the feud between the Douglas and Stewart kindreds, Captain James Stewart was slain fifteen years after he sent Morton to the scaffold. Twelve years later, in 1607, Lord Torthorwald, who had killed the captain, taunted his nephew about it, and did 'so inflame him, the old ulcer remaining uncured, as he avouched to have his life at all hazards', which he did, shooting Torthorwald dead in Edinburgh.[164] Both Captain Stewart and Torthorwald lived for years with the strain of the feud, and some clearly found this too much. The laird of Ardincaple complained that his enemy 'daylie awaittis all occasioun to revenge the same [his servant's murder]',[165] while Thomas Jack was so afraid that he was forced 'to abyd continewallie in his hous for feir of his lyff'.[166] When the privy council said of the feud between the Kerrs and Turnbulls that they were as 'violent and resolut in their humouris of revenge' as when it began,[167] they were describing a principle which was basic to the feud, and to its violent character. Revenge even travelled, and Arthour Forbes followed Gordon of Auchindoun to Paris where he contracted the 'Enfans de la Mat' to kill him. However, they only succeeded in wounding him. In fleeing from Auchindoun's party, one of the assassins dropped his hat, inside which were found the details of a rendezvous with Forbes. The Gordons then went to see another of their kinsmen employed as a gentleman in Charles IX's bedchamber. He told the story to the king, and Auchindoun was given a company of the royal archers who stormed the house where Arthour Forbes was staying, killing him and capturing his co-plotters who were all executed the next day, Forbes's own body being broken on the wheel.[168]

Why revenge was thought of this way had a great deal to do with attitudes to blood. A frustrated Tudor border administrator once exclaimed, 'I see none other than revenge for revenge and blood for blood'.[169] An eye for an eye is, of course, a very old concept, and the basis of most primitive justice, but while such specific retribution was no longer recognised, the idea of blood paying for blood retained a strong hold in a society which invested so many important properties in blood. Medical thinking throughout Europe was dominated by the idea that life itself was held in a man's blood. Honour and nobility were transferred through the blood, thus the king's belief that 'it is most certaine that vertue or vice will oftentimes with the heritage, be tranferred from the parents to the posteritie; and run on a blood (as the Proverbe is) the sicknesse of the mind becomming as kindly to some races, as these sicknesses of the body that infect the seede'.[170] John Ross told the king to his face that his 'Guysien blood' was the cause of his persecution of the presbyterians.[171] This sharing of a common blood had obvious implications for the feud. Revenge dictated that blood be shed in recompense, and ideally the blood of the killer or perpetrator of some infringement of honour was desirable, but if he was out of reach, then his blood might still be spilled by killing those who shared it, his kinsmen.[172] Hence blood took on an almost mystical importance — its shedding resembling a libation to the dead — so that when John Gordon of Gight was tried for murder in 1617, his lawyers pled that he was the legitimate 'avenger of blood' for a dead kinsman.[173]

The belief that 'it is certane that sanguis clamat, blood cryeth' was fundamental to the feud.[174] Even the crown accorded this idea some recognition in disciplining two lairds in 1616 for seeking vengeance 'notwithstanding the blood is now cold', the implication being that were it hot — that is, recently shed — then their behaviour would have been excusable.[175] Blood itself was thought capable of accusing a murderer. In *Daemonologie* the king wrote, 'In a secret Murther, iff the dead carkasse be at any time thereafter handled by the Murtherer, it will gush out of blood; as if the blood were crying to heaven for revenge of the Murtherer'.[176] So terrified were Muir of Auchindrain and his son of being put to this test that they chose to become outlaws instead.[177] Even when men did begin to turn away from the feud towards a justice imposed by God and king, their thinking did not radically alter, for, as Sir Robert Gordon observed, 'we sie that the Lord punisheth blood by blood, as such tymes and by such meanes as he thinketh expedient'.[178] Retribution would remain the basis of justice: 'thai that slayis will be slaine', wrote Birrel.[179]

Blood also had a highly effective visual impact in a society where symbol and ritual were important means of communication. In 1593 some poor women from Nithsdale travelled up to Edinburgh with the bloody shirts of their husbands, sons and servants who had been slain in a raid by the Johnstones. Carrying these gory objects, they paraded through the burgh exposing the king's inadequacy in providing protection or justice.[180] This presentation of blood was a common form of both demanding justice and presenting proof, and in barony courts people who had been assaulted brought bloodstained clothes before the judge.[181] Of course there were those willing to make more cynical use of such propaganda, and in 1588 the Aberdeen burgh council wrote a letter to its agents in Edinburgh about an attack on some of the town burgesses by the local Leslie family, instructing them to take their case to the king and privy council. They wanted bloody shirts presented to the crown, but warned that 'we micht not haiff the bludie sarks to send to you thair for ye men do the best ye can thairin and furnes sarks and put bluid thairon'.[182] Broken faith was likely to be subject to symbolic protests, and in the borders, 'If faith is broken a glove is paraded through his people on the point of a lance which so disgraces them that it is possible they will kill the man'.[183] While no evidence of that happening is known of, in 1598 the laird of Johnstone was judged to be guilty of breaking an assurance with Douglas of Drumlanrig, and, in a ceremony reminiscent of the degradation of nobility,[184] he was declared a 'mansworne man' and 'defamed and perjured'. To publicly emphasise this, 'his picture was drawn in blood, to signifye a murtherer and hung with his heels upwards with the name sett under his head, and INFAMY and PERJURYE written thwar his leggs'.[185] This same mixture of symbol and graffiti was at work when the murdered earl of Moray was drawn with all his wounds graphically displayed so that the picture could be presented to the king as a plea for justice, the king having refused to view the corpse itself.[186] Similarly, the earl of Mar paraded a picture of a murdered servant through the lands of the family who had killed him,[187] and at the funeral of the laird of Bargany a 'Banner of Rewendge' was carried 'quhairin was payntitt his portratour with all his wondis, with his sone sittand at his kneyis, and this deattone writtene betuix his handis, 'JUDGE AND REWENDGE MY CAUSE, O LORD' '.[188] Media exploitation is by no means a modern concept.

This visual reinforcement of the feud took other forms. The corpses of the dead earl of Moray and Lord Maxwell were left unburied for years by their kinsmen as a reminder to themselves of the vengeance they must seek.[189] Such a practice was a very old one in medieval Europe, and Bloch also described instances when 'the very corpse cried out for vengeance' by being left in this state.[190] One of MacDonald of Glengarry's sons was said to have been buried at the door of Kintail kirk so that his enemies and killers might step on his corpse each time they went to worship.[191] The MacGregors swore allegiance to the murderers of John Drummond by taking their oath in the presence of the dead man's head which had been place in Balquhidder kirk.[192] Corpses were often mutilated or ritually dismembered as though revenge was not satiated with death, but must further inflict shame on the body of an enemy. Duncan Buchanan's killers, 'eftir they knew he was deid, cuttit and manglit his haill body with durkis and swerids';[193] when the earl of Bothwell ambushed a party of Humes in 1584, he 'killed all three, but hewed Davy Hume . . . all to pieces';[194] and in 1605 the master of Crawford and his men slew one of his cousins, slashing him with a score of sword strokes, and then later returning to the corpse to cut its throat and dismember it.[195]

Not all feuds were violent all of the time, but most of those for which a sufficient degree of information can be gathered experienced some degree of violence (see Table 5 of page 278). Some feuds were more violent than others, as were some men, like the 4th earl of Caithness whose enemies said of him that he 'lived too long for these adjacent cuntries, wher he had been the instrument of eivill dissention and shedding of much blood'.[196] The majority of men were not like that, but most lords and lesser men who found themselves in a feud were prepared to use violence. A small minority of feuds appear to have displayed no violence at all, although the figure might be higher if more were known about a large number of feuds for which there is so little information that no evaluation of their conduct is possible. Between 1616 and 1617 the earls of Perth and Linlithgow were feuding over some local issue, but nothing is known about what happened.[197] Other feuds which appear to be non-violent on the basis of crown sources are revealed to be very violent from private sources, and therefore one has to remain suspicious of non-violent feuds which may be the product of scant records. On the other hand it would be quite wrong to imagine that such a thing was impossible, or that the intention in every feud was to maximise violence, something which was obviously not the case or sixteenth-century Scotland would have been anarchic.[198]

Property violence most often occurred as an accompaniment to inter-personal violence. Again this might be a reflection of reporting since murders were more likely to arouse comment than barn-burning, but while there was probably more property damage than the sources suggest, the intent of the feud was still to kill or wound people: destroying their property was only a second best. The level of that damage varied enormously. In 1602 Walter Currour of Inchedrour complained that his neighbour, John Gordon of Avarchy, had committed twenty-three separate attacks on him since 1598. These included a number of crimes against persons: a local government official had been killed, on five occasions Inchedrour's servants had been attacked, one had been forcibly evicted from his house, three were robbed, and he himself had been assaulted twice. For the duration of three years his mails and duties for certain lands were appropriated by Avarchy, his house was broken into and occupied, another of his houses was vandalised and stripped of its timber, his mill was wrecked and all the gear from it stolen, a barn was burned, crops were spoiled, horses stolen, grain was scattered and his salmon cobbles were broken.[199] As in most of these reports, some exaggeration must be allowed for, but it still adds up to a catalogue of economic disaster.

In areas like the borders or highlands cattle raiding was integrated into the local economy. One man gained and another lost only to try and make up his losses from someone else. No doubt some years were worse than others, or better, but some sort of equilibrium was maintained except for the few individuals who were ruined. Where feuding also existed a more destructive attitude prevailed. In 1613 Menzies of Pitfoddels and Forbes of Monymusk burned one another's corn with the result that the economy of that locality lost two harvests.[200] One cannot measure the impact of all these feuds upon the economy of the entire kingdom, but surveys of Kintyre in 1596 and 1605 showed a rise in waste land from 23% to 41% as a direct result of the MacDonald-MacLean feud.[201] Devastation on this scale was not typical, at least not outside the highlands or borders, but those regions were in themselves very large proportions of the kingdom and its population, they were not peripheral. The earl of Moray filed a damages complaint against the earl of Huntly to the sum of £800,000 for only five raids conducted by him during the years of the feud between Huntly and his family.[202] In 1613 Robert Maxwell, the heir to the forfeited Maxwell lordship, looked back over his father's and brother's long feuds, and found himself £40,000 in debt with no means to help 'my present miserie' and the 'distressit hous of Maxwell'.[203] In 1579 a MacLean attack on Gigha resulted in a number of slaughters, but they also 'brint and distroyit the houssis and cornis on most of the island' so that ' . . . a greit multitude of honest houshaldaris ar compellit to beg thair meit and put to utter povertie for evir'.[204] How far this held back Scotland's economic progress is difficult to estimate, but the long gap between the disappearance of feuding in the lowlands and a significant economic take-off makes one suspicious of too close a relationship. What the feud did do was cause localised hardship by periodically reducing food surpluses and diverting labour into rebuilding. Tying men up in both offensive and defensive roles rather than in production was less serious since there was a manpower surplus anyway, as is evident in the numbers seeking foreign service and in vagrancy.

Interpersonal violence was the main business of feuding. Full-scale battles took place in some of the larger feuds, but the likes of Glenlivet or Dryfe Sands were highly unusual, and numbers were swollen by the legitimising effect of the crown backing one side openly with commissions. The body count was also very high in the feuds between the MacDonalds and MacLeans, the MacLeods and Mackenzies, the MacGregors and Colquhouns, and the earls of Caithness and Sutherland, all of which were highland feuds. Clashes between substantial bodies of armed men were not, however, confined to that region, even if the more spectacular examples were. In 1601 the earl of Cassillis with a force some two hundred strong ambushed the laird of Bargany in the open fields outside Ayr where he was cut off from his own men before a lance 'straik him throw the craig and throw the thropill', and killed him.[205] These incidents were not always so deliberate as this had been. When John Graham, a senator of the college of justice, was walking with his friends between Leith and Edinburgh, they noticed Graham's bitter enemy, Sir James Sandilands, with the duke of Lennox and a large company coming up behind them. Seeing them brandishing their weapons, Graham's company attacked, and in the skirmish which followed he and another gentleman were killed. In fact Sandilands and Lennox had been on their way to play golf, and the supposed weapons were golf clubs.[206] Spontaneous violence like this was often the spark which began a feud, or, as in this case, it was all the more likely to erupt where one already existed.

Culzean was murdered in a very carefully planned assassination, and the only witness to it, a schoolboy who had unwittingly carried messages for the killers, was himself put to death by them a few years later.[207] The earl of Eglinton was another victim of a plot hatched weeks before his murder in 1585 by men contracted to do it by the earl of Glencairn.[208] More chilling was the capture in 1586 of MacLean of Duart and forty of his clan by MacDonald of Kintyre while they were guests of the latter. After burning two of the MacLeans alive when they resisted capture, MacDonald had the rest, with the exception of Duart himself, 'ilk ane beheadit the dayis following, ane for ilk day, till the haill nomber was endit'.[209] In 1593 a party of Gordons went to the home of Abercrumbie of Pitmedden, dragged him outside, shot him dead, and 'with their drawin swords, cuttit him all in peeces; and as monsteris in nature, left nocht sax inche of his body, airmis, legis, and heid undevydit, and cut assunder'.[210] Donald Mackmaroch Roy was taken by some Mackenzies who, 'not content to put him to ane simple death, bot to buit thame in his blude and be a strange exemple to satisfie thair cruell and unnaturall heartis', they cut off his hands, his feet and lastly his head, and 'having cassin the same in a peitpott, exposit and laid out his careage to be a prey for doiggis and revenus beistis'.[211] Equally savage were the MacFarlanes who in 1619 captured William Buchanan who had recently won a court case agaist them, stripped him, tied him to a tree, slashed him with dirks, cut out his tongue, slit open his belly, took out his entrails, entwined them with those of his dog, and then cut his throat. Even the hardened earl of Glencairn who was called out to investigate this was horrified by what he found.[212]

Glencairn's horror was genuine, and Buchanan's fate was certainly worse than that of most feud victims. Such barbarism was not really typical of the feud, and was in fact closer to the forms of execution practised by early modern governments throughout Europe. Feuding was, however, an essentially violent means of resolving disputes, and one ought not to allow Gluckman's enthusiasm for the peaceful resolution of conflict in feuding societies to obscure that underlying fact. Yet precisely because feud is most commonly perceived as private violence, either as self-help justice or, in less sophisticated explanations, as evidence of the intrinsic anarchy of feudal society, it is rarely understood. In the grand scheme of institutional development and of the evolution of the state the feud and its violence is largely seen as an obstacle to be surmounted, not as a phenomenon to be made sense of. In this interpretation feud is largely the product of the lack of state authority, and its place in early modern history in particular is to extol the merits of the absolutist state and to emphasise the degeneracy of late feudal power structures. This is a powerful argument and one not easily challenged, although there seems little doubt that the growth of state power resulted in far greater violence of a quite different nature from that found in medieval Europe, but it obscures analysis of private violence in the context of a feuding society itself rather than in that of the society which replaced it. Strong kinship and powerful lordship clearly were related to the degree of authority held by the crown, and both did contribute to the level of violence. The high profile and the power enjoyed by aggressive young men, and the widespread carrying of weapons certainly contributed to the inflammable relations between these competing social organisms. Yet here one is pursuing something of a circular argument: society was violent so men organised themselves into defensive relationships to protect themselves from that violence, but those very relationships were themselves responsible for sustaining the violence by making offensive actions worthwhile, by making it more likely that violence could be sustained over a longer time, by dragging more people into it, and by setting up the trigger situations where confrontation would quickly lead to violence. Having said that, however, one must also ask whether the violence would have been even greater without these bonds, for both the kindred and the lord at least imposed both restraints and order on its employment. Yet as an explanation of violence this is still unsatisfactory, placing too much emphasis on sociological and political conditions. Here the violence of the feud is little more than the inevitable result of a stage of development in society between the anarchy which precedes any social organisation at all, and the later abolition of private violence by the state. Alongside that structural framework one must also place a sustainable ideology which made private violence not only obligatory, but reasonable. That ideology had itself evolved to persuade men not to seek out conflict by making the consequences of that conflict too terrible to risk, but in doing so it denied men the freedom to distinguish between issues confronting them. Every issue, however small, was a measure of a man's honour. The freedom to choose an alternative to violence was not always there, and where it was, the road to peace was fraught with its own difficulties. In a social and intellectual environment which was so conducive to private violence it took far more effort and soul-searching to find an alternative means of resolving disputes, or to put a stop to the bloodshed, than it ever did to become entangled in the feuds in the first place.

NOTES

1. L. Stone, *The Crisis of the Aristocracy, 1558–1641,* Oxford, 1977, p. 108.

2. J. R. Hale, 'Sixteenth Century Explanations of War and Violence', in *Past and Present,* 50, 1971, p. 13.

3. K. Wrightson, *English Society 1580–1680,* London, 1982, pp. 55, 62–65 and 162; and A. Macfarlane, *The Justice and the Mare's Ale: Law and Disorder in Seventeenth Century England,* Oxford, 1981.

4. J. A. Sharpe, *Crime in Seventeenth Century England, A County Study,* Cambridge, 1983, especially pp. 115–140. Also 'Domestic Homicide in Early Modern England', in *The Historical Journal,* 24, 1, 1981, pp. 29–48. See too J. Samaha, *Law and Order in Historical Perspective; The Case of Elizabethan Essex,* London, 1974.

5. L. Stone, 'Interpersonal Violence in English Society, 1300–1900', in *Past and Present,* 101, 1983, pp. 22–33. L. A. Knafla, 'The Reality of Violence in Elizabethan England: A Perspective from the Star Chamber Proceedings, 1558–1625', a paper presented to the 2nd International Colloquium of the Association for the History of Crime and Criminal Justice at Maastricht, May, 1984. To be published in H. A. Diederiks and P. Spierenburg (eds.), *Collective and Daily Violence.*

6. *R.P.C.,* iv, p. 500.

7. *State Papers and Miscellaneous Correspondence of Thomas, Earl of Melrose,* Abbotsford Club, Edinburgh, 1837, i, p. 273.

8. J. Spottiswoode, *History of the Church of Scotland,* Edinburgh, 1820, ii, p. 465.

9. D. Calderwood, *The History of the Kirk of Scotland,* Edinburgh, 1842, v, p. 359.

10. See Chapter 7 below.

11. *C.S.P., Scot.,* x, p. 137. See too the comment that 'these controversies will hardly be decided but by the ordinary provocation in use here *a legibus ad arma*', *C.S.P. Scot.,* viii, p. 212.

12. *C.S.P., Span.,* iii, p. 396. Although Spanish Naples was said to be a place where 'there are robberies and crossed swords (every day) as soon as darkness falls', quoted in F. Braudel, *The Mediterranean and the Mediterranean World in the Age of Philip II,* Glasgow, 1973, ii, p. 737.

13. R. Birrel, 'The Diary of Robert Birrel', in *Fragments of Scottish History,* (ed.) J. G. Dalyell, Edinburgh, 1798, p. 46.

14. For some cautionary points on the value of quantification, see B. Lenman and G. Parker, 'State, Community and Criminal Law', in V. A. C. Gatrell, B. Lenman and G. Parker (eds.), *Crime and the Law: the social history of crime in western Europe from 1500,* London, 1980, pp. 11–46.

15. Hence the problems encountered by Patrick Rayner, Bruce Lenman and Geoffrey Parker in their attempt to quantify crime in early modern Scotland, see *Handlist of Records for the Study of Crime in early modern Scotland (to 1747),* compiled by P. Rayner, B. Lenman and G. Parker, List and Index Society, Special Series, 16, 1982, 3, p. 5.

16. *R.P.C.,* ii to iv.

17. *R.P.C.,* iii to v.

18. *R.P.C.,* v, pp. 198–253.

19. J. M. Brown, 'Taming The Magnates?', in G. Menzies (ed.), *The Scottish Nation,* B.B.C., 1972; J. M. Brown, 'Scottish Politics 1567–1625', in A. G. R. Smith (ed.), *The Reign of James VI and I,* London, 1973; J. M. Wormald, *Court, Kirk and Community, Scotland 1470–1625.* London, 1981; A. Grant, *Independence and Nationhood, Scotland 1306–1469,* London, 1985.

20. Brown, 'The Exercise of Power', in Brown (ed.), *Scottish Society in the Fifteenth Century;* J. M. Wormald, *Lords and Men,* Edinburgh, 1985.

21. M. Lee, *John Maitland of Thirlstane and the Foundation of Stewart Despotism in Scotland,* Princeton, 1959, p. 123.

22. *R.P.C.,* iv, p. 825.

23. Sir J. Melville of Halhill, *Memoirs of His Own Life,* Bannatyne and Maitland Clubs, Edinburgh, 1827, pp. 383–384.

24. *C.S.P., Scot.,* x, p. 14.

25. *Ibid.,* xiii, part 2, p. 1118.

26. *Ibid.,* viii, p. 79.

27. D. Hume of Godscroft, *A General History of Scotland from the Year 767 to the Death of King James,* London, 1657, p. 363.

28. *C.S.P., Scot.,* x, p. 46; and see also *C.S.P., Scot.,* v, p. 370, for a similar comment ten years earlier.

29. Melville, *Memoirs,* p. 384. When writing of medieval Germany, Du Boulay made the observation that 'Anarchy is perpetuated if no-one has overmastering strength', see 'Law Enforcement in Medieval Germany', p. 346. While one can understand why this might appear to be true, it is too crude, and allows for no middle ground between the modern state and the stateless society.

30. Wrightson, *English Society, 1580–1680;* P. Laslett (ed.), *Household and Family in Past Times,* Cambridge, 1972; A. Macfarlane, *The Origins of English Individualism,* Oxford, 1978; L. Stone, *The Family, Sex and Marriage in England 1500–1800,* Pelican, 1979. Most recently R. A. Houlbrooke, *The English Family, 1450–1700,* London, 1984, continues the attack on English kindreds and stresses the nuclear family, and the uniqueness of the individual's kindred.

31. Regions in which the decline of kinship was less marked are discussed by M. E. James, *Family, Lineage and Civil Society,* Oxford, 1974; S. J. Watts, *From Border to Middle Shire: Northumberland, 1586–1625,* Leicester, 1975; P. Williams, *The Tudor Regime,* Oxford, 1979.

32. J. L. Flandrin, *Families in Former Times; Kinship, Household and Sexuality,* Cambridge, 1979; and see J. Bossy, 'Blood and Baptism: Kinship, Community and Christianity in Western Europe from the Fourteenth to the Seventeenth Centuries', in D. Baker (ed.), *Sanctity and Secularity: The Church and The World,* The Ecclesiastical History Society, Oxford, 1973, pp. 129–43.

33. Wormald, 'Bloodfeud, Kindred and Government in Early Modern Scotland', p. 71; Wormald, *Lords and Men,* Chapter 5.

34. Sir R. Gordon, *A Genealogical History of the Earldom of Sutherland,* Edinburgh, 1813, p. 187. My italics.

35. J. Napier, *A Plaine Discovery of the Whole Revelation,* Edinburgh, 1593, p. 106.

36. Scottish Record Office, Breadalbane Muniments, G.D., 112/39/301.

37. *R.P.C.,* iv, p. 283.

38. *Criminal Trials in Scotland from 1488 to 1624,* (ed.) R. Pitcairn, London, 1833, iii, p. 21.

39. Gordon, *Sutherland,* pp. 256–257.

40. R. Rollock, *Select Works,* (ed.) W. Gunn, Wodrow Society, Edinburgh, 1844–49, i, p. 52.

41. Philpotts, *Kindred and Clan,* p. 2.

42. Gluckman, *Custom and Conflict,* pp. 14 and 22.

43. M. Bloch, *Feudal Society,* London, 1978, pp. 134–142. Also see G. Duby, *The Chivalrous Society,* London, 1977, pp. 134–148; D. Sabean, 'Aspects of kinship behaviour and property in Rural Western Europe before 1800', in J. Goody, J. Thirsk and E. P.

Thomson (eds.), *Family and Inheritance in Western Europe, 1222–1800,* Cambridge, 1976.

44. Whitaker, 'Tribal Solidarity and National Politics', in Lewis (ed.), *History and Anthropology,* p. 270.

45. Wormald, 'Bloodfeud, Kindred and Government in Early Modern Scotland', p. 67; and Wormald, *Lords and Men,* p. 79.

46. W. Fraser, *Memoirs of the Maxwells of Pollok,* Edinburgh, 1875, ii, pp. 154–155, no. 152.

47. Stone, *The Family, Sex and Marriage in England, 1500–1800,* pp. 98–100 and 116–118, is more traditional, while J. A. Sharpe, 'Domestic Homicide in Early Modern England', shows that in Essex only 25% of homicides were domestic compared to 50% today. Similar points are made by B. H. Westman, 'The Peasant Family and Crime in Fourteenth Century England', in *The Journal of British Studies,* 13(2), 1974, pp. 1–18.

48. For a general discussion, see R. Marshall, *Virgins and Viragos, A History of Women in Scotland from 1080–1980,* London, 1983, pp. 87–104. For a church court, see *Stirling Presbytery Records, 1581–87,* (ed.) J. Kirk, Edinburgh, 1981. Evidence from the Netherlands using church court records suggests a low level of marital violence, H. W. Roodenburg, 'Beating Spouses: Marital Violence and the Consistory of the Reformed Church of Amsterdam, 1579–1630', paper contributed to the 2nd International Colloquium of the I.A.H.C.C.J. at Maastricht, May, 1984. To be published in Diederiks and Spierenburg (eds.), *Collective and Daily Violence.*

49. *R.P.C.,* iii, pp. 34–35.

50. For example see *R.P.C.,* iv, pp. 175–176 for the Henderson brothers and pp. 295–296 for the Somerville family.

51. See below, pp. 76–79.

52. Bloch, *Feudal Society,* p. 225.

53. Gordon, *Sutherland,* p. 329.

54. See for example Lee, *John Maitland of Thirlstane,* p. 284.

55. Wormald, 'Bloodfeud, Kindred and Government in Early Modern Scotland', p. 72.

56. *C.S.P., Scot.,* v, p. 34.

57. *Melrose,* i, pp. 30–31.

58. *Report of the Historical Manuscripts Commission on the Laing Manuscripts preserved in Edinburgh University,* London, 1914, 1925, i, p. 83.

59. Hume, *History,* p. 344, where the laird of Wedderburn tells Morton that 'if his Chiefe should turn him out at the foredoore, he would come in againe at the back-doore'. An equally profound quotation from the Anglo-Saxon Chronicle is 'No relative is dearer to us than our lord'.

60. *C.S.P., Scot.,* iv, p. 561.

61. For English lordship in the late Tudor period see M. E. James, *English Politics and the Concept of Honour, 1485–1642, Past and Present Supplement* 3, 1978, especially pp. 17–22; M. E. James, *A Tudor Magnate and the Tudor State: Henry 5th Earl of Northumberland,* Borthwick Paper No. 30, York, 1966; M. E. James, 'The First Earl of Cumberland and the Decline of English Feudalism', in *Northern History,* i, 1966, pp. 43–69. For a discussion of this theme in a European context, J. Powis, *Aristocracy,* Oxford, 1984, pp. 51–57.

62. Gordon, *Sutherland,* p. 267.

63. T. Craig, *Jus Feudale,* (tr.) J. A. Clyde, Edinburgh, 1934, i, p. xi.

64. A. H. Williamson, *Scottish National Consciousness in the Age of James VI,* Edinburgh, 1979, p. 133.

65. *C.B.P.*, i, p. 408.

66. For the church, see below, Chapter 7. Powis rightly argues: 'That aristocratic following were on occasion drawn into violence is not in doubt. But the claim that they were *intrinsically* violent is another matter. It is not self evident that great noblemen, their kinsmen and their clients had much to gain from participating in indiscriminate civil mayhem', *Aristocracy*, p. 59.

67. J. M. Brown, 'Bonds of Manrent in Scotland before 1603', University of Glasgow Ph.D. thesis, 1974, and in the published form, J. M. Wormald, *Lords and Men*.

68. *Report of the Royal Commission on Historical Manuscripts*, London, 1870, iv, 'Erskine-Murray M.S.', p. 527.

69. W. Fraser, *The Elphinstone Family Book*, Edinburgh, 1897, ii, p. 264.

70. S.R.O., Inventory of Scottish Muniments at Haigh, N.R.A. 237, i, box C, 9/May/1578, Crawford to Lord Ross. For other letters like this, see Fraser, *Maxwells of Pollok*, p. 73, No. 54, Lennox to Pollok; *Correspondence of Sir Patrick Waus*, (ed.) R. Vans Agnew, Edinburgh, 1887, i, p. 94, Cassillis to Vaus of Barnbarroch.

71. *H.M.C.*, iii, p. 419.

72. *C.B.P.*, ii, p. 775.

73. Waus, *Correspondence*, ii, p. 380.

74. Fraser, *Maxwells of Pollok*, ii, p. 167, No. 171. On another occasion Pollok criticised a magistrate for the way in which he had treated one of his men, accusing him of being unfair, and telling him that 'The dweill maid sowteris schiptmen, quha can nather steir nor row', pp. 165–166, No. 168.

75. *Historical Account of the Principal Families of the Name of Kennedy*, (ed.) R. Pitcairn, Edinburgh, 1830, p. 26.

76. Leslie, *Historie of Scotland*, i, p. 103.

77. S.R.O., Atholl MS., National Register of Archives, 224/1633.

78. *C.S.P., Scot.*, x, p. 453. J. Russel-Major has shown that similar complaints were made in France, 'The Crown and the Aristocracy in Renaissance France', in *American Historical Review*, 69, (1963–64), p. 638.

79. Leslie, *Historie of Scotland*, i, p. 96.

80. Craig, *Jus Feudale*, i, pp. 583–610.

81. *R.P.C.*, iv, p. 349.

82. *C.S.P., Scot.*, xiii, Part 2, p. 864.

83. Pitcairn, *Kennedy*, p. 21.

84. Gordon, *Sutherland*, pp. 197–200.

85. For Tuscany, see the career of the first duke of Montemarciano in Braudel, *The Mediterranean*, pp. 749–751, which includes a fairly idealised view of banditry. M. E. James, in *Change and Continuity in the Tudor North: the rise of Thomas First Lord Wharton*, York, 1965, p. 8, writes that 'behind the decorous facade all great lords were bound in a close mafia with the upland thieves, and patronised and protected border lawlessness'. Similar relationships existed on the Welsh marches, P. Williams, 'The Welsh Borderland Under Queen Elizabeth', in *Welsh Historical Review*, i, 1960, pp. 19–36. For elsewhere in Europe, see M. Weisser, 'Crime and Punishment in Early Modern Spain', in Gatrell, Lenman and Parker (eds.), *Crime and the Law*, pp. 82–83; and A. D. Wright, 'Venetian Law and Order: A Myth?', in *Bulletin of the Institute of Historical Research*, 53, 1980, p. 193. For a more detailed study of banditry, E. J. Hobsbawm, *Bandits*, London, 1969, is the most useful. More recent research on early modern banditry was presented in papers at the 2nd International Colloquium of the I.A.H.C.C.J. in Maastricht, May, 1984 by F. Egmond on 'Bandits as savages' and J. Sundin on 'Bandits and Guerilla Soldiers'.

86. See J. A. Inciardini, A. A. Bloch and L. A. Hallowell, *A Historical Approach to Crime*, Beverly Hills, 1977, Chapter 4, 'The Godfather Syndrome'.

87. *C.S.P., Scot.,* ix, pp. 306, 453, 463, 619 and 716; xiii, Part 2, pp. 620, 659 and 661; *R.P.C.,* iv. p. 372; vi, p. 1; Pitcairn, *Criminal Trials,* ii, pp. 52, 402–403 and 410; Calderwood, *History,* v, pp. 71 and 169–170; Spottiswoode, *History,* iii, p. 422; Birrel, 'Diary', pp. 27–28; S.R.O., Bruce of Earlshall Muniments, G.D., 247/182/1.

88. Angus was also in his early thirties, but he died shortly afterwards.

89. Duby, *The Chivalrous Society,* p. 115. Also of use is D. Herlihy, 'Some Psychological and Social Roots of Violence in the Tuscan Cities', in L. Martines (ed.), *Violence and Civil Disorder in Italian Cities, 1200–1500,* London, 1972, pp. 129–154; and S. M. Wyntjes, 'Family Allegiance and Religious Persuasion: the Lesser Nobility and the Revolt of the Netherlands', in *The Sixteenth Century Journal,* xii, No. 2, 1981, p. 50, where young men's aggression was channelled into an alternative form of violence in iconoclasm.

90. *R.P.C.,* vii, p. 509; viii, p. 271; Pitcairn, *Criminal Trials,* ii, p. 532.

91. *R.P.C.,* vii, p. 425. Within two years, however, this same Lord Maxwell was accused by the king of 'youthfull ryott and insolence', and was executed in 1613, *R.P.C.,* vii, p. 539.

92. S.R.O. Inventory of Scottish Muniments at Haigh, N.R.A. 237, i, box C, 3/Nov/1591, Ogilvy to Crawford, and the reply is undated.

93. *R.P.C.,* vii, p. 60; Pitcairn, *Criminal Trials,* iii, pp. 61–65.

94. *R.P.C.,* xi, p. 439; xiii, p. 769; Pitcairn, *Criminal Trials,* iii, pp. 443, 479–481 and 542.

95. R. H. Harding, *Anatomy of a Power Elite; the Provincial Governors of Early Modern France,* Yale, 1978, pp. 71–80.

96. D. Moysie, *Memoirs of the Affairs of Scotland from 1577 to 1603,* Bannatyne and Maitland Clubs, Edinburgh, 1830, p. 78.

97. For a summary of these men's careers, see below, Chapter 8. This estimate is based on *The Scots Peerage,* (ed.) J. Balfour Paul, Edinburgh, 1904–14. Unfortunately most of the careers of younger sons are unknown.

98. Pitcairn, *Kennedy,* p. 12.

99. D. Caldwell, 'Royal Patronage of Arms and Armour Making', in D. Caldwell (ed.), *Scottish Weapons and Fortifications, 1100–1800,* Edinburgh, 1981, p. 82. Of England, Stone writes of a peak in the stockpiling of weapons between 1550 and 1660, *The Crisis of the Aristocracy,* p. 106; and J. Cockburn, in 'The Nature and Incidence of Crime in England, 1559–1625', highlighted the significance of fire-arms in violent crime, in J. Cockburn (ed.), *Crime in England, 1550–1800,* London, 1977.

100. *C.S.P. Scot.,* xiii, Part 1, p. 57; Pitcairn, *Criminal Trials,* i, Part 2, p. 89.

101. For Cawdor, see below, pp. 165–166, and for the others, *R.P.C.,* vi, pp. 178 and 519. Just how many of the nobility had ordnance, and what its quality was is unknown, but Spynie was certainly not alone in having a petard (an explosive device which was fixed to doors or walls), as the earl of Cassillis brought one home from Italy, Pitcairn, *Kennedy,* pp. 21–22.

102. *C.S.P., Scot.,* viii, p. 109.

103. *R.P.C.,* v, p. 236.

104. See below, 156 ff.

105. Pitcairn, *Criminal Trials,* iii, pp. 43–47; Calderwood, *History,* vi, p. 704.

106. *R.P.C.,* iv, p. 457.

107. Birrel, 'Diary', p. 56.

108. Pitcairn, *Criminal Trials,* iii, pp. 393–394.

109. *Ibid.,* p. 394.

110. *C.S.P. Scot.,* xii, p. 92; xiii, Part 1, p. 398.

111. Campbell, *Honour, Family and Patronage,* p. 193.

112. Karsten, 'Blood, Revenge and War among and the Jibaro Indians', in Bohannan (ed.), *Law and Warfare,* p. 316; and Black-Michaud, *Cohesive Force,* pp. 178–184.

113. Stone, *The Crisis of the Aristocracy,* pp. 107–113, and for by far the best discussion of this subject, M. E. James, 'English Politics and the Concept of Honour, 1485–1642', quote from p. 1.

114. F. R. Bryson, *The Point of Honour in Sixteenth Century Italy,* New York, 1935; J. Cooper, 'Introduction' to J. Cooper (ed.), *The New Cambridge Modern History, Vol. iii, The Decline of Spain and the Thirty Years War,* pp. 23–27; Harding, *Anatomy of a Power Elite,* pp. 68–71, where honour is closely related to royal service.

115. See M. Keen, *Chivalry,* New Haven and London, 1984.

116. Precedence disputes were fairly common, although the whole point of having a system of precedence was to avoid them, e.g. Lord Hume and Lord Fleming at the 1587 parliament when Hume challenged the latter to 'the singular combat', but they 'wer not suffered to fecht, albeit they war baithe weill willing', *C.B.P.,* i, p. 273; Moysie, *Memoirs,* p. 65. In Russia a points system was used to try and prevent any doubts over precedence, see D. H. Pennington, *Seventeenth Century Europe,* Singapore, 1980, p. 93, on the Russian 'mestnichesto'.

117. *C.B.P.,* ii, p. 712. In medieval Europe the other obligation to dead kinsmen was to pray for them 'since the bond of kinship is the most effectual means of securing mutual support in salvation', Bossy, 'Blood and Baptism', in Baker (ed.), *Sanctity and Secularity,* p. 136.

118. Keen, *Chivalry,* pp. 33 and 69. This sharing of honour was crucial to the survival of the kindred because the economics of primogeniture divided it by wealth, denying the majority of kinsmen access to that wealth, J. Goody, *The development of the family and marriage in Europe,* Cambridge University Press, 1983, pp. 121–122. Honour was not, therefore, as intangible as Stone suggests in *The Crisis of the Aristocracy,* pp. 107–108. Black-Michaud, in *Cohesive Force,* p. 178, writes that 'In feuding societies honour and power are synonymous ... a man's prestige ultimately summarizes all those qualities which differentiate him from other members of the same society and together constitute his qualifications for leadership'.

119. Birrel, 'Diary', p. 24.

120. Hume, *History,* p. 424.

121. L. Mair, *Primitive Government,* Harmondsworth, 1970, p. 40; and S. Roberts, 'The Study of Dispute: Anthropological Perspectives' in J. Bossy (ed.), *Disputes and Settlements,* Cambridge, 1983, p. 9.

122. Keen, *Chivalry,* p. 103.

123. F. A. J. Ianni and E. Reussi-Ianni, *A Family Business: Kinship and Social Control in Organised Crime,* New York, 1972, p. 20.

124. *C.B.P.,* ii, p. 463. Sir Robert showed exactly what he meant by this in 1596 when he responded to the theft of his own property by raiding into England and killing four men, prompting Sir John Carey, the deputy governor of Berwick, to comment in a letter to Burghley that all this was 'for one shepe hogg that was taken from Sessfords sheppherd, so highlie was Sessfordes honor toiched therein', *C.B.P.,* ii, p. 167.

125. Gordon, *Sutherland,* p. 258.

126. *Ibid.,* pp. 144–145. Sir Robert says that in contrast to this the English contest 'for the wall'.

127. *R.P.C.,* ix, p. 371, note.

128. *R.P.C.,* x, p. 165.

129. N. Davies, *God's Playground, A History of Poland,* Oxford, 1981, p. 352.

130. *C.B.P.*, ii, pp. 462–463.

131. For the duel, F. R. Bryson, *The Sixteenth Century Italian Duel: A Study in Renaissance Social History*, Chicago, 1938. Cooper, 'Introduction' to *The New Cambridge Modern History*, iv, pp. 23–25, describes the spread of the Italian duel, particularly to France where the nobility were said to be 'the most violent and insolent in the world'. Harding, *Anatomy of Power*, pp. 77–80 and 253–254, also discusses duelling in France where some 6,000 noblemen were estimated to have been killed in duels in the later years of the sixteenth century. Many critics thought that duelling cheapened honour by trivialising it. While Harding thinks that feuding was stimulated by duels, H. C. Lea, *The Duel and the Oath* (University of Pennsylvania, 1974), suggested that the abolition of feuding had been responsible for the growth of duelling in the first place.

132. S.R.O., Buccleuch Muniments, G.D., 224/1059/17.

133. Pitcairn, *Kennedy*, pp. 16–17.

134. *R.P.C.*, x, pp. 76–77.

135. *C.S.P., Scot.*, vi, p. 475.

136. Spottiswoode, *History*, ii, p. 228; Hume, *History*, p. 344.

137. Moysie, *Memoirs*, p. 111; Birrel, 'Diary', p. 31.

138. See below, p. 249.

139. Quoted in James, 'English Politics and the Concept of Honour', p. 14. Moslem 'honour' societies have experienced this same conflict, Kieffer, *The Tausug*, pp. 53–54.

140. Pitcairn, *Kennedy*, p. 125.

141. Birrel, 'Diary', p. 60.

142. Quoted in G. M. Fraser, *The Steel Bonnets*, London, 1971, p. 30.

143. *H.M.C.*, vi, 'Menzies M.S.', p. 697, No. 83.

144. Gordon, *Sutherland*, p. 182.

145. Quoted in Broude, 'Revenge and Revenge Tragedy in Renaissance England', p. 41.

146. *C.S.P., Scot.*, xi, p. 35.

147. Kieffer, *The Tausug*, pp. 68–70.

148. Karsten, 'Blood, Revenge and War among the Jibaro Indians', in Bohannan (ed.), *Law and Warfare*, p. 310.

149. Chagnon, 'Yanamamo: The Fierce People', in Spradley and McCurdy (eds.), *Conformity and Conflict*, p. 261.

150. Birrel, 'Diary', p. 32.

151. Broude, 'Revenge and Revenge Tragedy in Renaissance England', pp. 39–42.

152. Campbell, *Honour, Family and Patronage*, pp. 193–203.

153. Flandrin, *Families in Former Times*, p. 16. The missionaries wrote that the natives 'kill one another like Barbarians and are not willing to pardon nor even to discuss any arrangements until they are avenged. And not only do they make war on him who has done the injury, but also, in general, on all his kinsfolk, as far as the third degree of relationship'.

154. Gordon, *Sutherland*, pp. 188–189; *The Historie and Life of King James the Sext*, (ed.) T. Thomson, Bannatyne Club, Edinburgh, 1825, p. 217.

155. Leslie, *Historie of Scotland*, i, p. 101.

156. *R.P.C.*, v, p. 248.

157. See Black-Michaud's arguments on this, *Cohesive Force*, p. 28.

158. Pitcairn, *Kennedy*, p. 64.

159. *Ibid.*, p. 59.

160. Melville, *Memoirs*, p. 385.

161. Gordon, *Sutherland*, p. 299.

162. *R.P.C.*, iv, p. 655.

163. *R.P.C.,* xii, pp. 588–589.

164. For the deaths of Morton and Captain James Stewart, see below, p. 114; for Torthorwald, see *R.P.C.,* viii, pp. 128, 144 and 153; Spottiswoode, *History,* iii, p. 40.

165. *R.P.C.,* v, p. 74.

166. Fraser, *Maxwells of Pollok,* ii, p. 137, No. 156. Similar confinement was resorted to in Albania, see Wormald, 'Bloodfeud, Kindred and Government in Early Modern Scotland', p. 57, note 12.

167. *R. P.C.,* ix, pp. 352–353.

168. Gordon, *Sutherland,* pp. 170–171.

169. *C.B.P.,* ii, p. 189.

170. *Basilikon Doron,* p. 30.

171. *Historie,* p. 317.

172. In the Albanian case Whitaker has pointed out that bloodfeud was 'not merely vengeance, but an offering to the soul of a dead man', in 'Tribal Structure and National Politics', in Lewis (ed.), *History and Social Anthropology,* p. 266. The Tausug talk of a 'debt of a soul', Kieffer, *The Tausug,* p. 67.

173. Pitcairn, *Criminal Trials,* iii, p. 419.

174. Gordon, *Sutherland,* p. 194.

175. *R.P.C.,* ix, p. 639.

176. Pitcairn, *Criminal Trials,* iii, p. 190. Pitcairn discusses this in some detail, pp. 182–199. The idea was, of course, much older than the sixteenth century, and in *The Nibelungenlied,* p. 137, the author makes the comment that 'Now it is a great marvel and frequently happens today that whenever a bloody-guilty murderer is seen beside the corpse the wounds begin to bleed'.

177. Pitcairn, *Kennedy,* p. 125.

178. Gordon, *Sutherland,* p. 283.

179. Birrel, 'Diary', p. 46.

180. *Historie,* pp. 296–297; Spottiswoode, *History,* iii, pp. 445–446; Calderwood, *History,* v, p. 256.

181. R. A. Mactaggart, 'Assault in the Later Baron Courts', in *Juridical Review,* 7, 1962, p. 104.

182. *Aberdeen Council Letters, Vol. 1, 1552-1639,* (ed.) R. B. Taylor, Oxford, 1942, pp. 31–34.

183. Leslie, *Historie of Scotland,* i, p. 101.

184. Keen, *Chivalry,* p. 175.

185. *C.B.P.,* ii, p. 538; Birrel, 'Diary', p. 46.

186. *C.S.P., Scot.,* x, p. 641.

187. *Ibid.,* pp. 631 and 636; *Historie,* pp. 346–347. Curiously the author of the *Historie* thought 'this forme is rare, and was never usit in Scotland before', although the same source describes one being carried at Carberry in 1567, p. 13. This may have been the 'Darnley Memorial Portrait' or one like it.

188. Pitcairn, *Kennedy,* p. 68.

189. *R.P.C.,* v, pp. 444–445. Moray was killed in 1592, and Maxwell a year later, but both corpses were still unburied in 1598.

190. Bloch, *Feudal Society,* p. 126.

191. R. Chambers, *Domestic Annals of Scotland,* Edinburgh, 1859, i, pp. 368–372.

192. *R.P.C.,* iv, p. 455.

193. *R.P.C.,* v, p. 381.

194. *C.S.P., Scot.,* vii, p. 330.

195. *R.P.C.*, vii, p. 143.

196. Gordon, *Sutherland*, p. 177.

197. *R.P.C.*, x, p. 608; xi, p. 34; *Melrose*, i, p. 297.

198. In England, Stone believes most combats outside those involving the rapier to have been relatively harmless, *The Crisis of the Aristocracy*, p. 118; and Williams thinks men 'drew back from death blows', *The Tudor Regime*, p. 220.

199. *R.P.C.*, vi, pp. 501–505.

200. *R.P.C.*, x, pp. 172–173; Pitcairn, *Criminal Trials*, iii, p. 258.

201. D. Gregory, *History of the Western Highlands and Islands*, Edinburgh, 1975, p. 269.

202. S.R.O., Moray Muniments, N.R.A., 217/2/4/80.

203. W. MacDowell, *History of the Burgh of Dumfries with Notices of Nithsdale and the Western Border*, Edinburgh, 1872, pp. 293–294; Fraser, *Maxwells of Pollok*, ii, pp. 193–194, No. 197.

204. *R.P.C*, iii, pp. 135–136. Similar devastation took place in the feud between Sir Rory MacLeod of Harris and Donald Gorm of Sleat in which the two clans 'wer bent headlong in against one another with spoills and cruell slaughters, to utter ruin and desolation of both ther cuntries, untill all the inhabitants were forced to eat horses, catts, and other filthie beasts', Gordon, *Sutherland*, pp. 244–245.

205. Pitcairn, *Kennedy*, pp. 45–48.

206. *Historie*, p. 267; *C.S.P., Scot.*, xi, p. 49; Calderwood, *History*, v, pp. 223–224; Spottiswoode, *History*, ii, pp. 427–428.

207. Pitcairn, *Kennedy*, pp. 56–58; Pitcairn, *Criminal Trials*, iv, pp. 127–181.

208. See below, pp. 87–88.

209. *Historie*, p. 217; Gordon, *Sutherland*, p. 187. This incident probably inspired the 1587 legislation against murder under trust.

210. Pitcairn, *Criminal Trials*, iii, pp. 78–79.

211. *R.P.C.*, iii, pp. 505–506.

212. *R.P.C.*, xi, p. 635; Pitcairn, *Criminal Trials*, iii, pp. 547–548.

# 2

# *Peace and Persuasion*[1]

The illusory nature of peace has never stopped men looking for it, and in sixteenth-century Scotland that search was as much a preoccupation as was the violence which forced it to recede from men's grasp. A feuding society even more than a non-feuding society can never be at peace: to be so it would have to become something else, it would have to rid itself of feuding altogether. Yet that did not mean that individual feuds could not be pacified, and that enemies could not lay down their weapons and become friends. Violence may have been unavoidable, even respectable in the sense of being accepted in social behaviour, but it was rarely desirable. Even the most excessive violence of the feud represented more often than not an enraged cry for justice, it was not simply bloodletting for its own sake. Vengeance was self-help justice, however subjective it may have been, and while the violence could become a self-perpetuating cycle of apparent meaninglessness, justice, or the lack of it, remained its root cause. Of course, that justice simply meant wanting to have things one's own way as much as it meant any adherence to objective truths, and this does not somehow raise feuding to some higher moral level. Justice was many things, but for most men it was winning, and being seen to be right.

That justice may have been measured in the blood of one's enemies, and that was the currency which brought most satisfaction. Yet the desire for peace was an equally powerful one, and most feuding societies have evolved means of both achieving peace and ensuring satisfaction.[2] This dual necessity to have justice and peace could create irreconcilable tensions, unless the peace itself was demonstrably just, and because that could rarely be achieved by forcefully winning, compromise was necessary. However, in an honour society compromise can read like defeat since it implies that a man cannot attain the justice he has demanded. Making peace, therefore, was a long, slow business of persuasion, concession, and ultimately of compromise, the dynamics of which were themselves part of the fabric of a feuding society.

Yet perhaps the more obvious place to look for justice was in the law. Scottish law and the Scottish law courts were, after all, rapidly evolving and appeared to have the infrastructure and the personnel capable of dealing with the issues of a feud. The sixteenth century had seen a rapid growth in the development of a legal profession, and an interest in Scots law, both civil and criminal.[3] However, that increasing subtlety and expertise was in itself an obstacle, and the justice court in Edinburgh was 'characterised by excessive technicality'.[4] This was a complaint common throughout Europe, and had increasingly turned men away from the courts towards privately arranged settlements.[5] How litigious the Scots were in comparison to Englishmen or Castilians is unknown, but one suspects that like them their enthusiasm was tempered by the realisation that they were being asked to pay more, wait longer, and receive a judgement based more on points of law than on what they regarded as justice.[6]

There were other reasons for being dissatisfied with the courts, or for distrusting them. If the crime was a capital offence, then clearly an execution was not going to be any more acceptable to a kindred than murder would have been. In a feuding society like Scotland the law was simply seen as a weapon with a cutting edge of its own for pursuing vengeance.[7] Neither the law nor the judges who enforced it were ever thought of as objective and somehow above the world of the feud. The crown official who wrote to a session judge asking that 'ye will gif attendance that I get na wrong' knew very well that the most effective means of using the law was to put pressure on those who administered it, and he offered suitable favours in return.[8] The assize too was suspect in a society of powerful loyalties to kindred, lord, or dependant. When at the trial of John Ross of Ballivot in 1600 his lawyers repeatedly raised objections to the presence of men on the assize who were kinsmen of the pursuers, or of other men Ballivot was at feud with, they were not making technical points.[9] Judges and assizes were themselves too much a product of a feuding society in which obligations to friends and kinsmen, and extensive corruption, made it impossible for the law to be seen as the repository of anything other than a partisan kind of justice.

If such difficulties existed in the central courts, they were magnified in the local courts where the bulk of the law was practised and executed. There in the localities enormous hereditary judicial powers were invested in men who exercised those powers in an intensely personal way. Sheriff courts, regality courts, stewartry courts, bailie courts, and barony courts all had criminal jurisdictions of varying degree. The regality courts were virtually independent of royal justice, having the right to repledge cases from royal courts, and to try all crimes except treason, but including in some the four pleas of the crown: murder, rape, arson and robbery.[10] Those powers could themselves be the cause of a local feud, and they were certainly manipulated in the interests of the lord who exercised them[11]. Dame Jane Hamilton claimed before the privy council that she was unable to get justice locally in a dispute with her estranged husband, the earl of Eglinton: 'he being a grit man and judge in the cuntrie quhair he duellis, sche can get na remeid nor redress againis him by way of captioun or atherwayise as he war ane privat persoun'.[12] Patrick Crawford of Auchinames also appealed to the privy council to adjudicate in a case between himself and the commissioners of Glasgow who had summoned him to answer for the non-fulfilment of a contract. Auchinames did not believe this was the issue at all, and thought he was being invited to Glasgow because the Cunningham family was strong there, and could 'the better effectuate the gret malice and deidlie feid' they held against him.[13] Confidence in local justice was very low, unless one's own lord or kinsman was dispensing it. The law was highly personalised, and was seen to be so. Auchinames may have been quite wrong in how he perceived his summons to Glasgow, but one can understand why he saw it that way. This personal justice is emphasised by the case of William Douglas of Cavers, the sheriff of Roxburgh, a man who could not do his job properly, 'being knawne unable and sua corpolent as he mycht not travell'.[14] This fat judge trying to ride around his border sheriffdom was the other side of Scottish law from the sophisticated and highly trained lawyers of Edinburgh. It was in the hands of men like Cavers, with their heritable powers, and their local interests and loyalties, personally enforcing their version of legal justice, that the great responsibility for local peace lay.

An objective law, however, was not what men expected. While a man might complain that a judge was corrupt, or a friend of his enemy, he himself would have employed the same means had they been available. Judgement itself was not a solution, and in common with other European societies it was recognised that disputants were 'brought together by love or separated by judgement'.[15] This point was made in a letter from Lord Herries to John Johnstone of Greenhill in 1585 in which he tried to persuade the latter to free his man rather than try him in court:

> Quhairfor Johne, I desyr yow to lat this pure man to libertie as ye wald I suld do for yow. Utherwayis I will think ye do over lytill for me, and I will haif the les to do with yow in tyme cuming, and seik the nixt remeid. This gentill man is my freind quhom I man do for, and ye are ane man that I have to do with to, and gif ye lat him nocht to libertie, I can nocht think yow to be freind.[16]

It was outside the law as it was found in the courts that men sought the peace that only friendship and love could guarantee. Bridging that gulf between bloodfeud and friendship was impossible under the law, and far from easy outside it.

The reasons why feuding parties might decide to pursue peace obviously varied. No doubt some had just had enough and wanted to end the violence, and if this was so, there were great advantages in the assurance system described below which did just that, but did not conclude the feud. It was possible to remain in a state of feud without actually feuding, a situation which had great advantages in that honour remained intact. The problem was that in an honour society no-one wanted to appear too keen to establish peace, involving, as it must, compromise. More commonly, therefore, the initiative for that peace came from kinsmen, friends, and neighbours who were concerned that the feud was disrupting the locality. Alternatively that pressure might come from the crown. In either case such pressure could be sufficient to persuade men that they should at least explore the possibility of peace.

As in war, the first stage in pacifying a bloodfeud was to achieve a ceasefire. This could be attained by two means: by imposed acts of caution, or by mutually agreed acts of assurance. The assurance was a guarantee in the form of written contracts that neither side would harm the other. Lord Sempill gave assurance that neither he, his kinsmen, his dependants, tenants nor servants would molest Sir John Maxwell of Pollok, his brothers, kinsmen, etc., 'for quhatsumevir caus, occasioun, or trubles fallin furth and committit betuix us in ony tymes bygain', and he promised to observe this 'be my honour, lawtie, and fidelitie'.[17] Such a contract was both private and voluntary, entered into by both sides at mutual consent, and often exchanged for an assurance from the other side. Financial penalties were written into the terms should the assurance be broken. These amounts varied according to the status of the principals and the level of trust between both sides, but they could be very substantial, as in the £10,000 the earl of Crawford assured the master of Glamis for in 1579.[18] As in the Sempill case, honour was also involved, being forfeited if the assurance was broken, this being the reason for the symbolic humiliation of the laird of Johnstone in an incident cited in the previous chapter.[19] Given the importance of honour, this aspect of the assurance should not be under-estimated, although the additional financial penalty would not have been necessary if honour alone had been thought sufficiently binding. Concern that they might incur the pains of their assurance unwittingly prompted the lairds of Caprington and Craigie to add a clause to their agreement that 'sudden tuilyies' between their servants would not be considered an infringement of it.[20]

Assurances were not entirely beyond crown influence. In 1587 murder under trust was made a treasonable offence by parliament.[21] The act was largely a shocked response to the MacLean massacre earlier that year,[22] but it also gave the crown a greater say in penalising those who did abuse assurances. As was mentioned above, the crown might itself act to put pressure on the parties to give assurances in the first place, as it did with two Kennedy lairds in 1582.[23] Furthermore, the parties might themselves bring the crown into the agreement by asking the privy council to register it, thus making it a witness to the assurance, and a party in the recovery of any financial penalties which might have to be pursued at a later date.[24]

The assurance, however, was only a short-term agreement, most being made for a year or less. That between Lord Livingston and the laird of Carse was registered with the privy council on 27 March 1583 and was to last until the last day of November of the same year.[25] Many simply fell into abeyance unless the parties concerned really wanted to prolong the peace, or unless the same pressure was applied by other members of the community as had been the year before. Even during the period of assurance relations between the two sides could remain very tense. Lord Hamilton had to recognise this when he found difficulty in arranging a meeting among the gentlemen of the border marches because of 'the sundry quarrells and feads standing amongst thame, which they be assured to certain dayes, not yet expired, yet hath no will to cum togedder suddenly in any place'.[26] Others were less careful, and incidents real, imagined, or contrived took place which led to the collapse of the assurances. In Glasgow in 1581 John Pollok of that Ilk broke his assurance with Sir John Maxwell of Nethir Pollok when he 'chasit and followit thame on horsebak to have slayne thame with swordis, and dischargit pistolettis at thame'.[27]

This dependence on voluntary good will was the weakness of assurances. The loss of honour involved in behaving as the laird of Pollok did could easily be offset by that gained in fulfilling the honour-bound obligations of the bloodfeud, while actually collecting the financial pains could be very difficult, and where they were paid the price might be thought worth the vengeance extracted. Assurances were also to make the crown increasingly uncomfortable from the 1590s as they appeared to legitimise the subject's right to wage private war.[28] From the crown's point of view acts of caution were preferable since it was more directly involved. That involvement, however, stopped at ending the violence, and gave the crown no right to interfere in the search for a settlement. A caution, therefore, might follow a complaint made to the privy council by one or both parties about the activities of the other, or it might arise from a crown initiative to try and cool down a dispute. In form it was very similar to the assurance, but the principal of the act found surety for his behaviour from friends, and it was they who were bound to pay the crown should the promise not to harm the other side be broken.[29] Acts of caution were not only used to temporarily pacify a feud, but had a far wider application in keeping the peace, particularly among people of middle-ranking status groups, and between unequal rivals.[30]

The cautioners themselves were acceptable on the basis of their responsibility and their relationship with the principal. A large proportion were kinsmen, like the three Hamilton lairds who stood caution for William Hamilton of Sanquhar in 1576, or neighbours, as in the case of the other party in this dispute, John Wallace of Cragy whose surety was given by George Crawford of Lefnoreis.[31] The crown's concern with having the fines paid in cash probably explains the large number of burgesses who figure in the giving of surety. Thus when Uthred MacDowell of Garthland had to find surety in 30,000 merks not to harm his Gordon neighbours, he went to Robert Gourlay, an Edinburgh burgess, for help. Gourlay may have been a relative, but it is very probable that he was simply better able to guarantee the cash than any of MacDowell's Galloway kinsmen, and that the relationship was a business one.[32] Surety from noblemen was less acceptable, even if they could pay the money. When the earl of Caithness complained to the privy council that he had been outlawed and charged to ward in Blackness Castle in spite of having found surety from the earl of Huntly, the council refused to accept it from Huntly 'or ony utheris of his degree and rank', and told him to find surety from someone more accountable.[33]

Acts of caution were also difficult to enforce, which was the implicit reason for not accepting noblemen as surety. Being a crown measure gave them slightly more legal status, but the pains and the means of enforcing them were much the same as in assurances. This time the penalties fell on kinsmen, friends, dependants, or creditors who could try and recover the sum from the principal themselves, and there was certainly a value in daring men to risk inconveniencing such people through reckless behaviour. They therefore had a vested interest in seeing that a lord, relative or friend behaved, just as there was a responsibility on the part of the principal not to involve them in any material loss. However, for those determined enough the price could be met, and it was widely known how inefficient the crown was anyway in uplifting such fines.[34] For the principal himself the punishment was outlawry or horning, but the entire horning process was a shambles with civil and criminal law confused, and no-one quite sure what the status of an outlaw was. The result was that most outlaws walked about freely, knowing that the greatest threat to them came not from the crown, but from enemies who tried to exploit their legal vulnerability. Intromitting with property and attacks on their person were likely, but that was expected in feuds anyway, and, in effect, getting someone horned was seen as nothing more than another hostile tactic. Cautions also involved honour in an effort to better enforcement, and acts specified that 'reproof, dishonour and infamy' would fall on those who broke them, but even less attention was paid to this than to a promise voluntarily given in an assurance.[35] In spite of the weight of the crown behind them, cautions remained little more than short-term means of bringing peace to a feud — they too were for limited periods[36] — in which success rested largely on the good will of the parties involved.

The parties to a feud having been persuaded to recognise a truce between them, the next step would be for those with an interest in peace to move forward to mediation or arbitration. Some would reject this out of hand. Indeed almost everyone was honour-bound at least initially to reject peace, and the feud would either be actively renewed, or continue under restraint by having the acts of assurance or caution periodically renewed. In this state the parties were in a state similar to cold war. However, both mediation and arbitration had long histories in Scotland, having survived both the influx of Norman feudal law and the influence of the medieval church whose own canonical law encouraged arbitration, and whose procedures were largely adopted by secular arbitrators.[37] The lawyer David Moysie relates that 'gif the meanest gentleman that hes his kynsman or neir freind murthered enter into trysting with the committeris freindis, the offeris ar maid be the committeris of the deed, quhilkis ar deliberatlie resolvit upone be him, his kyn and freindis'.[38] What Moysie thought of this loss of business for his own profession he does not say, but his description is accurate. Justice was not yet monopolised by the professional, but remained the business and the responsibility of the community.

What Gluckman called the pressures of 'common residence', along with other cohesive bonds like kinship, lordship, and dependence acted together to create webs of co-operative relationships with an interest in peace.[39] In 1595, during the feud between the earl of Montrose and Sir James Sandilands, it was reported that 'the great men of the west have comperit upon it'.[40] One of those men, Lord Loudon, wrote to a dependant asking for his advice on whether the bloodfeud should be pursued by the party he had an interest in, or 'tane up and freindfullie agreit be the adwyis of freindis'. He also asked Maxwell of Pollok to accompany him to a meeting where he had been asked to advise one of the principals of the feud as 'I culd nocht gudlie gif ansuer thairto without the adwyis of my maist speciall freindis'.[41] This 'guid counsale and adwyis' of friends[42] was being sought by Sandilands of friendly lords like Loudon, whose own servant had been killed in the feuding, and he in turn was seeking advice from his circle of friends and dependants. Here the structures and dynamics of a feuding society are seen at work, not in pursuing violence, but in a widespread discussion of how best to achieve justice.

Lordship was a highly effective means of persuading men that they should make peace.[43] As Craig of Riccarton observed, it was a duty of good lords to adjudicate quarrels among their dependants.[44] James and Patrick Graham told the laird of Johnstone that after the slaughter of their father they were left 'in the protectioun and favouris of your maisterschippis', and would abide by his will in the matter of their feud with the killers of their father. If he would not make any agreement for them, then 'gif they wald offer unto us all the geir thai haif in the warlds, we wald nocht accept it gif we culd haif your maisterschippis favouris utherwayis'.[45] Revenge was clearly what the Grahams wanted, but if their lord decided that a negotiated settlement was more in his interests they would have no choice but to obey since a feud could not be sustained without him. However, they would also be expecting him to get them a good settlement, for that was his duty as their overlord, and for him to fail in that would be to raise questions about his ability to be an effective lord. The Regent Morton explained this to Queen Elizabeth in 1573 in an answer to a letter about why he had not made peace with the Hamiltons at the end of the war. Morton may have been regent of Scotland with high political stakes to play for, but he was also a Douglas lord, and the Hamiltons had murdered Johnstone of Westraw, a Douglas dependant. He told the English queen that 'I have not heard of any sufficient offer wherby the party grieved might be satisfied, or I relieved of the shame of dishonour of the world, which I could not fail to incur if I should lightly overpass the loss of such a friend and servant'.[46] Exercising good lordship was a serious and important matter even for men with powers and responsibilities which projected them into an arena much greater than their own locality or dependency.

The earl of Atholl was giving the best of advice to Menzies of that Ilk when he wrote to him about a quarrel he was having with a neighbour. Atholl counselled that he should not 'seek the circumstances of the law', but instead get the help of his own lord who would mediate with his enemy's overlord for a much quicker and more satisfactory solution.[47] Those men who ignored the peace negotiated for them by their lords could very easily find themselves isolated in a hostile environment, with no protection other than what they could muster themselves.[48] When a number of Grahams and Irvines killed a kinsman of the laird of Johnstone in 1582 they found themselves without a lord to mediate for them, and had no choice but to accept an unfavourable peace in order to avoid a feud with such a powerful man. They expressed 'full repentance in our hairttis', 'crawis forgiveness for Godis sake', and offered substantial compensation.[49] Occasionally, the pressure worked in the opposite direction as when the earl of Errol found himself being forced into negotiations with the Earl Marischal by a number of local lairds who were losing patience with his obstinacy.[50]

Where a lord himself did not mediate, arbitration took place. Some men had their own particular arrangements for arbitration, like the earls of Caithness and Sutherland who agreed to appoint the earl of Huntly to be their hereditary arbitrator.[51] In the islands a 'brieve' was 'a kynd of judge amongst the islanders, who hath ane absolute authoritie and censure they willinglie submitt themselves when he determineth any debatable question betuein partie and partie'.[52] In 1582 the Kerr kindred made a self-regulating bond in which 'having considderit quhat inconvenientis hes and may fall out among us be resoun of melling in utheris bluid and in speciale be the crewell slawchter of David Kerr ... ', it was agreed to outlaw those members of the kindred responsible. Furthermore, this was to apply to all future disagreements among them, and even their chief was to submit to the authority of four Kerrs chosen to consider complaints made against him by the kindred.[53] All of these were special cases, although the brieve had a significance beyond the limitations of the other two. In the majority of cases, however, the form observed was fairly standard, having been arrived at by a mixture of custom and the influence of Roman and canon law. The general outlines given by Sir James Balfour of Pittendreich in his *Practicks* were recognisable in most arbitrations of the later sixteenth century in both civil law and in the settlement of bloodfeuds.[54]

Agreement to accept arbitration was usually signalled by the signing of a submission in which the signatories bound themselves, their kinsmen, friends and dependants to observe the terms of the decision.[55] Each side then nominated arbitrators, and, according to Balfour, any free man over the age of twenty-one who could hear and speak was eligible.[56] Balfour also says that an uneven number was named in order to ensure a majority opinion,[57] but this was not the case in most feud arbitrations where each party named the same number of men. A quorum was also decided. Those who accepted the task of arbitration were likely to be kinsmen or friends, though lawyers might also be chosen, particularly if they were also one of the former. The session judge, Vaus of Barnbarroch, acquired a reputation as a good arbitrator, well known for 'your accustomet maner of doings for your freindis',[58] but not everyone could afford to hire such expertise, or could call upon it among their clientage. The great majority of arbitrators were in fact laymen, although it ought to be remembered that the layman's knowledge of the law, particularly among the landed elite, was fairly high, and many of them were either judges or held lesser positions in local courts. Yet it was not for their knowledge of the law that men were primarily asked to be arbitrators, for what was at issue was not necessarily points of law. When Alexander Spens murdered Andrew Burnet, the arbitration was conducted by Burnet's six sons, his brother-in-law, and his sister's son on the one side, and by Spens's own brother and two other kinsmen. Both sides assumed responsibility for their entire kin, the Burnets specifying that they did so for the 'relict, remainder, bairnis, kin frendis and four branches of the said umquhile Andro'.[59] The unequal distribution of the arbitrators, coupled with their relatively low status, suggests that this was not a formal arbitration committee, but an informal meeting of two families to hammer out an agreement. Even at this level, with men who were not important lairds or lords, the need to include so many kinsmen in the settlement was recognised, and usually an effort would be made to have them all sign the submission before any discussion got under way. More commonly arbitrators were of an equal number, as in the eight each in the committee appointed by the lairds of Glenorchy and Menzies to pacify their feud.[60] Apart from kinsmen and friends, lords might take on the role of arbitrators, as in 1574 when the earls of Morton and Angus acted on behalf of the Westraw family,[61] or in 1585 when the master of Glamis's wife represented her husband in an arbitration to determine the compensation one of his servants should pay for killing John Frost.[62]

A submission by the earls of Caithness and Sutherland in 1589 details a procedure to be followed by the arbitration committee which was typical for the period. Here both earls were 'obleist and sworne to stand, abyde and underly and fulfill the decreit delyvrit' by the arbitrators chosen by them and by their oversman, Huntly. Balfour thought the use of an oversman dated from the parliament of 1426,[63] but this may only have been the recognition of an existing practice designed to break a deadlock in negotiations. Usually the committee elected one of their own number to act as oversman, often before they did anything else, but in this case Huntly held the position under the terms of a previous agreement. This submission then went on to set a specific date by which time all claims against the other party for redress had to be submitted. A date was then agreed limiting the time the committee had to reach a solution, failing which Huntly was to take over, and he too was given until a further date to deliver his decreet. The submission finally defined the committee's terms of reference, excluding certain issues from them which were to be settled by other means. Regardless of whether the final decreet arbitral was delivered by the committee, or by Huntly, it was to be equally binding. Provisions were made for the election of replacement arbitrators should any have to retire, and it was made quite clear that if either side failed to turn up at a meeting, or walked out of one, then the remaining members of the committee could go ahead and deliver a binding decreet. Finally, it was to be registered in the books of council and sessions, and to have the same authority as an act or decreet of those lords.[64] This last practice was also found in later medieval England by Edward Powell, and his conclusion that it signified a recognition that out of court settlements were only effective if they could not be questioned or overturned in court might equally be applied to Scotland.[65]

Arbitration itself was a difficult business. In 1587 a tryst arranged between the earl of Huntly and the Earl Marischal ended in a fight, and with the slaughter of a Keith gengleman by William Gordon of Gight.[66] Less dangerous, but equally frustrating, were those who did not even turn up for the preliminary stages before a submission was made.[67] Huntly himself wrote to the council about his efforts to mediate in the feud between Caithness and Sir Robert Gordon, telling him that

> ... to end a quarrell beteuin tuo pairties of such qualitie, deiplie grounded, and enracined for many other preceiding particular debates, without disgrace or wrong to either syd, wes almost impossible without extraordinaire discretion and indifference; considering how the smallest circumstances wer sufficient to put all out of frame and temper.[68]

Huntly, of course, knew what he was talking about, being himself one of the most touchy and uncompromising magnates in the kingdom. The laird of Garleis wrote despairingly to Vaus of Barnbarroch that his attempts to negotiate on behalf of his servant were foundering as 'I haif causit him maik all the offeris that hie can to the partie, and thai will on nae wyis excep thame'.[69] John Crichton of Frendraucht was equally exasperated with the problems of reconciling the apparently irreconcilable, and wrote, 'we haiff delt and yit sall dell quhat in us lyis to satisffeye my lord of Erroll his lordschippis desyir, provyding we cut nocht my lord Merschael his lordschippis thrott'.[70] In some cases a settlement was just not possible, and in 1608 the arbitrators for the earl of Mar and the laird of Colquhoun went home after eight months of trying to find peace, protesting that they were not to blame, but that the principals themselves had wanted them to fail.[71]

In each of these cases the arbitrators had to face the fact that the will to succeed was essential on both sides, and that without compromise a settlement was impossible. Yet in spite of all the hazards many settlements were arrived at, though some, like that described in a twenty-six page decreet arbitral between Colin Mackenzie of Kintail and Robert Munro of Foulis, were clearly the product of long, hard bargaining and very detailed discussion.[72] What actually took place in these discussions is unknown. Some hints of the kinds of claims, counter-claims and reasoning survive in letters like that sent in 1589 by Lord Forbes to the earl of Huntly in which he listed a number of demands, and in which Huntly's own responses to these have been noted in the margin.[73] On the whole Huntly did not find them unreasonable, but a reply by Morton to a similar letter from Sir Thomas Kerr of Ferniehirst was much less conciliatory.[74]

Balfour wrote that 'Arbiteris may not deliver as they think reasonabill, bot efter the lawis of the realme' unless special conditions were written into the submission.[75] In practice the layman's sense of reason and justice had priority over legality. However, while arbitrators were free to discuss each case on its merits, the solutions they adopted followed fairly standardised principles. Compensation or assythment was usually at the core of the agreement. According to Balfour this was settled on the principle that

> the assythment or kinbuit maid or adjudgit to be payit be the committaris of slauchter, to the kin, bairnis and freindis of ony persoun that is slane, is gevin to thame in contentatioun of the hurt, damnage and skaith sustenit be thame throw the wanting of the persoun that is slane, and for skaith incurrit be thame thairthrow, and for pacifying of thair rancor.[76]

Unlike the earlier *Regiam Majestatem* which set out fixed rates of compensation for varying crimes and victims of crimes in a form typical of the early medieval period,[77] Balfour offered only guidelines which were to be borne in mind by the arbitrators. Thus the nature of the crime, the wealth and status of the killer and his victim, and the number and age of their children had all to be taken into account when deciding the amount of assythment to be paid. That amount would also be affected by the need not only to compensate one side, but by the equally important necessity of not leaving the other side feeling unduly resentful.[78] Justice was not to be seen as a means of victimising or punishing a killer and his kinsmen, but as a means of restoring peace and friendship to the two families by compensating the one for its loss.[79]

Cash was the commonest form of assythment. David Fyvie of Drumbillo agreed to pay 500 merks on behalf of the killers of David Malcolm of Drumbillo, the money being divided between Malcom's wife and son;[80] the Spens kindred paid 800 merks to six Burnet brothers for the loss of their father;[81] John Cok, an Edinburgh baxter burgess, accepted 200 merks on behalf of his daughter whose husband had been killed, and on behalf of the rest of his son-in-law's kin from John Crombie, a maltman burgess of the same burgh;[82] and the master of Forbes offered 4,000 merks for the slaughter of George Gordon of Gight and his servant which the earl of Huntly was to distribute among the wives, daughters, kinsmen and friends of the two men.[83] In each of these cases different sums of money were arrived at to meet specific social needs, and no doubt they also reflected the social strengths of the parties, and the negotiating skills of the arbitrators. Settlements, therefore, were not always fair in an objective sense, but they did reflect the price each side put upon peace.

The division of any money among a kindred was also likely to vary according to circumstances, but Balfour did provide some governing principles. The relative needs of the family were taken into account, and while 'the air sould have his part thairof with the rest of the bairnis', that amount should be 'not sa mekil as ony of thame', and unmarried daughters 'sould ressave twice als mekil as ony of the sons'. Wives and bastard children were recognised, but not grand-children unless their own parents had died since the slaughter and made an assignation of their claim to them.[84] Those who needed to be compensated most, younger sons and unmarried daughters, received most, while the rights to assythment do not appear to have extended beyond the nuclear family, and any illegitimate offspring. That does not mean than other kinsmen were not compensated. Brothers, uncles, nephews and brothers-in-law acting in their wives' or children's interests were all found involved in arbitration, but their claims to part of the assythment were weaker. Like most lawyers Balfour was being too tidy, and claims to be treated seriously in the proceedings would always receive attention if the bloodfeud was to be successfully pacified. Thus while John Frost was found to be largely responsible for his own death at the hands of Lady Hume's son, she agreed to pay 300 merks to be 'ane help and support' to his wife and children.[85] Lady Hume was recognising a moral and social responsibility, and ensuring that the Frost family would not cause her or her son any trouble in the future. By no means did the whole kindred or its four branches receive compensation, but a rule of thumb pragmatism guided arbitrators more than rights under the law. Similarly, while kinsmen had no obligation under the law to help in the payment of assythment, some were willing to rally round, or to make loans. In the Spens-Burnet case it was the killer's elder brother who raised the 800 merks by transferring the liferent of lands held by his wife from a previous marriage to George Spens, another kinsmen and an Edinburgh burgess.[86] Lords might also make payments on behalf of their men, as Lord Livingstone did in 1576 when he paid 700 merks to the family of a man killed by his servants.[87]

Assythment was not only paid for slaughter, but was widely employed in barony courts to settle assault cases.[88] In 1595 Lord Forbes accepted an offer of 1,800 merks from the earl of Argyll for damages done by his men in a number of raids on Forbes's lands.[89] For the mutilation done to his right hand by John MacKie and his brother, Fergus MacDowell received 200 merks,[90] and in 1579 James Wotherspoon of Bighouse paid £100 to two men 'in full contentatioun and assythment for the hurting, mutilatioun, and making thame impotent'.[91] Here compensation was being granted for property damage, for affecting a man's ability to work and fight, and for ruining two men's sex lives, and in each case one can assume that similar considerations of status as well as the nature of the injury were taken into account in deciding on a sum.

Compensation was not only paid in cash. In the Johnstone of Westraw case the money agreed upon was not to be paid to Johnstone's family directly, but to the earl of Morton who was to use it to redeem lands mortgaged by Johnstone during his lifetime, and only then was the remainder to be divided up. Again the social implications of the killing for the family had been considered, and the opportunity was being taken by their kinsmen to ensure the recovery of the entire Westraw estates rather than allowing them and the money to be dissipated.[92] Much the same thinking was behind the decreet between John Ross of Craigie and Peter Oliphant of Turingis in which the former was allowed to make a compulsory purchase from the Oliphant family at an agreed price.[93] In the decreet involving Lord Livingston and the Moffet brothers he also promised to infeft the elder brother in some of his own lands.[94]

Satisfaction could not be achieved by assythment alone. There was a sense in which the whole business of compensation was dishonourable, appearing to be a neglect of the obligation to extract vengenance, and a sale of honour.[95] Had the agreement ended there, with the payment of money or land, the killers and their kinsmen would have been able to claim a moral victory, and the kindred which accepted compensation would have appeared weak and shameful. Homage offered a way out of this problem which was both symbolic and practical. In homage a man not only took the place of the dead man by becoming bound to his kinsmen, but the status quo in honour was restored to equilibrium. The honour lost in the failure to attain blood vengenance was regained in the public humiliation of one's enemies in the homage ceremony. Homage itself, with the presentation of a naked sword by the killers to the kinsmen of their victim represented a form of ritual revenge. John MacKie of Myrton and his brother had to go to Kirktown parish church, and 'cum in, but thair schone, haiffing thair naikit suordis in thair handis, and thair first to craiff god, secundlie the pairtie, thirdlie the congregation forgiffnes for committing of the said mutilatioun'.[96] God, the victim and his kinsmen, and the community were thus all satisfied by this public repentance and shame. Another document even draws attention to the element of shame involved in this, referring to the 'gret rependance and humiliatioun'[97] which was integral to this 'ancient custume'.[98] Homage also had the attraction of being widely understood.[99] The powerful Hamilton brothers had to 'do the honoris'[100] to the earl of Angus at Holyrood, 'comming the whole bounds of the inner court bare headed; and sitting down on their knees, delivering him the sword for the slaughter of Westraw'.[101] With even lowlier submission some Grahams and Irvines wrote to the laird of Johnstone, offering to go in 'our lynning claythis to sit doune upon oure kneis and desyre forgiveness for Godis caus, and in toiken of homage and repentance take our naikid swordis be the poyntis in our handis and offer thame'.[102] Nor was this ceremony confined to the landed community, as in 1618 Andrew Henderson, the son of an Edinburgh merchant, did homage to another merchant burgess in front of the privy council for having mutilated his hand nine years before.[103]

While homage was an integral part of assythment — 'the custom of the realme' one decreet called it[104] — formal bonding was less common. Presumably men realised that for a dependency relationship to be effective it had to be entered into freely. However, a bond of manrent was given by William Edmonstone of Duntreath to James Stewart of Doune for killing his father,[105] and John Douglas of Erchemoston was ordered by a decreet arbitral to bond himself to Dalzell of that Ilk for having murdered his uncle.[106] Both these cases involved the loss of close kinsmen, but the earl of Angus received a bond of manrent from John Kennedy of Blairquhan in 1578 for having so injured one of his servants that the man could no longer work for him,[107] and a later earl of Angus received the manrent of the captain and an entire company of Edinburgh guards in 1597 after a goldsmith of the burgh had accidentally killed his master stabler.[108] The point of establishing such lordship over all these men was not to put them in a position of servitude, but to reinforce the good relations between them which the peace settlement was intended to create. Instead of enmity between them it was expected that there would exist the same mutual obligations as were typical of those between lords and men.[109]

In all the feuds and settlements discussed so far the loss, or skaith, has been on the one side, but in a great many feuds both sides suffered from the killing and material damage. In the Caithness-Sutherland settlement Caithness claimed that Sutherland's men had slain ten of his people, and he also listed extensive material losses which he had sustained. For his part Sutherland claimed for the deaths of six men, and for similar property damage. Unlike the Icelandic sagas where killings were set off against one another by number and status,[110] each case was to be dealt with on its own merit. The kinsmen of the dead were to approach the two earls with their claims, and they were bound to satisfy them. Claims for the material destruction were similarly dealt with.[111]

Regardless of whether both sides had suffered loss or not, every feud-settlement offered something to both sides. In their decreet arbitral the Burnets 'frelie fra thair hairtis remittis and forgives safar as in thame lyis' the Spens kindred for the murder of their father, and received the killer and his kinsmen in kindness as though the event had never happened. All civil and criminal actions against him were dropped, he was to be freed immediately from the tolbooth where he was being held, and was to be given a letter of slains from the Burnets as evidence of their forgiveness of him. By this mixture of Christian forgiveness, good neighbourliness, and self-interest, justice was done, and the relationship of feud was replaced by that of outward friendship. Both sides 'faithfullie binds and obleiss thame to stand and remane to perpetuall amitie and freindschipp ... as gif the said slauchter had never beene quhitted nor maid'.[112] The letter of slains, which was usually subscribed by the four branches of the dead man's kin, was the guarantee for the killer that the bloodfeud was ended for ever.[113] The language of these documents was far more than rhetoric, and reflected the very real hopes of those to whom it applied, and of the arbitrators who had framed the settlement. The earls of Caithness and Sutherland agreed that 'all bypast injuries wer forgiven on either syd', and that 'old grieffs and grudges should no moir be revived, bot bureit hencefoorth, together with the memorie of these later tymes'.[114] In their case, however, the peace did not last for long. The Humes and Wauchopes agreed to live in 'godlie peace and brotherlie societe' with one another,[115] and the Gordons of Lochinvar promised the MacDowells that 'all rancor and malice of the hairtis consaivit and borne' against one another would be removed 'sua that the memorie of it [the feud] salbe forgot and extinguisheit in all tymes heirefter'.[116] These promises were not made lightly, they were essential to the peace men were trying to make. In a feuding society memory served to fuel future conflicts, and it was important that the bloodshed was both forgiven and forgotten. For the kinsmen of the dead this was at least as difficult as homage was for the killers, involving a delicate trade in honour. That trade was only thought worth while if a genuine peace was achieved and social relations returned not simply to a sort of mutual toleration, but to friendship, kindness and love.

The letter of slains was only half, though the more difficult half, of the means by which a man re-established himself in the community. Slaughter also broke the king's peace, and pursuit before the law was an option that a family might resolve upon as the best means of acquiring a vengeful justice. In order to avoid being taken to the criminal courts, or being outlawed, men bought remissions or limited respites from the king. This gave the killer breathing space to come to an agreement with his enemies, and, of course, it was a source of money for the crown. It was not, however, a sale of justice. Since the fourteenth century no remission could be granted, or be upheld in a court of law unless a letter of slains was also produced.[117] In 1575 the Regent Morton granted a remission to John Smith and his brothers for the murder of Henry Moffet on the grounds that their father had 'satisfied the kinsmen and friends of the said Henry'.[118] The system was certainly open to corruption and abuse, and it was loosely interpreted, but its intention was to add the weight of crown authority to private bloodfeud settlements. Forgiveness from the king was only to follow forgiveness from the kinsmen of the victim. Further encouragement was given to this by the use of respites. Morton granted one of these to Thomas Gilbert that 'in the meantyme he may laboure to satisfie the pairtie offendit'.[119] Here the crown was being paid for keeping the case out of court long enough for assythment to be offered and peace made, following which a full remission would be granted. Punishment was not the king's business, peace was, and the crown realised as much as the kindreds that peace could be better achieved by settlements negotiated locally by those most closely involved.

This does not mean that the crown played a merely passive role in the enforcement of justice. On some occasions crown permission was sought before a party accepted assythment.[120] The crown might also be asked to play the part of an arbitrator, as in 1587 when Scott of Branxholm and Tweedie of Drummelzier submitted their feud to the king.[121] Involving the king in the arbitration, or in the registration of an arbitral, conferred greater authority and greater legal legitimacy on the agreement.[122] Direct intervention by the king was fairly common, especially in noble feuds, and at a convention in 1602 James mediated in feuds between Lennox and Argyll, Ochiltree and Loudon, Huntly and Errol and a number of lesser ones. The king too was an overlord with a responsibility to use that lordship and his personal relations with his nobility to pacify disputes.[123] Some feuds did reach the criminal courts where a defendant who saw that the assize was likely to convict him might ask to be taken into the king's will in order to avoid a mandatory sentence. In 1598 Mathew Stewart of Dunduff took this route in the course of his trial for the attempted assassination of the earl of Cassillis. While the king's will was by no means a guarantee of a lighter punishment, James in this instance handed the matter over to Cassillis who was satisfied with Stewart's banishment. The king himself asked for a thousand merks.[124] The crown might also try to force two parties towards an agreement, as the Regent Morton did in the feud between the Haitlie and Burnfield families in the 1570s. However, while the privy council could outlaw Alexander Burnfield for failing to answer to it 'tuiching the removing of the deidlie feid and contraversay betuix thame and certane of the surname of the Haitleis',[125] its means of enforcement remained very limited. Cautions and horning were the privy council's principal responses, and their effectiveness has already been demonstrated. This was not simply a matter of crown weakness, for it had never been intended that the crown would interfere greatly in such affairs, and there was no reason to believe that the crown could have offered a better means of restoring peace to local communities than those that already existed within them.

Yet it was the limitations in the effectiveness of private justice which were partly responsible for a change in how feuds were handled towards the end of the century. The failure to make a lasting peace in a feud arose for a number of reasons. The necessity of involving as many kinsmen as possible in the settlement was not always observed, more by neglect or intransigence on the part of individuals than by intent. The murder of Lord Torthorwald in 1608 was committed by a man who had refused to subscribe to a submission signed by the rest of the kindred in preparation for negotiation with the Douglases.[126] Inclusion of so many kinsmen was essential, and the law made it as difficult as possible for rogue kinsmen to operate by denying the right of a single individual to either pursue for assythment, or grant a letter of slains.[127] In 1580 the privy council was in the middle of making arrangements for settling a quarrel between Colin Campbell of Glenorchy and James Menzies of that Ilk, when on the date laid aside for discussing the issue Glenorchy's son turned up and said that his father was too old to travel in such bad weather, but that he had been sent in his place. The council, however, refused to go any further, saying that a feud was far too important to be discussed without the presence of one of the principals.[128] In fact, according to Balfour, a decreet arbitral had no authority at all if all the principals were not present at its reading.[129] No excuse was to be given to men to say at a later date that they had not been party to a settlement, and would therefore refuse to recognise it.

This principle had to be observed even in the case of minors. When the Ancrum branch of the Kerr family made their peace with the laird of Cessford, they took him by the hand, but protested 'always that thair dewtie of freindschip micht be reservit to the bairnis of the said umquhile William at their perfyte age, to do in the mater, tuiching the said slauchter as salbe then thocht expedient be freindis'.[130] The important feuds between the Cunningham and Eglinton families and the Lyon and Lindsay families were delayed for years so that the young earl of

Eglinton and the young Lord Glamis would be old enough to assent to the peace.[131] Where care was not taken to include minors, as in the Maxwell-Johnstone feud, disaster could follow, and in this case the 9th Lord Maxwell ignored the peace made with the Johnstones by his kinsmen, and murdered the laird of Johnstone in 1608.[132]

Settlements could founder if one side failed to fulfil the terms of the decreet. How legally binding a decreet arbitral was is not entirely clear, although Balfour thought that if the principals were of age and had sworn to obey its terms, and it was neither contrary to the law nor had been influenced by a corrupt arbitrator, then it was binding.[133] More importantly, the feud would be revived if the terms were not strictly adhered to. In 1577 the Scott kindred broke off their agreement with the Kerrs, signed in 1564 and ratified ten years later, saying that it was 'newlie gewin up, freindschip dischargeit, and deidlie haitrend and grudge proclaimit'. The Kerr chief complained to the Regent Morton that 'thair is na place left now to renew that deidlie feid nether for thingis bygane nor to cum', but after investigation the privy council discovered that George Kerr had failed to marry Janet Scott as had been agreed — marriages sometimes were included in a peace settlement as a means of further binding the two kindreds together[134] — thus incurring a penalty of 1,000 merks. The Scotts' complaint was upheld, and the council offered to help mend the broken fences by 'sum mid and indifferent way'.[135] Here a solution was found before relations deteriorated any further, but events did not always turn out so fortunately.

While relating the tale of Finn in *Beowulf*, the writer warned of those who would 'fetch the feud to mind and by taunting words awaken the bad blood'.[136] In that sense feuds were eternal, and the peace was little more than a temporary calm between a succession of disputes linked together in the kin memory and consciousness into a single feud.[137] It was too easy to awaken 'the old rancour and malice',[138] or 'the old dissensions that had long slept'.[139] For many the fear and the suspicion remained that the feud 'lyis still living among them, readie to burst furth upon the least occasioun'.[140] In some cases the peace lasted for hours rather than years, as in the reconciliation arranged by Sir John Kennedy at which one of the men suddenly attacked the other as they came to shake hands, 'to his disgrace and that of his convoy'.[141] The feud between the Buchanans and Colquhouns was laid to rest, but shortly afterwards Robert Colquhoun went and brutally murdered Duncan Buchanan, having found himself unable to accept that the feud was over.[142] More commonly the problems of living together in a local community threw men into repeated competition and conflict, and new feuds between the same families broke out over quite different issues. The great feud between the Cunningham and Montgomery families in north Ayrshire broke out in the 1570s after half a century of peace between them.[143] Peace lasted only for as long as it took to find a new issue over which to quarrel.

When writing of the search for peace in medieval Germany, F. R. H. Du Boulay argued that 'Without durable institutions, every initiative is an expedient', and that the attainment of peace was a 'task of persuasion'.[144] The same could be said of early modern Scotland. There the persuading was done by those within the community who sought to replace conflict with co-operation, and to a limited extent by the crown as it tried to reinforce those pressures. The crown's role was decidedly secondary, and amounted to little more than imposing, where it could, limited periods of non-violence, offering to act as a mediator, persuading men to talk to one another, occasionally serving as an arbitrator or oversman, and adjudicating in broken agreements. In none of these roles, however, was its position institutionalised. The greater part of persuasion was done by the combined voices of local kinsmen, friends, lords and dependants who wanted peace in their community (see Table 6 on page 279). Such pressure could be resisted, and often was for very long periods, but it was a reasonably effective means of reducing violence and securing a just peace. At least it was the best that such a society had to offer. Yet feuding itself could not be talked out of existence. William Asheby was partly right when he wrote that 'the Scottish nature is hardly reconciled',[145] since that national psychology was a product of social and ideological factors which made it very difficult to make and keep the peace. The competing desires for peace on the one hand, and for honour and power on the other, co-existed uneasily in men's minds. A man would pursue his own feud with all the vengeful violence expected of him, and at the same time offer to help his neighbour to make peace in his quarrels. There was a tension in that kind of behaviour which demonstrates the recognition of a whole range of obligations and responsibilities which were not always reconcilable, but which were always taken seriously.

## NOTES

1. An earlier version of this chapter was published as 'Peace and Persuasion: Pacification Procedures in the Early Jacobean Bloodfeud', in *Police and Policing,* The Past and Present Society, 1983, for the Past and Present Society Colloquium, 6 July 1983.

2. See, for example, Gluckman, 'The Peace in the Feud', in *Custom and Conflict;* S. Roberts, 'The Study of Dispute: Anthropological Perspectives', in Bossy (ed.), *Disputes and Settlements,* pp. 1–24; and Wormald's comments on this in 'Bloodfeud, Kindred and Government in Early Modern Scotland'.

3. A. A. M. Duncan, 'The Central Courts Before 1532' and Lord Cooper of Culross, 'The Central Courts After 1532', in *Introduction to Scottish Legal History,* Stair Society, 20, Edinburgh, 1957, pp. 321-324 and 341-349; G. Donaldson, 'The Legal Profession in Scottish Society in the Sixteenth and Seventeenth Centuries', *Juridical Review,* 1976, pp. 1–19; P. Stein, 'The Influence of Roman Law on the Law of Scotland', *Juridical Review,* N.S. 8, 1963, pp. 205-245; H. L. McQueen, 'Jurisdiction in Heritage and the Lords of Council and Session after 1532', *Stair Society Miscellany,* ii, (ed.) D. Sellar, Stair Society, 35, Edinburgh, 1984, pp. 61-85.

4. J. I. Smith, 'Criminal Procedure', in *Introduction to Scottish Legal History,* p. 437.

5. I. Rowney, 'Arbitration in Gentry Disputes of the Later Middle Ages', in *History,* 67, 1982, p. 367; Lenman and Parker, 'The State, the Community and the Law in Early Modern Europe', in Gatrell, Lenman and Parker (eds.), *Crime and the Law,* pp. 21-22; Roberts, 'The Study of Dispute: Anthropological Perspectives', in Bossy (ed.), *Disputes and Settlements,* p. 17.

6. For England, see J. A. Sharpe, ' 'Such Disagreement betwyx Neighbours': Litigation and Human Relations in Early Modern England', in Bossy (ed.), *Disputes and Settlements,* pp. 167–187, where he argues that the point of litigation was very often to force an out of court settlement by way of arbitration. For Castile, see R. L. Kagan, 'A Golden Age of Litigation: Castile, 1500–1700', in Bossy (ed.), *Disputes and Settlements,* pp. 145–166. For cost and efficiency generally, Lenman and Parker, 'The State, the Community and the Criminal Law in Early Modern Europe', in Gatrell, Lenman and Parker (eds.), *Crime and the Law,* pp. 18–20. See below, pp. 198–9, for the comments of some Scottish poets on the law.

7. Kagan makes a similar point for Castile, 'A Golden Age of Litigation', in Bossy (ed.), *Disputes and Settlements,* p. 159; and J. Casey, in 'Household Disputes and the Law in Early Modern Andalusia', in Bossy (ed.), *Disputes and Settlements,* p. 189, quotes one Spanish book of conduct which said that 'Litigation is war'.

8. Waus, *Correspondence,* i, p. 137.

9. Pitcairn, *Criminal Trials,* ii, pp. 138–145. The categories of witnesses who could be dismissed are discussed by D. M. Walker in 'Evidence', in *Introduction to Scottish Legal History,* pp. 306–307; and also of interest is I. D. Willock, *The Origins and Development of the Jury in Scotland,* Stair Society, 23, Edinburgh, 1966. Williams, in 'The Welsh Borderland', p. 27, draws attention to the poor reputation of juries in a similar social context, and the same kind of objections are raised in *Njals Saga,* pp. 304–305.

10. I. A. Milne, 'The Sheriff Court Before the Sixteenth Century', C. A. Malcolm, 'The Sheriff Court: the Sixteenth Century and After', and P. McIntyre, 'The Franchise Courts', all in *Introduction to Scottish Legal History,* pp. 351–355, 356–362 and 374–383.

11. See below, pp. 73–75.

12. *R.P.C.,* ii, pp. 303–304.

13. S.R.O., Inventory of Craigans Writs, G.D., 148/37/271.

14. *R.P.C.,* iv, p. 63.

15. M. Clanchy, 'Law and Love in the Middle Ages', in Bossy (ed.), *Disputes and Settlements,* p. 47.

16. W. Fraser, *The Annandale Family Book of the Johnstones,* Edinburgh, 1894, ii, p. 274, No. 361.

17. Fraser, *Maxwells of Pollok,* p. 320, No. 162.

18. *R.P.C.,* iii, p. 233.

19. See above, p. 29.

20. *R.P.C.,* v, p. 467.

21. *A.P.S.,* iii, p. 451, and see Irvine and MacDonald, 'Criminal Law', in *Introduction to Scottish Legal History,* pp. 290–291. Such killings were also seen as particularly anti-social in other feuding societies, Black-Michaud, *Cohesive Force,* pp. 240–241.

22. See above, p. 32.

23. *R.P.C.,* iii, pp. 503–504.

24. As in Lord Somerville and William Graham in 1584, *R.P.C.,* iii, p. 677.

25. *Ibid.,* p. 561.

26. *C.S.P., Scot.,* x, p. 207.

27. *R.P.C.,* iii, pp. 436 and 455. For another example, see Hay and Scott, *R.P.C.,* iii, pp. 380, 388 and 404.

28. See below, p. 243.

29. For the evolution of surety, see Duby, *The Chivalrous Society,* pp. 53–54. See also J. Balfour, *Practicks,* (ed.) P. McNeill, Stair Society, 21, 22, Edinburgh, 1962–63, ii, pp. 518–519, on 'Anent Lawburrowis'; and J. I. Smith, 'The Transition to the Modern Law, 1532–1660', in *Introduction to Scottish Legal History,* p. 25.

30. An analysis of the acts of caution registered by the privy council in 1588 reveals that 81% were exclusively between members of rural society, 10% were exclusively between urban parties, and 9% were mixed. None of the cautions involved peers, and while 78% involved a man of lairdly status on one side at least, only 15% had a laird on both sides, and only 4% had burgesses on both sides. The remainder were largely between men of unequal status, and 20% of the cautions had a woman as one of the parties. *R.P.C.*, iv.

31. *R.P.C.*, ii, pp. 493–494.

32. *R.P.C.*, iv, p. 403.

33. *Ibid.*, p. 689.

34. See below, pp. 254–255.

35. *R.P.C.*, ii, p. 397.

36. For example, *R.P.C.*, iii, pp. 208–209.

37. Lord Cooper of Culross, 'From David I to Bruce, 1124–1329; The Scoto-Norman Law'; and Smith and MacDonald, 'Criminal Law', in *Introduction to Scottish Legal History*, pp. 9, 11 and 299–301; Stein, 'The Influence of Roman Law on the Law of Scotland', pp. 205–245; Balfour, *Practicks*, ii, pp. 411–417; T. Hope, *Major Practicks*, (ed.) J. A. Clyde, Stair Society, 3, 4, Edinburgh, 1937–38, ii, pp. 58–63. Wormald discusses mediation in 'The Exercise of Power', in Brown (ed.), *Scottish Society in the Fifteenth Century*, pp. 61–65, and 'Bloodfeud, Kindred and Government in Early Modern Scotland'. For a useful comparison, see E. Powell, 'Arbitration and the Law in England in the Late Middle Ages', in *Trans. Royal Hist. Soc.*, 33, 1983, pp. 49–67.

38. Moysie, *Memoirs*, p. 61.

39. Gluckman, 'Peace in the Feud', pp. 8 and 14.

40. *C.S.P., Scot.*, xi, p. 632.

41. Fraser, *Pollok*, ii, pp. 179–180, No. 185.

42. *Ibid.*

43. Wormald, *Lords and Men*, pp. 126–127.

44. Craig, *Jus Feudale*, i, p. 608. For some comments on the criminal liability of lords for their servants' behaviour, see T. B. Smith, 'Master and Servant', in *Juridical Review*, N.S. 3, 1958, pp. 215–217.

45. Fraser, *Annandale*, ii, p. 274, No. 362.

46. *C.S.P., Scot.*, iv, p. 626.

47. *H.M.C.*, vi, 'Menzies M.S.', p. 693, No. 37, p. 696, No. 86, and p. 707, No. 206.

48. See, for example, Waus, *Correspondence*, ii, pp. 521–523.

49. Fraser, *Annandale*, ii, pp. 45–46, No. 48.

50. *Miscellany of the Spalding Club*, Spalding Club, Aberdeen, 1841–52, ii, 'The Erroll Papers', pp. 285–292.

51. Gordon, *Sutherland*, p. 200, and see pp. 181–183 and 197; *C.S.P., Scot.*, xi, p. 849.

52. Gordon, *Sutherland*, p. 268. For an interesting comparison, see the role of the leopard-skinned chief among the Nuer, Evans-Pritchard, *The Nuer*, pp. 163–164.

53. *H.M.C.*, *Laing*, i, p. 33. For another self-regulatory bond, see *H.M.C.*, vi, 'Ross M.S.', p. 717, No. 16. D. V. Kent and F. W. Kent mistakenly thought that the Peruzzi example they uncovered was unique, 'A Self Disciplining Pact Made by the Peruzzi Family of Florence, (June, 1433)', in *Renaissance Quarterly*, 34, 1981, pp. 335–355.

54. Balfour, *Practicks*, ii, pp. 411–417; and see also *Regiam Majestatem*, (ed.) T. M. Cooper, Stair Society, 11, Edinburgh, 1947, ii, pp. 105–110; Craig, *Jus Feudale*, i, p. 29.

55. For an example, Waus, *Correspondence*, ii, pp. 480–481. English forms are discussed by Rowney, 'Arbitration in Gentry Disputes', pp. 368–369; and Powell, 'Arbitration and the Law', pp. 53–54.

56. Balfour, *Practicks,* ii, p. 412, cii.

57. *Ibid.,* p. 412, ciii.

58. Waus, *Correspondence,* ii, p. 349. Another of Vaus's friends did warn him that 'ye haif ane guid counsale to giff to ane freind, taik pairt of it to your hs self. quiet your hous with your nychtbouris, and keip baith honour and proffit . . . the first conqueis of the warld is to have your hous in quietnes', *Ibid.,* ii, p. 489.

59. S.R.O. Register of Deeds, 1/41/335b. The place given to cognatic kinsmen here is not unusual, see also R.D., 1/14/306.

60. *H.M.C.,* vi, 'Menzies M.S.', p. 707, No. 206.

61. S.R.O., R.D., 1/14/50. 1/14/31, 1/44/359b.

62. Ibid, 1/25/155.

63. Balfour, *Practicks,* ii, pp. 412–413.

64. See, for example, S.R.O., R. D., 1/36/24.

65. Powell, 'Arbitration and the Law', p. 62.

66. *Spalding Society,* ii, 'The Chronicle of Aberdeen', p. 59; Moysie, *Memoirs,* p. 154; *C.S.P., Scot.,* ix, p. 531; S.R.O., Moray Muniments, N.R.A., 217/2/3/245.

67. See the master of Oliphant's letter to Vaus of Barnbarroch in Waus, *Correspondence,* i, p. 93.

68. Gordon, *Sutherland,* p. 295.

69. Waus, *Correspondence,* i, p. 281.

70. *Spalding Miscellany,* ii, 'The Erroll Papers', p. 288.

71. *R.P.C.,* viii, p. 79.

72. S.R.O., R.D., 1/13/459.

73. S.R.O., Forbes Collection, G.D., 52/1089.

74. Fraser, *Annandale,* i, pp. 42–44, Nos. 45 and 46.

75. Balfour, *Practicks,* ii, p. 415, xxi.

76. *Ibid.,* p. 516, ci.

77. *Regiam Majestatem,* pp. 278–279. This included the *Leges inter Brettos et Scottos,* see Wormald, 'Bloodfeud, Kindred and Government', p. 59, note 18.

78. Balfour, *Practicks,* ii, p. 517, civ.

79. See Wormald on this, 'Bloodfeud, Kindred and Government in Early Modern Scotland', pp. 72–77.

80. S.R.O., R.D., 1/30/63b.

81. S.R.O., R.D., 1/44/335b.

82. S.R.O., R.D., 1/39/172.

83. S.R.O., R.D., 1/22/49.

84. Balfour, *Practicks,* ii, p. 517, ciii, civ, cv.

85. S.R.O., R.D., 1/25/155/

86. S.R.O., R.D., 1/45/206b. This contrasts with Finland where payment and receipt of compensation involved all male members of a family with an additional sum for a widow for 'bed robbery', Lenman and Parker, 'The State, the Community and the Law in Early Modern Europe', in Gatrell, Lenman and Parker (eds.), *Crime and the Law,* p. 24, note 26.

87. S.R.O., R.D., 1/15/241.

88. Mactaggart, 'Assault in the Later Baron Courts', pp. 123–125.

89. *H.M.C.,* vi, 'Argyll M.S.', p. 630, No. 223.

90. Waus, *Correspondence,* ii, pp. 480–483.

91. *R.P.C.,* iii, p. 206.

92. S.R.O., R.D., 1/14/50.

93. S.R.O., R.D., 1/15/121, and see 1/36/302 for a similar case.

94. S.R.O., R.D., 1/15/241.

95. Assythment or compensation has been interpreted as a satisfactory or honourable evasion of kin responsibilities, B. Malinowski, *Crime and Custom in Savage Society,* London, 1978, pp. 115 and 118–119.

96. Waus, *Correspondence,* ii, p. 482.

97. *H.M.C.,* iv, 'Wauchope M.S.', p. 537.

98. *Historie,* p. 152.

99. S.R.O., R.D., 1/14/50.

100. See Craig's comments, *Jus Feudale,* i, p. 181.

101. Calderwood, *History,* iii, p. 346; J. Balfour, 'Annales of Scotland', in *The Historical Works of Sir James Balfour,* (ed.) J. Haig, Edinburgh, 1824–25, i, p. 363; Waus, *Correspondence,* ii, pp. 479–480.

102. Fraser, *Annandale,* i, pp. 45–46, No. 48.

103. *R.P.C.,* xi, pp. 318–319.

104. S.R.O., R.D., 1/13/322.

105. Brown, 'Bonds of Manrent', appendix, p. 509, No. 7.

106. Ibid., p. 375, No. 12.

107. S.R.O., R.D., 1/13/322.

108. Chambers, *Domestic Annals,* i, pp. 394–395.

109. This is discussed in greater detail by Wormald, *Lords and Men,* pp. 127–30.

110. See, for example, *Njals Saga,* p. 154.

111. S.R.O., R.D., 1/36/24.

112. S.R.O., R.D., 1/34/24.

113. For an example, S.R.O., Mackintosh Muniments, G. D., 176/166 from David Rose in Lyn to John Rose in Ballivat, and for Balfour's comments, *Practicks,* ii, p. 517, cviii.

114. Gordon, *Sutherland,* p. 204.

115. *H.M.C.,* iv, 'Wauchope M.S.', p. 537. Compare this with Rowney's gentry expressing a desire to be 'ful frendes', 'Arbitration in Gentry Disputes', p. 371.

116. S.R.O., R.D., 1/36/302.

117. Smith and MacDonald, 'Criminal Law', in *Introduction to Scottish Legal History,* pp. 297–299; C. H. W. Gare, 'The Effect of a Pardon in Scots Law', in *Juridical Review,* 1980, pp. 18–23.

118. *Registrum Secreti Sigilli Regum Scotorum,* (eds.) M. Livingston and others, Edinburgh, 1908– , vii, p. 58, No. 379.

119. *Ibid.,* p. 56, No. 375.

120. *Report of the Historical Manuscripts Commission, Various Collections,* Hereford, 1901–13, v, 'Duntreath M.S.', p. 42.

121. *R.P.C.,* iv, p. 225.

122. For example, in 1601 the privy council arranged to discuss the interpretation of a decreet between the earl of Atholl and Stewart of Gairntullie, *R.P.C.,* vi, pp. 299–300.

123. *C.S.P., Scot.,* xiii, Part 2, p. 940.

124. Pitcairn, *Criminal Trials,* ii, pp. 39–40.

125. *R.P.C.,* ii, pp. 302, 534, 625 and 630; iii, pp. 35 and 562.

126. *R.P.C.,* viii, p. 514.

127. Balfour, *Practicks,* ii, p. 517, cvi. This principle is also found in the Icelandic bloodfeud and is the point of the tale of Amendi the Blind in *Njals Saga,* pp. 226–227. Amendi was a blind bastard who slew his father's killer because he had not thought him worth considering for assythment. 'It is a warning to others in similar circumstances never to rebuff those who are so close of kin.' On bastards in Scotland, Balfour wrote that they

were entitled to half the amount in compensation as legitimate children, *Practicks,* ii, p. 517, ciii.

128. *R.P.C.,* iii, p. 297.

129. Balfour, *Practicks,* ii, p. 414, cvi.

130. *R.P.C.,* v, p. 273.

131. See below, p. 100.

132. Maxwell had grudgingly assented to this peace in 1605, *R.P.C.,* vii, pp. 38, 58 and 64–65; Spottiswoode, *History,* iii, p. 165, but it was clear that he had been forced into it by the crown and by Lord Herries during his minority.

133. Balfour, *Practicks,* ii, p. 413, cvii, cviii, p. 415, xxiii, p. 417, xxxiv, xxxv. There is no evidence of corrupt arbitrators for this period in Scotland, but Powell has found some English examples, 'Arbitration and the Law', p. 57.

134. See, for example, between the earls of Argyll and Huntly, below, p. 171.

135. *H.M.C., Laing,* i, pp. 27–28; *R. P.C.,* ii, pp. 643 and 665.

136. *Beowulf,* p. 85.

137. Evans-Pritchard, *The Nuer,* pp. 154–155, 'A Nuer is proud and wants a man's body in vengeance and not his cattle'. See also Black-Michaud, *Cohesive Force,* p. 16.

138. Gordon, *Sutherland,* p. 236.

139. Spottiswoode, *History,* ii, p. 206.

140. Gordon, *Sutherland,* p. 261.

141. Pitcairn, *Kennedy,* p. 42.

142. *R.P.C.,* v. pp. 491–493.

143. See below, pp. 85–86.

144. Du Boulay, 'Law Enforcement in Medieval Germany', p. 347.

145. *C.S.P., Scot.,* x, p. 196.

# 3

# *Local Issues*

Central government was something that most men living in sixteenth-century Scotland would not have closely identified with. The Stewart monarchy, the protestant church, and Scots law did create common loyalties and values, but this was still a society in which the locality, even more than the nation, shaped men's lives. That locality was understood in both a structural and an existential sense. The tangible side to it was castle or tower house, baronial court, church, village, cultivated lands, grazing pasture, water and woods.[1] Within this physical environment most people were born, lived and died. It was also where family and friends were, where lord and man formed their bonds, where loyalty was forged and pride was invested. In 1584 the earl of Atholl wrote to Walter Stewart of Minto asking him to talk to a cousin of his who was oppressing a Mr. Thomas Jack, vicar of Eastwood, a man who lived well beyond Atholl's bounds, who did not share his Stewart surname, but who was 'oure native cuntrey man'.[2] Bonds like these allowed even the humblest of men to strongly identify with their own homes, and with their lord's domain. There were exceptions, but if a man's name was Campbell, and he lived in Argyll, one had more than his address.

The idea that the necessity of social living prevents feud in the local community is a powerful one. There are good reasons for arguing that 'feud between neighbours is unlikely',[3] and where good lordship also existed, that eventuality was further limited. Yet if friends were to be found in the community where one lived, so were enemies, and even the kindred itself could be the source of deadly rivalries. Where neighbour meant the neighbouring lord and his dependants, the causes of tension were as great as the motives for peace, and the competition which inspired that tension, in effect the issues of local politics, was resolved in feud.

Land was, of course, an immense source of conflict in all pre-industrial societies, and the 'territorial imperative' has roots which are both biological as well as sociological.[4] Whether the context is Ottonian Saxony or twentieth-century New York, the impulse to protect and to enlarge territorial control is a powerful one.[5] James VI himself observed that the 'maist pairt' of feuds

> haith arysen upoun contraversie of marches, teinds, or casting of faill and diwott, or such lyk occasionis, the beginning whereof oftentymes carryed perhaps small schaw of inconvenience however thaif afterward tryed to bring very hard and troublesome, and dangerous sequellis and eventis.[6]

As J. P. Cooper and B. Coward have shown for England during this period, land ownership was giving rise to an even higher degree of litigation and quarrelling than before as inheritance patterns changed, and as a rising legal profession exploited the many technicalities of the law.[7] Similar problems existed in Scotland where, in contrast to the fifteenth century, the landed community was extremely tense and unstable. Feudal law was straining under a variety of new market conditions and new attitudes among the landowners. What the effects of high inflation, an increased population in the noble kindreds, the feuing movement, the transfer of church lands and of teinds to secular owners, a re-evaluation of kindly tenure, the mid-century upheavals, and the possible rise of the lairds all had on the land market has not been fully explored, but one can suggest that it was all very destabilising.[8] There too the competitive instincts of the landowners in a society where forced possession was still as good, or better, than documentation were not easily channelled into the courts where a legal profession, only just emerging from the shadow of the medieval church, had to wrestle with unclear charters, forgeries, forfeitures, escheats, wadsets, varying forms of tenure, and long memories. Much of this was settled by law as the vast evidence of the Acts and Decreets bears witness, but legal actions were expensive and protracted, and mediation did not always work. The high number of cautions registered by the privy council in which men promised not to molest a rival in his possession of his lands suggests a considerable degree of tension among both landowners and tenants. Where that tension breached the limits of patience and tolerance, or where men believed the issue could be forcefully resolved, feud was likely to break out.

The entangled state of the law covering land transfer was highlighted by the feud between the Sandilands and Graham families. In 1579 the 1st Lord Torphichen, head of the Sandilands family, died, and in his will made over to his wife the heritable rights of the Halyards in Lothian. However, there also existed a second disposition in favour of the tenants and labourers of the land, ' . . . and that fraudfullie to collect in great sowmes of money'. Torphichen's wife later married John Graham, a senator of the college of justice, and she transferred the Halyards to him. By exploiting his position in the session court, Graham was able to have the rights of the tenants nullified, but the fact that his brother had bribed one of the notaries working on the case was discovered. An investigation followed in which other damaging loopholes were found in Lord Torphichen's rents, and in those of Sir James Sandilands, the tutor of the second lord, and an influential courtier. The notary was hanged, and while Graham himself avoided any punishment, he had incurred the wrath of the Sandilands family. A bitter bloodfeud followed in which John Graham was killed, Sir James Sandilands almost died from wounds, and the earl of Montrose, chief of the Grahams, narrowly avoided being slain in Edinburgh.[9]

In the highlands, where the competition for land still had a colonising aspect to it, outbreaks of feuding were less technical in their origins. A long-standing inheritance dispute over Strome Castle and lands in Lochalsh, Lochcarron and Lochbroom was at the heart of the feud between the Glengarry MacDonells and the Mackenzies of Kintail. In 1582 the latter launched a devastating attack on their enemies, capturing Strome itself along with a large number of MacDonells, including the chief, Glengarry. About thirty of these prisoners were then put to death by the Mackenzies, who

> band thair handes with thair awin sarkis, and cruellie and unmercifullie, under promise of sauftie of thair lyffes, cassit murther and slay thame with dirkis,

appointing that thay suld not be bureit as Christian men, bot cassin furth and eitten be doiggis and swyne.[10]

Glengarry himself was eventually released after a hazardous imprisonment, and his castle was returned, but the feud continued for another twenty years before Mackenzie of Kintail eventually achieved his ambitions by a mixture of law and force.[11] On the fringes of the highlands Campbell expansion into the lands of Coupar Angus Abbey brought them into conflict with the Ogilvy family who felt this was a threat to their own influence in the area. Again the friction between the Angus Campbells and their Ogilvy neighbours existed long before violence broke out, and the question of the abbey lands was tied up with both internal Campbell politics and the Crawford-Glamis feud in Angus. When in 1590 the Campbells threatened further expansion by re-opening an old case against the Ogilvies, resentment spilled over into violence, and four Campbells were murdered during the summer of 1591. Retaliation was swift and savage as the Campbells and their dependant clans ravaged Ogilvy territory 'with sic barbarous crueltie, not sparing wyffis and bairnis, bot murthourit and slew all quhome they fund thairin', while also carrying away a great amount of booty. These raids in August and September were a terrible lesson to the Ogilvies, who also lost their case before the king, who in adjudging a settlement shortly afterwards laid most of the blame on them. Even in far away Angus the Campbells were a very dangerous foe to incur a feud with.[12]

As is the case in most quarrels between neighbours, tension is highest at boundaries, whether they be the borders between states, or the ill-defined march lands of adjoining estates. Sir Robert Gordon wrote of the earl of Huntly that he was 'a good and just neighbour (and chiefly in his marches, wherein most commonlie great men offend)'.[13] The earl of Perth and Lord Livingston, however, feuded over march lands in Menteith between 1615 and 1617, and while neither of these men was particularly bellicose, they were both willing to risk royal displeasure over marginal lands on the periphery of their estates.[14] Such an issue was as important to them as to obscure lairds like Haig and Halyburton who were called to account in 1610 for feuding over marches between their lands.[15] Those lands themselves may have been of doubtful economic value, but their symbolic significance was understood by everyone. A man who showed little interest in protecting these lands was inviting a neighbour to be even more aggressive about territory which was important.

One of the most contentious issues arising within the landed community during this period was that of the ownership of teinds, and the attendant question of how they were to be gathered. This latter point was sufficiently disruptive to warrant the only significant rural legislation passed in parliament during the king's reign, with five acts being passed between 1579 and 1617 which gave increasing rights to those subject to the teinds over the owners.[16] This was a seasonal problem which occurred at the end of the harvest when those with teind rights turned up for the 'leading of the teinds', and arguments might develop over the proportion taken, or over who had a right to the teinds. Perthshire was a particularly troublesome area. In 1572 Lord Ruthven and Bruce of Clackmannan both appeared armed on the fields 'quhairupoun grit blude shed, deidlie feid and utheris inconvenientis happynnit'. A year later the privy council pre-empted a repetition of this by appointing a neutral to gather the teinds until ownership was decided.[17] In 1580 Lord Ruthven clashed with Lord Oliphant in an incident which left a number of men dead, and had arisen out of differences over teinds,[18] while in that same year Oliphant was disputing teinds with Moncrieff of that Ilk.[19] The crown's tactic of intervening and uplifting the crops for itself usually worked, but when it did this in a case involving the Hume lairds of Coldenknowes and Manderston in 1619, the former compensated himself for what he saw as his losses by raiding Manderston's barns.[20]

A more detailed look at how a teind confrontation could escalate is described by the contemporary Kennedy historian. The earl of Cassillis had been in the practice of employing the laird of Bargany, his most powerful dependant, and the laird of Girvanmains to act as his tacksmen in gathering the teinds from one another's lands. However, having suspected for some time that the two lairds were in collusion to defraud him, he obtained a decreet from the court of session in his favour, and prepared to uplift the teinds himself. Bargany and Girvanmains found out in advance about the earl's plans, and when he and his men turned up on the latter's lands, he found the enclosures armed against his entrance. Frustrated by this, Cassillis went back to court, and obtained a decreet allowing him to intromit with the entire standing crop of one of Bargany's tenants. This time his men arrived first, but were only half way through the job when Bargany appeared with a larger following, and forced them to hand over the crop. In an exemplary display of Sabbatarianism both sides let the next day, a Sunday, pass without incident. Then on the Monday Cassillis led a large armed force to Bargany's lands to collect the remainder of the unshorn crop. Once there he found the enclosures, along with the neighbouring houses, held against him by a few hundred mounted men, hagbutters and a number of basses (a lightweight cannon), and these were soon reinforced by Lord Ochiltree and his men. In time Cassillis could have outmatched this with his own forces, and a very ugly confrontation looked likely. Fortunately, neither side really wanted bloodshed, and when Lord Cathcart turned up with a compromise, both Cassillis and Bargany accepted it, leaving the tenant, John McAlexander, to 'schoir his cornis in peace'. It was a narrow escape in which common sense and good neighbours ensured that a feud did not erupt, but any thoughts that it was all a game of bluff and counter-bluff ought to be dispelled by the fact that a few years after this incident the Bargany family paid a bloody price for challenging the earl's lordship.[21]

Quarrels between landlords and tenants were also common, though most of these did not become feuds because of the disparity of power between the two.[22] Where the tenant was a powerful man himself, confrontation was more likely. When the earl of Atholl tried to dispossess Campbell of Glenorchy of land in Perthshire before the expiry of the latter's tack, Glenorchy refused to move. Atholl then ejected all of Glenorchy's tenants, and prevented him from drawing rents. Glenorchy retaliated by taking his case to Perth Sheriff Court, but when he was awarded six cows in compensation, Atholl's men simply stole them back again.[23] In 1578 the feud between the Gordons and the Forbes was revived when the earl of

Huntly ordered a large number of Forbes tenants to leave lands his family had acquired in feu at an earlier date.[24] When the earl of Cassillis began evicting many of his kindly tenants in Galloway, his lordship was challenged by the Galloway lairds who agreed that 'quhome on that ewer me Lord beganne to dispossess, that thay suld all defend him, with thair horse'. This they did, trapping the earl in one of his castles, and forcing him to make a number of concessions.[25] Whether these disputes, and others like them, were symptomatic of wider changes taking place within the rural community one does not know. Many lairds may have been flexing their muscles, either individually like Glenorchy, or collectively, like the Galloway lairds, to signal a new awareness of their own status. Alternatively, such actions may have been entirely defensive, reflecting a more aggressive and materialistic estate management on the part of superiors, a trend which had been commented on by Sir Richard Maitland a few decades earlier.[26] Sir Thomas Craig also commented on this:

> The removing of husbandmen and indwellers is an incident of everyday occurrence, and is often the cause of bitterly contested litigation owing to the conflict between the quities pleadable by both sides.[27]

As a civil lawyer who made most of his money from litigation in the land market, Craig knew what he was talking about, although one has to avoid painting too dark a picture of rural relations.[28]

If the majority of tenants were vulnerable to aggressive behaviour, the same was true of women. In 1588 William Johnstone complained to the privy council that ten years before his mother had obtained a decreet upholding her rights to the lands of Wamphray from which his eldest brother had excluded her since 1567, but that it had never been obeyed. Three years later Lady Wamphray was still trying to get her lands back from her son.[29] Lady Innermeith was also the victim of her own family when her former husband attacked her lands and occupied her lands and home of Reidcastle.[30] Women were by no means all passive and defensive in such quarrels, and the countess of Erroll was only one of a number when she had to give caution that she would not harm her male neighbour.[31] Some went even further, and in 1616 two border ladies held a 'Course of War', following which they hired a gang of local ruffians to slaughter a number of Douglas of Drumlanrig's sheep.[32] However, these were exceptions, and the unmarried, usually widowed, female landowner was more commonly seen as a soft target in the eyes of acquisitive neighbours, or of her own family, and for her the best defence lay in marriage.[33]

Land, of course, was not the only resource in a locality over which men competed. When writing of the bedouin, E. L. Peters argued that 'feud is competition for preferential access to natural resources', and that 'as long as these natural resources are scarce and competition continues, the pattern of feuding stays'.[34] This cannot be uncritically applied to the Scottish context, but quarrels over natural resources, one of which was land and its produce, were among the commonest origins of feuds. Water was another resource, and, while it was not scarce, the best fishings and the construction of dams did arouse intense competition. In 1609 Innes of Innermarcky and Innes of Blackhills were warned not to convocate their men in pursuit of a quarrel over the bigging of a mill dam.[35] Lundy of Balgony was warned in 1616 not to build a dam on a part of the Water of Leven as its ownership was being contested by Lady Bass whose armed men had also been seen on the site.[36] Lord Oliphant complained in 1611 that the master of Tullibardine had brought his men to a mill dam and destroyed it,[37] and in 1588 Tait of Adamhill complained that Wallace of Cragy had blocked his passage to a water-gang and a mill dam.[38] Fishing rights were the immediate origin of the great feud between the earls of Huntly and Moray in the 1580s,[39] and the commendator of Cambuskenneth and Murray of Touchadam fell out over rights associated with fishing at the mouth of Doven Water.[40]

In February 1588 trouble broke out within Aberdeen over disputed fishing rights and teinds in Banff. These were claimed on the one hand by Alexander Cullen and Alexander Rutherford, two prominent burgesses and councillors who had the backing of the burgh establishment, and Thomas and John Leslie, burgesses who had retained strong links with their rural kinsmen and their chief, the laird of Balquhane. A confrontation at the place of the fishings was followed by the burgh denying entrance to its precincts to John Leslie of Balquhane who then 'declairit his feid' against Aberdeen. The two Leslie burgesses were tried by the burgh council, and found guilty of having 'purchest lordship' against it, for which they were fined and stripped of their freedom of the burgh. Both sides began intensive lobbying of the privy council in Edinburgh, and tried to attract the sympathy of the earl of Huntly, while the laird of Balquhane's son attacked a party of Aberdeen men at the beginning of March, injuring a number of them, and then at the end of the month he broke into Cullen's country property, looting it and killing two servants. By the summer Huntly had succeeded in pacifying the dispute, but the raising of tensions in the locality had made it a dangerous six months, especially for the burgh, whose provost shortly afterwards gave Huntly a bond of manrent in the hope, no doubt, that his lordship would protect Aberdeen from such a threat in the future.[41]

Peats, as a source of fuel, were another natural resource over which neighbours were likely to quarrel. When Wemyss of that Ilk and Scott of Balwery set about gathering certain 'turves', or peats, in defiance of one another, the privy council had to intervene by sending the sheriff of Fife to collect them until ownership could be decided.[42] Thirty years later, in 1615, the Earl Marischal and Douglas of Glenbervie were warned off by the crown following a similar disagreement.[43] The dangers of failing to find a solution to these neighbourly contests were demonstrated in 1621 when Douglas of Drumlanrig and Douglas of Cashogle fell out over peats lying in a moss belonging to Drumlanrig's brother. Cashogle had had the right to lift peats from the moss until he and the Drumlanrig Douglases fell out over some other matter. However, he defied the ban imposed on him, and sent his servants to collect peat as usual. After they had been turned back on two occasions, he went himself with a larger force of armed men, and was met by Drumlanrig who barred his entry to the moss. A fight broke out in which a number of men on both sides were wounded, and one of Cashogle's servants was killed.[44]

Such disputes over peats were likely to arise given the customary and ill-defined rights which often determined access to and ownership of the mosses in which they lay, but in 1613 there was serious friction between the Fife lairds of Cambo and Largo over coal fields to which they had both laid claim.[45]

Fixed property was not a major issue in local feuds, possibly because ownership was more clearly proven by the fact of occupation. However, escheats were usually left to local enforcement, and were consequently a source of irritation to those who often suffered under an arbitrary act of horning. Certainly those who were the victims of the system could have the greatest of difficulty in getting their property back. Alexander Porterfield complained to the privy council in 1579 that the earl of Glencairn was denying him access to his father's castle in spite of a decreet in his favour a year before. Glencairn did eventually leave Duchal, but not before he had wrecked the place.[46] It was the rightful owner who finally burned a house down to spite his rival in a feud between the Bruce lairds of Clackmannan and Fingask in 1600–1601.[47] On the borders a quarrel between the Kerrs and Scotts over Spielaw castle threatened to revive their old feud, and caused the 'breaking of many staves and shot of many 'pistollis' '.[48]

Nor was the sacred exempt from such profane struggles. Feuding over seating arrangements in local churches took place in Scotland just as it did in England,[49] although the issue had less to do with ownership than with prestige and status, and often arose when the local kirk became too small to accommodate the number of lairds who thought they should be the pre-eminent people in the congregation. Andrew Wood of Largo and Robert Lundy of Balgony feuded over a seat in Largo kirk for over a decade, during which time Largo destroyed the seat installed by his rival, both men defied the presbytery and the crown, and church life was so disrupted that the congregation was unable to meet for worship.[50] Similar disputes took place between Kerr of Cessford and Haig of Bemerside in 1599,[51] and between Sir John Wood of Fettercairn and Stratoun of Lauriston from 1612 to at least 1622.[52] In fact, as a place of meeting, and one of the focal points of the community, the church and its yard had always been a place of potential violence.[53] In 1591 John Hoppringle of Muirhouse and his followers went to the churchyard at Stow, and killed there a David Taylor.[54] In 1593 the earl of Morton and Lord Maxwell scuffled in St. Giles, and the Edinburgh magistrates had to be summoned to prevent a serious incident.[55] In 1612 the Lochie and Hair families lined up in a kirkyard to settle their differences, and only the timely arrival of the sheriff of Dumfries prevented bloodshed.[56] Nor were ministers themselves immune from feud. In 1576 the minister in Ancrum refused to baptise the child of a man who was thought to keep images in his house. When the mother died shortly afterwards, supposedly of grief, 'the husband conceived a deadly feud against the minister'.[57] On 4 July 1586 Thomas Burnet went at night to the home of the minister of Birse kirk, next to the church, and assaulted his wife. Then on 20 September he returned with his father and a dozen of their friends, and finding the minister himself, John Lindsay, at study in his glebe, they savagely beat him, and left him for dead. Furthermore, the assailants 'in thair preconsavit malice and haitrent' continued to 'ly at awaitt' for him, so that he and his wife 'dar not oppinlie resorte nor repair in the cuntrey', while he could not 'repair to his awne kirk for discharge of his office thairat for feir of his lyff'. As a result of this both sides were made to assure one another.[58] However, in December of that year the minister at Dalmeny had to give caution not to harm one of his parishioners,[59] and, while there was none of the scandalous behaviour found among the Venetian clergy,[60] ministers were certainly not always the victims of local quarrels. What the issues were in these two cases is unknown, but while one might have expected religion itself to be contentious in local society,[61] examples are very rare. A duel did take place in Edinburgh when an argument developed between two men over the number of the sacraments, one man asserting that there were seven, and the other 'but two, or else he would fight'. They did, and both died as a consequence of their combat.[62] More common was the attitude conveyed in a complaint that 'never a nobleman will countenance the ministry, such excepted as has private quarrels to debate that will be contented for some time to receive their assistance for palliation of their proper designs'.[63]

Almost as important as local resources were local jurisdictions. While lordship was not a jurisdiction in the formal sense, it was similar in that power and authority were invested in the man who was lord over his neighbours. The competition to possess such status was, therefore, intense.[64] As one would expect, an issue like this was the preserve of the landed elite, particularly the nobility, but there was enough fluidity within local power structures to ensure a constant round of manoeuvring and aggression to weaken a rival's lordship and strengthen one's own. Here the divisive, competitive forces within lordship took precedence over its cohesive aspects, and feud between lords soon followed. Lords were highly sensitive to any erosion of their lordship. In 1575 Sir Mathew Campbell of Loudoun, sheriff of Ayr, went to the lands of James Chalmer of Gaitgirth, intimidated his tenants, and 'mannassit and compellit thame to renunce to him thair kyndlie maister' in an effort to undermine Gaitgirth's authority, and take possession of the lands.[65] While land may have lain at the root of that quarrel, a more serious feud almost broke out in 1613 between the earls of Argyll and Huntly purely over lordship. When some old charters were discovered by Argyll showing him to have claims to the lands dwelt in by Huntly's dependant, Alan MacDonald Duy, pressure was put on MacDonald to change his allegiance to his feudal superior. Coming as it did less than a decade after the ending of the great feud between these two earls, a highly dangerous situation evolved, but while a score of MacDonalds died in fighting within the clan, the peace was preserved.[66] In 1618 the earl of Sutherland was faced with dissension among his dependants when the earl of Caithness undermined his authority over MacKay of Strathnaver. Careless lordship by Sutherland, who had left MacKay outside his council, was to blame, and Caithness found the snubbed dependant willing to listen to his offers of better terms. MacKay was soon joined by others, like John Gordon of Enbo who was aggrieved over the earl's handling of a teind quarrel he had an interest in. However, Caithness's duplicity, and Sutherland's desperation to avoid bloodshed and an expensive campaign, persuaded the latter to open negotiations with

MacKay. The latter forced the earl to recognise him as his principal dependant, but Enbo was excluded from the agreement since, as a Gordon, it was thought 'ane evill exemple, that the Earle of Southerland his owne vassallis should come under his other vassalls protection and accord'.[67] This same attitude was expressed by Cassillis when he denounced Kennedy of Bargany because he had dared to 'mak him ane pairty, within his awin cuntrey'.[68]

While lordship could be destabilising and disruptive in a locality, it was no more so than the more formal jurisdictions through which political control was exercised. Royal offices and commissions were as much a means to local predominance as lands or men as they offered the prospect of enhanced authority, profit, and the legitimisation of private actions.[69] This last was probably the most important where local rivalries already existed, as it allowed the holder of such offices and commissions to act in the king's name, and to compel neutrals to support him. The balance of power in a locality could thus be altered through such jurisdictions, which meant that it was worth while courting favour from the king, his courtiers, and officers of state. Court and country were thus joined in patronage networks which made the placing of support in the localities important to the men at court (a side of the relationship which is explored later), and the competition for local office of great significance to those whose power base lay there. Offices created to enforce order became themselves the root of the disorder which flowed from feuds born out of competition for them.

Holding court, whether baronial, bailey or whatever, on the land of a man who claimed exemption from it was intended to be provocative. Such a situation arose when either the holder of the office sought to extend his influence in a locality, or when another man felt that his prestige had grown sufficiently for him to be slighted by appearing to be under the jurisdiction of another. In 1612 the earl of Angus and Kerr of Ferniehirst came close to blows when the latter held a court on the earl's lands, claiming to do so as heritable bailie. Challenges were exchanged, but crown intervention defused the quarrel.[70] In 1598 the tenants of the lordship of Coupar took both the earl of Atholl and Lord Ogilvy to court because they were tired of being the subject of a feud between them over who had bailey rights to Coupar.[71] The right to hold bailie courts in the regality of Arbroath caused friction between the marquis of Hamilton and the master of Ogilvy which 'wer lyke to breed a greate deall of mischeiffe'.[72] Even an admiralty court in Galloway was able to divide two local families for over three decades, with one side holding court in 1600 at Loch Ryan in defiance of the other, and of the crown.[73]

The manner in which such courts and other royal commissions were exploited explains why so much effort was put into getting them. Men were expected to manipulate such positions in their own interests, and even if they did not, others would claim that they had in order to discredit them. It was well known that it was 'a hard thing indeed to subject one great man to another in 'feude' with him that by authority under colour of justice oppress him'.[74] In 1588 Thomas Cuming of Altyre was able to present sufficient evidence, real or contrived, to persuade the privy council to exempt him from the authority of James Dunbar of Cumnock, sheriff of Elgin, because of the 'deidlie feid' between them. However, this did not stop Cumnock who arrested one of Altyre's servants, and executed him for theft. Even after being denounced by the council he continued to exercise his office, and the feud was continued by Cumnock's successor who in 1619 wrote of the 'inimitie and deadly feud standing unreconcilie' between Altyre and previous sheriffs.[75] In 1596 the sheriff depute of Dumfries, Kirkpatrick of Closeburn, complained that the sheriff of Dumfries, Crichton of Sanquhar, had broken off friendship with him, allied himself with Closeburn's enemy, Douglas of Drumlanrig, and intended to exploit his authority against him. Since the agreement had been made, Sanquhar had already taken one of Closeburn's men prisoner, and when another had been sent with a missive, the sheriff had executed him for alleged theft. This time Sanquhar was arrested, and Closeburn was exempted from his jurisdiction.[76] Only a few years before this Closeburn had complained to the privy council that Drumlanrig had obtained a new commission of justiciary which clashed with his own authority, and that it was intended to 'cullour and cloik the wicked and mischevous deidis' of the Douglases.[77] In 1616 Francis Hay murdered a member of the Gordon family after losing a fencing match to him. On hearing of this, Gordon of Gight gathered his men, went to the home of the Hays of Brunthill, broke in, beat up the family who lived there, and captured Francis. He was then taken to Aberdeen, to the sheriff depute, John Gordon of Clubbisgoull, tried before an assize of Gordons and their friends, found guilty, and taken outside to a clumsy execution. The killing infuriated the earl of Erroll, not because his man had been executed by the sheriff depute, but because the Gordons had so obviously made use of their power to prosecute the feud through an office they controlled.[78]

It was not only shrieval offices which were open to such manipulation. In 1576 the earl of Cassillis (the 4th earl of Crossraguel fame) went to the home of George Cory, seized him and his brother, and plundered his house. For two weeks the brothers were held without charge under Cassillis' authority as bailie of Carrick. An order from the privy council to release them was ignored, and only after further lobbying by their friends did the earl agree to bring them before the council for an inquiry.[79] In 1593 Robert Galbraith of Culcreuch conspired with the laird of Buchanan to get a commission against the Macgregor clan, but which they both used to oppress the MacAulay clan with whom they had private quarrels.[80] In 1608 the earl of Crawford's commissions were suspended when it became apparent that he intended to use them to pursue his feud with Sir David Lindsay of Edzell.[81] Not everyone had genuine motives for making these complaints, however, and occasionally the government saw through what was simply an attempt to weaken a rival by undermining his local authority.[82]

The long and violent feud between the Maxwell and Johnstone families on the west marches was intimately tied up with court politics, with Spain and England, and with government policy on the borders after 1603, but between the two families themselves much of the quarrel centred on control of the west wardenry. In 1573 Lord Maxwell was appointed as warden of the west marches, an office which he regarded as virtually his by right, but which had been temporarily lost due to his own minority, and the civil war. Complaints soon followed from the laird of Johnstone that Maxwell was exploiting the office, but he easily swept aside

Johnstone's objections, and retained the office until 1577 when he resigned after an argument with the Regent Morton. Within the year the regency came to an end, and he was restored to office, but a government report later in 1578 accused him of negligence in his administration of justice. Maxwell defended himself by claiming that he had insufficient power, having 'only the title of warden' due to the many exemptions held by local barons and lairds which 'made the office needless and contemtable'.[83] There was little doubt, however, that Maxwell was treating the wardenry as a private domain, governing it in his own interests. Thus one man complained in a letter to a friend, 'I will persew na thing befoir the Warden, becais they men ar his Lordschippis servandis, and I knaw he will be a parsiall judge'.[84] Maxwell's demands for greater authority were turned down, but his replacement by Lord Herries, another Maxwell, was unlikely to assuage the resentment of other families in the wardenry. Herries found it impossible to hold the office without putting a strain on his relations with the family chief, and resigned in August 1579, allowing Morton to secure the appointment of the laird of Johnstone. Maxwell then set about making it impossible for Johnstone to administer the wardenry, fighting broke out, and the feud between the two kindreds intensified. As Johnstone was now firmly tied to Morton's clientage, it was no surprise that following his fall at the end of 1580 Maxwell was given back his old office in 1581. He was, however, a close friend of the duke of Lennox, and following the Ruthven Raid in 1582 was deprived in favour of Johnstone who succeeded in holding onto the office when Arran resumed power in 1583. This, and Arran's own quarrel with Maxwell over lands in Renfrewshire, brought the latter into open rebellion in 1584, and in a savage war fought throughout the south-west in 1584–85 Maxwell broke the power of the Johnstone warden, while also exposing the weakness of Arran's regime, and precipitating its overthrow in October 1585. The laird of Johnstone died within two years of this, having been held prisoner by Maxwell, and 'for grieff of the great victorie, that his enemie had obtenit over him'.[85] The completeness of Maxwell's victory ought to have guaranteed his power from 1585, but his involvement in catholic conspiracies which brought him out in rebellion in 1587–88 gave the Johnstones the opportunity to recover. They in turn allied themselves too closely to the earl of Bothwell, and were in rebellion when Maxwell proceeded against them as warden in 1593, the office having in the meantime changed hands again on a number of occasions, but he was soundly defeated and killed at Dryfe Sands. The feud continued after 1593, claiming the lives of another Johnstone warden in 1608 and of his murderer, the 9th Lord Maxwell, who was executed in 1613, but the jurisdictional issue had by then become less important than vengeance itself. The two families did not make their peace with one another until 1623, by which time the wardenry itself was defunct.[86]

Burghs and their offices were also the object of intense competition. St. Andrews narrowly avoided an outbreak of violence in the 1590s over the provostship,[87] competition over the provostship in Dumfries exacerbated the feud between Lord Maxwell and the laird of Johnstone in 1584,[88] and in 1606 in Glasgow there was fighting between the supporters of the ousted provost, Sir

Mathew Stewart of Minto, and his successor, Sir George Elpinstone.[89] Tension existed in Ayr in 1578 over the growth of Campbell of Loudoun's influence there,[90] in Leith in 1588 due to a feud with the earl of Bothwell who was using his office as lord admiral to interfere with the burgh's shipping,[91] and in Aberdeen in 1590 between rival factions who wanted to reduce the power of the earl of Huntly there.[92] Often the authority of burghs was usurped, or disregarded by rural neighbours, such as when the earl of Crawford rode into Dundee and freed his men from the tolbooth,[93] but burghs could also be tough in defending their jurisdictions, as when Perth magistrates led an attack on the home of the Bruce laird of Clackmannan, and succeeded in firing it and forcing the laird to surrender.[94] The rural localities had no monopoly on feuding.[95]


In all of the feuding discussed so far competition has been between corporate groups which were distinguishable as clans or kindreds. Yet just as bonds within lordship could fracture, thus disrupting the locality, so the kindred could divide, making its internal feuding the politics of the locality. Around 14% of the feuds identified were between kinsmen sharing the same surname.[96] Kindreds were not monolithic power structures, blindly following a chief, and always working to common ends, and the power of the kindred itself could become a source of competition, or the kindred could become so large that cadet branches began to pursue independent ambitions of their own. Certainly feud within the kindred, or within close degrees of kinship, was avoided where possible. When accused by Kennedy of Bargany of plotting against him, Kennedy of Culzean replied that as 'sister-son' to Bargany's house, he was 'owr neir cumit tharof to craiff thair bluid'.[97] Of course, such a reply could be expressing a conventional value rather than an actual opinion, and where reasons could be found kinsmen were slain. Both the younger laird of Bargany and the laird of Culzean were murdered by rival branches of the Kennedy kindred. Such feuds could be particularly bloody, as Sir Thomas Craig explained, for 'so far from acting as a protection against discord, community of blood often intensifies the bitterness of family quarrels, and the most violent hate of which human nature is capable occurs between brothers and sometimes between father and son'.[98] Similar points have been made by more modern commentators: 'Conflict and competition begins within the family,' wrote Lucy Mair,[99] and Gluckman also drew attention to the 'Dispersal of the vengeance groups' which divided loyalties within the kindred.[100] Whether this was any more intense in sixteenth-century Scotland is unknown. Pressure on the land from younger sons may have been a little more intense, and in France a greater emphasis on primogeniture does appear to have intensified rivalries within the family in the course of the sixteenth century.[101] Yet Sharpe's analysis of domestic homicide in early modern England suggests that killings within the family were half as common as they are today, and this picture has been confirmed for the medieval period.[102] Such figures are not available for Scotland, but one suspects that the English findings are relevant, and in discussing family feud it should be borne in mind that in the great majority of cases families did not kill one another, and that most kindreds which experienced feud were large social units and did not inhabit a domestic environment.

Feuds between fathers and sons certainly were rare. In 1590–91 old Lord Forbes was drawn into a feud between his sons over inheritance. When he was persuaded by his younger sons to disinherit the master of Forbes, the latter responded by taking his father prisoner, and some raiding took place between the brothers.[103] In 1588 the master of Sempill complained that he was being oppressed by his father, Lord Sempill, who was denounced by the privy council,[104] and in 1616 the privy council had to discipline both Sir Thomas Kirkpatrick of Closeburn and his eldest son, as their arguments over family debts were threatening the peace of the locality.[105] Lord Somerville, however, was saved from feuding with his eldest son after he accidentally shot his younger brother when the king told him 'he was a madman; that having lost one son by so sudden an accident should needs wilfully destroy another himself', and a family reconciliation followed.[106] The earl of Caithness did cause the death of his eldest son, starving him to death in the dungeons of Girnigo,[107] and Sir James MacDonald was accused of trying to murder his father, MacDonald of Dunivaig.[108]

Feuds among brothers, most commonly over their inheritance, were more numerous. In 1592 John Colquhoun was executed for his part in the slaying of his brother, the laird of Luss.[109] In 1604 George Meldrum was found guilty of having conceived a feud against his brother, attacking him, and taking him prisoner, and was sentenced to be beheaded.[110] Robert Tinto of Crimpcramp complained that his two brothers and his mother came to his home, broke in, beat up his wife, stole his documents, silver and gold, and shot him in the arm.[111] The earl of Cassillis incarcerated his brother in Dunure dungeons when he uncovered a plot to murder him, and relations between the two were always icy.[112] In 1613 the MacNeills of Barra fell out among themselves when two sets of sons born of different mothers began warring for their father's favour. Widescale raiding and slaughter followed, with the clans of the two women, the MacDonalds and MacLeans, becoming increasingly involved.[113]

Feuds of this nature were certainly more likely in the highlands where inheritances were often settled as much by might as by right.[114] The most dramatic example documented is that of the MacLeods of Assynt whose internal squabbling resulted in the deaths of fourteen of the twenty-eight male descendants of Angus Moir MacLeod, the clan chief, who was murdered by his brother, John, some time before the middle of the century. He was succeeded by his son, Donald Caim, who was himself slain in a dispute with MacLeod of Lewis, and, as he had no sons, leadership of the clan passed to Tormot, his younger brother. Tormot then quarrelled with another brother, Angus Beg, who killed him, before being slain himself by a bastard brother, Alexander. Neither Tormot nor Angus Beg had any issue either, which suggests that all the brothers may have been relatively young at the time, and the new laird of Assynt was John Reawigh, the eldest of Angus Moir's three surviving, legitimate sons. The bastard Alexander was murdered by the kinsmen of Angus Beg's wife. This ended the first succession feud, and John Reawigh survived as the clan chief for fifteen years, dying peacefully, and leaving the rule of Assynt to his brother Neil until his own sons came of age. However, the last of Angus Moir's sons, Hucheon, resented this, and a struggle for power in the clan broke out between the two brothers who both ignored the interests of their nephews. When Hucheon captured Neil, he succeeded in extracting from him a promise to share power in Assynt, but once free Neil renounced it, took Hucheon and one of his sons prisoner when they came to see him, and murdered them both. This murder was followed by a rebellion within the clan which resulted in Neil being sent to Edinburgh where he was tried and executed in 1581. Angus MacEan, the eldest son of John Reawigh, then tried to rule, but was lame in one leg, and was deposed by a combination of Hucheon's surviving sons, and the illegitimate sons of Neil. They had therefore excluded all the sons of John Reawigh who made no effort to assert themselves in the future, and Neil's legitimate sons. Of these, the elder died while being held in the earl of Caithness's notorious· dungeons at Girnigo, and Donald Bane was in Ross under the tutorship of the laird of Foulis. Hucheon's eldest son, Neil, was then named captain of the clan, and the cousins divided up the lands among them, but now they quarrelled, and two of the bastards, Tormot and Allister, were killed. Donald Bane then returned from Ross with Allister's son Angus, and they revenged these deaths by slaying John Hucheon, one of Neil's brothers. A truce was arranged by the earl of Sutherland which left Neil as laird of Assynt, and this was cemented by a marriage between Neil's daughter and Angus. However, Donald Bane was far from satisfied with this, and within a year Angus had killed his father-in-law, while he killed Neil's brother Rory, and then captured and executed the last of Hucheon's sons, Angus. Further fighting continued until in 1609 Donald Bane's leadership of the clan was finally recognised by everyone, including the senior branch of the family which had descended from John Reawigh.[115] This feud is not typical in the degree of destructiveness it inflicted within the family, although to some extent one is at the mercy of records for the west highlands, but it does demonstrate just how terrible a feud within the family could be.

The length of the Assynt feud, spreading over more than one generation, widened the feud to include cousins, and, as one would expect, feuding became more common as relations grew more distant. Robert Bartilmo of Kirkshaw murdered his uncle Patrick Bartilmo in 1601,[116] the laird of Bomby had to give assurance that he would not harm his kinsman, William MacClellan of Auchlean in 1608,[117] and in 1614 George Leslie of Crechie had to promise to keep the peace with his nephew, Leslie of Wardes.[118] Such strains probably arose from many of the same issues which have always divided families, but in a feuding society they were more dangerous. The rivalry within the Lindsay kindred over long-standing jealousies between the earl of Crawford's family and that of the laird of Edzell was about more than just bickering within the kindred. Because of the political role of the kindred in the locality and beyond, it was also a struggle for real power. In 1605 the master of Crawford killed and hewed to pieces Edzell's brother, Sir David Lindsay of Balgays, and a few years later Edzell's son killed the master's uncle, Lord Spynie, in Edinburgh.[119] In the north-east the Innes kindred split over leadership of the clan a quarter of a century earlier, and in 1580 the laird of Cromy was stabbed to death in Aberdeen by his rival, Innes of Innermarcky. Four years later Cromy's son had his revenge when he tracked Innermarcky down, killed him, and became chief of the kindred, having, it was claimed, sent his enemy's head to the king as proof of his success.[120] On the borders the Kerrs, Scotts and Humes all experienced feuds within the surname, and the Turnbulls sustained a bloody struggle for over twenty-five years.[121] In the west MacLean of Duart attacked MacLean of Coil's castle in 1579, ejecting Coil and his kinsmen from it, and executing his former tutor. In 1596 Coil was still complaining of oppression by his chief.[122]

The origins of most feuds are elusive (see Table 7 on page 279). While a case could appear to be about a killing, the context in which the killing took place may have been a quarrel over land or jurisdiction. Very often the underlying cause was forgotten about as honour and vengeance maintained a conflict which was simply about feuding itself. Yet in those cases where an initial cause can be identified with relative confidence, local issues predominate, and it would not be rash to assume that most of those unidentified followed a similar pattern. Control of wealth, measured in land and other natural resources, of manpower, and of offices was what gave a lord or laird pre-eminence in a locality, a pre-eminence which had its rewards in the fear and recognition it inspired among neighbours, and in the wider political world. It also inspired jealousy in others, and triggered competition with them. This drive for power was more than simple greed: standards of living had to be protected, younger sons and daughters had to be provided for, dependants had to be maintained, status had to be visibly displayed in ostentatious consumption, and the inheritance of the lineage had to be expanded, or at the very least maintained, as a duty which was self-perpetuating.

The men who were the leaders of local society represented interest groups of varying sizes, each with ambitions which were usually commensurate with the limits of their own and their competitors' power. Unlike today, when corporate or interests groups can shift wealth, distribute patronage, and change officials by elections, either within themselves, or in competition with others in the community, the sixteenth century had no such mechanisms for effecting change except through personal relationships. These either took the form of co-operation, that is in bonds of one sort or another, favours or deference, or in conflict, in the threat of feud, or actual feuding. The killing, burning and stealing which accompanied it did not mean that local society was anarchic, or breaking down, and did not mean that it was dominated by bad and ruthless men. These were simply the tools employed in resolving competitive politics in a society which had few other means of doing so, and which was saturated in the values of the bloodfeud.

The tensions in local society were all potential feuds. Most were resolved peacefully, in arbitration and compromise, but almost every lord and a great many lairds participated in at least one feud in their lifetime. To have escaped the feud would have been almost impossible, and, unless one was blessed in having remarkably reasonable neighbours, it would have required an abdication of responsibilities, and a meek and ruinous submission to the demands of others to avoid feuding. However, more than a tough defence was expected, and aggressive competition was necessary if power was to be held onto. To refuse to compete was to invite predators and lose support which naturally gravitated to those lords who could deliver. Feud in this context was not an aberration, but a symptom of vitality in the distribution of power. That power was not so structured and apportioned that it was closed off to ambition, but rather it remained fluid and there for the taking. Those who did try to take may have been reaching for no more than the increase in wealth and status which fishing rights or some minor jurisdiction might give them in the community, or, like the earls of Moray and Caithness, their ambitions may have been more regional. Whatever the scale, their actions, and the opposition they encountered, reveal a society in which the distribution of power was neither so rigid that it could not be shifted about, or so rotten that newcomers could carve their way into it with ease. Instead it was excitingly volatile, and hence potentially explosive. There clever and tough men like Mackenzie of Kintail and Johnstone of that Ilk could do well by changing the status quo of their localities, while others like the earl of Moray, Kennedy of Bargany, or Kerr of Ancrum were smashed by the very men they sought to displace or dislodge. However, these local feuds were rarely fought out in isolation, but were often linked to the wider political environment, and to the politics of the royal court where local and national issues were meshed in a complex web of loyalties, rivalries and factional conflict. That is a theme which is picked up in Part Two, but before then it will be useful to anatomise in detail the history of one local feud.

## NOTES

1. For the best descriptions of Scottish local society, which was essentially rural in character, see M. H. B. Sanderson, *Scottish Rural Society in the 16th Century,* Edinburgh, 1982; and I. Whyte, *Agriculture and Society in Seventeenth Century Scotland,* Edinburgh, 1979.

2. Fraser, *Pollok,* ii, p. 157, No. 156.

3. Black-Michaud, *Cohesive Force,* p. xvii, and see too, Gluckman, *Custom and Conflict,* p. 19. To some extent this depends on what exactly one means by 'neighbour'.

4. R. Ardrey, *The Territorial Imperative,* London, 1970.

5. J. K. Leyser wrote of the 'perennial feuds' among the ninth-century German nobility which sprang from land fragmentation caused by inheritance laws, 'The German Aristocracy from the Ninth to the early Twelfth Century. A Historical and Cultural Sketch', in *Past and Present,* 41, 1968, pp. 25-33. A New York gang member described a gang quarrel as 'You have a certain piece of land, so another club wants to take your land, in order to have more space, and so forth. They'll fight you for it. If you win, you got the land; if you don't win, then they got your land. The person that loses is gonna get up another group, to help out, and then it starts up all over again'. Yablonsky, 'The Violent Gang', in J. Endleman (ed.), *Violence in the Streets,* London, 1969, p. 234.

6. *R.P.C.,* viii, p. 621. When parliament established justices of the peace in 1609 it made similar observations, *A.P.S.,* iv, pp. 434-435.

7. J. P. Cooper, 'Patterns of Inheritance and Settlement by great landowners from the fifteenth to the eighteenth centuries', in Goody, Thirsk and Thomson (eds.), *Family and Inheritance;* B. Coward, 'Disputed Inheritances: Some Difficulties of the Nobility in the Late Sixteenth and Early Seventeenth Centuries', in *Bulletin of the Institute of Historical Research*, 44, 1971, pp. 194–215. See too E. Le Roy Ladurie, 'A System of Customary Law: Family Structures and Inheritance Customs in Sixteenth Century France', in R. Forster and O. Ranun (eds.), *Family and Society*, Baltimore, 1976.

8. For the fifteenth century, and in particular for his comments on demography, see Grant, *Independence and Nationhood*, pp. 127–130 and 140–143. Sanderson has, of course, analysed feuing in *Scottish Rural Society in the 16th Century*. The rise of the lairds in Scotland is an assumed thesis which has never been put to the test that the English gentry have, see J. Habakkuk, 'The rise and fall of English Landed Families, 1600–1800: 111. Did the Gentry Rise?' in *Trans. Royal Hist. Soc.*, 31, 1981, pp. 195–217.

9. *Historie*, pp. 256–257; Spottiswoode, *History*, ii, pp. 413–415; Birrel, 'Diary', p. 29.

10. *R.P.C.*, iii, pp. 505–506.

11. *R.P.C.*, iii, pp. 505–506, 541–543, 548 and 555–557; vi, p. 461; Gordon, *Sutherland*, p. 248; Pitcairn, *Criminal Trials*, ii, p. 413.

12. *R.P.C.*, iv, pp. 682–684 and 687–688; *C.S.P., Scot.*, x, pp. 566–567, 569–570, 572–573, 575 and 585. For a more detailed explanation of this very interesting case, see E. J. Cowan, 'The Angus Campbells and the Origin of the Campbell-Ogilvie Feud', in *The Journal of the School of Scottish Studies, University of Edinburgh*, 25, 1981, pp. 25–37.

13. Gordon, *Sutherland*, p. 479. Of Romagna, John Larner wrote that 'From time to time private wars over boundary disputes and rights of pasturage would break out between rural communes and even on the plains, boundary disputes at harvest time were likely to lead to killings between communities', Larner, 'Order and Disorder in Romagna', in Martines (ed.), *Violence and Civil Disorder*, pp. 40–41.

14. *R.P.C.*, x, pp. 362 and 607; xi, pp. 54 and 178; *Melrose*, i, p. 297.

15. *R. P.C.*, ix, p. 8.

16. See Whyte, *Agriculture and Society in Seventeenth Century Scotland*, p. 97.

17. *R.P.C.*, ii, p. 273.

18. *R.P.C.*, iii, p. 329; *Historie*, p. 80; Pitcairn, *Criminal Trials*, i, Part 2, pp. 89–92.

19. *R.P.C.*, iii, p. 311.

20. *R.P.C.*, xii, pp. 81 and 89.

21. Pitcairn, *Kennedy*, pp. 36–38.

22. Much of the business of barony courts involved disputes between landlords and tenants, Sanderson, *Scottish Rural Society in the 16th Century*, pp. 14–15; Whyte, *Agriculture and Society in the Seventeenth Century*, p. 45.

23. *R.P.C.*, iv, p. 687.

24. *A.P.S.*, iii, pp. 112–114.

25. Pitcairn, *Kennedy*, pp. 36–38.

26. *The Penguin Book of Scottish Verse*, (ed.) T. Scott, Penguin, 1970, p. 178.

27. Craig, *Jus Feudale*, i, p. 548.

28. Thus see Sanderson on evictions arising from feuding, *Scottish Rural Society in the 16th Century*, pp. 162–165.

29. *R.P.C.*, iv, pp. 273–274 and 654–655.

30. *R.P.C.*, iii, pp. 125, 155, 171–172, 188–189, 211, 217–218, 230, 276, 278 and 361.

31. *R.P.C.*, iv, p. 385. See too Lady Ross, *Ibid.*, p. 315.

32. Pitcairn, *Criminal Trials*, iii, pp. 380–389.

33. Marshall, *Virgins and Viragos*, pp. 47–48 and 162, has some comments on this.

34. Black-Michaud, *Cohesive Force,* p. xxvii.

35. *R.P.C.,* viii, pp. 320 and 589.

36. *R.P.C.,* x, 657–658.

37. *R.P.C.,* ix, p. 235.

38. *R.P.C.,* iv, p. 328.

39. See below, p. 147.

40. *R.P.C.,* viii, p. 128.

41. *Aberdeen Council Letters,* (ed.) Taylor, pp. 7–47; *R.P.C.,* iv, pp. 203ff; Moysie, *Memoirs,* p. 66; *Spalding Miscellany,* ii, 'The Chronicle of Aberdeen', p. 58; Brown, 'Bonds of Manrent', appendix, p. 469, Nos. 71 and 72.

42. *R.P.C.,* iv, p. 8.

43. *R.P.C.,* x, p. 354.

44. Chambers, *Domestic Annals,* i, pp. 520–521; Pitcairn, *Criminal Trials,* iii, pp. 500–501.

45. *R.P.C.,* x, pp. 5 and 27.

46. *R.P.C.,* iii, pp. 195–196; S.R.O., Glencairn Muniments, G.D., 39/1/25/112.

47. *R.P.C.,* vi, pp. 167 and 197–198.

48. *C.B.P.,* i, p. 460.

49. C. Haigh, *Reformation and Resistance in Tudor Lancashire,* Cambridge University Press, 1975, pp. 53–54.

50. *R.P.C.,* vii, p. 424 through to refs. in *R.P.C.,* x.

51. *C.S.P., Scot.,* xiii, Part 1, p. 373.

52. *R.P.C.,* x, p. 208.

53. I. B. Cowan, 'Church and Society', in Brown (ed.), *Scottish Society in the Fifteenth Century,* p. 113, where he comments that Church life was often 'violated by the effusion of blood'.

54. *R.P.C.,* iv, pp. 574 and 689.

55. *C.S.P., Scot.,* xi, p. 42; *Historie,* p. 263.

56. *R.P.C.,* ix, p. 490.

57. *The Booke of the Universall Kirk of Scotland: Acts and Proceedings of the General Assemblies of the Kirk of Scotland from the Year MDLX,* (ed.) T. Thomson, Maitland Club, Edinburgh, 1839–45, i, p. 364.

58. *R.P.C.,* iv, pp. 118, 119 and 120.

59. *Ibid.,* p. 132.

60. Wright, 'Venetian Law and Order: A Myth?', pp. 193–212.

61. G. Donaldson, *Scotland, James V–VII,* Edinburgh, 1971, p. 40.

62. Birrel, 'Diary', p. 42; Chambers, *Domestic Annals,* i, p. 285.

63. *C.S.P., Scot.,* xiii, Part 1, p. 557.

64. Wormald, *Lords and Men,* p. 27, has argued however that when men changed lords 'it did not usually create a conflict of loyalties'.

65. *R.P.C.,* ii, p. 464. This feud was still active in 1582, *R.P.C.,* iii, p. 503.

66. *R.P.C.,* x, pp. 818–820.

67. Gordon, *Sutherland,* p. 354.

68. Pitcairn, *Kennedy,* p. 38.

69. However, it was private power which remained at the base of a man's authority, and this was often the case even in England where 'the order keeping forces of the state remained firmly in private hands', James, *English Politics and the Concept of Honour,* pp. 43–44.

70. *R.P.C.,* ix, pp. 372–374, 394 and 398–400; x, p. 156.

71. S.R.O., Airlie Muniments, G.D., 16/41/108. This feud is mentioned as early as 1593, and was unresolved in 1606, *C.S.P., Scot.,* xi, p. 102; *R.P.C.,* v, pp. 523 and 552; S.R.O., Airlie Muniments, G.D., 16/41/129, G.D., 16/41/134.

72. Balfour, 'Annales', ii, p. 54.

73. *R.P.C.,* iii, p. 317; vi, pp. 84 and 87–88; x, pp. 394 and 622.

74. *C. S.P., Scot.,* xii, p. 52.

75. *R.P.C.,* iv, pp. 283–284; *H.M. C.,* vi, 'Cuming M.S.', p. 688.

76. *R.P.C.,* v, pp. 378–379.

77. *R.P.C.,* iv, p. 735.

78. *R.P.C.,* x, p. 496.

79. *R.P.C.,* ii, pp. 486–488.

80. *R.P.C.,* v, pp. 74–76.

81. *R.P.C.,* viii, pp. 117–118.

82. *R.P.C.,* vi, pp. 227–228.

83. Spottiswoode, *History,* ii, p. 259. For the actual investigation, *R.P.C.,* iii, pp. 73–86.

84. Fraser, *Pollok,* ii, p. 146, No. 142.

85. *Historie,* p. 210.

86. For a more complete discussion of this feud, see K. M. Brown, The Extent and Nature of Feuding in Scotland, 1573–1625, University of Glasgow Ph.D., 1983, ii, pp. 451–548.

87. Melville, *Autobiography and Diary,* p. 210.

88. *Historie,* p. 209; *R.P.C.,* iii, pp. 767–768; Spottiswoode, *History,* ii, pp. 325–326.

89. *R.P.C.,* vii, pp. 233–235, 240–247 and 249–250.

90. *R.P.C.,* iii, pp. 44–45.

91. *C.S.P., Scot.,* ix, p. 641; *Extracts from the Records of the Burgh of Edinburgh, 1573–89,* Burgh Record Society, Edinburgh, 1882, p. 150.

92. *R.P.C.,* iv, pp. 533–534; Moysie, *Memoirs,* p. 118; *Historie,* p. 331.

93. *R.P.C.,* iii, p. 572–574.

94. *R.P.C.,* v, pp. 6–8 and 80–81.

95. This is discussed at greater length in K. M. Brown, 'Burghs, Lords and Feuds in Jacobean Scotland', in M. Lynch, *The Early Modern Town in Scotland,* forthcoming, 1986.

96. See Appendix, p. 278, Table 4.

97. Pitcairn, *Kennedy,* p. 23.

98. Quoted in Wormald, 'Bloodfeud, Kindred and Government', p. 69, and see her comments, pp. 69–70.

99. Mair, *Primitive Government,* p. 10. Black-Michaud parallels killings within the family with incest, and shows that the response of the community to them was quite different from normal killings, *Cohesive Force,* pp. 228–234.

100. Gluckman, *Custom and Conflict,* p. 12.

101. Harding, *Anatomy of a Power Elite,* pp. 165–166. See too Wright, 'Venetian Law and Order: A Myth?', p. 193.

102. Sharpe, 'Domestic Homicide in Early Modern England'; and see too Westman, 'The Peasant Family and Crime in Fourteenth Century England'.

103. *R.P.C.,* iv, pp. 497 and 617–618.

104. *Ibid.,* pp. 248–250.

105. *R.P.C.,* x, pp. 606–607, 646 and 678–681.

106. Chambers, *Domestic Annals,* i, pp. 191–192.

107. Gordon, *Sutherland,* pp. 107–108.

108. Pitcairn, *Criminal Trials,* iv, p. 6.

109. Birrel, 'Diary', p. 29; Balfour, 'Annales', i, p. 392.

110. Pitcairn, *Criminal Trials,* ii, pp. 428–430.

111. *R.P.C.,* v, p. 215.

112. Pitcairn, *Kennedy,* pp. 20–21.

113. *R.P.C.,* x, pp. 6, 42 and 817.

114. For a similar society, see K. Nicholls, *Gaelic and Gaelicised Ireland in the Middle Ages,* Dublin, 1972, p. 25.

115. Gordon, *Sutherland,* pp. 262–266. This appears to disprove Peters' point that 'feud is excluded from the corporate group', Black-Michaud, *Cohesive Force,* p. xiii.

116. *R.P.C.,* vi, p. 203.

117. *R.P.C.,* viii, p. 98.

118. *R.P.C.,* x, p. 259.

119. *R.P.C.,* vii, p. 143, and for Spynie's death, *R.P.C.,* vii, p. 383.

120. *Spalding Miscellany,* ii, 'The Chronicle of Aberdeen', p. 52; Chambers, *Domestic Annals,* i, pp. 154–157.

121. See, for example, the Turnbulls, *R.P.C.,* ii, p. 591; iii, pp. 302 and 619–620; vi, p. 4; Pitcairn, *Criminal Trials,* ii, pp. 509–511.

122. *R.P.C.,* iii, pp. 132–135; v, p. 354.

# 4

# A Local example:
# The Cunningham–Montgomery Feud

The feud between the Cunningham and Montgomery families in north Ayrshire has a reputation of having been both very long and very bloody. The locality in which most of it took place was bounded in the south by the River Irvine with the burgh of Irvine at its mouth, by the sea to the west, and by hills to the north and the east. Much of the land there was hill and bog, with the more fertile and populous areas being concentrated in the Irvine Valley, the Garnock Valley and along the coast. The bailiery of Cunninghame and the regality of Kilwinning Abbey were both contained within it, and were the major administrative and judicial jurisdictions for the district. There the Cunningham and Montgomery kindreds had long been dominant, and except for a brief hiatus in the early fifteenth century, the chiefs of the Montgomeries had been bailies of Cunninghame since 1366. During the fifteenth century both chiefs became lords of parliament, as Lord Montgomery in 1444 and Lord Kilmaurs in 1450, and were raised to the earldom of Glencairn for the latter in 1503, and the earldom of Eglinton for the former in 1507. Competition between them was fairly muted throughout this time, but in 1509 the Cunninghams challenged the 1st earl of Eglinton's right to the office of bailie, and in the 1520s fighting broke out. By 1536 peace had been made between them, and the Montgomeries soon found themselves tied up in a quite different feud with the Boyds. However, their dominance of local offices had been enhanced by James V, and the Cunninghams were forced increasingly to look elsewhere for aggrandisement.[1]

Four decades of peace followed the settlement of that earlier feud in the 1520s and 1530s, and there is really no connection between it and the feud at the end of the century. During the Reformation and the civil war that peace held. Alexander, 4th earl of Glencairn, was one of the protestant stalwarts and an uncomprising king's man who emerged as the major threat to the earl of Morton in the regency election of 1572. In contrast, the 3rd earl of Eglinton was a catholic, and continued to support Queen Mary until 1571. Yet in spite of these differences over national issues, the locality remained largely undisturbed, and it was only with the end of the war that local tensions began to be raised.[2]

It was Kilwinning Abbey which provided the fuel for the conflict. By the 1570s Montgomery dominance of local patronage was almost complete, and even the abbey had fallen under their influence, with Eglinton being granted the offices of chamberlain, justiciar and bailie of the abbey lands in 1552, and acquiring feus from it in 1566. This had been largely helped along by the commendator, Gavin Hamilton, a kinsman of Eglinton's first wife, but he died in 1571, and was succeeded by Alexander Cunningham of Montgreenan, Glencairn's youngest son.[3] The appointment reflected Glencairn's position in the government, and was probably a recognition of his part in the king's service. Not until after the death of 'the good earl' in 1574 could Eglinton begin to make an effective challenge to this frustration of his ambitions.[4]

In fact it was Montgreenan whose behaviour was the more aggressive in refusing to infeft Eglinton in those abbey offices he had held for the previous twenty years, and in seeking to have him stripped of them by the session court.[5] Angered by this, Eglinton's younger son, Robert Montgomery of Giffen, attacked one of Montgreenan's tenants in 1576, driving the man and his family from their home. Giffen was denounced, but six months later Eglinton himself led an attack on the abbey at Kilwinning and garrisoned it during the commendator's absence.[6] Montgreenan decided to continue using the law, and complained to the privy council who ordered Eglinton to vacate the abbey, or to come and explain himself.[7] The earl took the latter course, hoping no doubt to retain control while the case was argued out before the council and the courts. Meanwhile a number of powerful neighbours approached both Eglinton and Glencairn, and persuaded them to sign a bond agreeing to settle any differences between them by arbitration.[8] Clearly there was local concern that the confrontation might escalate. When both sides did appear in Edinburgh a few days later Eglinton was again warned to leave the abbey, and both were told not to use it, or any of its buildings, as fortifications.[9] Six weeks later Eglinton returned to complain that the commendator had gone ahead and outlawed him in spite of his obedience to the council's instructions and his finding surety for his behaviour. The horning was reduced, Montgreenan was himself outlawed for having fortified the abbey, and shortly afterwards he too gave caution.[10] A combination of local and crown pressure, and much restraint on both sides had thus ensured that a dangerous incident had been defused.[11]

The underlying issue still remained unresolved. A year later, in the summer of 1578, Eglinton arrested Hugh Girvan, one of Montgreenan's servants, in a move which was clearly designed to test his own authority as bailie of the abbey's regality court. Girvan himself, with the backing of the commendator, complained to the privy council that he was to be tried for his life by 'ane verray suspect assyis' composed of those 'that dar not utherwayis declair except that thay knaw it to be his [Eglinton's] pleasour'. This, he declared with unconscious humour, would be unfair because a weighty matter like his life deserved better consideration, as 'in caise it be taiken fra him be thair weikit moyne and pretences, [it] can nevir be recoverit be na reductioun of thair proceedings'. The arrest, he claimed, had followed a slander against him which had since been withdrawn before the church to the satisfaction of everyone except Eglinton who would already have executed him had Montgreenan not intervened. He reminded the council that 'it is notourlie knawin quhat inimitie' there was between the earl and his master who was presently trying to have Eglinton's judicial authority reduced by the session, and had already had his own servants and tenants exempted from it 'for sindrie caussis baith of deidlie feid and utheris'. Girvan then delivered a thinly veiled threat from the commendator that if this affair was not satisfactorily dealt with, 'greit inconvenienties may fall to the trubill of the haill cuntrie, speciale betuix sa greit surnames, being a deidlie feid of auld'. Montgreenan was not really linking his case with the feud of forty years before, but his manipulation of history made an effective point, and the council set a date for the case to be heard by the lords of council and session.[12]

A compromise appears to have followed, for nothing more was heard of Girvan, and in 1580 Montgreenan gave Eglinton infeftment in his offices.[13] Three years later further agreement was reached on the administration of the regality when the commendator promised to maintain the abbey tolbooth, make available irons in the bellhouse, and erect gallows whenever Eglinton required them.[14] He also appointed two of the earl's servants as directors of the chancellory and chapel, granted tacks for teindsheaves in 1581, and for land a year later.[15] What Eglinton gave Montgreenan is unknown, but the two seemed to have formed a working relationship which preserved local peace.

That peace was also pursued on a wider front. In 1580 the 5th earl of Glencairn died, having taken little part in his brother's quarrel with Eglinton, but his son, James 6th earl of Glencairn, was a more aggressive man who had already acquired a reputation for tough dealing in local issues. Two years later Glencairn responded to persuasion from the duke of Lennox and the earl of Arran to assure Eglinton not to pursue him 'in law or besyde the law' for anything which had occurred between them.[16] Shortly afterwards they were ordered by the privy council to seek a more permanent solution to their feud,[17] but within a few weeks of this is was the government itself which fell following the Ruthven Raid in which Glencairn took an active part. He was soon disillusioned with the new government, and when it in turn collapsed a year later both Glencairn and Eglinton responded to the king's call for them to come to his assistance in St. Andrews.[18] Nothing more was heard of a peace settlement from the crown, although there seemed to be little dividing the two families when Eglinton died in 1585.

The effort by Lennox and Arran to formally reconcile Glencairn and Eglinton was largely politically inspired, both earls being thought sympathetic to their faction, but it revealed a concern on their part that these two potential supporters remained rivals. One contemporary thought that in 1583 'bayth the parties semit fullie to be satisfeit and aggreit in all poyntis',[19] but below the surface ill-feeling remained. That same source relates that the Cunninghams 'be the interventioun of a wicked instrument of that surneyme, kindlit up a new rancor in the hartis of the rest of that famelie', so that a party of them went one Sunday morning to the Montgomeries' kirk and attacked them. A Montgomery was wounded in the fighting, and one of the Cunninghams was killed before they were driven off.[20] The whole nature of the feud had been quite dramatically altered.

The initial Cunningham response to this death was to try and make a case at law, but their accusations were immediately dismissed. Following that, a number of them approached Glencairn with a plot to 'be avenged upon the fattest of the Montgomeries', and he agreed to it.[21] A band was then drawn up by the earl and his kinsmen under which 'whomsoever wald tak the turne in hand and performe it, he suld not onlie be sustenit upoun the common expensis of the rest, bot suld be menteynit and defendit by thayme all from danger and skayth'.[22] Glencairn himself signed this 'upoun the fayth of ane nobill man', along with Alexander

Cunningham of Craigends whose idea it appears to have been, David Cunningham of Robertland who was the 'wicked instrument' responsible for the earlier attack, Alexander Cunningham of Aiket, John Cunningham of Ross who was Glencairn's younger brother, his uncle Montgreenan, and John Cunningham of Corsehill. Glencairn swore to be responsible for 'materis succeidant upoun the said interpryse', and to guarantee them his protection 'to the hasart of my lyff, landis, and the lyffis of all that will do for me'.[23] Here was the shadier side to Scottish lordship.

In the months which followed, throughout the remainder of 1585 and the early part of 1586, Glencairn kept in touch with the plotters by letter, but lived away from the locality to avoid any suspicion being attached to him. From his castle in Finlayston he wrote to them:

> Cusingis, I haue ressauvit zour letteris, and persaweis that ze ar reddie with zour commownaris anenttis the lytill particulare pertening to me: and willis me to haue myne reddie, quhilk, I assure zoe sal be; for I pray zow put me to sum poynt, and appoint me ane tyme of meitting to that effect. I am glad of our freindis gud mening in that caus, quhilk salbe rememberit to me, incaise he haue to do quhairin I may pleasoure zow.[24]

The most cryptic parts of the letter were explained by the anonymous Cunningham traitor who revealed them at a much later date, writing that it was meant to be 'mistie and generall' in case it was taken en route. According to him it had been agreed at the first meeting that the murder of Eglinton would be referred to as 'the lytill particulare' and the plotters as 'Commowneris'.[25] However, in spite of these preparations difficulties soon developed, with the important and powerful cadet houses of Glengarnock and Caprington showing very little enthusiasm for the murder. Furthermore, Eglinton, whose every move had been shadowed, was thought to suspect something, and Montgreenan wrote to his nephew that 'I sie nothing bot this mater is oppinit up be sum to thame, or ellis thai suspect the saymn; and leist thai suspect me'.[26]

In fact the killing was carried out with remarkable ease. In the last week of April 1586 Eglinton set out on a journey to join the court at Stirling. Apparently he had no idea of the Cunninghams' plans, and was accompanied by only a small retinue of servants. After leaving Eglinton Castle he stopped off at the tower of Neil Montgomery of Langshaw to dine, but Langshaw's wife was a Cunningham — evidence that the two families were not always hostile[27] — and she sent word to neighbouring kinsmen about the earl's movements. When he left Langshaw later in the day he was followed and ambushed as he crossed a small burn, where 'The horsemen ran all on him, and unmercifullie killit him with shots of gunnis and strokis of swords'. John Cunningham of Clonbeith delivered the *coup de grâce* at close quarters with a pistol. A few of his fleeing servants were also surrounded and 'hewed to pieces' without mercy.[28] The 'lytill particulare' had been attended to, and a few days later Thomas Randolph wrote home to England that 'This is likely to stir up some new mischief among those in the west parts, so that they are free from no part, if this revenging world continue'.[29]

At this point it is worthwhile interrupting the narrative of the feud to try and analyse what is meant when one talks about kindreds like 'the Cunninghams' or 'the Montgomeries'. In north Ayrshire there was no doubt that it was these two families, and to a lesser extent the Boyds, who were dominant. The only other sources of power were the abbey, prior to the Reformation, and the burgh of Irvine, but it was largely controlled by Eglinton.[30] However, not everyone was drawn into the Cunningham-Montgomery confrontation. While Lord Boyd's major interests were further south, around Kilmarnock, he held sizeable estates in the north, and was a neighbour of both kindreds. Since his family's feud with the Montgomeries had ended, the two had become friends, but he had also avoided becoming an enemy of their rivals. Thus one finds lesser lairds like Blair, Crawford, Hunter, Fairlie, Boyle and Fraser attaching themselves to him in an effort to keep out of the growing rift between the two major kindreds of the locality.[31] Some of these men were faced with extremely complex problems of loyalty which made the presence of a third and largely neutral lord a great advantage. John Blair of that Ilk, for example, had had a grandmother who was the daughter of the first Eglinton earl, his mother was a daughter of one of the Cunningham lairds of Glengarnock, his wife was a daughter of Glencairn's enemy, Lord Sempill, and his sister was married to Montgreenan. Here were community allegiances which could so divide loyalties that the spread of feud was inhibited.[32]

It was the earl of Eglinton, however, who had been the most successful in securing the patronage of the locality. Yet at this time the immediate Eglinton family was in danger of extinction. Hugh Montgomery, the 3rd earl, died in 1585 leaving two sons and two daughters. The eldest son, the 4th earl, was slain in 1586 while still only a young man, and he left only a baby son to succeed him. His brother, Robert Montgomery of Giffen, was both master of Eglinton and tutor to the young earl, and it was upon him that responsibility for the feud came to rest. His own marriage produced only one daughter whom he married to his nephew, the 5th earl, and that marriage in turn was fruitless. After 1586 there was only one adult member of the Eglinton family, and by the time the young earl had come of age, Giffen himself had only a short time to live.[33]

The Montgomeries could, however, boast a number of substantial cadet houses who gave active support throughout the remaining years of the feud. Hugh Montgomery of Hessilhead participated in both the more violent aspects of it, and in the earlier stages of the reconciliation which the crown began to push from 1599. After his death, some time before 1606, his son Robert continued to participate in the discussions leading to peace, although he had a separate feud with the Cunningham laird of Glengarnock which complicated matters.[34] Neil Montgomery of Langshaw was especially keen to compensate for his wife's part in Eglinton's murder — he is said to have sent her to safety in Ireland — and took a hand in all of the kindred's doings up until the settlement of 1609, having been opposed to it to the end. However, he did not entirely break with his wife's family, and he guaranteed protection to Montgreenan's wife after his death, and was doing business with another Cunningham family in 1600.[35] Sir Robert Montgomery of

**Map of north Ayrshire and west Renfrewshire showing castles and tower houses of nobles and lairds involved in the Cunningham-Montgomery feud.**

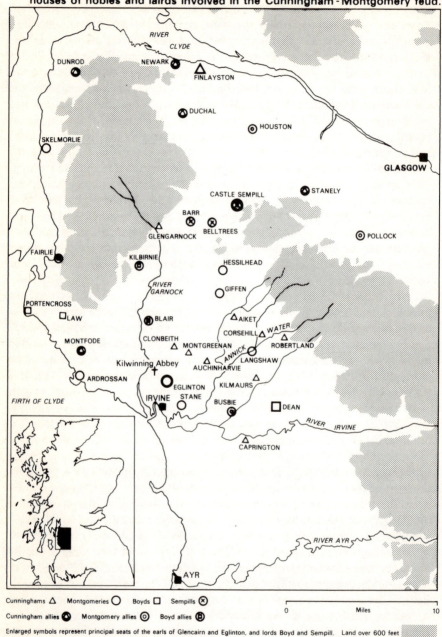

Cunninghams △   Montgomeries ○   Boyds □   Sempills ⊗

Cunningham allies ▲   Montgomery allies ◉   Boyd allies Ⓑ

Enlarged symbols represent principal seats of the earls of Glencairn and Eglinton, and lords Boyd and Sempill.   Land over 600 feet

0          Miles          10

Skelmorlie was said to have been the man the Cunninghams most feared, and had a quarrel with them which pre-dated that of the rest of his kinsmen. This had originated in the 3rd earl of Eglinton's gift of the Giffen estates to his younger son at the expense of the widow of the previous incumbent, a daughter of Maxwell of Stanely. The dispute between the Montgomeries and the Maxwells led to Stanely's slaughter, followed by that of Sir Robert's father and elder brother. Naturally the Maxwells had turned to Glencairn for protection, and the two feuds were conducted simultaneously, although the Maxwells were still at feud with Skelmorlie in 1613. Like Langshaw, Skelmorlie was present at every stage of the main feud from 1586–1609.[36] A number of lesser lairds made fleeting appearances in the records of the feud,[37] while the more important laird of Braidstone only played a part in the latter stages of the settlement when he was asked 'to assist the said agreement'.[38]

The Eglinton house also had a number of cognatic relations from whom it received limited support. Lord Boyd had one daughter married to Hessilhead, and another had been married to the murdered earl, and while dying before him had borne his only child. It was Boyd who played an important part in persuading the older earls of Glencairn and Eglinton to sign the 1578 bond. However, he died in 1590 without having played any part in the feud in the four years since the earl's murder. Thomas, 6th Lord Boyd, was a participant in the violence of 1591, and in 1604 was suspected of harbouring a number of outlawed Montgomeries. Chronic ill health probably restricted his activities, but the Boyds had no obligation to help the Montgomeries, particularly as Gilles Boyd, the wife of the 4th earl, had already died, and the tutorship had gone to Giffen.[39] The west Renfrewshire family of Sempill were also allied by marriage to the Montgomeries, and had a history of feud with the earls of Glencairn which stretched intermittently back to the 1530s. Of the 3rd Lord Sempill's daughters, one married the elder laird of Skelmorlie who was slain by the Maxwells, another married the younger Hessilhead, and his eldest son, the 4th lord, married the youngest daughter of the 3rd earl of Eglinton. Like Boyd he took part in the events of 1591, but he was much more involved in the negotiations for peace, having a feud of his own to settle with Glencairn which took a few weeks longer than the Montgomeries' own one did. On the whole, therefore, his interest in prosecuting a feud with the Cunninghams grew more from his own rivalry with them than from any deeply felt obligations to his children's in-laws.[40] Apart from these major allies by marriage, the Muir laird of Rowallan was married to a daughter of Hessilhead's. However, the Muirs, who were also largely in west Renfrewshire, were divided. The Caldwell branch were firmly on the Montgomery side as the laird of Caldwell had been slain by the Cunninghams in 1570, but Rowallan had a history of bad relations with Lord Boyd, and Muir of Thornton does appear as a friend of Glencairn.[41] The marriage of the 3rd earl of Eglinton's eldest daughter to a son of Lord Seton's meant that one of their sons, Alexander Seton, became sole heir to the Eglinton estates and earldom, and in 1606 he and his brothers were caught up in some fighting with Glencairn in Perth.[42] Giffen had married a daughter of the powerful Campbell of Loudoun, and he was described as being at feud with the Cunninghams in 1588. He was also present at various stages of the conflict and the peace negotiations in a largely supporting role.[43]

Friends and dependants made up the rest of the Montgomeries' supporters. Houston of that Ilk, another west Renfrewshire laird, was the most important of these. In 1576 Houston's brother had killed a servant of Glencairn's, and he in turn was ambushed by the master of Glencairn, the future 6th earl. The laird and a number of his followers were taken prisoner, his brother was wounded, and two servants were killed. In 1582 the crown tried to persuade both sides to make peace but to no avail, and Houston remained an enemy of the Cunninghams and an ally of the Montgomeries throughout the remainder of their feud.[44] John Pollok of that Ilk was a rival of the Maxwells of Pollok who sided with the other Renfrewshire Maxwells against the Montgomeries, and it was he who killed Clonbeith.[45] James Mowat of Busbie was an Eglinton dependant who was active throughout the feud,[46] and minor support was given by Ralstoun of that Ilk, Dunlop of that Ilk, Fergushill of Fergusland, Lindsay of Crevock and, surprisingly, Robert Cunningham of Whithirst who all had their own axes to grind against Glencairn and then to the 5th earl until the conclusion of the feud, and a handful of lesser

The Montgomery interest was a fairly strong one, and by the standards of the locality it was a very powerful one. While the Eglinton family itself was small, three of the four principal Montgomery lairds gave consistent support to Giffen, and then to the 6th earl until the conclusion of the feud, and a handful of lesser lairds are also known to have been loyal. Affinal kinsmen were much less prominent, but at the very least their being related by marriage neutralised them, and where interests converged, as with Lord Sempill, more positive help was forthcoming. In addition to these men, the Montgomeries had the backing of a number of friendly and dependent lairds from in and around the locality. This alliance of men was bound together by a mixture of common interest, kinship, dependency and perhaps outrage at the murder of the earl. Disentangling that motivation is virtually impossible; it is not certain, for example, that Skelmorlie, whose family had been a cadet branch since the fourteenth century, was more interested in his feud with the Maxwells than in avenging the murder of his chief. Kinship there looks tenuous, and perhaps it was, but whatever welded this alliance together — and it was certainly more than merely self interest — it proved effective enough in waging a feud with a kindred which was potentially the more powerful.

Unlike the earls of Eglinton whose lands and kinsmen were all in north Ayrshire and west Renfrewshire, Glencairn had estates in Dumbartonshire and in Renfrewshire, his seat at Finlayston castle being in the latter, and in Galloway from where he took his title. While it was thought of Eglinton that 'his power of himself is not greate', the Cunninghams were thought to be 'men of fayre landes and of greate power of their own surname'.[48] Within the immediate Glencairn family there were certainly more of them. Glencairn himself was a very tough man in his handling of local affairs, and while he distanced himself from the murderers very successfully, he continued to give what protection and support he could from afar, and was involved at every stage of the peace negotiations. His brother, John

Cunningham of Ross, had been present at the murder, acquired a remission for it, and remained deeply involved in the feud.[49] His younger brother, William, rector of Inchcailleoch, is never mentioned, and none of Glencairn's own sons was ever involved in any aspect of the feud. Of the earl's uncles, Andrew Cunningham of Syid and James Cunningham, Prior of Lesmahagow, were both kept at a distance, but Montgreenan was obviously a principal character in the feud, and was killed himself by the Montgomeries in 1591. Thereafter his son, James, continued to be prominent for the remainder of the feud, until its settlement in 1609.[50] Moving back a generation, to those houses erected by Glencairn's grandfather, one finds that both of the families settled in the locality were supportive. The laird of Corsehill had been one of the plotters against Eglinton, he was also one of the murderers, and was outlawed. His lands were badly ravaged in his absence, and one of his sons, Patrick Cunningham, was slain by the Montgomeries between 1586 and 1588. He himself died before 1599, but his son Alexander appeared at every step of the negotiations over the next decade.[51] The remaining family was that of Watterstoun, or Carlung, which appears to have had a separate quarrel with the Mongomeries in 1582. Archibald Cunningham, the heir to the laird, was killed at some unspecified date, but the laird of Watterstoun showed a declining interest in the feud as the years passed.[52]

Three of the most important Cunningham lairds showed very little interest in the feud at all. Of these the laird of Glengarnock, whose cadetship stemmed from the late thirteenth century, and who was described in 1577 as 'a greate man of the Cunynghames', was pre-eminent. This was recognised by Glencairn when he later married his eldest daughter to Glengarnock's heir, but between 1576 and 1582 the laird sided with Houston of that Ilk against the earl. During the next few years he drifted closer to Glencairn again, and fell out with the Houstons who killed his grandson and bastard son 'in feid' in 1589. Thereafter his and the earl's interests were entwined, but his status was usually recognised in that he was summoned separately from Glencairn and the others, and in 1607 when it was claimed by Hessilhead that he had a feud of his own with him, Glengarnock denied it, unless Hessilhead 'wald qualifie a feid'.[53] The laird of Caprington's lands lay much further south in Kyle, and like Glengarnock he had disapproved of the plot to kill Eglinton in the first place. Apart from accompanying Glencairn before the privy council in 1586, and being included among his friends in 1599, he largely distanced himself from the conflict.[54] Similarly, the laird of Craigends took no further part in the feud after his initial part in sponsoring the idea of the murder, and his relations with Glencairn were strained by a quarrel over lands which raged between them for over twenty years.[55]

A much greater commitment to the feud was found among the families who lived at the centre of the conflict, in the Irvine valley. Alexander Cunningham of Aiket had been one of the original conspirators, he was present at the killing, was outlawed, his estates were ruined, and he was murdered himself in 1602. Over the next seven years his sons and his grandson continued to participate in the settlement procedures.[56] David Cunningham of Robertland was also a plotter and a murderer, he too was outlawed, and his estates were taken over by Giffen.

However, he fled abroad to Denmark where he found service with the future wife of the king. He returned with her in 1590, was granted a remission, and a knighthood, and was appointed her master stabler. He and — after his death — his son were present at each stage of the settlement.[57] John Cunningham of Clonbeith first appears as the man who delivered the killing blow to Eglinton, and within a few years he had been brutally done to death in Lord Hamilton's house where he was sheltering. His son made only fleeting appearances in the records of the feud over the next twenty years, but was present at the reconciliation in 1609.[58] A further twenty lairds took part at some stage or other of the feud's history in the years after Eglinton's death, although the laird of Auchenharvie was not one of these, and even failed to turn up when summoned as one of Glencairn's friends in 1608.[59]

Of those families connected to Glencairn by marriage, by far the most significant was that of Lord Hamilton. Glencairn's grandmother had been the daughter of the Hamilton earl of Arran, and he married one of his own daughters to Lord Hamilton's eldest son, and another to Hamilton of Libberton. On two occasions Hamilton came close to actively taking sides with the Cunninghams: the first arose over a quarrel with Giffen about the escheat of Robertland's property which Hamilton tried to protect, and the second occurred when Clonbeith was killed in his house. After that event it was said that Lord Hamilton 'consauvit and beris ane deidlie haitrent, malice and inimitie' against the Montgomeries, and had become an 'assistair and partaker with the Erll of Glencarne in all his actionis and querrellis aganis thame'. However, Hamilton held back from joining the feud himself, and the only other reference to Hamilton interference was in 1608 when the earl of Abercorn took a hand in the latter stages of the peace negotiations.[60] Glencairn was also related to the Gordons of Lochinvar through his mother, and his own wife was a daughter of Campbell of Glenorchy, but both these marriages had been made in the context of the family's other possessions, and these affinal kinsmen were too distant to be of any active assistance.[61]

Of the Cunninghams' allies or dependants, the Maxwells were the most involved in the feud. Apart from what has already been said about their conflict with the Skelmorlie Montgomeries, members of the Newark family were present at Eglinton's murder, and they were regularly included in the settlement procedure.[62] Porterfield of Douchall was yet another west Renfrewshire laird with whom Glencairn had fallen out, and in fact he destroyed Douchall house, but Porterfield later drifted back into Glencairn's dependency, and appeared as one of his friends in 1609.[63] That status was also recognised in Boyd of Clerkland and Arnot of Lochrig who made brief appearances along with Glencairn in the later years of the feud.[64]

Clearly the Cunningham kindred was larger than that of their rivals, and almost inevitably it was less manageable. The kindred was also less committed to north Ayrshire, and Glencairn himself did not reside there. However, the earl's own family did play a significant part in the conduct of the feud, as did a large number of Cunningham lairds. They drew little support from other families in the locality, or in neighbouring ones, partly because of Glencairn's tendency to quarrel with too many people, and partly because additional support was not needed. To an extent they could also count on Lord Hamilton, and the sort of influence he could wield in their interests was invaluable. While Glencairn's protection of the murderers was apparently less than they might have hoped for, no-one is known to have raised objections to his lordship. More serious was the lack of enthusiasm among a number of kinsmen for the feud, and the defensive posture the Cunninghams found themselves adopting after 1586.

Analysis of the anatomy of these two kindreds or alliances shows that their internal politics were complex. While it is convenient to do so, whole families cannot be lumped together under their lords and chiefs, and treated as monolithic power blocs. A wide range of personal friendships and rivalries, of interests, and of temperament were at work within the dependencies as well as between them, and while those subtleties cannot always be enlarged upon, they ought at least to be recognised.

Traditional accounts of how the Montgomeries responded to Eglinton's murder describe a 'scene of bloodshed and murder in the west, that had never been known before'.[65] In assessing how accurate this is, one encounters those problems of sources and reporting discussed already in connection with violence. The slaughter of an earl would be recorded, but the deaths of less important men could easily have failed to find their way into written evidence. Yet one has to be equally suspicious of accounts which relate that 'in the heat of their resentment' the Montgomeries 'killed every Cunninghame, without distinction'.[66] In fact evidence of indiscriminate violence is slight. Not until 1591, five years after the killing, was there widespread fighting between the two kindreds when 'between these two, twenty or thirty persons [were] slain in one day and nothing accounted of'.[67] However, this source can be shown to be suspect in its exaggeration of other violent episodes, and as it was written from Berwick it is possible that the tale had been distorted. Certainly there was trouble in the locality throughout the summer and autumn months of 1591 when a number of men from both sides were ordered to find caution, and Glencairn was warded for a short time. In the following spring the earl, Lord Sempill, Muir of Caldwell and Pollok of that Ilk were again in trouble with the privy council for maintaining their men in arms throughout the winter, and the unrest continued through to November of 1592 when both sides again had men in the field.[68] One casualty of this period was Montgreenan who was shot dead outside his house, and it may have been the killing of Glencairn's uncle which sparked off the fury of the following months.[69] That murder was very probably a response to the collapse of the Montgomeries' legal case against the murderers in the spring of 1591, but the kind of general conflict of 1591–92 in which an unknown number of people were thought to have died was not typical of the feud, and on the whole revenge was more selective.

A list of Eglinton's killers, or at least the more important ones, can be pieced together. Glencairn himself was not there, but he did promise that as 'it is fallen out that the said Erle of Eglintoun is slane', he would protect the killers.[70] These were the Cunningham lairds of Robertland, Clonbeith, Polquhern, Aiket and his brother, Glencairn's brother Ross, Corsehill and his son, Bordland and a son or servant, two brothers of Maxwell of Newark, and Ryburn of that Ilk. Of these, all but Clonbeith and Ryburn are known to have been outlawed, and while Montgreenan was not a murderer, he was widely suspected of having had a hand in its planning.[71] Over the next sixteen years only four of these men were murdered in reprisal for their part in the killing, and apart from those slain in 1591–92, and a servant of Glencairn's who died in a street brawl in Perth in 1606, no-one else was killed on either side between 1586 and 1609. Corsehill's son was slain within two years of the murder by either Langshaw or Giffen,[72] and Clonbeith was killed at much the same time by Pollok of that Ilk.[73] As early as 1587 Montgreenan was complaining that Giffen was pursuing him for his life, and a year later Giffen and Langshaw tried to ambush him outside his house. Three years later they, or other members of the Montgomery kindred, finally did succeed in killing the commendator.[74] Eleven years later Aiket was also shot dead outside his house.[75] In all it was not a particularly bloody record, and both sides continued to show considerable restraint in their use of violence.

However, violence can take other forms. Once outlawed, most of the killers either fled abroad, or took refuge with kinsmen and friends outside the locality. That did not always guarantee security, as Clonbeith discovered, but it did leave families and estates exposed to the Montgomeries. In August 1586, four months after Eglinton's murder, the wives, children and tenants of Aiket, Corsehill and Bordland complained to the privy council that Giffen and his friends were systematically oppressing them in the name of the commission they had against the murderers. Many of their houses had been burned, including Corsehill which had been delivered up to the Montgomeries when the laird was horned, property had been vandalised, goods had been stolen, and the raids had 'alluterlie wrakit and distroyit the pure tennentis and labouraris of the grund' who had also been robbed and forced to pay their rents to their persecutors. It was feared that their next move would be to cut and remove the standing corns, thus totally ruining everyone. Furthermore, the donators of their husbands' escheats were looking for their claims to be fulfilled. The council responded to this plea for help by ordering Giffen not to destroy any houses in his possession, but to garrison and maintain both Aiket and Robertland towers at a cost that would be borne by those families.[76] By 1592 parliament recognised that these estates were completely wasted and censured the privy council for exceeding its rights,[77] but in 1596 the council was still receiving complaints of raids by the Montgomeries in which burning and looting continued to be practised, and tenants were warned not to work for the Cunninghams or they would 'mak thameselffis to repent it'. This time a harder line was taken against the Montgomeries who had been allowed a decade of oppressive vengeance by a sympathetic government.[78]

How does one measure the impact of this violence on a locality? Eglinton's murder sparked off a conflict in which as few as four men are known to have died, but in which the actual numbers could have been more than thirty. It also resulted in intensive raiding and destruction in the Irvine Valley on the Aiket, Robertland, Clonbeith and Bordland estates which had long-term economic consequences for them and their owners, and inflicted short-term misery on the families who lived there. This was a society better able to face suffering than our own, in which the bad weather and harvests of the 1590s were as likely to grind people down as a feud, but while life did go on, the quality of it was undoubtedly lowered by such effective revenge. Yet north Ayrshire did not drift into local warfare, except in 1591–92, and the feud was conducted within fairly tight guide lines in which only legitimate targets were recognised, that is the killers of Eglinton and their lands. Why some feuds appear to have been contained within these sort of rules, and why others became much more indiscriminate is unknown, although lowland feuds were more inclined to the former. Had the Montgomeries spread their vengeance to include all Cunninghams, and had Glencairn initiated a more aggressive response to what was a rout of his kinsmen within the locality, then the feud would have taken a quite different course. This refusal by both sides to discard all restraint was what allowed such societies to avoid anarchy. All forms of conflict have rules built into them, and it was this evolved common sense and self-interest which contained the violence of this feud within limits which were largely acceptable to both sides.

While pursuing this violent revenge, the Montgomeries did not neglect to exploit the formal organs of the law. Giffen quickly established himself as the leader of his kinsmen, fending off an attempt by the Boyds to obtain tutorship of his nephew, and paid the two great court brokers, Chancellor Maitland and Treasurer Glamis, for the ward and non-entry of his brother's lands and offices.[79] He also complained to the king who had Eglinton's killers outlawed, ordered that they be tried in the justice court, and gave Giffen the right to intromit with Robertland's and Aiket's houses and lands.[80] This led to the first clash with Lord Hamilton who claimed that he had the escheat of these lairds, but Giffen defeated him, and had his rights confirmed by parliament in 1587.[81] During 1587–88 Montgreenan complained to the privy council that Giffen was harrassing him, but the council agreed with Giffen that he could hardly be asked to assure his brother's killers, and the commendator, who was under suspicion, lost his case.[82] Shortly afterwards Giffen was granted a commission giving him all his brother's offices in the bailiery of Cunningham and the regality of Kilwinning.[83]

In the two years after the murder Giffen was clearly able to exploit widescale outrage at the slaying of an earl, but March 1588 was the high-water mark of his campaign. In 1589 Lord Hamilton re-opened his case against Giffen over the Cunningham escheats and won.[84] Giffen ignored the order to hand these properties over until March 1591 when he was given a discharge for returning Robertland to the now restored laird, and later that year he was obliged to give Lady Aiket caution for her safety.[85] During 1592 the Montgomeries found themselves in as much trouble as their rivals for failing to reduce the conflict which had been simmering throughout the year, and Giffen himself was outlawed on a civil matter of not having paid his brother's debts.[86] In June 1592 parliament completed Robertland's restoration, and Giffen was discharged from Aiket's house. In that same parliament the king stated that he had not given remissions to any other of the murderers, but Glencairn immediately rose to protest that this declaration should not prejudice the rights of any of his friends who actually held remissions, clear evidence that the king had granted privy ones.[87]

Over the next few years Giffen struggled to keep his enemies at the horn, thus making them more vulnerable to vengeance killings, while Glencairn stepped up his efforts to have the hornings suspended. In 1593 Giffen had Aiket and Ryburn summoned to answer concerning alleged remissions they held.[88] In 1596 he complained to the privy council that more remissions had been granted in spite of the king's promises, and in contravention of recent legislation. If this were true, he warned, he and his kinsmen would be 'frustrat of justice', and 'it will discourage all men to seik redress be ordour of justice heirefter, bit rather to seik thair privat revenge at their best advantage', but no decision was made, and the case was handed over to the justice general.[89] It would appear, therefore, that Glencairn, who had the better court connections, was succeeding in getting remissions for his kinsmen by exploiting the king's willingness to grant privy ones, both in the hope that a reconciliation could be achieved and for money, and because the passage of time had reduced the amount of sympathy the Montgomeries had initially enjoyed. The fact that no effort was ever made to bring any of the murderers to trial suggests strongly that Giffen's interest in having them horned had nothing to do with seeking justice at law, and was only a tactical ploy which made oppression and murder both easier and legitimate in the eyes of the law. As the crown's own thinking about feud altered throughout the 1590s (one is anticipating much of Part Three in what follows), and as a campaign against feuding got under way, that course became less acceptable, and the king lent his authority not to one side so that it could exact private punishment from the other, but to the search for a permanent peace between them.

Apart from the ineffective attempt in 1582 there were no crown initiatives to pacify this feud until 1595 when it was included among others in a general attack on feuding. Then it was recognised as one of the three major feuds in the kingdom, and one in which the king himself had an interest. In accordance with the recent act concerning feuding, both the young earl of Eglinton and Glencairn were summoned along with their friends to appear before the privy council on 15 and 17 January, 1596 to submit their feud to private arbitration.[90] The Montgomeries replied to this with excuses which amounted to a refusal to come, making this immediately a trial of strength between their honour and the king who 'is very earnest because he thinks, if he pass over this first order and suffer himself to be disobeyed, he will find difficulties hereafter in others'. He therefore sent word that unless the Montgomeries appeared within eight days they would all be horned and he would ride out himself to take their houses. This had the desired effect and they rode up to their Seton kinsmen's house outside Edinburgh to await the king's will.[91] Glencairn did not even bother to send excuses at first, and simply failed to appear. A week later one arrived, and then having heard of the king's mood he himself turned up on the 29th and was put in ward. A further week passed before he was freed, having been punished 'by the purse' which 'is kept quiet'.

Assurances from both sides were intended to follow, but none were made, and everyone finally went home with nothing achieved.[92]

The king returned to the problem in 1598 with further legislation (the chronology of this anticipates some of the reforms discussed in Part Three), and early in 1599 both Glencairn and Eglinton were again summoned to come and assure one another, and to begin negotiating a peace settlement.[93] This appears to have been obeyed, and the exclusion of Glencairn and the known murderers from the Cunningham summons may have been instrumental in hastening these preliminaries. A summons was then issued for a second meeting at the end of March, but this time all the principal characters were included, and this too seems to have taken place.[94] However, the 1598 act did no more than nudge parties in a feud towards a submission, nothing more, and without the will to make peace it could not be attained. In the locality, therefore, the conflict continued, with Glencairn having his men's exemption from the jurisdiction of the burgh of Irvine confirmed in 1601 because of Eglinton's influence there,[95] and in 1602 Aiket was killed. It was not until after the 1604 legislation had been passed that the privy council returned to the feud, taking precognition from both earls within a month of that, and insisting that assurances were continued.[96]

While both earls were extremely reluctant to end the feud, much of the pressure to continue it came from their supporters, and with the crown becoming increasingly impatient that created difficulties for them. In March 1604 both Eglinton and Lord Sempill were relieved of responsibility for any of their men who broke assurances if they brought them before the council, and in the months following Glencairn sought similar concessions on individual cases. However, the council refused him the same general exemption after a debate in which a number of noble consellors argued that 'it was not reasonable to snaire the nobilitie of Scotland with sik bands as mich draw thame to sik inconvenientis'. In spite of that pleading Lord Advocate Hamilton had his way, and Glencairn's request was refused, although he was permitted to continue making individual applications which were treated on their merit.[97] On 1 July 1606 an incident took place during the sitting of parliament in Perth which typified the kind of happening Glencairn had in mind. He and his friends were walking along the high street when they encountered Sir Alexander Seton, Eglinton's heir, and his retinue. The principals all passed one another peacefully, but then the servants began to jostle for room, a fight broke out, a number of men were hurt, and one of Glencairn's servants was killed. The fact that this had taken place during a sitting of parliament made it especially outrageous in the eyes of the crown, but while the Setons were thought to have been responsible, the incident was played down and some 'rascall servandis' were blamed.[98] The king himself was furious, fearing that this would revive 'that new mortifeit monster of deidlie feud' which he had been claiming was well under control before he went to England in 1603. Glencairn was prevented from opening up a private prosecution, but in spite of threats to do so itself the crown was also reluctant to take the case to court, and it restricted itself to ensuring that both sides renewed their assurances.[99]

The incident did prompt the privy council to initiate another round of trying to achieve a settlement. The fact that Eglinton was no longer a minor had removed a major obstacle to peace, and both he and Glencairn were summoned to Stirling.[100] At the end of August 1606 they both appeared with their friends, but they were no more willing to talk about peace than at any other time in the decade since the king had first summoned them to Edinburgh. Glencairn simply stated that he had no feud with Eglinton and could not submit it, while Eglinton said that as he had only just reached his majority he had not had time to consult his kinsmen. Only Lord Sempill was willing at that time to make a submission. Faced with this the privy council were at something of a loss, and after giving Eglinton a month in which to discuss the matter with his friends and kinsmen, they wrote to the king asking for advice.[101]

The intervention of the ruthless earl of Dunbar seemed to be the king's answer, and by January 1607 he had bullied both sides into signing submissions. The earl of Abercorn persuaded the few remaining malcontents to sign during the next few months, and even the laird of Braidstone who had taken no part in the feud was given sixty days from the receipt of letters from the council to return from the continent and make his submission.[102] By the end of February all but Hessilhead had submitted, and he was denounced, and on the 24th the arbitrators, who were a mixture of distant kinsmen and friends, also subscribed.[103] Within a week the committee had broken up as Glencairn had instructed his side that since the submission did not concern him alone, 'bot everie ane of his freindis had thair awne particulair interesse and had gevin thair clames hinc inde', then an oversman would have to be appointed for each of them separately. Eglinton's side refused this condition, which does appear to have been a wrecking tactic, and broke off the discussions.[104]

The king at that point became sole oversman. Assurances were renewed yet again, and a meeting took place in August 1608 which was attended by the principals and a number of friends who were included to 'assist the said agreement'. Finally both parties were summoned to appear on 16 March 1609 to hear the crown's decreet arbitral.[105] While the decreet itself has not been found, the form of that last meeting was recorded. On arrival at the council house a list of those present was checked off, and then each party was led separately into the council chambers. There they were lectured on the trouble they had caused, and on the great lengths the crown had gone to in order to pacify the feud. They were reminded of the king's right to act as sole oversman under the terms of the feud legislation, and were asked to declare their willingness to forgive the other party and to abide by the decision the king had reached. Once both sides had been through this they were brought together, and the declaration was repeated. The terms of the decreet were then made known to them, following which they shook hands, declaring that 'thair chopping of handis sould be als sufficient for all those of ather side quho wer absent and were guiltie of the said bloodis as gif thay were present and had chopit handis with thame'. Further handshaking took place between Glencairn and the Setons, and arrangements were made to conclude his feud with Lord Sempill as soon as possible,[106] a fact which was accomplished shortly afterwards.[107]

When he heard this news the king wrote to the privy council acknowledging the 'very speciall and acceptable service done to us', although he exaggerated when he told them that it was 'the last that remainit in that whole kingdome of ony consequence'.[108] For the lowlands that was true, and while it took some fourteen years to accomplish, the peace it brought to north Ayrshire and to the kindreds involved in the feud was a victory for the crown, for its legislation, and for the men who served it. The nature of that legislation, the composition of these men, and the reasons why the crown changed in its policy of dealing with feuding during these years is examined in detail in later chapters, but the fact that it was done at all was clearly a victory for central government over local politics. There was no doubt that the lords and kindreds themselves did not want to end the feud, or were unable to find a way of ending it to the satisfaction of their honour. Of course kings had intervened in local politics before, but rarely in order to implement a policy throughout the localities, and never in a way that permanently changed the nature of local politics. Local peace was now very much royal business, local politics would in future have to be conducted differently, and competition would have to be resolved by other means. That did not mean that society had altered such that royal government played a domineering role in daily living, it had not, and the aggregate power of the localities remained stronger than the crown, but the crown had shown that it could play a useful part in local affairs, and that was being accepted gradually, even if grudgingly.

Local studies are extremely tempting to the historian looking for answers to wider questions, and this is no exception. That this was only one locality should, therefore, be borne in mind. Yet it is one which demonstrates the complexity of local society, in this case of its politics and of the relationships of the people who practised those politics. Localities were not simply dominated by solid political interests, instead the picture is more fragmentary. Lordship, kinship and friendship did create dependencies with great cohesion and strength, but these did not negate individuality, and neither loyalty nor obedience was automatic or unquestioning. To identify the mavericks, the obstinate and the indifferent kinsmen and dependants is not to argue that lords were weak and ties of kinship equally weak, but the opposite, since those who were ultimately loyal to the ideals of lord and family followed with greater free will than they are often credited with. Secondly, local politics were very much the politics of conflict and confrontation as we have seen, and the tool of that conflict in this society was violence, actual or threatened. That did not mean that life was intolerable, although for some it may have seemed so at times, and the violence of major feuds like that between the Cunninghams and the Montgomeries, and of all the sub-feuds which interacted with it, was itself an integral part of that society. Yet it was a violence contained within social rules: there was no anarchy, and only in the mythology it later generated did it appear that there was. Finally, while local society could at times find the human resources to punctuate feud with peace, it could not find a way of guaranteeing that peace, or of competing without threatening it. A peace that was permanent required a shift in how men thought about their world, of the place of violence in it, and of how they coped with rivals and enemies in a world without it.

Peace had to become more highly valued than honour and power, and it had to be institutionalised by a coercive authority. By the time that process was completed local politics had been irrevocably changed, and the feuding society had disappeared.

## NOTES

1. Further details of these years can be gleaned from Fraser, *Memorials of the Montgomeries, Earls of Eglinton,* i and ii, Edinburgh, 1859; G. Robertson, *A Geneological Account of the Principal Families in Ayrshire,* i and ii, Irvine, 1823–25; *The Scots Peerage,* iii for Eglinton and iv for Glencairn.

2. Useful information on the political careers of these men is found in Donaldson, *All The Queen's Men.*

3. *R.S.S.R.S.,* iv, Part 1, p. 161, No. 724; *Scots Peerage,* iv, p. 241.

4. *R.P.C.,* ii, p. 566.

5. *R.P.C.,* iii, p. 143; S.R.O., Eglinton Muniments, G.D., 3/1/80/739.

6. *R.P.C.,* iii, p. 1.

7. *Ibid.,* p. 1.

8. Brown, 'Bonds of Manrent', appendix, p. 544, No. 65.

9. *R.P.C.,* iii, p. 1.

10. *Ibid.,* pp. 11, 23 and 24. Eglinton's surety of £1,000 was given by Lord Boyd.

11. This, of course, was not surprising, and the majority of local disputes would be resolved like this without escalating to a violent level.

12. *R.P.C.,* iii, p. 143. Girvan claimed that the feud had continued by proxy between Eglinton and a dependant of Glencairn's.

13. S.R.O., Eglinton Muniments, G.D., 3/1/80/739.

14. S.R.O., Eglinton Muniments, G.D., 3/1/80/740, 3/1/80/743.

15. S.R.O., Eglinton Muniments, G.D., 3/1/80/747, 3/1/20/205, 3/1/87/834.

16. Fraser, *Memorials of the Montgomeries,* ii, pp. 223–224.

17. *R.P.C.,* iii, p. 508.

18. *R.P.C.,* iii, pp. 506–508; *C.S.P., Scot.,* vi, pp. 542 and 572.

19. *Historie,* p. 238.

20. *Ibid.,* This may have sparked off the violence reported the following summer when fifteen or sixteen people were reported slain, *C.S.P., Scot.,* vii, p. 232.

21. *Historie,* p. 238.

22. *Ibid.*

23. Fraser, *Memorials of the Montgomeries,* ii, p. 226.

24. *Ibid.*

25. *Ibid.,* pp. 225–226.

26. *Ibid.*

27. Thus one also finds for example that in 1585 Langshaw set in wadset in a five merk piece of ground Patrick Cunningham in Bordland. Feud was disruptive, but not to the extent that all other social and economic relationships were excluded. S.R.O., R.D., 1/49/63.

28. Moysie, *Memoirs,* p. 57; *Historie,* p. 240; Robertson, *Ayrshire Families,* i, pp. 295–296.

29. *C.S.P., Scot.,* viii, p. 329.

30. S.R.O., Eglinton Muniments, G.D., 3/1/15/27. Eglinton was both coroner and chamberlain of the burgh.

31. For the bonds see Brown, 'Bonds of Manrent', appendix, pp. 396–397.

32. W. Paterson, *History of the County of Ayr*, Paisley, 1847–52, ii and iii. Blair did, however, have a feud with the neighbouring laird of Kilbirnie, Pitcairn, *Criminal Trials*, i, p. 71; *Accounts of the Lord High Treasurer of Scotland*, (eds.) T. Dickson and Sir J. Balfour Paul, Edinburgh, 1877–1916, xiii, p. 116.

33. *Scots Peerage*, iii, pp. 440–444.

34. *R.P.C.*, iv, pp. 94–95, 675 and 709; v, pp. 539 and 543; vii, pp. 233 and 324; viii, pp. 252 and 262–263.

35. Robertson, *Ayrshire Families*, i, pp. 298–299; *R.P.C.*, iv, pp. 94–95, 234, 256, 704 and 709; v, pp. 539, 543 and 584; vii, pp. 233–234 and 296–297; viii, pp. 138–139, 252 and 262–263; S.R.O., Glencairn Muniments, G.D., 39/5/72.

36. S.R.O., Eglinton Muniments, G.D., 3/1/30/303, G.D., 3/1/31/313; Fraser, *Memorials of the Montgomeries*, i, p. 156ff; Robertson, *Ayrshire Families*, i, p. 297; ii, p. 329; S.R.O., Craigend Writs, G.D., 148/215, 148/216; Pitcairn, *Criminal Trials*, i, Part 2, p. 133; *R.P.C.*, v, pp. 271, 539 and 543; vii, pp. 296–297; viii, pp. 138–139, 252 and 262–263; x, p. 112.

37. *R.P.C.*, v, pp. 271, 539 and 543; vii, pp. 233–234 and 296–297; viii, pp. 138–139, 252 and 262–263.

38. *R.P.C.*, v, pp. 539 and 543; vii, pp. 233–234; viii, pp. 138–139, 252 and 262–263.

39. *The Scots Peerage*, v, pp. 161–163; and Paterson's *History of Ayrshire* for the genealogies of lesser families; Brown, 'Bonds of Manrent', appendix, p. 544, No. 65; *R.P.C.*, iii, p. 11; iv, p. 704; vii, p. 8. The Boyds may have temporarily held the Eglinton tutorship before Giffen acquired it.

40. Hay wrote of the Sempills: 'They be allyed with th'erles of Eglinton, and have bene sometyme in controversy with the Cunnyhames, and overmatched with that surname; men sufficient hardy, their lyvinge not great, and of late hurte'. *Estimate of the Scottish Nobility During the Minority of James the Sixth*, (ed.) C. Rodgers, London, 1873, p. 23. Pitcairn, *Criminal Trials*, i, p. 164; *R.P.C.*, ii. pp. 12 and 155; vii, pp. 160, 233–234 and 296–297; viii, pp. 221–222. A bond of friendship followed their reconciliation, *Miscellany of the Maitland Club*, ii, Edinburgh, 1840, pp. 394–395.

41. *R.P.C.*, iv, pp. 98, 704 and 747; v, p. 543; vii, pp. 233–234 and 296–297; viii, pp. 138–139, 252 and 262–263; Wormald, 'Bloodfeud, Kindred and Government', p. 77.

42. *R.P.C.*, viii, pp. 221–222.

43. S.R.O., Glencairn Muniments, G.D., 39/5/68; *R.P.C.*, iv, p. 704; viii, pp. 138–139.

44. *R.P.C.*, ii, p. 576; iii, p. 503; iv, p. 248.

45. Robertson, *Ayrshire Families*, i, p. 298; *R.P.C.*, iv, p. 747.

46. S.R.O., Eglinton Muniments, G.D., 3/1/54/514; *R.P.C.*, iv, pp. 94–95; vii, pp. 233–234 and 296–297; viii, pp. 252 and 262–263.

47. *R.P.C.*, v, pp. 271 and 543; vii, pp. 296–297; viii, pp. 138–139, 252 and 262–263. Dunlop had given a bond to the earl of Eglinton in 1559, Brown, 'Bonds of Manrent', p. 448, No. 5.

48. *Estimate*, pp. 10 and 12.

49. Fraser, *Memorials of the Montgomeries*, ii, pp. 227–228; Robertson, *Ayrshire Families*, i, pp. 295–299; *R.P.C.*, v, p. 269; vii, pp. 296–297; viii, pp. 138–139, 252 and 262–263.

50. For Montgreenan's son, *R.P.C.*, v, pp. 539 and 543; vii, pp. 296–297.

H

51. Fraser, *Memorials of the Montgomeries,* ii, pp. 227–228 and 266; Robertson, *Ayrshire Families,* i, pp. 295 and 298; *R.P.C.,* iv, pp. 94–95; v, p. 543; S.R.O., Glencairn Muniments, G.D., 39/5/68.

52. *R.P.C.,* iii, p. 503; v, p. 539; viii, pp. 1, 138–139 and 549.

53. *Estimate,* p. 22; Pitcairn, *Criminal Trials,* i, Part 2, pp. 182–183; *R.P.C.,* v, p. 248; vi, p. 731; vii, p. 324; viii, pp. 138–139.

54. Fraser, *Memorials of the Montgomeries,* ii, p. 227; *R.P.C.,* v, pp. 269, 539 and 543.

55. S.R.O., Glencairn Muniments, G.D. 39/1/91; S.R.O., Craigend Writs, G.D., 148/27/205; *R.P.C.,* iv, p. 415; v, p. 649.

56. Fraser, *Memorials,* ii, pp. 226–228; Robertson, *Ayrshire Families,* i, p. 295; *Historie,* p. 240; *R. P.C.,* iv, pp. 94–95; v, pp. 269 and 543; vii, pp. 233–234 and 296–297; viii, pp. 138–139, 252 and 262–263.

57. As above and *Historie,* pp. 239–240. In 1597 objections were raised to Robertland appearing as an assessor at the trial of the laird of Duntreath as the latter was third of kin to Eglinton: Pitcairn, *Criminal Trials,* ii, pp. 13–14.

58. Robertson, *Ayrshire Families,* i, pp. 295–298; Fraser, *Memorials,* ii, pp. 229–230; *R.P.C.,* v, pp. 539 and 543; vii, pp. 233–234 and 296–297; viii, pp. 138–139, 252 and 262–263.

59. For Auchinharvie, *R.P.C.,* v, pp. 539 and 543; vii, p. 549; viii, pp. 138–139.

60. Fraser, *Memorials of the Montgomeries,* ii, pp. 229–230; *Scots Peerage,* iv, pp. 241 and 245–246; *R.P.C.,* viii, pp. 138–139.

61. *Scots Peerage,* iv, pp. 242 and 244.

62. *R.P.C.,* v, p. 269; vii, pp. 296–297 and 324; viii, pp. 138–139, 252 and 262–263.

63. S.R.O., Glencairn Muniments, G.D., 39/1/62. 39/1/112, 39/1/112, 39/1/118; *R.P.C.,* iii, pp. 195 and 556.

64. *R.P.C.,* vii, pp. 233–234 and 296–297; viii, pp. 138–139, 252 and 262–263.

65. Robertson, *Ayrshire Families,* i, pp. 296–297. See also W. Paterson, *From Ayrshire's Story,* Midlothian, 1977.

66. Robertson, *Ayrshire Families,* i, pp. 296–297.

67. *C.S.P., Scot.,* x, p. 574.

68. *R.P.C.,* iv, pp. 701, 704 and 709; *C.S.P., Scot.,* x, pp. 812 and 819.

69. He was dead by August 1591.

70. Fraser, *Memorials of the Montgomeries,* ii, pp. 227–228.

71. Moysie, *Memoirs,* p. 57; Robertson, *Ayrshire Families,* i, p. 295; *Historie,* p. 240; Fraser, *Memorials of the Montgomeries,* ii, pp. 227–228; *R.P.C.,* iv, p. 94; v, p. 269.

72. S.R.O., Glencairn Muniments, G.D., 39/5/68 and above, p. 93.

73. Fraser, *Memorials of the Montgomeries,* ii, pp. 229–230.

74. Robertson, *Ayrshire Families,* i, p. 297. The commendatorship was granted to the senator of the college of justice, Mr. William Melville, who in 1604 resigned it in favour of the 5th earl of Eglinton so that the Montgomeries finally got their hands on it after all. S.R.O., Eglinton Muniments, G.D., 3/1/77/689, 3/1/77/699, 3/1/77/701; *Registrum Magni Sigilli Regum Scotorum,* (ed.) J. M. Thomson, Edinburgh, 1822–1914, v, Part 2, pp. 709–710, No. 2085.

75. *C.S.P., Scot.,* x, pp. 812 and 819.

76. *R.P.C.,* iv, pp. 94–95.

77. *A.P.S.,* iii, p. 611.

78. *R.P.C.,* v, p. 271.

79. S.R.O., Eglinton Muniments, G.D., 3/1/20/204.

80. *Historie,* p. 240; *R.P.C.,* iv, pp. 94–95 and 98; v, p. 269.

81. *R.P.C.*, iv, p. 215; *A. P.S.*, iii, p. 479.
82. *R.P.C.*, iv, pp. 223–234 and 226.
83. S.R.O., Eglinton Muniments, G.D., 3/1/15/129.
84. *R.P.C.*, iv, p. 387.
85. *R.P.C.*, iv, pp. 601 and 675.
86. *R.P.C.*, iv, p. 760; S.R.O., Eglinton Muniments, G.D., 3/1/20/207.
87. *A.P.S.*, iii, pp. 610–611.
88. *R.P.C.*, v, p. 105.
89. *Ibid.*, pp. 269–270.
90. *C.S.P., Scot.*, xii, p. 99; *R.P.C.*, v. p. 248.
91. *C.S.P., Scot.*, xii, pp. 102, 122 and 136.
92. *R.P.C.*, v, p. 261; *C.S.P., Scot.*, xii, pp. 134, 136 and 142.
93. *R.P.C.*, v, p. 523. The legislation is discussed in Chapter 9.
94. *Ibid.*, pp. 539 and 543.
95. *R.P.C.*, vi, p. 698.
96. *Ibid.*, p. 600; vii, p. 153.
97. *R.P.C.*, vi, pp. 604 and 818–819; vii, pp. 549 and 557 (though this was suspended, p. 9), p. 160.
98. *R.P.C.*, vii, pp. 221–223; Spottiswoode, *History*, iii, pp. 175–176; *Melrose*, i, p. 17; Balfour, 'Annales', ii, p. 17.
99. *R.P.C.*, vii, pp. 498, 247, 646 and 288.
100. *Ibid.*, pp. 233–234.
101. *Ibid.*, p. 249.
102. *Ibid.*, p. 296; Balfour 'Annales', ii, p. 16.
103. *R.P.C.*, vii, p. 324. Glencairn's arbitrators were Lord Cathcart, a nobleman from neighbouring Renfrewshire; Porterfield of Duchal, a client of Glencairn's who was also from Renfrewshire; Blair of that Ilk, a local laird who had strong marriage bonds with both sides; Maxwell of Nethir Pollok, a kinsman of Glencairn's Maxwell allies; and Otterburn of Reidhall and Fleming of Berrochane. For Eglinton were Sir James Douglas of Drumlanrig, a border laird with distant kinship with Eglinton and who was a brother-in-law to Skelmorlie; Sir William Grier of Lag, who was married to the sister of Montgomery of Braidstone's wife; Sir John Bruce of Kincavill, Sir John Wallace of Cornell and Andrew Kerr, a younger brother of the earl of Lothian. The family connections are found in *Scots Peerage*, iv, pp. 238 and 413; v, p. 498; vii, pp. 125 and 129.
104. *R.P.C.*, vii, p. 328.
105. *R.P.C.*, viii, pp. 138–139.
106. *Ibid.*, pp. 262–263.
107. *Ibid.*, pp. 292 and 585–586; Chambers, *Domestic Annals*, i, p. 395.
108. *R.P.C.*, viii, pp. 569–570.

*Part Two: Politics and Feud*

# 5

## *Feud, Faction and the Court*

The feuding society was essentially a localised society in which the participants lived in neighbouring communities, and the issues were those of local politics. However, early modern Scotland was not only a society lived at a local level, but had a political centre which gave those scattered and disparate localities a nexus where they could identify with one another and express their political unity. That centre was occupied ideologically by kingship, and physically by a royal court composed of the king, his family, the nobility who came to counsel and lobby him, his officers of state and lesser administrators, and his household. That court was most often found in Edinburgh, but it was often at Stirling or Falkland, or at less commonly used royal and private residences. Its nature also changed as personnel came and went, when the king and his household separated themselves from all or some of the administration, or during the king's minority when there was no household and the king himself was little more than a passive object of other men's ambitions and schemes. Yet whatever its particular composition or whereabouts at different times, the court was the kernel of political life. There major policy decisions were made, wealth and office could be acquired or lost, and patrons or clients were cultivated on a scale which went beyond the parameters of a man's own locality. In one sense the court — which by English or French standards was very small and impoverished — was itself another locality with resources and offices to be competed for by those who inhabited it. Those who did go there went for a variety of reasons, but the pursuit and protection of power was the major interest of the political elite who influenced court politics, the great magnates, the high officials and the courtiers. There the competition was extremely intense because the stakes were high, and men did not leave their honour, their friends and dependants, or their weapons at home when they went to court. Nor did they forget their feuds. Local alliances and animosities were therefore very important in shaping court politics, and the reverse was often just as true. Even the proximity of most noblemen to the court — only a handful lived more than a day or two's ride from the major royal residences — meant that local politics could not be forgotten at court. In fact combinations of local power were quite capable of violently intruding themselves upon the centre. The feuding society, therefore, embraced Scottish political life in its entirety, from locality to court. An understanding of how feuds shaped the course of politics, delineated the rules of conduct in political life, and contributed to how political issues were approached is crucial if the politics of the last years of the Stewart royal court are to be explained.

Yet the sixteenth century was a period of fundamental debate and change in political ideologies, language and loyalties. Throughout much of Europe the long-established adherence to lords and kindreds was put under enormous strain as rival churches and self-confident princes claimed that it was to them that obedience was first owed. Church, state, lord and family all had to compete for loyalty. That conflict was not, of course, an even one, and some societies were more vulnerable to the erosion of traditional or feudal values than others. In Scotland one finds a society well prepared to resist such erosion, where both the social environment and the ideology of a feuding society had retained their vitality. However, Scotland was also a country which produced George Buchanan and Andrew Melville and in which political thinking was at its most radical, both in the debate over the rights of subjects and princes, and in that concerning the nature of the church.[1] The existence of two parallel political ideologies, the one emphasising loyalty to lord and kindred, the other requiring commitment to a confessional stance, and both existing in the context of greater or lesser obedience to the crown, makes Scottish politics in the latter half of the century particularly complex. In resolving those complexities Scottish politicians did not necessarily make clear-cut decisions when faced with apparently irreconcilable choices. Hence the often confusing political alignments one finds from the Reformation through to the end of the civil war in 1573. Where there was tension, politicians might place one loyalty before another, but neither was predominant, and party, faction and family all existed as vehicles for political action. As long as that was the case, feud remained sufficiently potent to shape the course of politics, and continued to be manipulated as a highly effective tool in the hands of the more adept politicians.

Scotland approached the last quarter of the sixteenth century at war, and as Gordon Donaldson has demonstrated, the parties of the civil war of 1567–73 (arguably the war dates from 1559) were shaped by a combination of factors which included religion and thoughts on the legitimacy of Mary's abdication, but in which kinship and feud were also prominent.[2] That there were such a multitude of factors influencing political loyalties is hardly surprising. Historians of the French Religious Wars have long recognised that the opposing sides there were not neatly divided by single issues. The well-known comment by the Venetian Ambassador that 'these civil wars are born of the Cardinal of Lorraine to have no equal, and the Admiral (Coligny) and the house of Montmorency to have no superior'[3] may have been a somewhat simplified analysis, but it was clear that contemporaries did not just see the wars as confessional conflicts. In discussing the French wars Donald Kelley understood their origins to lie both in the issues of religion and political ideology, and in the 'amplified continuation of social violence beyond legal control'.[4] Harding, however, placed greater emphasis on the wars as the cause of social violence.[5] The social effects of warfare in mid-sixteenth century Scotland are largely unknown, but while there is little evidence of feuds evolving out of wider political confrontations, it is clear that, as in France, war did escalate the violence of existing feuds.

In Scotland the rivalry of the Douglas and Hamilton families underwrote many of the major political confrontations of the century. Even after the victory of the king's party in 1573 it continued with the Regent Morton exploiting his power to force a humiliating feud settlement on the Hamiltons, and then in 1579, following the end of the regency, uniting with the Argyll faction to drive them out of the country.[6] This destruction of the once great Hamilton family has been described as 'a somewhat primitive and barbaric way to govern a country',[7] while the politics of feud are often seen as little more than the reactionary behaviour of a disorderly and irresponsible nobility.[8] Yet while civil war may have exacerbated divisions, heightened political violence and left a number of open sores within the political community, feuding was not simply caused by that war. The roots were much deeper in Scottish society itself. Feud occupied a central and natural place in Scottish politics, and was not simply an aberration created by the fracturing of the political community in the thirty turbulent years which had followed James V's death in 1542.

During the civil war George Gordon, 5th earl of Huntly, 'An Erle of greate power, and of the most revenue of any Erle in the land',[9] led the Marian party north of the Tay, and was opposed by William, 7th Lord of Forbes, who adhered to the king's party. However, the Gordons and Forbes were 'harbouring deadlie fead, of long rooted betuin them',[10] and political division was intensified by the breakdown of the marriage between the master of Forbes and Huntly's daughter, an event which disrupted the fragile peace which existed between them.[11] The first major engagement between the two was at Tulliangus in October 1571 when Huntly's brother, Gordon of Auchindoun, routed the Forbes, inflicting very heavy casualties on them.[12] Following this the master of Forbes went south, was granted a commission of lieutenancy by the Regent Mar, and levied troops with which he hoped to reverse his family's defeat.[13] At stake, therefore, was the immediate course of the war in the north, and the possibility of undoing Huntly's regional dominance. However, within two weeks of leaving Mar, Forbes had again been defeated, and this time even more decisively. At Crabstane, which was fought on 20 November, the master of Forbes was himself taken prisoner, and his troops were decimated, thus effectively ending any local opposition to Huntly.[14]

In the wider context of the war, however, Huntly's party was less successful, and in February 1573 he signed the Pacification of Perth in which he recognised the king and the regency government. The Pacification was just what one would expect from a feuding society with both sides agreeing that what had been done in the war should not be the cause of future quarrels. In other words there were to be no feuds arising from the war.[15] Yet Huntly had not been defeated locally, and any aspirations the Forbes had of exploiting the victory of the king's party were quashed when Auchindoun attacked Lord Forbes in Aberdeen during the sitting of the conference at Perth, and once again achieved a victory.[16] It was partly because of this that Auchindoun was sent to France during the Morton regency, his actions having put him outside the terms of the Pacification.[17] Huntly himself suspected that Morton wanted to murder him, and obeyed the regent's order that he should temporarily ward with his kinsmen in Galloway, well away from his own power base.[18] Nevertheless, it was not until 1574 that Morton visited Aberdeen, and no serious attempt was made by him to reward the Forbes family at Huntly's expense.[19] It was only after the death of Huntly in 1576 that the two families appear to have recommenced hostilities, although it is unclear if this was due to greater confidence on the part of Lord Forbes now that his enemy was dead, or to

Auchindoun's more aggressive leadership of the family during his nephew's minority.[20]

The end of the regency in 1578 offered the Gordons their first glimmer of political rehabilitation since 1573. It also gave Lord Forbes the opportunity to bargain with Morton who had largely ignored him throughout his period as regent. When parliament met in July 1578 in Stirling, the Forbes complained that a number of their kinsmen were in the process of being evicted from kindly tenancies they held in lands owned by the 6th earl of Huntly. The earl, or more probably Auchindoun acting in his interests, had taken the case to the court of session, but the Forbes argued that they were being victimised for their opposition to the Gordons during the war. The complaint was in all likelihood a valid one, and they went on to point out that they had suffered greatly in the king's cause without reward or compensation, while their rivals had been confirmed in all their rights. In bringing the feud to parliament, Lord Forbes was thus letting Morton know what the price of his support in the struggle with the Atholl-Argyll faction would be, but more seriously he was questioning the basis upon which peace had been agreed in 1573, and was threatening to re-open the old scores which had been settled by the Perth Pacification. Knowing that this was not a simple matter of redistributing patronage, parliament appointed a commission to investigate the complaint.[21]

When parliament met again in November 1578, Morton was once again the dominant figure in the Scottish government, but now he shared his power with Atholl and Argyll. The commission's report was favourable to the Forbes, the Gordons were found to have brought dishonour on the king by breaking the Pacification of Perth, and while a final decision on what to do about it was postponed until the spring, it was expected that Huntly would at least face a heavy fine.[22] However, the Gordons were not to become the regime's victims, and throughout 1579 the government was more interested in crushing the Hamiltons, the family who had been the Gordons' major allies during the war. Such a development might have been expected to be a prelude to an attack on the Gordons too, but when at the beginning of the new year a skirmish took place on the shore at Dundee between the Gordons and the Forbes in which Sir George Gordon of Gight and Forbes of Tollie were among the slain, the privy council decided to try and make peace. Claiming that it desired to find 'sum mid and indifferent way' to prevent 'the trubling of the gude and quhiet of the haill cuntrie', the council began looking for a means to end the feud.[23] This probably reflected the tension in the privy council between Morton and Chancellor Argyll into whose faction the Gordons had eased themselves, and when the arbitration committee was announced in April the Gordons had nominated Argyll and his friends to represent them, while Lord Forbes had named Morton and a number of his allies.[24] The feud was becoming a trial of strength between the two major factions in the government.

Like most arbitrations this one produced no immediate results, and with Morton's fall at the end of the year, and the rise of Esmé Stewart who brought so many former Marians back to court, the Forbes case was lost. Further fighting did take place between the two families in the summer of 1581 which the privy council took some interest in,[25] but more importantly parliament delivered its final verdict on the feud in November. Two acts relating to the feud were passed, the 'Act anent the debatable cause between the Gordons and Forbes' and the 'Act of compromise between the Gordons and Forbes'. Now in a much stronger position politically, Huntly was able to get parliament to agree that the claims the Forbes had made in 1578 were against the 1573 Pacification, and Lord Forbes was forbidden ever to raise the matter again. As for the matter of Huntly's tenants, the court of session was ordered to proceed with the case, and it was declared that parliament's interference in 1578–79 had been a frustration of justice.[26] Such a complete Gordon victory can only be seen as a result of Morton's execution seven months before, and it marked the end of the period of political eclipse the Gordons had suffered since 1573. Since then there had always been the possibility that Morton would try to replace the earl of Huntly with Lord Forbes in the north, but his unwillingness to test the Gordons' strength, and his general insensitivity to his own supporters left the status quo intact. After 1578 there was the faint hope for the Forbes that Morton could be persuaded to act more decisively in the north, but it was the more vulnerable Hamiltons the new regime attacked. The division in the government, in effect a split within the former king's party, allowed the Gordons to join the anti-Morton faction, and his fall guaranteed Huntly's continued regional domination. Peace was made between the two kindreds in 1582–83, and while the feud broke out again in 1589, and continued until 1597 against a similar background of Gordon opposition to royal government, the context was a quite different one, being largely unrelated to the issues of the civil war.[27]

Until 1578 Morton's power had lain in the fact that he held the office of regent, and in the military victory his party had secured in 1573. That victory was unlikely to be reversed by the queen's party, but Morton's failure to build up a large clientage and his interference in the local politics of other noblemen created enough dissent to break up the old party alignments of the war. The earl of Argyll's 'deadlie inimitie' with Morton spanned the greater part of the regency, during which Morton had done all he could to humiliate the man who was clearly his most powerful rival. The regent's meddling in Argyll's feud with his neighbour Atholl persuaded these two to sink their differences, and carry out the coup at Stirling at the beginning of March 1578. In late 1580 Morton lost power a second time, but on this occasion it was not to a coup mounted from the localities, and his enemies were found in a faction within the privy council and the court.[28] The coup and the faction had re-emerged as the means by which power was seized or transferred, and feud had come to occupy an even more central position in political life.

Coups or raids in which possession of the king's person was seen as the means of legitimising the authority of a faction or an individual punctuated Scottish political history from 1578 until 1594. Successful coups took place twice in 1578, in 1582, in 1583 when the king himself co-operated in it, in 1585, and in 1593, while failed attempts were made in 1584, 1591, 1592 and 1594. The 1589 rebellion might also be interpreted as a coup which misfired, forcing the conspirators into more open confrontation with the government. The propaganda which accompanied such events was in the usual language of feudal revolt, that is to say it was claimed that it was being done in the king's good service. That was how the Ruthven Raid was justified, but on the fall of the regime a year later the actions of the plotters were condemned as *lèse majesté*.[29] The age of the king himself was, of course, a crucial factor in determining the ease with which a coup could be carried through. In 1578 the twelve-year-old king easily gave way to the fiction created by Argyll and Atholl that he was prepared to take the yoke of government upon himself. In 1582 James was frightened by the Ruthven Raid, his tears prompting the master of Glamis to say harshly, 'Better bairns greet than bearded men'.[30] However, James was old enough to resent what had happened to him, and a year later he eagerly conspired against his own government, facilitating Arran's return to power. He was unable to protect Arran against the exiled lords when they stormed into Stirling in 1585, but he was no longer a pawn, and imposed some of his own conditions on the triumphant faction. In 1589 he rejected Huntly's suggestion that together they should overthrow Chancellor Maitland and his colleagues, and he was bitterly determined to punish Bothwell for the raids he attempted against him between 1591 and 1594. The coup was essentially a tool of minority politics, and became of decreasing use as the king grew older, a fact Bothwell failed to understand. Even his successful coup of 1593 could not last because the king would not accept it as a legitimising action, and Bothwell's only real option was to kill James.

The military nature of these events introduced a level of violence into Scottish politics, but that violence was minimal. Argyll and Atholl gained control of the king without bloodshed in 1578, they lost him weeks later when the earl of Mar seized control of Stirling Castle with very little fighting, and when the two factions faced one another outside Stirling later in the year they agreed to a compromise rather than do battle. The Ruthven Raid and the Stirling coup of 1585 were again relatively free of violence, and while some fighting took place during the 1589 rebellion, Huntly shied away from a battle at Brig O' Dee when faced by the king. Even Bothwell's raids were not particularly violent, although the cost was high for those of his men who were caught by the king and were hanged. Melville of Halhill was quite right to comment that 'It had bene sendle sean in any contre, sa many gret alterations to be maid, as hes bene in Scotland laitly in the Kingis tym, with sa little bludschedding'.[31]

This reluctance to indulge in violence during political struggles was also reflected in an unwillingness to make use of the machinery of the state to kill opponents. Chancellor Maitland was reported to have said after the 1589 rebellion that he 'had rather the noblemen of this conspiracy would fly, that they might put them to the horn and banish them, than to try them and shed their blood, wheron will grow everlasting feuds'.[32] There was no possibility of the king permitting executions of the principals of the rebellion anyway, but as was pointed out at the time, the example of the earl of Arran was a salutary reminder of how feuds could follow political executions. As a former mercenary, Arran brought a degree of ruthlessness to Scottish politics which earned him a reputation for 'rage and unlimited violence',[33] and it was he who was largely responsible for the executions of Morton in 1581 and Gowrie in 1584. There is little doubt that these deaths were contrary to the assumed rules that governed political life in Scotland, as Morton was the first peer to be executed since Lord Hume in 1516, and the first earl since Ormond in 1455. Throughout the fifteenth century there appeared to be a strong tradition of minimising political violence, which contrasts sharply with the experience of England.[34] Morton's apparent paralysis in the months after his arrest was thought by one commentator to stem from the fact that he believed 'the Nobility would never give way to such extremity, which was an ill precedent and preparative against themselves'.[35] For Gowrie at least that was true, and he was a victim of a precedent he himself encouraged. Arran, however, did not establish a new norm in violent behaviour; instead he was remembered as 'a man full of violence, and when he was in place of rule executed it with much cruelty'.[36]

One obvious reason why noblemen were unwilling to shed blood in this manner was that they were 'so linked by blood or allied one with another'[37] that they had no desire to break such bonds, even when their kinsmen or friends might have opposed them politically. The other reason is that given by Maitland, that the rewards of government office or position at court were not worth the price of a feud. The earl of Montrose found himself at feud with the earl of Angus, Morton's nephew, because in 1581 'the sentence of gyltenes was prononcit aganis him be the said Montrose, as Chancellor of that jure'.[38] Montrose also incurred a feud with the earl of Atholl because of his part in Gowrie's execution, Atholl having married Gowrie's daughter, 'and with her he entred the feades of her father'.[39] The king himself was the subject of a murder plot in 1600 in which Gowrie's sons tried to avenge their father's death in 1584. Spottiswoode's claim that Alexander Ruthven attacked the king, crying out to him that 'You remember how you used my father and now you must answer for it', is what one would expect in this society.[40] Of Arran himself it seemed to Melville of Halhill 'passing strange that he was left so lang on lywe',[41] but in fact Arran was forced to live in seclusion after 1585 in constant fear of his many enemies. On 2nd November 1596 he was met on the road by one of Morton's nephews and by two other Douglases whose fathers he had put to death, and they 'killed the same Captain and cut him in pieces for the deaths of the Earls of Morton, Gowrie and others their friends'.[42] In 1608 Arran's own nephew took his own revenge on Lord Torthorwald who had done this deed, stabbing him to death in an Edinburgh street, and it was not until 1613 that the feud between the two families was pacified.[43]

Scottish politics were notoriously violent, but the violence was rarely channelled through the state apparatus. Most of it worked its way up into national politics from local and personal roots. Thomas Fowler reported to Burghley in 1589:

> It is the accustomable fassyon of this contry, [and] specyally amonge the best sort, to styk or sh[oot] with a pece or pistoll such one as the Chance[lour] if he give them cawse of offence ... [44]

The Scots' reputation for indulging in bloody politics was even passed on to Philip II by Mendoza in 1582 who told him that 'people there are not only accustomed, for slight causes, to shed the blood of private persons, but do not hesitate to kill their kings'.[45] Mendoza's evaluation may have been based on a reading of Scottish history; and in the more recent past there had been the murders of Darnley and the regents Moray and Lennox, Chancellor Glamis was shot dead in 1578, Chancellor Atholl was probably poisoned in 1579,[46] and Morton had been executed in 1581. In each of the post-war cases feuds were at the root of the violence, and feud also accounted for the later slaughter of the earl of Moray and Lord Maxwell, both of whom were politically involved at the court as well as in their localities. The fact that local issues and existing feuds were so important in introducing violence into the politics of the court and government may have been more pronounced that elsewhere, although that is far from certain. Certainly political violence was not exclusive to Scotland. In France Henry III complained that 'We are nearly always ready to cut each other's throats. We Carry daggers and wear mail shirts, even breast plates, under our cloaks . . . '[47] Henry himself fell to the assassin's knife, and assassins also accounted for Coligny, the duke of Guise and Henry IV, who had avoided eighteen previous attempts on his life. Elsewhere, examples of political violence are not difficult to find, and within two weeks of Lord Glamis's slaughter in 1578 Juan de Escobedo was murdered in Madrid by agents of Antonio Perez.[48] Fowler may have been correct to say of the failed Ruthven regime that 'They were far overshot, and England also to think two earls and some other penmen might govern the estate of Scotland, when their affairs during the King's minority are more governed by the spear than by the pen',[49] but that was neither unusual nor unique in contemporary Europe.

An experience of the continental wars may explain why the earl of Arran made his enemies 'daft with feare'.[50] Captain James Stewart was the younger son of Lord Ochiltree who returned to Scotland in 1579 after some time spent serving as a mercenary in Europe, and he was by all accounts clever, ambitious, daring and still relatively young.[51] Although Captain Stewart's father was an ardent supporter of Morton, the master of Ochiltree had been in trouble with the regent between 1574 and 1576, and after his death a year later Morton cheated his widow out of her lands, and granted them to one of his Douglas kinsmen.[52] There may, therefore, have been personal reasons for the captain becoming 'Morton's special enemy',[53] but he also found good patrons at court who secured for him a share of the forfeited Hamilton estates, and an appointment as a gentleman of the newly formed bedchamber in 1580.[54] He was thus being drawn into the faction formed in the bedchamber around Esmé Stewart, and backed by Chancellor Argyll, and then also Lord Ruthven, the treasurer, who was probably Captain Stewart's patron. This court faction persuaded the captain to accuse Morton of treason before the privy council in December 1580, and following the success of this ploy he was admitted to the privy council, made captain of the king's guard, created earl of Arran, and granted a number of lucrative gifts.[55] During his period of power, which lasted until the autumn of 1585 with a break during the Ruthven regime of 1582–83, Arran put to death Morton, Mr. Archibald Douglas, Douglas of Mains, and a number of other Douglases and Douglas servants, as well as Gowrie.[56] Both Morton and Gowrie were in no doubt that Arran was personally determined to kill them. Morton sensed he was as good as dead as soon as he was told Arran was in charge of the trial, and Gowrie told the court which tried him that he was the victim of 'warldly revenge' and of 'my malicious adversarie'.[57] Morton forgave Arran before his execution, and Gowrie prayed that 'my blood may satiate and extinguish the bloodie rage and ire of the courteours',[58] but as we have already seen, their kinsmen and friends were less charitable.

Gowrie's reference to courtiers is an important one. Morton's fall in 1580 resulted from his failure to gain the king's confidence, to make good use of patronage, or to build up a strong faction, and it was the manipulation of these more subtle weapons as much as the use of violence and naked power which was increasingly important as the king grew older. In a poem in which he advised his son how to behave at court, Sir Richard Maitland wrote, 'He reulls weill that weill in court can guyde'.[59] That kind of power was derived from a personal relationship with the king, and there was some substance to Hume of Godscroft's assertion that after 1578 Morton hung onto power 'merely by the King's countenance; and if that were once taken away from him, the rest would prove but easie'.[60] James was still young, but now that the minority was officially ended, even a child's favour was worth cultivating. Esmé Stewart soon demonstrated that as 'his name, his kindred, his carriage, his commission from friends in France, his comelinesse, his observance, his person did procure him credit with the King'. Those astute enough to recognise the importance of this 'did privately insinuate with him', and 'openly thrust him forward into the King's favour'. Esmé was thus able to alienate Morton from the king 'whose eare hee now had'.[61] The man who was so placed could both influence the king's opinion and affect the flow of patronage, a fact which annoyed Melville of Halhill who scolded the king in later years because gifts were obtained 'be the persuasions of sic as had your ear, and not to best deservers'.[62] Who the king spent time with mattered greatly, and when in 1593 Maitland's enemies thought that the chancellor's fall was imminent, they 'were agast' when James rode to his home, and 'dynit with him, and conferred long'.[63] Relatively minor household officials, like the masters of the royal stables, 'are thought to be over often in the King's ear and so well heard by him that many plots devised be oftentimes by this means defeated', and hence their removal was a matter of great importance for a rival faction.[64] In 1580 Robert Bowes reported that

> The strife in the nobility and others about the King at present is raised and nourished by the inordinate desire occupying each several party and faction to attain and hold the ear of the King, which they would turn to their own advantage and for their private respects.[65]

Intimacy was power, and a whole string of successful courtiers recognised that from Esmé Stewart through to the duke of Buckingham. Arran persuaded the young king that

> he wald find it a faschious busynes to be encombit with many contrary opinionis; but willit him to tak his pastym at hunting, and he suld tary in and heir us, and report again at his Majestie retournyng, all our oppinions and conclusions.

In time Arran was able to ensure that the king 'tak na man's advice but his awen'.[66] After Arran's fall no-one else achieved such a monopoly until Buckingham, although between 1585 and 1589 Huntly did appear to have it within his grasp. To be 'ane of the Kingis chiefe mynonis' as Walter Stewart, Prior of Blantyre, was described, or 'the king's minion' as Alexander Lindsay was, or to be called, as Sir George Hume was, 'ane of his upstart courtiers', was a recognition of power, and was not simply derogatory.[67] Chancellor Maitland was well aware of the threat posed by such men, and 'wald have wraked his Majesteis trewest myngnons' had he been able to.[68] Even after 1603 the earl of Dunbar continued to return to London as often as possible because he knew that his power lay in the king's confidence.

The court, therefore, was an important place. There noblemen, royal officials, household servants, those of the chamber and others who had come to pay court to the king mixed in an entangled web of friendship, faction and feud. To neglect the court was dangerous as it could result in an enemy being given the freedom to ruin one's reputation with the king, or to divert patronage away, thus affecting a man's ability to reward clients and dependants. Local power as much as a place in government, or in the king's affections, were all to some extent influenced by a man's performance at court. When Sir Robert Melville was absent from court his enemy 'tak occasion to callomniat' him,[69] while Maitland also suffered during one of his absences when 'a great number of faltis wer layit out against him'.[70] Opinion was easily swayed, and in Maitland's case 'The court at this tyme beguid to mislyk the chanceller'.[71] The earl of Angus' friends were worried that his distaste for the court might weaken his power to the detriment of their own interests, and so they told him 'to frequent the Court more, and to make his residence at it'.[72] The competitiveness which the court encouraged usually took the form of rumour and conspiracy which was designed to ruin reputations, but it could also spill over into violent clashes wherever the court happened to be. Thus in 1588 a quarrel between Bothwell and the master of Glamis resulted in their taking to the streets of Edinburgh to resolve their differences.[73] It was a tense, highly charged atmosphere in which men with deadly feuds were forced to come together, and which itself produced new feuds. In 1585 the privy council warned that those attending court were to 'contene thameselffis in honest behaviour and quietnes', and must not attack one another 'for auld feid or new' under pain of death, but such a proclamation was impossible to enforce.[74]

Some idea of the court's place at the very centre of political life is glimpsed in James Melville's remark that when in 1588 pestilence and a poor harvest struck, 'the commoun clamer of the peiple was against the Court'.[75] Within the court itself power was conceived of in concentric circles centred on the king's person. Among the most important of those who could enter that first circle were those of the king's own household and the gentlemen of the bedchamber.[76] In 1578 the privy council decided that 'the tyme is not yit proper and convenient to erect his Hienes house with all the officiares and servandis belonging thairto' on grounds which were a mixture of cost, the king's age, and the political context.[77] Over the next two years, however, the household grew in size, and the king had appointed to serve him personal servants like William Murray, son of the comptroller, and Sir William Murray, who had been especially sent to France for his education so that he would be properly prepared for royal service.[78] Then in September 1580 the privy council decided that the time had come to appoint a lord chamberlain and first gentleman of the bedchamber along with twenty-four ordinary gentlemen of noble and baronial rank, all with 'the moyen to leif on thair awin, being personis knawin to have bene affectionat to his Hienes sen his birth'.[79] Within a month Lennox became chamberlain, and the chamber he presided over was full of men hostile to Morton.[80] Three months later Morton had been brought down, and the power of the chamber, which was to last for the remainder of the reign, had been established.

Having a presence in the chamber was a means of access to the king which could have dramatic political consequences, or more normally influenced the flow of patronage. Access was crucial, and one of the responsibilities of these gentlemen was to accompany the king when out riding, surrounding him with their own persons both as added security, and to enhance his dignity.[81] When in his residence they were even more important, and at Stirling, for example, the king was approached through the guard chamber to the presence chamber and on into the bedchamber where only the most privileged were permitted to attend.[82] Both the offices of chamberlain and captain of the guard were important politically. Esmé Stewart's power base remained the chamber even after Morton's fall, and his son, Ludovick, 2nd duke of Lennox, succeeded to his father's office of chamberlain, and demonstrated its value when in 1593 he facilitated Bothwell's successful entrance to the king's apartments. Through his life Lennox enjoyed great intimacy with James on account of his office, and became one of the grandees of the Jacobean court. Lennox's position gave him enormous influence in the distribution of patronage, but the guard captaincy had more obvious advantages, and when Huntly acquired it in 1588 he employed his own men before writing to Philip II and telling him that he could now be 'master of the king'.[83] In 1581 Arran had assumed the office, thus consolidating his newly acquired influence with the king, and another soldier, Colonel William Stewart, succeeded him, exploiting his position to carve out a political career, and to become trusted with some of the king's more sensitive diplomatic business. It was also an office the master of Glamis was determined to have on his return to Scotland in 1585, and which his enemies were equally determined to oust him from. Apart from these offices the chamber and the household were the first stage in political influence and personal fortune for a large number of the king's most trusted advisers and servants.[84]

Those within the chamber in particular had a level of access to the king which could be manipulated to guide the flow of patronage which was the currency binding court factions together in webs of clientage and friendship. In 1590

> Ther was emulation betwn the consaill and the chamber; the consaill compleyng, that the chamber wer the devysers of every wrange that was done, be causing his Maiestie subscyve sindre hurtfull signatours and commissions; and get past for them selves and ther frendis, the best and maist proffitable casulties.[85]

For men like Chancellor Maitland and Treasurer Glamis who were outsiders to the chamber, this was a very real political threat, especially as only a year before both their lives had been threatened by a rebellion with which the chamber had had a great deal of sympathy. The courtiers wanted rid of many of the privy council, and the appointment of 'others mair frendly for them placit in ther rowmes', and while they were unable to achieve this, Maitland was equally frustrated in his efforts to curb their influence.[86]

The council-chamber relationship was the axis on which Jacobean court politics often turned. As early as 1579 the privy council told the young king not to write to them 'in furtherance or hinderance of ony particular personis actionis and causis ... bot suffer thame to do justice in all actionis privlegit to be decydit be thame'.[87] In ending the regency so prematurely, the Scottish nobles had made the king himself the fount of patronage at an age which was too easily exploited, a fact. the council drew attention to a year later when they warned that lives were being imperilled by people casually seeking the king's signature.[88] Later in 1580 the privy council again condemned 'the importunitie and bauldnes of privat personis' who were pressing the king for his signature, and they decreed that all papers had to be subscribed by royal officials or their deputies in the relevant offices. Furthermore, the newly appointed chamberlain, Esmé Stewart, was ordered to purge the household of those known to be guilty of causing such 'Great inconvenience'.[89] By doing this, the council allowed Lennox to tighten his own control of patronage, but after Morton's fall in December 1580 he rapidly assumed a dominant position on the privy council as well. Early in the new year the council complained that the king was still 'daylie fascheit' with the 'indiscreit behaviour' of those seeking favour, and they highlighted an aspect of James's character which would plague Scottish and English governments for decades when they pointed out that 'his Hienes bountefull gude natoure hes bene abusit greatlie'. The result had been confusion, the loss of much-needed revenue, and, for Lennox and his friends, the draining away of patronage which they needed to consolidate their political position. It was therefore decided that until the king reached his majority all suitors should present the king with short written supplications which he would place in 'his awin cabinet' until the Wednesday of each week when he would discuss them with the relevant royal official, and

> sic as his Hienes upoun ressonable consideratioun grantis, that it may be written on the bak *Aggreit;* and sic as beis refusit, to be written on the bak *This may not be.*

These would then be returned to the party who were not to raise it again, and they would serve as evidence to the privy council when presented with them.[90] Privy letters, however, continued to plague the council, and in 1585 Arran, who was powerful in the chamber and held the office of chancellor, sought to further secure the monopoly his own faction had over royal letters. The privy council ordered that letters of summons were to be regarded as invalid unless they were signed by at least four officers of state, one of whom had to be the chancellor, the treasurer or the secretary of state.[91] Apart from the political motivation in such legislation it was recognised that these letters, which contained pains of treason, could be too easily exploited by parties at feud. Parliament too recognised this and it ratified the act after Arran's fall, criticising those who had been 'making a cloak of his highnesses name and authority to collour their private revenge'. It also took steps to prevent junior officials bypassing their superiors by slipping papers before the king for his unwitting signature.[92] There was a similar mixture of self-interest and public concern in the privy council's cancellation of a number of commissions of justiciary in 1582 because of the means by which they had been obtained,[93] and in 1590 when the council declared that persons holding these commissions had acquired them

> for thair awne particulair proffeit and using of revengement upoun personis aganis quhome thair professit evill will and inimitie, as planelie appeiris be the deidlie feidis and quarrellis that heirupoun hes fallin oute amangis sindre nobleman and utheris.[94]

The objection to this did partly arise from a desire to reduce local tensions, but it was equally inspired by the councillors' need to satisfy their own clients and friends by ensuring that their local disputes were handled favourably by the partial distribution of patronage. The whole point of having royal office, or having friends, kinsmen and patrons in office, or close to the king, was to seek rewards, and to enable men to manipulate 'the colour and shadow of the Kings authority for their owne private ends, and to fulfill their owne malice, and revenge'.[95]

After Arran's fall the king's refusal to allow himself to be monopolised frustrated the privy council's efforts to reduce chamber influence. Chancellor Maitland strongly advised James 'not to be over famylier nor of easy acces',[96] except, of course, in the case of himself and his allies, but the king would have none of it. James almost succumbed to Huntly and his chamber friends before 1589, but his accessibility prevented the evolution of the kind of control the Cecils were able to create in England. The result was greater political freedom, but the price was greater competition, factionalism and political feuding. That reached its heights during the Maitland years when the split between council and chamber was at its most intense, and the Octavian regime which followed in 1595–96 foundered on its efforts to reduce the cost of running the court, a policy the chamber successfully resisted.[97] Thereafter the separation of the two was less clear-cut as a number of important courtiers took up places on the privy council, but the tension remained, and the council failed to impair the power of its rival. In 1600 Sir Robert Cecil received a report that 'The King is now so affected to his Chamber and they so feed his humour' that the privy council were becoming redundant.[98] That may have been an exaggeration, although it was one Cecil had to evaluate carefully when considering his own future, but the clamour for attention in the presence chamber remained as great as ever, and the bedchamber was still the centre of the patronage network. That same year Alexander Stewart was denounced for assaulting one of the king's ushers for 'halding him at his Majesteis chalmer dur at tyme quhen his Hienes desyrit to be quyet'.[99] Two years later Stewart wrote an apology to the king, telling him that

> I beying at your Majesteis dur, the preis of the pepill thrust me haiff in, and the said Mr Alexander put bak the dur in my faice and hurt me, and I thocht he had done it

upoun sum partycular evill will, albeit I durst nocht declair the samin to your Majestie for feir of my lyff.[100]

In 1601 the privy council tried to prevent a repetition of this unseemly behaviour by devising stricter rules to govern who had a right to be in both the presence chamber and the bedchamber or cabinet. The 'confusit nowmer of personis of all rankis quha hes entres in his Majesteis bed chalmer' was to be reduced, but access to the presence chamber was to remain unrestricted to noblemen, their eldest sons, and privy councillors, while 'nane presume to enter in the cabinet quhill he be callit for be his Majestie'.[101] Six months later it became clear that James was still highly accessible when the masters of the household were commanded to prevent members of the household from seeking the king's signature.[102] Familiarity remained the hallmark of James's kingship, and he persistently refused to be cut off from people either by the administrative bureaucracy of the privy council, or by attempts to formalise the household.[103] The politics of his court therefore remained relatively free and competitive.

It was also notoriously corrupt. The king's own poverty forced him to sell favour, but corruption had a symbiotic relationship with faction and feud as courtiers sold what influence they had to suitors, and as the profits of office lay not in salaries, but in the potential for exploitation. In this, of course, the Scottish court was little different from the French or English courts where similar practices operated on a larger scale.[104] After 1603 abuses in England became more pronounced as James allowed the practices of the Scottish court to graft themselves onto an already corrupt system.[105] As Linda Levy Peck has pointed out in discussing the corruption of James's English court, corruption was not necessarily a dysfunctional, destructive presence within political life, and it only really became dangerous to the crown when it was monopolised, as it was by the duke of Buckingham in the later years of the reign.[106] That also applied to Scotland under the Regent Morton and the earl of Arran. Morton's corruption was one source of his unpopularity, his enemies claiming that he 'set his haill study how till gather geir',[107] while his friends shifted the blame to his household which was accused of 'receiving and taking bribes, from such as had suites to him for obtaining access to him'.[108] Even more notorious was Arran whose wealth grew spectacularly during his period of power, chiefly from the spoils of the forfeited Hamilton and Ruthven estates.[109] Arran's greed was insatiable, and as his wealth was acquired in the form of escheats, it was particularly dangerous. The rich Ruthven estates were sufficiently tempting to guarantee Gowrie's execution, the bulk of which he acquired himself, the remainder being divided among some others 'to get ther votis and consentis that he [Gowrie] mycht be wrackit'.[110] According to Melville, Arran

maid the haill subiectis to trimble under him, and every man dependit upon him; daily inventing and speaking out of new faltis against dyvers, for the escheitis, landis, benefices, or to get budis; vexing the haill wretes and lawers to mak sur his giftis and conkiss.[111]

Melville was clearly overstating his case against Arran, but in substance he was correct, and the result of such greed was, as in the case of Morton, too narrow a base of support. Morton neglected to follow the advice that he should 'bestow part of his gold unto samany of them as he beleved wer wonnable',[112] and Arran failed to satisfy his allies who 'all thought it reason, that they should (at least) have their share of the spoil in a fit proportion; but they could not have it any wayes proportionable to their esteem of themselves'.[113] Thus Morton in 1581 and Arran in 1585 found themselves isolated and vulnerable to their enemies.

More commonly the spoils system could not be monopolised and it operated with greater fluidity. James himself was accused of carelessness in his distribution of gifts, and of having 'heaped gift upon gift till a sort of greedy cravers' surrounded him.[114] In this world where 'All men dois for advantage',[115] there was little that did not have a price. Both the queen's revenues and the gifts sent at Prince Henry's baptism were plundered, fines paid by Huntly for his rebellion in 1589 were secretly pocketed, pledges held for the behaviour of highland chiefs were released in 1590 following a bribe to the chamber, and when Bothwell found himself in trouble in 1591, some councillors 'went about to draw commodite fra him to be his frendis'.[116] In 1601 the earl of Cassillis was able to have his killing of the laird of Bargany legitimated by having the privy council declare the latter to have been at the horn at the time, and that he had a commission for his capture, 'Bot yit how evir the ten thousand markis gewin to the Thesaure was that quhilk did the turne'.[117] The corruption continued after the union, and in 1609 it was discovered that Lord Scone had been approached by a syndicate who 'made sute for the last tak of the customes', offering him a thousand crowns 'to be thair frend' with an additional income to act as their 'new undertaker'.[118] For once there was royal disapproval, and Scone, who was more corrupt than most, lost the comptrollership, but he survived that, and did make his fortune at court which was the aim of so many men there. In common with court poets elsewhere, Scottish poets often put such success down to good luck,[119] but there was more at play in the game of courtiers than either dishonest corruption, or good luck.

The bonds which drew men together in Scottish society, those of kinship and lordship, did not dissolve in the world of the court, although they may have been overlaid by those of clientage and faction. The seventeenth-century courts of absolutist rulers which made noblemen dependent upon the court and what the king could offer there were at a far remove from the Scottish court before 1603. The origins of that process have been identified by C. Stocker in France where he identified royal office holding as 'the best form of maintenance',[120] and Stone described the English nobility as 'a set of shameless mendicants'[121] because 'the authority of the magnate over the local gentry was now coming to depend less upon his territorial power than upon his influence in London'.[122] Nor, it has been claimed, was kinship a very important factor in politics in England, alliances between kinsmen being 'as fragile and volatile as any other sort'.[123] In Scotland, too, the court has been seen as a magnet which 'drew men away from their traditional loyalties'.[124] Thus many of Esmé Stewart's followers, whose relationship with him was largely an economic one, were 'wyse enough for their awen proffit, bot cairles of his standing'.[125] Nor was there ever any shortage at court of those prepared 'to please them that had the cheif handling'.[126] Sir Richard Maitland bemoaned the passing of kindness at court,[127] and Alexander Montgomery warned of untrustworthy patrons,[128] but one has to treat Maitland's nostalgia, and Montgomery's bitterness, with some suspicion. Even in England, where customary bonds may have been looser than elsewhere in western Europe, Lord Burghley counselled his son to promote the interests of kinsmen 'in all honest actions' as it would 'doubel the bond of nature'.[129] The inter-connection of court and country there may have been less dominated by the power of the former than has been thought,[130] while in France the debate between *fidélité* and economic factors in determining clientage is far from exhausted.[131] The whole question of how far the court and royal patronage had penetrated localities and broken up the bonds there between lord and man, or among kinsmen, is not yet settled, and one would certainly not expect Scotland to be to the fore in such a process were it taking place on a European scale.

The attraction of the court with its potential for economic and political opportunity need not have been antithetical to the maintenance of powerful bonds between lords and dependants, or to local interests. Government and the royal household was there to be exploited in much the same way that the church had been by noble families prior to and immediately after the Reformation in Scotland. This 'colonization'[132] was referred to by the king himself who complained that he had for years been troubled by 'solliciters, recommending servants unto me more for serving in effect their friends that put them in, then their master that admitted them'.[133] Melville, too, drew attention to this fact: 'Officers and servandis ar not chosen for ther qualites, bot at the instance of this or that frend or courteour' so that there was 'ane extraordinary number' employed when 'twa or anew in every office'.[134] In 1583 when the king escaped from the Ruthven regime he dismissed a number of his servants as they were 'favoreis of the erle of Mar', one of the Ruthven Raiders.[135] By 1589 it was being reported that all the king's close servants were clients of the earl of Huntly,[136] and the Octavians were accused of causing 'his Maiesties awen domestikis to folow and depend upon them'.[137] Even the king's guards had to be warned not to 'taikis pairt with divers his Majesties subjectis . . . quhilk ar under deidlie feid and querrell with utheris'.[138] Private interests pervaded crown offices, and thus the earl of Errol asked a session judge for 'Justice with fauvoris'.[139] Such favours were as much a currency of exchange among men at court, or involved with royal government, as were the more obvious economic considerations.

If the local dependency was the stable base of a lord's power, and the court clientage an additional layer to that power which was formed from a mixture of loyal kinsmen and dependants as well as more materialistically motivated men, the faction was the uniting of one such web of interests with others. Unlike the dependency, it was highly unstable, being thrown together by lords, or powerful crown officials, in order to pursue short-term political objectives. The long-term alliance between the earls of Huntly and Errol which was sealed by repeated bonds of friendship was not factional, but grew out of the established policies of both families for the peace of their localities, and was reinforced by religious issues which made them the basis of a catholic party.[140] Nor were the alliances between the earls of Angus and Morton, or Lords Maxwell and Herries, factional since the first two were both Douglases, and the latter were both Maxwells. Kinship was an assumed political bond, faction defied natural bonds, and crossed kindred lines, feud, local interests, or religious party. As Bowes wrote, 'The end of feuds and entry into bands are often the beginning of great actions'.[141] Both the 1585 coup and the 1589 rebellion were in part factional, the first involving an alliance between the Hamiltons and Douglases, the latter an alliance between the earls of Huntly and Bothwell. Scottish politics were not, therefore, divided into stable, identifiable parties founded on religion,[142] or on the bilateral lines found in England during the period of Cecil-Essex rivalry.[143] Instead the political world was highly volatile. Lord Hunsdon was staggered by the whirlpool of change which confronted him, and wrote to Burghley that 'The factyons ar suche amonge the nobell men, as yt ys almoste an impossybyllyte too wryght any sertenty of them'.[144]

In the political language of Scotland 'faction' was an abusive word, used largely by those in positions of power and office to criticise their rivals on the outside seeking to displace them. Such a usage had a long history outside Scotland; in republican Rome friendly alliances were called *amicitia*, hostile ones *factio*.[145] The breakdown of the regency in 1578 was interpreted by Balfour as the re-emergence of faction at the forefront of political life, while to Hume, Morton's enemies were a faction 'glewed together by nothing but common discontentment'.[146] The Marians were 'the dregs of the old faction', Bothwell and 'sic as wer malcontents' formed a faction, the Brig O' Dee rebels were 'a new faction, wherof the Erle of Huntly was cheifest', and Maitland was 'a man of a contrary faction and disposition in all business of the Common-weale'.[147] Melville of Halhill thought that factional politics were legitimate during a royal minority, but thereafter he criticised men who were 'bot factious, faischious, ambitious, gredy, vengeable, warldly, wretchit creatours', while boasting that he himself was 'never esteamed a factioner'.[148] Moysie implied much the same when he related how the earl of Mar asked the earl of Angus to 'come upone thaire faction' in 1584, but Angus refused, declaring that 'he wald folow the Kingis will'.[149] In reality, however, those within government were sustained by faction as much as they were threatened by it, although there is little doubt that the period between 1578 and 1595 was more intensely factional than the years before then when party was more prevalent, while after 1595 politics settled down into a more stable condition. As long as factions were so competitive, feud was found at the heart of court politics, and local disputes and quarrels ran up and down the bonds which linked court with country, binding and welding them into conflicts which straddled both.[150] How this operated in practice can be seen from the three examples which follow.

On 17 March 1578 Lord Glamis, who was then chancellor, was shot dead on the streets of Stirling in the midst of a fight between his own kinsmen, the Lyons, and those of the earl of Crawford, the Lindsays. The two families had a long history of recurrent feud, and they were at the time unreconciled 'for auld bludeshed betuix thais tua houssis',[151] but at the time they appeared to be under assurance to one another. Thus when Glamis and Crawford met in the narrow wynd leading up to Stirling Castle they studiously tried to avoid an incident, but 'thair servands in pryde strave for the best part therof', a struggle broke out, and in the subsequent fighting Glamis was shot from an upstairs window.[152] Crawford was immediately arrested and warded in the castle on suspicion of murder, and from there he wrote to his friends that this was 'the maist vechtie mater that ewer I haif haid or is hable to haif ado standing upon my honour, leif and heritage'.[153] It was widely suspected that Crawford had in fact set up the killing of a man who was one of the most respected politicians in the country, and had been a close ally of the recently deposed Regent Morton. Preparations were made to try Crawford for treason, but insufficient evidence could be found, the earl was released on surety, and the case dragged on until November 1579 when it appears to have been dismissed, following which Crawford gave assurance on pain of £10,000 that he would not harm Thomas Lyon, master of Glamis, and applied for a licence to leave the country.[154]

During this time the master of Glamis pursued Crawford in the courts, and in spite of repeated mutual assurances in 1580 and 1582, 'deadly feude, and divers murders' occurred between these two neighbouring Angus families.[155] In 1579 the earl complained in a letter to one of his friends that Glamis had sent one of his 'mest speciall interpryssouris to haiff murderit us in our bed',[156] and it was said of the master of Glamis that so determined was he to have vengeance that 'Crawford all his life was glad to stand in a soldier's posture'.[157] In 1583 English estimates of Crawford's power suggested that it was 'tyed shorte by the feade he hath with the master of Glames and his frendes'.[158] However, in April of that year it was Glamis who complained to the privy council of 'a greit nowmer of gentlemen and utheris slaine' by the Lindsays, and of 'divers slauchters' which Crawford had been allowed to commit because of the king's 'owersycht and delay usit in justice'.[159] The reasons for Glamis thinking that, and for now expressing it, were largely political.

When Lord Glamis was killed in 1578 Crawford was already inclining to the side of the Argyll-Atholl faction, and it was Atholl who benefited most from Glamis's death, succeeding to the vacant chancellorship. While the master of Glamis continued to lean towards Morton, Crawford benefited from his fall, becoming in time a close ally of Lennox.[160] When Lennox had Glamis fined the huge sum of £20,000 for killing one of Crawford's men, he firmly tied the earl to his own faction which was formed from a number of former Marian families, and drove Glamis into the hands of his most extreme enemies.[161] The latter was, therefore, one of the leading figures in the Ruthven Raid in August 1582 which drove Lennox from power. Crawford retired from court, preparing once again to go abroad, while Glamis, who was now a privy councillor, sought to prevent it, and to have his enemy pursued at law.[162] The collapse of the Ruthven regime in July 1583 once again reversed the situation with Crawford being quick to ally himself with the earl of Arran. Arran, however, initially favoured a reconciliation between Crawford and Glamis, as he had in 1581, but throughout the remainder of the summer Glamis resisted.[163] He was in fact plotting with the earl of Mar to wrest power back from Arran, but when they attempted a coup in April 1584 it failed miserably, forcing them to flee into exile, and leaving one of Glamis's kinsmen to be executed along with Gowrie.[164] Crawford was by this time one of Arran's staunchest supporters, and he and Montrose were the only earls still close to him when his fall came in the autumn of 1585, following which the earl was ordered to ward himself.[165] For Glamis the coup brought him high rewards as his senior position in the faction which engineered it was recognised. He was re-admitted to the privy council, was appointed captain of the guard and lord treasurer, was granted a pension, and over the next few years was appointed to other offices and commissions, and received further grants and gifts.[166] With the rich Glamis estates in his control, the backing of his kindred — a relatively small one — and these offices, Glamis stood on the threshold of unrivalled power in the government.

The king's determination not to allow the 1585 coup to be a means of allowing the victorious faction to persecute their enemies was reflected in his handling of the Crawford-Glamis feud. Both sides were brought to assure one another, and pressure was brought to bear on them which resulted in a reconciliation in June 1587 when they 'soupit togither' in Chancellor Maitland's house.[167] The recent appointment of Maitland to the vacant chancellorship had, however, put a strain on the fairly good working relationship he and Glamis had arrived at over the preceding two years, since the latter had wanted the office for himself.[168] This tension affected their ability to meet the rising challenges coming from the earls of Huntly and Bothwell who had their own reasons for wanting rid of both men. Over the next year these two grew in influence, while also competing with one another, and Huntly succeeded in persuading the king to strip Glamis of the captaincy of the guard, and to grant it to Crawford's younger brother, Alexander Lindsay. Glamis saw this as a further reduction of his power, and as particularly offensive in that the beneficiary was a Lindsay. So 'heichlie movit' was he by the loss that the king finally gave the office to Huntly himself, and bought Glamis off with a gift.[169] The affair had also brought Glamis into conflict with Bothwell who took the side of the Lindsays, engaged in some 'braggingis' with Glamis, and provoked him into marching out with his friends onto the streets of Edinburgh to confront the earl and the master of Crawford. Fortunately, the king was able to intervene in time to prevent bloodshed, and warded both men for their misconduct, although not before having an unseemly argument with Bothwell.[170]

This struggle towards the end of 1588 over the guard prefigured that in the following spring when Crawford joined Huntly and Bothwell in their rebellion against the chancellor and his friends, of whom Glamis was still thought to be one. Crawford's alignment was consistent with his adherence to Lennox and Arran, but his catholicism was not militant, and his principal motivation seems to have been the hope that Glamis might be overthrown. Thus, when at an early stage of the rebellion Glamis's house was sacked, and he was captured, it was expected that 'they will never keep him alive if it were but Crawford's feud with him'.[171] Crawford's allies, however, had no desire to kill Glamis whose own rivalry with Maitland was of potential use to them, and when they refused the earl's demands for blood he 'retired in discontentment'.[172] Following the collapse of the rebellion Glamis set about helping Huntly escape punishment, a ploy which made some suspicious of his whole part in the affair, and this frightened Maitland into an alliance with Bothwell. Crawford was convicted of treason by assize, and Glamis sought to have him executed, prompting Fowler to call him 'a perilous man', but no-one else would support this, and like the other rebels he was freed without punishment.[173]

For almost two years the feud was kept out of court politics, and by February 1591 there was again talk of peace between Glamis and Crawford.[174] Relations between Maitland and Glamis were, however, growing increasingly tense, and Bowes wrote that 'Sondry accidentes dailie falling do rather blow the cole, then quinche the fier of their displeasures'.[175] In particular Maitland was in the midst of forcing a matter through the court of session in favour of his nephew, and against the interests of the earl of Morton, Glamis's father-in-law.[176] Seeing that Glamis was on the point of making his peace with Crawford over the long-standing issue of the burgh of Forfar, Maitland encouraged Crawford to break off negotiations by lending his weight to the earl's case, thus managing to 'awake this sleping dogg to byte Glames'.[177]

Bothwell's fall later in the year removed Maitland's most implacable opponent, and he soon exploited the situation to have Glamis horned and deprived of his offices for failing to assure Crawford when ordered to by the privy council.[178] This open split between the two was facilitated by the alliance between the chancellor and Huntly towards the end of 1591 which greatly worried both the protestants and the English, and pressure was soon being put on Maitland to be reconciled with his rival.[179] Feeling sufficiently secure, he was unresponsive, and Glamis turned instead to Alexander Lindsay, now Lord Spynie and one of the king's favourites in the chamber, persuading him to try to bring Crawford round to forming a faction against the chancellor. The project drifted on through the winter, but Crawford and his other brothers were not interested, and Glamis's own fall was soon forgotten in the aftermath of the murder of the earl of Moray in February 1592.[180] Suddenly Maitland found himself highly unpopular and vulnerable, and he quickly patched up his quarrel with Glamis.[181] The two continued to bicker, but their uneasy alliance held throughout the three difficult years which followed, and after Maitland's death in 1595 Glamis continued in the offices to which he had been restored, including that of treasurer, until his retiral in 1598.[182] Crawford gravitated towards Huntly in 1592, but was unwilling to repeat his rebellion of three years previously. In 1595 he attempted once again to oust Glamis by joining with the earl of Mar against Maitland and his allies, but the earl's years at the centre of political life had long since passed.[183] The feud continued, although without the same political implications, and the date of its settlement is unknown.[184] As for the old adversaries, Crawford died in November 1607, and Glamis followed him three months later, their hatred of one another going with them to the grave. [185]

This interplay of court politics with local feud can also be seen at work in the feud between the earl of Bothwell and Alexander, 6th Lord Hume. Bothwell and the Humes of Manderston had rival claims to the lands of Coldingham priory which were in the hands of the latter.[186] In 1583 the earl quarrelled at court with David Hume, one of the laird of Manderston's sons, and while a violent incident was avoided at the time, some days afterwards Bothwell attacked the family when they were in the company of Lord Hume.[187] The attack took place close to where the king was staying, and was broken up by Colonel Stewart, following which both young noblemen were warded, and were forced to assure one another.[188] In spite of this Bothwell ambushed David Hume and two of his friends in September 1584, and 'killed all three, but hewed Davy Hume ... all to pieces'.[189] Lord Hume was then warded to prevent his seeking vengeance, and while preparations were made to try Bothwell, the case never came to law.[190]

Arran's refusal to support Bothwell in his claim to Coldingham finally persuaded the earl to leave court in March 1585, and later in the year he joined the exiled lords in the Stirling coup.[191] Yet he was quickly disappointed when Manderston was confirmed in his rights, the chancellorship which he desired was left vacant, and the captaincy of Edinburgh Castle was granted to Sir John Hume of Coldenknowes, thus frustrating another of his ambitions.[192] A year later a serious clash between Bothwell and the Humes was narrowly avoided over the gathering of the teinds of the property.[193] However, in the spring of 1587 the Humes gave way to pressure from the king to recognise Bothwell's claim to Coldingham, and with the marriage of his half-sister to the laird of Coldenknowes a degree of peace was restored to the east marches.[194]

More important to Bothwell by this time was his rivalry with Maitland. This too had roots in the Coldingham lands to which Maitland had a claim of his own which he revived in 1585, but had dropped again by 1587, and in his determination to become chancellor, an ambition fulfilled in the same year.[195] In November 1587 it was first rumoured that Bothwell was planning to murder Maitland.[196] His growing hatred of the chancellor drew him into alliance with Huntly in 1589, but he had no interest in the wider ambitions of the catholic earls, and was considered 'an undertaking man' as they term it here, but withall fickle, as no party is sure [of] him; feared on both sides, trusted on neither'.[197] The rebellion was even more unsuccessful for Bothwell than it was for the northern earls, and he surrendered to William Hume, the lieutenant of the guard, claiming that 'his rysing in armis wes to be revenged of the chancellor only'.[198] Like the other rebels, Bothwell was soon freed, but was not pardoned. Hume of Manderston supposedly offered to murder the earl in return for the restoration of Coldingham, but Maitland had his own reasons for seeking to make his peace with Bothwell.[199] In fact he tried to reconcile the earl and Lord Hume, but it proved impossible 'by reason of the youth and furious nature of both these lords, and both being well friended', and having 'bloudie handes and turbulant sprites'.[200]

Bothwell's temporary friendship with the chancellor was partly responsible for his being trusted with so much power during the king's and Maitland's absence from the country during the winter-spring of 1589–90. Before he left, the king arranged for Bothwell and Hume to recognise one another's zones of influence in the south-east,[201] but he would have been as surprised as anyone else to find on his return that the two were 'so well agreed betwixt them-selves as their late and earnest feede is turned into tender and familiar friendship', or at the very least they were talking about peace.[202] Those talks revealed that Maitland had been inciting them against one another for some time, in spite of the peace moves he had encouraged in 1589.[203] While Bothwell refused at the time to turn against the chancellor, he and Hume had arranged a reconciliation by the autumn in which the killing of David Hume and the question of Coldingham were both settled.[204]

Following Bothwell's arrest on a charge of witchcraft in the spring of 1591, and his subsequent escape from Edinburgh Castle in June, Lord Hume did not immediately try to exploit the situation. In fact immediately after the escape, for which the earl was outlawed, Hume proved to be his closest ally, and joined him on the borders, from where Bothwell declared that Maitland was behind this latest misfortune.[205] However, when Hume himself was denounced at the beginning of August, he saw no reason to be dragged down with the earl, especially as other border barons were declaring their allegiance to the king. After consulting with his friends he made his peace with James, and before the end of the month he and Maitland were reconciled by a bond of friendship.[206] The crown now encouraged Hume to revive his feud with Bothwell, which was made all the easier by the murder of George Hume of Spott by men working for James Douglas of Spott, a friend of Bothwell's.[207] Bothwell's raid on Holyrood in December failed in its attempt to kill Maitland 'whome he deidlie haittit', but Spott's killers were rescued.[208] The king, now even more determined to punish Bothwell, gifted Coldingham to his chamber servant, Sir George Hume, a brother to the murdered David Hume, and a nephew of the murdered Hume of Spott. He also granted Lord Hume other former properties of the earl, and gave him command of a company of horse raised to capture him.[209]

The successful palace coup by Bothwell and the Stewarts in July 1593 brought a temporary reversal in the fortunes of the Humes. The earl insisted that James should not see Maitland, Glamis, Lord Hume and Sir George Hume, and his properties, including Coldingham, were restored. However, he was unable, without keeping the king a prisoner, to enforce his terms on James, and complained that 'he could not get presence of his Maiestie, nor speik of him, for the Homes, quho were courtiers with the King'.[210] By the beginning of the autumn Bothwell's position had become untenable, and it was made impossible at court when Alexander Hume was elected provost of Edinburgh in a move to counter the earl's popularity there.[211] Shortly after this Bothwell challenged Lord Hume to a duel, but the latter wisely ignored it,[212] and it was not until April 1594 that they clashed when Bothwell led a large raid on Edinburgh. Outside Leith, Bothwell was met by the king and a much larger force assembled by Lord Hume and from among the townsmen by Alexander Hume. Although Bothwell defeated Lord Hume's mounted vanguard, he was forced to desert the field of what proved to be his last serious encounter with the king.[213] After the raid on Leith, Bothwell became increasingly desperate as allies left him, the laird of Johnstone being prised away by Hume, his plot to murder the king and Sir George Hume was uncovered by William Hume, and his associations with Huntly became public.[214] Lord Hume was granted a commission to hunt Bothwell and his supporters down, the earl's brother, Hercules Stewart, was captured and brought in for execution by William Hume, lieutenant of the guard, and this same William Hume killed one of Bothwell's servants in Dunfermline 'because he was a stryiker of Da. Home, his brother, when Bothwell slew him'.[215] By 1596 Bothwell's 'miserable plight' was such that he had no choice but to flee the country.[216] The king's victory had also been one for his chancellor, and for the Humes whose feud with Bothwell was put to such good use. Bothwell never returned to Scotland, and while his son failed to have his title restored, he did come to a compromise with the Humes in 1620–21.[217]

The very intense factionalism and feuding in court politics which had characterised the years from the end of the Morton regency to the defeat of Huntly and Bothwell in 1594–95 was very much reduced thereafter by the growth in the king's own control over court politics. However, in 1595 the court threatened to divide into bilateral factions which reached out into the countryside, and forced noblemen there to declare for one or the other. At the heart of the dispute were two relatively minor issues. The first involved the earl of Mar's criticisms of the financial administration of the crown which Maitland incorrectly interpreted as an attack on himself, thus forcing Mar to advise the chancellor's own removal at the end of 1594.[218] The ill feeling which this generated was then fused with a second issue in the spring when Maitland was suspected of being behind the queen's attempts to force James to remove Prince Henry from the earl's custody.[219] In fact while Mar and Maitland were pointedly cool with one another, the old chancellor had found himself the hostage of his own clients and of the queen, much to the king's anger.[220] In December 1594 it had been predicted that 'the feud is likely to be quickened with blood and to the trouble of the country',[221] and six months later that prediction had been fulfilled.

In Stirlingshire a quarrel had broken out among the Forresters of Garden, dependants of Mar's, and the Bruces of Airth and Livingstons of Dunipace, both of whom were also inclined to accept Mar's local dominance. The dispute appears to have been partly about the degree of influence the Forresters had with the earl, but was heightened by competition over a woman who was being wooed by a Forrester and a Bruce.[222] A fight took place in Stirling in April 1595,[223] but Mar was too preoccupied with the court to settle the affair, and 'as the ane preassit to prevayle above the uther, the factioun of thir two drew freyndis to parteis and factions'.[224] Then on 24 June one of the Forresters, who also happened to be a bailie of Stirling and one of Mar's servants, was murdered on the road to Glasgow by Livingston of Dunipace, Bruce of Airth and their friends.[225] The killing immediately opened old sores with the Livingstons with whom Mar's family had been at feud in the latter half of the 1570s, and with their Elphinstone allies with whom Mar had another dispute over land.[226] Yet the incident also had wider implications, and 'set all on fire' at court where Dunipace's recent attempt to solicit help from Maitland was soon being connected with the murder. A 'bloody end' looked likely as 'all sides are busy packing up all their small feuds for their advantage'.[227]

Mar called a meeting of his friends in Stirling within the week, and was well attended there by Lennox, Argyll, Morton and a large number of barons who swore to hazard 'life, land, and all' in his interest if he sought justice by law, a condition the king had also imposed on his support.[228] From there Mar led a large, armed procession through the lands of the killers, bearing the corpse of his servant, and displaying before him a banner on which the dead man had been painted 'to move the beholders to a great detestation of the fact'.[229] At court an attempt by some neutral men to quickly clear up the quarrel between Maitland and Mar was frustrated by the chancellor who failed to appear at the meeting they had arranged, declaring 'what should need agreement when there is no feud'.[230] It seems unlikely that the chancellor had anything to do with the killing, but he was clearly enjoying the discomfort it was causing Mar, and powerful court interests associated with Maitland and the queen were now gathering around Livingston of Dunipace and his friends to protect them.[231]

Throughout August and September those interests were ranged behind the killers in an attempt to persuade Mar to accept a quick out-of-court settlement. In mid-august Mar was asked to accept the banishment of the murderers in return for assuring the lives of their kinsmen, and this was linked with efforts to reconcile him with the chancellor.[232] By the following month homage to Mar and Forrester of Garden, and a thousand merks for the family of the dead man were also on offer.[233] The master of Elphinstone visited Mar to discuss assythment for Forrester and another of his servants who had been killed in revenge for the death of a Bruce, but Mar still suspected a plot which went beyond Dunipace and his friends, and Elphinstone left 'sore frome my hairt'.[234] Lord Livingston wrote to Mar swearing his innocence in the murder, and offering to allow any of his own people to face a just trial,[235] and Dunipace also wrote in a similar vein, offering to stand trial so long as Mar himself was not the pursuer, or to accept whatever reasonable terms Mar's friends wished to impose 'for assauging his lordship's grief'.[236] Further banishments and an increased assythment of two thousand merks were offered at the beginning of October,[237] but Mar was determined to find out the whole truth of the murder in court, and they were rejected as the others had been before them.

Faced with Mar's obstinacy, the king agreed to a trial, and it was set for 20 December.[238] The privy council was now faced with the dangers of a violent confrontation in Edinburgh as both sides prepared to go there in strength, and it forbade large retinues, while suspending the sitting of the court of session for a few days at the time of the trial to reduce the number of people likely to be in the burgh on business.[239] Meanwhile, Maitland's death in October had left the queen to champion Dunipace, which she did with almost suspicious determination. In the middle of December she asked Mar to postpone the trial, but he refused as 'it touches him so far in honour that he cannot satisfy her request'.[240] On 17 December both sides rode into Edinburgh in strength, and the government and the burgh steeled themselves for trouble, placing restrictions on movement and putting a heavy guard in the streets. The queen then intervened again on the day before the trial, threatening James with the prospect of her own friends being convened in Dunipace's defence. The king sent for Mar and persuaded him to accept a postponement of the trial to the next justice ayre in his locality, unless the king could first arrange a settlement. It was a victory for the queen who had shown uncharacteristic interest in the affair, and Mar went home disgruntled.[241] On 23 December the privy council ordered both parties to submit the feud according to the terms of the 1595 act concerning feuding, setting a hearing for the middle of February.[242]

The feud was still potentially dangerous, as one commentator observed: 'still I fear this matter of my Lord Mar [will] work more mischief for though the day of law be continued yet hatred diminishes nothing on either side, which (being so near neighbours) is fearful'.[243] Back in Stirling there was further fighting between Mar's people and the Livingstons, while a royal messenger was attacked, and the presbytery condemned the postponement of the trial, 'conceiving that justice was by that new puting off of that day illuded at the least'.[244] Mar's failure to discipline the men who attacked the king's officer, and his reluctance to assure the Livingstons lost him the king's sympathy,[245] but at the same time the crown was now hunting down the killers.[246] In May 1596 an Erskine and a Livingston were both denounced for fighting in a single combat.[247] The exchange of assurances, and the flight into exile of the killers reduced local tension by the summer of 1596, while better relations between Mar and the queen at court took the feud out of court politics.[248] The king's decision in the summer of 1598 to pass a new act designed to speed up the pacification of feuds greatly annoyed Mar who felt he was being pushed into a settlement 'against his honour', and he led the opposition to the act in the convention of the estates which sat in June.[249] James followed up the convention by persistently pressurising Mar into making a submission of the feud, but he held out long enough for James to pass him over in appointing a new chancellor, an office he was expected to be offered, and the submission was not made until February 1599. A settlement soon followed, and James was able to feast the two sides in April.[250]

In each of these three cases the locality and its politics figured prominently in the politics of the court. The disputes between Crawford and Glamis, Bothwell and Hume, and Mar and the Livingstons were all essentially local, but in each instance they brought their feuds with them to court, and the court intruded itself into their affairs. Court factions, therefore, formed around these local divisions, and the outcome of these local feuds could be decided by men at court. The exploitation of local differences allowed a man like Maitland, who was not a magnate, to out-manoeuvre most of his rivals. Alexander Montgomery wrote in a poem composed for Maitland, 'A cunning king a cunning chancellor chusis',[251] and there was no doubt that Maitland and the king himself were the best practitioners of a form of control which had always been practised by kings and their highest officers. Yet the locality could also be a point of vulnerability for men who operated at court, as the master of Glamis, Bothwell and Mar all discovered to their cost, while men who ignored the localities altogether, like Morton and Arran, could be overwhelmed by them. Court and locality were symbiotically united, with local magnates and court politicians, be they themselves noblemen, courtiers, or crown officials, feeding off one another in order to sustain or enhance their power in the arena of their choice. The local bonds of kinship, lordship, dependency and feud fused with those of patronage, clientage and faction to create an entire political fabric so interwoven that the one cannot really be understood without the other.

The point about feud and politics is not that politics were all about feuding — clearly that was not the case — but that Scottish politics were practised in the context of a feuding society. Nor does that mean that politics were anarchic, or the product of a self-interested, lawless nobility. Political life was dynamic, and social in nature, based on relationships of co-operation and of conflict. That conflict could make Scottish politics violent, but the implications of political violence for a feuding society were sufficient to have a restraining influence on the degree of violence men were prepared to employ. There are other kinds of political violence than feuding, and in Scotland these were rare. The amount of feuding in court politics also varied during this period. Until 1578 what feuds there were remained local as there was no division at the centre, but from the overthrow of the regency, feud and faction grew increasingly unchecked in court life. A number of factors contributed to this: the fact that authority resided in the person of a boy-king, the degree to which local interests could impose their power politics on the centre, the alternative sources of power in the privy council and the chamber, and the privatised and fractured nature of the patronage system. By the middle of the 1590s the king had created a powerful enough clientage of his own to be able to make it more worthwhile to seek entrance to it than to create factional opposition, although the dispute between Mar and Maitland threatened to create a bilateral situation similar to the Cecil-Essex one in England. From the end of the decade only petty faction survived, and with the decision to attack feuding itself in 1595, and more seriously in 1598, the local feud and the court faction wre prised apart. The union in 1603 accelerated that, making the division between court and country more pronounced, while also guaranteeing that the chamber was better placed to influence the king than was his privy council. A royal dependency was created which no longer needed to be so aware of the localities, but was increasingly cut off from them in the English court until they once again forced themselves into the foreground in 1637.

NOTES

1. For political ideas in Scotland, Williamson, *Scottish National Consciousness in the Age of James VI*, and R. Mason, Kingship and Commonweal: Political Thought and Ideology in Reformation Scotland, University of Edinburgh Ph.D., 1983.

2. Donaldson, *All The Queen's Men*, in which one suspects the degree of personal and local rivalry is still under-estimated.

3. Cited in J. H. Elliot, *Europe Divided*, Glasgow, 1977, p. 108.

4. D. R. Kelley, *The Beginnings of Ideology, Consciousness and Society in the French Reformation*, Cambridge, 1981, p. 201.

5. Harding, *Anatomy of a Power Elite*, pp. 71–80.

6. For the 1575 settlement, Calderwood, *History*, iii, p. 346; Hume, *History*, p. 322; *Historie*, p. 155; S.R.O., R.D., 1/14/40. For the basic details of Morton's dealings with the Hamiltons, G. Hewitt, *Scotland Under Morton*, Edinburgh, 1982, pp. 64–71.

7. Hewitt, *Scotland Under Morton*, p. 69.

8. This tends to be the line taken by Lee, *John Maitland of Thirlestane*, for example, p. 11.

9. *Estimate*, p. 7.

10. Gordon, *Sutherland*, pp. 164–165.

11. There had been a decreet arbitral between the two families in 1543, S.R.O., Gordon Castle Muniments, G.D., 44/14/7/4, and marriage alliances which accompanied the peace, *Scots Peerage*, iv, p. 59, and Gordon, *Sutherland*, pp. 164–165. For the divorce, *Scots Peerage*, iv, p. 69, and S.R.O., Forbes Collection, G.D., 52/1087. As well as being weaker than the Gordons, the Forbes appear to have been weakened by internal dissension, Gordon, *Sutherland*, p. 164, and Spottiswoode, *History*, iii, p. 169.

12. Gordon, *Sutherland*, p. 165; *Spalding Miscellany*, ii, 'The Chronicle of Aberdeen', p. 38; Spottiswoode, *History*, ii, p. 169; Chambers, *Domestic Annals*, i, p. 75. Lord Forbes's brother, Black Arthour, was among over a hundred men said to have been slain. Auchindoun was said to have followed up this victory by setting fire to Black Arthour's house at Towy, killing his wife and twenty-seven servants, Spottiswoode, *History*, ii, pp. 169–170.

13. Gordon, *Sutherland*, p. 166; Spottiswoode, *History*, ii, p. 70; S.R.O., Forbes Collection, G.D., 52/29, G. D., 52/30.

14. Gordon, *Sutherland*, p. 166; *Spalding Miscellany*, ii, 'Chronicle of Aberdeen', pp. 58–59; Spottiswoode, *History*, ii, p. 170.

15. *R.P.C.*, ii, pp. 193–200.

16. *Historie*, p. 139.

17. Gordon, *Sutherland*, pp. 170–171. An attempt was made by Arthour Forbes to murder Auchindoun in Paris.

18. *Historie*, pp. 150–151; *R.P.C.*, ii, p. 381.

19. See Hewitt, *Scotland Under Morton*, pp. 39–40, for Morton's dealings with Aberdeen.

20. *C.S.P., Scot.*, v, p. 253.

21. *A.P.S.*, iii, pp. 112–114.

22. *Ibid.*, pp. 164–165.

23. *R.P.C.*, iii, pp. 261, 262, 275 and 278; Gordon, *Sutherland*, pp. 174–175.

24. *R.P.C.*, iii, p. 278.

25. *Ibid.*, pp. 401–402.

26. *A.P.S.*, iii, pp. 230–231.

27. For the settlement, S.R.O, R.D., 1/20/386, R.D., 1/22/49. In 1589 the Forbes tried to get better terms, S.R.O., Forbes Collection, G.D., 52/1089, and fighting broke out again, *C.S.P., Scot.*, x, pp. 186–187. For the 1597 peace, see *C.S.P., Scot.*, xiii, Part 1, p. 56.

28. For a basic political narrative of the Morton regency, see Hewitt, *Scotland Under Morton*, Chapters 3 and 4.

29. *A.P.S.*, iii, p. 330; *R.P.C.*, iii, pp. 508–509 and 614.

30. *R.P.C.*, iii, p. 509, note.

31. Melville, *Memoirs*, p. 355.

32. *C.S.P., Scot.*, x, p. 4.

33. Hume, *History*, p. 364.

34. A. Grant, 'Crown and Nobility', in R. Mason (ed.), *Scotland and England*, Edinburgh, forthcoming.

35. Hume, *History*, p. 350.

36. Spottiswoode, *History*, iii, p. 40.

37. *C.S.P., Scot.*, x, p. 52.

38. *Historie*, p. 229.

39. *C.S.P., Scot.*, x, pp. 271 and 276.

40. Spottiswoode, *History*, iii, p. 84.

41. Melville, *Memoirs*, p. 405.

42. *C.S.P., Scot.*, xii, p. 360; Pitcairn, *Criminal Trials*, iii, p. 66.

43. *R.P.C.*, viii, pp. 128, 144 and 543; x, pp. 1 and 45; *Melrose*, i, p. 104.

44. *C.S.P., Scot.*, x, p. 68.

45. *C.S.P., Span.*, iii, p. 396.

46. There is contradictory evidence for Atholl. See Hume, *History*, p. 345; *R.P.C.*, iii, p. 184; *C.S.P., Scot.*, v, pp. 385, 570, 663, 671 and 683; Moysie, *Memoirs*, pp. 20–23; S.R.O., Atholl M.S., N.R.A., 224/1638, 16/March/c.1580, Queen Mary to the countess of Atholl.

47. Cited in D. Stewart, *The First Bourbon*, London, 1971, p. 34.

48. J. Lynch, *Spain under the Hapsburgs*, Oxford, 1981, i, p. 323. For England, Stone, *The Crisis of the Aristocracy*, p. 112, writes of a 'sinister background of rival court factions with their hired killers and 'cutters', of sporadic murder and violence in the countryside . . . '

49. *C.S.P., Scot.*, vi, p. 689.

50. Hume, *History*, p. 385.

51. For his character, *Ibid.*, p. 349, and Melville, *Memoirs*, p. 263.

52. For the treatment of the master of Ochiltree, *A.P.S.*, iii, p. 90; *R.P.C.*, ii, p. 531. In 1576 he came into Morton's will, but it is not known how he was punished. After his death in 1577 Morton persuaded his wife to exchange her lands for a pension, but the pension was not paid, and the lady complained to the privy council in 1579. She temporarily regained them, but in the same month as Morton's fall they were seized by Robert Douglas, Commendator of Whithorn, *R.P.C.*, iii, pp. 89–90, 141, 206, 275–276 and 292.

53. *C.S.P., Scot.*, vi, p. 12.

54. *R.M.S.R.S.*, p. 819, No. 2983; *R.P.C.*, iii, p. 323.

55. See *R.S.S.R.S.*, viii, for some of those gifts.

56. For the persecution of the Douglases, *R.P.C.*, iii, 348–349, 351, 365, 368, 369, 377–378, 389–390, 415, 425 and 624; Spottiswoode, *History*, ii, pp. 280 and 314; Moysie, *Memoirs*, pp. 31 and 48–50; Birrel, 'Diary', p. 23.

57. Morton was said to have exclaimed, 'I knowe then what I may look for', Spottiswoode, *History*, ii, p. 276. For Gowrie, *Bannatyne Miscellany*, Bannatyne Club, Edinburgh, 1827–55, i, 'The Manner and Form of the Examination and Death of William Earl of Gowrye, May 1584', p. 91, No. 92, pp. 100–101, No. 92.

58. Arran told Morton that what he had done was because of matters of state, not for personal reasons, but Morton was unconcerned, telling Arran 'It is no tyme to remember quarrelles. I have no quarrell to you or any other. I forgive you and all others as I will you forgive me', Spottiswoode, *History*, ii, pp. 278–279; also *C.S.P., Scot.*, vi, p. 22; Hume, *History*, p. 356. Gowrie's comment is in *Bannatyne Miscellany*, i, pp. 101–101, No. 92.

59. *The Maitland Quarto Manuscript*, (ed.) W. A. Craigie, Scot. Text Soc., New Series 9, Edinburgh, 1920, p. 16b.

60. Hume, *History*, p. 383.

61. *Ibid.*, p. 347.

62. Melville, *Memoirs*, p. 36.

63. *Ibid.,* p. 102.

64. *C.S.P., Scot.,* v, p. 498, and see p. 503.

65. *Ibid.,* p. 516.

66. Melville, *Memoirs*, p. 294.

67. *Ibid.,* p. 40; *C.S.P., Scot.,* x, pp. 102 and 575.

68. Melville, *Memoirs*, p. 376.

69. *Ibid.,* pp. 374–375.

70. *Ibid.,* p. 402.

71. Moysie, *Memoirs,* p. 96.

72. Hume, *History,* p. 429.

73. Moysie, *Memoirs,* p. 71; *C.S.P., Scot.,* ix, p. 640.

74. *R.P.C.,* iii, p. 751.

75. *The Diary of Mr James Melvill, 1556-1601,* Bannatyne Club, 34, Edinburgh 1829, pp. 148–49.

76. The ideas expressed here owe much to a lecture I heard Dr. David Starkey give in St. Andrews in 1983, and to the subsequent discussion.

77. *R.P.C. ,* ii, p. 694. The expense appeared to be the main reason, *Ibid.,* pp. 683–684, and *R.P.C.,* iii, pp. 35–36.

78. *R.S.S.R.S.,* vii, p. 391, No. 2384. Murray was appointed with a pension for life.

79. R.P.C., iii, p. 316.

80. *Ibid.,* p. 322, *C.S.P., Scot.,* v, p. 519. Morton was not present at court when this was done, *Ibid.,* p. 511.

81. *Ibid.*

82. *Stirling Castle,* H.M.S.O., 1948, p. 10.

83. *C.S.P., Scot.,* ix, pp. 621, 627, 635 and 638; Moysie, *Memoirs,* p. 72; Spottiswoode, *History,* ii, pp. 390–391.

84. For the careers of these men and others in the household, see Chapter 8. Colonel Stewart used his office as captain of the guard in 1583 to facilitate the king's escape from the Ruthven regime, Calderwood, *History,* iii, pp. 715–716.

85. Melville, *Memoirs,* p. 375.

86. *Ibid.,* pp. 375 and 391. Melville says that the chamber had 'gretest credit with the King his Maiestie' and 'put the chancelar schone out of conceat'.

87. *R.P.C.,* iii, p. 98.

88. *Ibid.,* p. 286.

89. *Ibid.,* p. 326.

90. *Ibid.,* p. 349.

91. *Ibid.,* p. 750.

92. *A.P.S.,* iii, p. 377.

93. *R.P.C.,* iii, pp. 326 and 510–511.

94. *R.P.C.,* iv, p. 522.

95. Hume, *History,* p. 350.

96. Melville, *Memoirs,* pp. 376–377.

97. They were specifically commissioned to do this, *R.P.C.,* iii, p. 758.

98. *C.S.P., Scot.,* xiii, Part 2, p. 618.

99. *R.P.C.,* vi, p. 186.

100. *Ibid.,* p. 862.

101. *Ibid.,* pp. 207–208.

102. *R.P.C.,* vi, p. 317.

103. On the day of his departure for England Mr. Robert Bruce sought an audience with the king, the details of which are of some interest in trying to determine how formalised the Jacobean royal household was, Calderwood, *History*, vi, pp. 217-218.

104. For France, see Harding, *Anatomy of a Power Elite*, pp. 136-137 and 167. For England, see J. Hurstfield, *Freedom, Corruption and Government in Elizabethan Government*, London, 1973; W. MacCaffrey, 'Place and Patronage in Elizabethan Politics', in S. T. Bindoff, J. Hurstfield and C. H. Williams (eds.), *Elizabethan Government and Society*, London, 1961. Also of interest is G. Parker, 'Corruption and Imperialism in the Spanish Netherlands: the case of Francisco de Lixalde, 1567-1612', in G. Parker, *Spain and the Netherlands*, Glasgow, 1979, pp. 152-161. For Europe in general, H. G. Koenigsberger and G. L. Mosse, *Europe in the Sixteenth Century*, London, 1979, pp. 234-237.

105. For a good analysis of corruption in James's English court, see L. L. Peck, 'Corruption at the Court of James I', in B. C. Malament (ed.), *After the Reformation, Essays in Honour of J. H. Hexter*, Manchester, 1980, pp. 75-94. On its importance to particular Jacobean politicians, see L. L. Peck, *Northampton, Patronage and Policy at the Court of James I*, London, 1982, and R. Lockyer, *Buckingham*, New York. 1981.

106. Peck, 'Corruption at the Court of James I', p. 77.

107. Melville, *Memoirs*, p. 259.

108. Hume, *History*, p. 335.

109. See *R.S.S.R.S.*, viii, where between 1581 and 1584 Arran, his wife and other members of his family benefit from a very generous list of gifts in the form of pensions and escheats.

110. Melville, *Memoirs*, p. 326.

111. *Ibid.*, p. 324. Hume also accused Arran of summoning men *super inquerendis,* and outlawing those who failed to appear, while imprisoning those who did until they bought their way out, *History*, p. 378.

112. Melville, *Memoirs*, p. 263.

113. Hume, *History*, p. 400. Robert Bowes had also predicted that Lennox was in danger of doing the same in 1580, annoying others who 'will soon disclaim to have all the fat taken from their beards', *C.S.P., Scot.,* v, p. 243.

114. Melville, *Memoirs*, p. 381.

115. Rollock, *Works*, i, p. 427.

116. Melville, *Memoirs*, p. 413. Melville says that Maitland made the most from the queen's estates, and that at the baptism gifts arrived from all over Europe, 'bot I say that they were schone melted and spendit'. For Huntly's fines, *Ibid.*, p. 224; the highland pledges, *Ibid.*, pp. 391-392; and Bothwell's fall, *Ibid.*, p. 397.

117. Pitcairn, *Kennedy*, pp. 51-52.

118. *Melrose*, i, p. 69.

119. In 'Ane invectione Against Fortun: Conteining ane Admonitione to his Friends at Court' Montgomery writes:

Quhen with a quhisk sho quhirles about her quheill,
Rude is that ratill running with a reill,
Quhill top our tail goes honest men atains.
Then spurgald sporters they begin to speill;
The cadger clims, neu cleikit from the creill;
And ladds uploips to lordships all thair lains:
Doun goes the bravest, brecking all thir bonis.
Sho works hir will; God wot of it be weill,

Sho stottis at strais, syn stumbillis not at stanis.

See *The Poems of Alexander Montgomerie,* (ed.) J. Cranstoun, Scottish Text Society, 9,10,11, Edinburgh, 1855–57, p. 130. See, too, Hume, 'Ane Epistle to Maister Gilbert Mont-creif' in *Poems,* pp. 76–77, and the anonymous 'Suppois I war in court must be', in *The Bannatyne Manuscript,* Hunterian Club, 1846, ii, p. 233. The writer of the *Historie* expressed this same sense of fatalism when he wrote that 'tyme in short space dois exalt men to digneteis and honors, and at another season dryvis thayme to extreme calamitie and miserie, and speciallie thois that hantis the courtis of Princis', *Historie,* p. 252.

120. C. Stocker, 'Office as Maintenance in Renaissance France', in *Canadian Journal of History,* vi, 1971, p. 33.

121. Stone, *The Crisis of the Aristocracy,* p. 217.

122. *Ibid.,* p. 134. Accoding to R. B. Smith, this had been true since the reign of Henry VIII, see *Land and Politics in the Reign of Henry VIII,* Oxford, 1970, p. 133.

123 Houlbrooke, *The English Family,* p. 45.

124. Williamson, *Scottish National Consciousness in the Age of James VI,* p. 134.

125. Melville, *Memoirs,* pp. 275–276.

126. *Ibid.,* p. 406.

127. *Scottish Poetry of the Sixteenth Century,* (ed.) J. Eyre-Todd, Glasgow, 1892, for example, 'Na Kyndnes at Court Without Siller'.

128. Montgomerie, 'The Oppositions of the Court to Conscience' in *Poems,* p. 128:
Syn everie minioun thou man mak
To gar thame think that thou art thairs,
Howbeit thou be behind thair bak
No furtherer of thair effairs.

129. Quoted in Lockyer, *Buckingham,* p. 35. See, too, Flandrin, *Families in Former Times,* p. 48, where he writes that in France 'family solidarities formed the thread of those clienteles which, in their struggles for power, formed the structures of political life'.

130. A. G. R. Smith, *The Emergence of a Nation State, The Commonwealth of England, 1529–1660,* London, 1984, pp. 124–125. See, too, Peck, *Northampton,* Chapter 3, on 'A Jacobean Patronage Network'.

131. For the most recent contribution, M. P. Holt, 'Patterns of *Clientele* and Economic Opportunity at Court during the Wars of Religion: the Household of Francois, Duke of Anjou', in *French Historical Studies,* xiii, No. 3, spring 1984, pp. 305–322. See, too, Harding on brokerage, in *Anatomy of a Power Elite,* pp. 31–37.

132. P. Anderson, *Lineages of the Absolutist State,* London, 1979, pp. 48–49, wrote of the 'colonization by grandee houses competing for the political privileges and economic profits of office, and commanding parasitic clientages of lesser nobles who were infiltrated into the state apparatus and formed rival patronage networks within it'.

133. *Basilikon Doron,* p. 32.

134. Melville, *Memoirs,* p. 380.

135. Moysie, *Memoirs,* p. 33.

136. *C.S.P., Scot.,* x, p. 17.

137. Melville, *Memoirs,* p. 390.

138. *R.P.C.,* iii, p. 549.

139 Waus, *Correspondence,* i, pp. 137 and 140. Such requests were not only in the earlier part of the reign, for example see Sir Andrew Kerr's letter to the clerk of the privy council in 1618, *R.P.C.,* xi, pp. 630–631.

140. For example, see the 1589 bond of friendship, Brown, 'Bonds of Manrent', appendix, p. 548, No. 90.

141. *C.S.P., Scot.*, x, p. 264.

142. Some attempt has been made to do this by J. G. B. Young, Scottish Political Parties, 1573-1603, Edinburgh Ph.D., 1976, but the results are unconvincing.

143. For faction in Tudor and early Stuart England, E. W. Ives, *Faction in Tudor England*, Historical Association, 1979; E. W. Ives, 'Faction at the Court of Henry VIII: The Fall of Anne Boleyn', in *History*, 57, 1972, pp. 169-188; D. Starkey, 'From Feud to Faction, English Politics circa 1450-1550', in *History Today*, 32, November 1982, pp. 16-22; S. Adams, 'Faction, Clientage and Party, English Politics, 1550-1608', in *History Today*, 32, December 1982, pp. 33-39; K. Sharpe (ed.), *Faction and Parliament*, Oxford, 1978.

144. *C.B.P.*, i, p. 298.

145. Syme, *The Roman Revolution*, p. 157: 'Roman political factions were welded together, less by unity of principle than by mutual services (*officia*), either between social equals as an alliance, or from inferior to superior, in a traditional and almost feudal form of clientage: on a favourable estimate the bond was called *amicitia*, otherwise *factio*. Such alliances either presupposed or provoked the personal feud — which to a Roman aristocrat, was a sacred duty or an occasion of just pride.'

146. Balfour, 'Annales', i, p. 364. Morton saw 'new factions to grow amongst the nobilitie, quho much repynned (according to their wounted maner) that they had no hand in the government'. Hume, *History*, p. 341.

147. *Ibid.*, p. 368; Melville, *Memoirs*, pp. 397-398 and 361; Hume, *History*, p. 430.

148. Melville, *Memoirs*, pp. 285, 268 and 358.

149. Moysie, *Memoirs*, p. 44.

150. This was also true elsewhere, for example in Spain where the feud between the duke of Alba and the prince of Eboli 'involved every quarrel over a sheep-run in the power politics of the court of Madrid', H. G. Koenigsberger, 'Western Europe and the Power of Spain', in R. B. Wernham (ed.), *The New Cambridge Modern History, vol. iii, The Counter Reformation and the Price Revolution, 1559-1610*, Cambridge, 1971, p. 243.

151. *Historie*, p. 149.

152. Calderwood, *History*, iii, p. 397; Melville, *Memoirs*, i, p. 264; *Historie*, pp. 148-149; Spottiswoode, *History*, ii, p. 206; Balfour, 'Annales', i, p. 364; Moysie, *Memoirs*, p. 4; Hume, *History*, pp. 341-342; *Spalding Miscellany*, ii, p. 44.

153. S.R.O., Inventory of Scottish Muniments at Haigh, N.R.A., 237/1. box C, Crawford to Ross, 9 May 1578.

154. S.R.O., Invent., Scot., Mun., at Haigh, N.R.A., 237/1. box C, 1578, licensing of Crawford's defence; N.R.A., 237/1, box C, 29 June 1578, royal warrant for surety of Crawford's servants; Pitcairn, *Criminal Trials*, i, Part 2, pp. 79 and 85, the latter of which was on 5 March 1579 when Crawford failed to appear; H.M.C., iii, 'Abercairny M.S.', p. 419, letter from Crawford to the laird of Abercairny asking for attendance at his trial on 3 November 1579; S.R.O., Invent., Scot. Mun. at Haigh, N.R.A., 237/1, box C, 5 November 1579 for the licence; and for evidence that he did go, see the warrant to the lords of justiciary, dated 1580, *R.P.C.*, iii, p. 233, for the assurance.

155. *R.P.C.*, iii, pp. 288 and 457; Hume, *History*, p. 405.

156. *Spalding Miscellany*, iv, 'The Dun Papers', p. 62.

157. Chambers, *Domestic Annals*, i, p. 118.

158. *Estimate*, p. 32.

159. *R.P.C.*, iii, p. 563.

160. He is described as a friend of Lennox's at the latter's fall, *C.S.P., Scot.*, vi, pp. 157 and 159.

161. *C.S.P., Scot.,* vi, p. 477.

162. *R.P.C.,* iii, p. 563.

163. Moysie, *Memoirs,* p. 36. *C.S.P., Scot.,* vi, pp. 566 and 575. When in December Chancellor Argyll opened up his own peace moves between the two men, Arran frustrated them, *Ibid.,* p. 686.

164. He was known to be plotting as early as September 1583, *Ibid.,* p. 597. For the executed Lyon, *C.B.P.,* i, p. 136.

165. Moysie, *Memoirs,* p. 54 and Melville, *Memoirs,* p. 350, relate that Crawford was with Arran at the fall of Stirling. *C.B.P.,* i, p. 215, for warding.

166. *Scots Peerage,* viii, pp. 285–286.

167. *C.B.P.,* i, p. 211; *C.S.P., Scot.,* viii, p. 364; *R.P.C.,* vi. p. 128; Calderwood, *History,* iv, pp. 613–614; *Historie,* p. 228; Moysie, *Memoirs,* p. 63.

168. See Lee, *John Maitland of Thirlestane,* pp. 117–119.

169. *C.S.P., Scot.,* ix, pp. 621, 627, 635, 638 and 647; Moysie, *Memoirs,* p. 71.

170. *C.S.P., Scot.,* ix, p. 640; Moysie, *Memoirs,* p. 71.

171. *C.S.P., Scot.,* x, p. 36; Moysie, *Memoirs,* pp. 74–75. Rumours that Crawford was plotting Glamis's murder had been circulating for over a month before the rebellion, *C.S.P., Scot.,* x, pp. 856–857.

172. *C.S.P., Scot.,* x, p. 58.

173. *Ibid.,* x, p. 102.

174. *Ibid.,* x, p. 459.

175. *C.B.P.,* i, p. 375; *C.S.P., Scot.,* x, p. 469.

176. *C.B.P.,* i, pp. 375–376; *C.S.P., Scot.,* x, p. 468.

177. *C.B.P.,* i, pp. 375–376; *C.S.P., Scot.,* x, p. 468.

178. *C.B.P.,* i, p. 383; *C.S.P., Scot.,* x, p. 590.

179. *C.S.P., Scot.,* x, pp. 592, 595 and 596. For Maitland and Huntly, see below, p. 154.

180. *C.S.P., Scot.,* pp. 595, 598, 600, 602, 608 and 627.

181. *Ibid.,* pp. 653 and 671.

182. They were in dispute again later in the year, *C.B.P.,* i, p. 405; *C.S.P., Scot.,* x, p. 776. Glamis lost the treasurership in 1595.

183. *C.S.P., Scot.,* x, p. 653; xi, pp. 151, 159, 169 and 509.

184. There was a struggle outside Edinburgh tolbooth in 1595 while the king was in the midst of mediating the two, *C.S.P., Scot.,* xi, pp. 517, 519 and 525. From about 1595 the master of Glamis lost the leadership of the Lyon kindred to his nephew, Lord Glamis, with whom he quarrelled, *Ibid.,* pp. 588 and 689. After 1596 the king began to put more pressure on both sides to settle, although he tended to favour Crawford, having never liked Glamis whom he ordered to be unceremoniously dismissed from his seat on the court of session in 1599 for non-attendance, and who was again warded for failing to assure Crawford, *Melrose,* i, p. 1; *C.S.P., Scot.,* xiii, Part 1, p. 497. For crown mediation 1596–99, *R.P.C.,* v, pp. 248, 475, 540 and 551; *C.S.P., Scot.,* xii, p. 142; xiii, Part 1, p. 444; S.R.O., Scot. Invent. at Haigh, N.B.A.m 237/1, box C, 8 June 1598. In 1599 there was further fighting between the two families, *C.S.P., Scot.,* xiii, Part 1, p. 525. In 1600 a servant of Lord Glamis tried to kill Sir John Lindsay of Ballinscho in Edinburgh, and then shot at Lord Glamis himself when he denied any knowledge of the incident. Two weeks later Lord Glamis killed the man, *R.P.C.,* vi, pp. 69, 91 and 239; *C.S.P., Scot.,* xiii, Part 2, pp. 884 and 891; Pitcairn, *Criminal Trials,* ii, p. 386. The last one hears of the feud was in 1602 when Lord Glamis chose exile rather than make peace with Crawford, *R.P.C.,* vi, pp. 311 and 367.

185. *Scots Peerage,* viii, p. 286; iii, p. 31.

186. See Lee, *John Maitland of Thirlestane*, pp. 60–61, and Donaldson, *James V–VII*, p. 191, for brief explanations of this complex issue.

187. *C.S.P., Scot.*, vi, pp. 658 and 666.

188. *Ibid.*, pp. 666 and 675; *R.P.C.*, iii, pp. 616 and 634.

189. *C.S.P., Scot.*, vi, pp. 329–330; Calderwood, *History*, iv, p. 200.

190. Calderwood, *History*, iv, p. 200; Waus, *Correspondence*, ii, pp. 307 and 311–312.

191. *C.B.P.*, i, p. 175.

192. *A.P.S.*, iii, p. 387; *C.B.P.*, i, p. 211; *C.S. P., Scot.*, vii, pp. 203 and 206.

193. *C.B.P.*, i, p. 231; *C.S.P., Scot.*, ix, p. 18.

194. *C.S.P., Scot.*, ix, p. 18; *C.B.P.*, i, pp. 231 and 559–560; S.R.O., R.D. 1/36/27b.

195. Lee, *John Maitland of Thirlestane*, pp. 60–61, comments on Maitland's claim.

196. *C.S.P., Scot.*, ix, p. 507.

197. *Ibid.*, ix, p. 677.

198. *Ibid.*, x, p. 70; Moysie, *Memoirs*, p. 77.

199. *C.S.P., Scot.*, x, pp. 110, 137 and 145.

200. *Ibid.*, pp. 146 and 148.

201. *R.P.C.*, iv, p. 423.

202. *C.S.P., Scot.*, x, pp. 273 and 279; *C.B.P.*, i, p. 353. Though not before there had been another clash between them at Leith, *C.S.P., Scot.*, x, p. 846.

203. *C.S.P., Scot.*, x, pp. 285 and 494; Melville, *Memoirs*, p. 373.

204. *C.S.P., Scot.*, x, pp. 307, 312, 365, 411, 413 and 494; S.R.O., Bruce of Earlshall Muniments, G.D., 247/180/1.

205. *C.S.P., Scot.*, x, pp. 536, 543, 546, 548 and 550; *C.B.P.*, i, p. 381; Spottiswoode, *History*, ii, p. 413; Moysie, *Memoirs*, p. 86.

206. *C.S.P., Scot.*, x, pp. 554–555 and 559; *R.P.C.*, iv, pp. 649, 662, 666 and 668; *C.B.P.*, i, p. 383; S.R.O., Lauderdale Muniments, N.R. A., 832/78.

207. The killing was actually done by other Humes. Spottiswoode, *History*, ii, pp. 417–419; *R.P.C.*, iv, p. 677; *C.S.P., Scot.*, x, pp. 572, 575 and 584; xiii, Part 2, p. 659; Melville, *Memoirs*, p. 397; *Historie*, p. 243.

208. In fact their rescue may have been responsible for the failure of the principal object of the raid, Moysie, *Memoirs*, p. 87; *Historie*, p. 243; Melville, *Memoirs*, p. 397; Birrel, 'Diary', p. 26.

209. *C.S.P., Scot.*, x, pp. 608, 741 and 781; xi, pp. 19 and 82. Bothwell was forfeited by parliament in June.

210. Spottiswoode, *History*, ii, p. 434; *C.S.P., Scot.*, xi, pp. 159–160; *C.B.P.*, i, p. 488; Birrel, 'Diary', p. 30.

211. *C.S.P., Scot.*, xi, pp. 170 and 188; *C.B.P.*, i, pp. 498 and 492; Moysie, *Memoirs*, p. 105. At this time Hume and Maitland also settled their differences over the teinds of Lauder kirk, S.R.O., R.D., 1/44/365b/ (380), R.D., 1/44/365b/(389b).

212. *C.S.P., Scot.*, xi, p. 188.

213. *C.B.P.*, i, pp. 523–525 and 525–527; *C.S.P., Scot.*, xi, p. 304; Spottiswoode, *History*, ii, p. 448.

214. *C.S.P., Scot.*, xi, pp. 284, 301, 369, 439 and 444.

215. *R.P.C.*, v, p. 137; *C.S.P., Scot.*, xi, pp. 536 and 541.

216. Spottiswoode, *History*, ii, p. 461.

217. *Ibid; C.S.P., Scot.*, xiii, Part 2, pp. 1029 and 1007; Moysie *Memoirs*, i, p. 122; *Melrose*, i, pp. 370–372. For an interesting discussion of a quite different aspect of Bothwell's career, see E. Cowan, 'The Darker Vision of the Scottish Renaissance: The

Devil and Francis Stewart', in I. B. Cowan and D. Shaw (eds.), *The Renaissance and Reformation in Scotland,* Edinburgh, 1983, pp. 125–140.

218. *C.S.P., Scot.,* xi, pp. 488 and 494–495, and see Lee's comments, *John Maitland of Thirlestane,* p. 285.

219. *C.S.P., Scot.,* xi, p. 545.

220. *Ibid.,* p. 567; Lee, *John Maitland of Thirlestane,* pp. 286–287.

221. *C.S.P., Scot.,* xi, p. 488.

222. Spottiswoode, *History,* ii, p. 465; *Historie,* pp. 546–547.

223. *C.S.P., Scot.,* xi, pp. 575 and 584.

224. *Historie,* p. 346.

225. *Historie,* pp. 346–347; *C.S.P., Scot.,* xi, pp. 624, 625 and 637.

226. For the Livingstons, *R.P.C.,* ii, p. 660, and the Elphinstones, *Scots Peerage,* iii, p. 537; *C.S.P., Scot.,* xii, p. 20.

227. *C.S.P., Scot.,* xi, pp. 584, 625 and 627.

228. *Ibid.,* pp. 630 and 625.

229. *Historie,* pp. 346–347; *C.S.P., Scot.,* xi, pp. 631 and 636–637; Spottiswoode, *History,* ii, p. 465.

230. *C.S.P., Scot.,* xi, p. 641.

231. *Ibid.,* p. 654.

232. *Ibid.,* pp. 579 and 690.

233. *C.S.P., Scot.,* xiii, Part 2, pp. 11 and 20.

234. *Report of the Historical Manuscripts Commission on the Manuscripts of the Earl of Mar and Kellie,* London, 1904, p. 45.

235. *Ibid.*

236. *Ibid.,* Dunipace did not, however, admit his guilt.

237. *C.S.P., Scot.,* xiii, Part 1, p. 33.

238. *H.M.C., Mar and Kellie,* p. 44.

239. *C.S.P., Scot.,* xii, pp. 79 and 88; *R.P.C.,* v, p. 242.

240. *C.S.P., Scot.,* xii, p. 92.

241. *Ibid.,* pp. 95–96, 97, 99–100, 101 and 114.

242. *R.P.C.,* v, p. 248.

243. *C.S.P., Scot.,* xii, p. 100.

244. *Ibid.,* pp. 101, 114 and 123.

245. *Ibid.,* pp. 123, 136 and 163.

246. *R.P.C.,* v, p. 303; *H.M.C., Mar and Kellie,* p. 46.

247. *R.P.C.,* v, p. 288.

248. For the earliest stages of this, *C.S.P., Scot.,* xii, pp. 240 and 282. Local difficulties, however, did remain, and another Bruce appears to have been killed in 1598, forcing Bruce of Clackmannan to withdraw his support from Mar as it had been given 'sa lang as ane Bruce was not in the feild or thair bluid spiltt', *H.M.C., Mar and Kellie,* p. 47.

249, *C.S.P., Scot.,* xiii, Part 1, pp. 214, 217 and 220; *C.B.P.,* ii, p. 538; and see below, pp. 241–242.

250. For details of the negotiations from June 1598 to April 1599, *C.S.P., Scot.,* xiii, Part 1, pp. 242, 278, 292, 362, 369, 375, 395, 404, 419, 422, 423 and 444. What looks like part of an assythment appears in S.R.O., Miscellaneous Accessions, G.D., 1/529/53. Tensions were briefly raised again over Falkirk in 1600, *C.S.P., Scot.,* xiii, Part 2, p. 726. For the clandestine return of one of the killers in 1609, *H.M.C., Various,* v, 'Duntreath M.S.', p. 114.

251. Montgomerie, *Poems,* p. 93. Morton had practised similar politics in the 1570s, see Randolph's comment that he 'nourishes discords' for private reasons, *C.S.P., Scot.,* v, p. 274.

# 6

# *Court and Locality: the Huntly–Moray Feud*

The murder of the 'Bonnie Earl of Moray' on 7 February 1592 was one of the great *causes célèbres* of James VI's reign. Yet the feud which was the reason for that killing had a significance far beyond that suggested by the romantic ballad which immortalised the relatively unimportant Moray. His killer, the 6th earl of Huntly, was the greatest magnate in Scotland, a close friend of James VI, and, after 1588, the leading catholic nobleman in Scotland. His determination to carry through a Counter Reformation, or at least to achieve the recognition of catholic freedom of conscience, involved him in continuous plotting with Spain and in three rebellions during the height of his feud with Moray and his friends. Huntly's great court influence also brought him into competition with the major court politicians, Chancellor Maitland, Treasurer Glamis and the earl of Bothwell, Moray's Stewart kinsmen. Finally, as a great territorial lord in north-eastern Scotland, and as lieutenant of the north, he enjoyed the power of a regional prince. That in itself brought Huntly into conflict with neighbouring lords like the earl of Atholl, another Stewart, and the earl of Argyll with whom he shared the government of the highlands. The tentacles of power which Huntly controlled were far-reaching, and the complex web of friends and enemies at the centre of which he sat meant that the exercise of that power sent tremors far beyond the boundaries of his own lands. The feud with Moray was in its origins a local concern, but because locality and court were so interwoven, especially where someone of Huntly's stature was involved, its implications went far beyond a quarrel over fishing rights on the River Spey. The feud, therefore, came to be about much more than local politics; its outcome would determine control of the highlands, and dominance of the court and of royal offices, and it embraced the struggle between the forces of the Counter Reformation and the protestant, largely pro-English interests within Scotland.

The local political background to this feud lay in the instability in the highlands created by the temporary weakening of the two families the crown had used to govern the highlands since the mid-fifteenth century. The Campbell earldom of Argyll, whose earls controlled most of north-west Scotland, sank into a divisive minority in 1584 during which the Campbells drifted 'the closest they ever came to fragmentation'.[1] In the east the death of the 4th earl of Huntly in 1562 while in rebellion against Queen Mary, and of the 5th earl in 1576 after defeat in the civil war, had shaken the power of the Gordons. The assassination of the Regent Moray in 1570 ended the threat he posed to Gordon hegemony in the building up of the Moray earldom, but his ambitions were to be revived in the 1580s by others who had been encouraged by this demonstration of Gordon vulnerability.[2] It was this belief that the Gordons could be successfully challenged, and the determination of the 6th earl of Huntly to restore the power of his family which lay at the root of his feud with his neighbours.

In spite of these setbacks George Gordon, 6th earl of Huntly, inherited at the age of fourteen the most powerful earldom in Scotland. Educated as a catholic in France, he returned home in the early 1580s where he quickly identified himself with the conservative Lennox and Arran regimes, and established himself as a major figure at court. By 1587 it was being said of him that he was 'indeid ane greit curteour and knawis mair of the Kingis secreittis nor ony man at this present doithe', and that he 'lay in his hienes chalmer', a privilege bestowed only on the closest of the king's intimates.[3] Even after his treasonable dealings with Spain became known six months later, James's 'extraordinary affection to Huntly' remained, and the earl could 'persuade his majesty to any matters to serve his own particular or friends'.[4] Such favouritism brought Huntly marriage to the 2nd duke of Lennox's sister, the vice-chamberlaincy, which gave him effective control of the chamber during Lennox's minority, the commendatorship of the lucrative abbey of Dunfermline, and in 1589 the captaincy of the guard.[5] With such unrival!ed influence in the chamber and at court, and with his enormous regional power, which included the lieutenancy of the north, he was in a position of strength which made him second only to the king.

When making excuses for Huntly after the 1589 rebellion, the king said he was 'but young, merry, disinterested in matters of state', and 'easily led to evil or good'.[6] This appearance of carelessness may have been cultivated; in 1583 Hay had noted that Huntly had been 'slowe to engage himself in any faction or quarrel of state' until he had consolidated his power base in the north and at court where he concentrated on his relationship with the king, 'to whose humor he dothe wholly blende and apply himself'.[7] Therefore allegations that he was 'shallow witted', and 'a most semple man' who was only saved from himself by 'shrewed counsellors ... whose advice he follows' seem doubtful.[8] He was, however, 'hot and hardy',[9] and while this rarely took the form of personal bravado, Huntly made good and frequent use of the force which was his to command. The bloody reputation he acquired and the tight security with which he surrounded himself were only one side of the man, that of the archetypal warring magnate, but he was also a man of educated and sophisticated tastes, with a deep personal commitment to catholicism.[10]

In contrast James Stewart, 2nd earl of Moray, was lacking in either conviction or in any understanding of the responsibilities of lordship. He had appeared at court at much the same time as Huntly, having been a client of Arran. It was this powerful patron who secured for the younger son of Lord Doune, himself a recent arrival to nobility, the wardship and marriage of the daughters of the late Regent Moray. By marrying the eldest daughter himself, James Stewart acquired the earldom of Moray which he shared with his wife.[11] The story of his physical attractiveness had substance to it, and he was described as 'the maist wirlyke man bayth in curage and person, for he was a cumlie personage, of a great stature and strang of bodie lyk a kemp'.[12] His personality was less agreeable, and he was a gambler with heavy debts, his marital relations were strained, and his lordship was poor and often absentee.[13] While he was deeply envious of Huntly, he could never hope to match him, his power being 'not comparable to the uther, as all men knawis'.[14]

Map of Scotland showing the distribution of power among
the principals of the Huntly - Moray feud.

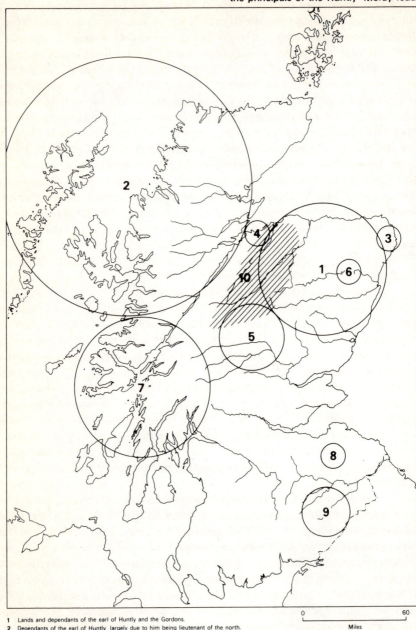

0        60

Miles

1   Lands and dependants of the earl of Huntly and the Gordons.
2   Dependants of the earl of Huntly, largely due to him being lieutenant of the north.
3   Lands and influence of the earl of Errol.
4   Lands and influence of the earl of Moray.
5   Lands and dependants of the earl of Atholl.
6   Lands and influence of Lord Forbes.
7   Lands and dependants of the earl of Argyll and the Campbells.
8   Lands and influence of the earl of Bothwell.
9   Influence of the earl of Bothwell, largely due to him being keeper of Liddisdale.
10  Region of greatest conflict in which were the lands of those clans who changed sides during the feud.

The rivalry between Huntly and Moray arose over the common issue of lands and their profits. This concerned an old dispute over the Moray earldom which Huntly's grandfather had been granted in 1548, but which was lost to Lord James Stewart fifteen years later.[15] Closely bound up with this was the bishopric of Moray. Moray and his wife had succeeded in getting their hands on certain pensions from the fruits of the diocese, but were frustrated in their ambitions to enlarge on these when in 1584 Huntly drew up a contract with the bishop in which he offered his protection in return for the pensions Moray was seeking.[16] Further entangled in this was the lordship of Spynie with its lands and castle, and the rich Spey fishings. The quarrel over the fishings had been going on between the Gordons and the Regent Moray's widow since the 1570s, and in 1586 it was still Dame Annas Keith who was involved in litigation with Huntly. The legal tussle continued, but that year also saw the Gordons killing two of Moray's servants on Speyside,[17] and the summoning of the countess of Moray to have her titles to Spynie reduced.[18] By then relations between the two earls had already reached the point where the differences between them were unlikely to be settled in a court of law.

South-west of Huntly's domain lay the lands of John Stewart, 5th earl of Atholl. He was another young and ambitious nobleman, and although described as 'a man of lyttle valuer or accompte',[19] he could still put a large number of men in the field. He too had exploited the difficulties of the Gordons, and had attracted the support of Mackintosh of Dunnachtan away from Huntly.[20] However, throughout the 1580s Huntly exchanged bonds of manrent and maintenance with a long list of lords and chiefs throughout the north-east and the highlands in an impressive reconstruction of Gordon power.[21] Many of these were men traditionally dependent upon the earls of Huntly, or fairly independent highland chiefs who thought it wise policy to at least recognise the primacy of the king's lieutenant, if not of Huntly himself. Others were discontented with their own lords, and of these the Campbell lairds of Lochnell and Glenorchy, who had been ousted from the management of Argyll by the lairds of Ardkinglass and Cawdor, were the most important. While that had implications for the future, the switch from Atholl's lordship to Huntly's by Drummond of Blair on the grounds that the former was not taking him into his confidence had more immediate results.[22] In 1587 Atholl sent raiding parties against Drummond and Menzies of Wemyss, who he thought should also be within his sphere of influence, in an effort to woo them back to his protection. Huntly responded to this by outlawing the raiders, both lords began levying their forces, and when an order arrived from the king telling them to settle by law, Huntly refused to give assurance, and insisted on his rights to deal with the matter in his own courts. That was to be the tone adopted in all Huntly's local affairs, and, not wanting any confrontation, the privy council oversaw a hastily arranged arbitration which found in his favour.[23]

At the same time as he was establishing his authority throughout the highlands, Huntly was embarking upon more grandiose schemes. In May 1586 he wrote to Philip II offering his services, and from then until the Armada two years later his activities were the subject of speculation in Spain, England and throughout

Scotland.[24] Although Lord Maxwell continued to be seen as the leading catholic nobleman in Scotland, his defeats in 1587-88 and Huntly's growing power made the latter more and more the focus of catholic hopes. In February 1588 he was one of the principal figures in a move to bring down Chancellor Maitland, Treasurer Glamis, and those other government figures who had secured their positions in the 1585 coup.[25] Discontent with their rule was the ostensible reason for the demonstration that Huntly and his friends manufactured, but as a catholic agent later informed Mendoza, 'Reform in the administration is now the professed aim of all our enterprise, until the arrival of your support enables us to promote openly the Catholic religion'.[26] What the Scottish catholics did not know was that Philip II had already concluded that 'the necessary forces are not now in hand', and Spanish policy towards them was largely to string them along in the hope that the arrival of the occasional agent or subsidy would maintain enthusiasm.[27] When Huntly went north to prepare his defences for a Spanish landing, the groundwork had been laid for a catholic rebellion, and while Huntly and his northern allies were able to prevent the premature fiasco which ruined Lord Maxwell in the south, they were unable, as Parma himself observed, to maintain their preparedness after the failure of the Armada.[28]

Whatever suspicions the king harboured about Huntly, it made no difference to their relationship, and in fact James's own equivocal diplomacy encouraged catholic aspirations in Scotland. Early in 1589 he appointed the earl to the captaincy of the guard, but shortly afterwards letters from Huntly and other catholic earls to Parma were brought from England to the king. Huntly was deprived of the captaincy, and arrested and warded, but the affair was not treated very seriously by James, who was more hurt than angered by Huntly's duplicity, and the earl was freed and restored to favour eight days later, on 14 March.[29] Protestant neurosis reached new heights at this, and Chancellor Maitland in particular was both furious and frightened. However, there was no St. Bartholomew Day Massacre, and instead both Huntly and the earl of Errol tried to persuade James to go north with them, and lead an army against his own government of which they argued the king had been a prisoner since 1585. James refused, and they parted amicably, his friendship with Huntly still being such that 'the wourld thinkes he is bewitched with him'.[30] Once in the north, Huntly, Errol and Crawford came out in open rebellion, while in the south Bothwell attempted a simultaneous insurrection. Bothwell's ambitions had little to do with those of the catholic earls, being more concerned with the removal of Chancellor Maitland, but his supporters were unenthusiastic, and the rebellion collapsed almost immediately. The northern earls had more success, were able to occupy Perth and Aberdeen, capture Treasurer Glamis, and field a larger army than the king when he marched against them. However, apart from Errol the rebels had no wish to fight James, and on 17 April they decided to capitulate. The Brig O' Dee rebellion, as it came to be known, was over.[31]

If the campaign of the rebellion was characterised by shadow boxing, the punishment of the principal rebels continued the charade. The king was publicly critical of Huntly's judgement, but of little else, and their friendship endured, while the nobility either pleaded his case as kinsmen and allies, or were 'affrayde to tacke him in blud' and risk feud with the Gordons. He was also protected by Glamis whose life he had saved from Crawford, and who saw the opportunity of getting Huntly's support against Maitland. When faced with the charges against him, Huntly simply pleaded guilty to them all, being fully confident of what the king's will would be, and after a short period in ward he was freed. All that had been lost was the lieutenancy of the north, and by July he was again dominating the court.[32] Of the others, Errol was pardoned, Crawford admitted some of the charges against him and was found guilty of the remainder by assize but was granted a remission, and only Bothwell proved intransigent, denying all accusations, but being found guilty by assize. His reputation as 'a bloody man infected with all notiryous vyces' was now well established, but Maitland now needed him to counter the threat from Glamis and Huntly, and, like Huntly, he was freed but without a pardon 'to hold them in awe'. Policy also affected these decisions, and Lord Maxwell, who had been in ward since his rebellion in 1588, was freed, thus letting both England and the church know that James would not be a prisoner of their ambitions, but was prepared to be conciliatory towards his catholic subjects.[33]

This setback for Huntly was clearly a great opportunity for Moray, who remained loyal to the king without actually joining the royal army. When Huntly had first been warded in March over the Parma correspondence, Moray had moved quickly to have him horned, although the messenger who executed the letters was fortunate to escape from Banff alive. The Gordon response to this was to begin raiding Moray's lands, and his servants were soon writing him complaining letters about what they were having to endure from 'limmerers' who were exploiting his continual absence. Furthermore, not only was Moray away from home, but his bailie could not be found, and his chamberlain would not take responsibility for such affairs until he and his family had been guaranteed protection.[34] Clearly Moray was failing in his lordship by leaving his people to face the Gordons while he dallied at court. Even there he achieved little, failing to capitalise on Huntly's defeat. By June Huntly had moved onto the offensive on both fronts. Moray's servants were driven from Speyside, their fishing cobbles were smashed, an attack on Darnaway itself was feared, and one servant felt indignant enough to write to his master telling him that 'The country is masterless at present'.[35] Huntly had also secured bonds of manrent from Mackintosh of Dunnachtan and Innes of Innermarky, and had renewed his bond of friendship with Errol.[36] At the same time the legal case against Moray was driven home, and the beleaguered earl was warded in Stirling Castle facing a complete rout at the hands of his over-mighty rival.[37]

That Moray's feud with Huntly was able to survive beyond the summer of 1589 was due entirely to the intervention of the earl of Bothwell in his affairs. While Huntly and Bothwell had been allies in the rebellion in the spring, they had been rivals only months before that, 'even to stabbing and shooting one another', and they quickly reverted to that position.[38] Now an ally of Maitland, Bothwell had his aspirations rewarded in the autumn when he and Lord Hamilton were left in

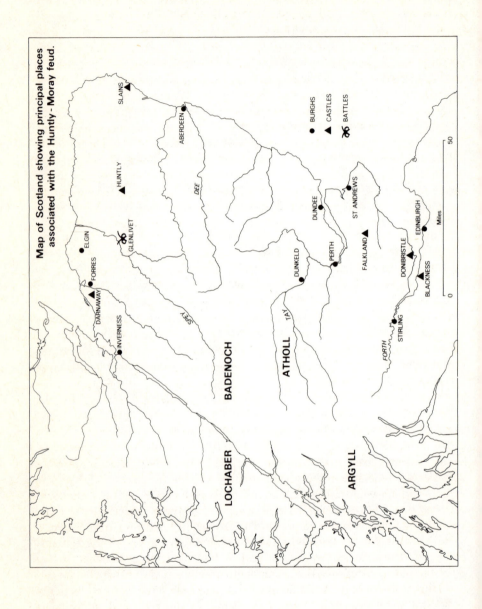

Map of Scotland showing principal places associated with the Huntly - Moray feud.

● BURGHS
▲ CASTLES
✕ BATTLES

effective control of the government while the king and his chief officers of state left for Denmark to complete James's marriage.[39] This recognition of his kinship with the king was what Bothwell had wanted since 1585, and coming within months of his rebellion it represented a considerable breakthrough for him, but he knew very well that the king remained suspicious, that his alliance with the chancellor was likely to be temporary, and that his failure to secure much support from among his own dependants during the rebellion had seriously exposed the shallowness of his lordship. Having been grafted onto the old Hepburn earldom, Bothwell lacked a kindred of his own to form the nucleus of a following, and while he could do little about that in his locality, he was determined to use his enhanced influence to create a Stewart faction at court. Apart from a few business transactions between them, relations between Bothwell and Moray appear to have been restricted to meeting at court, and there is no sign of any political affinity before the winter of 1589-90. Then in November 1589 Bothwell went to the home of another Stewart earl, to Atholl, to discuss mediating between Moray and Huntly. He returned in the spring when Huntly's side made it clear that they were not interested. However, he was able 'to complete the band amongst the Stewarts against Huntly', which appears to have been his real intention anyway, as his interference in the feuds between Huntly and Moray and between Errol and Atholl left them 'vorse nor he founde it'.[40] This new alliance of Bothwell, Atholl and Moray united Huntly's court and local enemies against him, and with both the king and Maitland absent, the threat they represented was a very powerful one indeed.

Moray now had the court backing he needed to strike back at Huntly, and Bothwell himself 'pretendeth some interest' in the questions related to the Moray bishopric and the Spey fishings. When Huntly failed to respond to summons, letters of horning and treason were issued against him, and when the king returned home in May, it was widely expected that he 'proposed to shew Murray — being a Steward — all the favour he can'.[41] In fact James was not at all happy at the prospect of a strong Stewart faction, and within days of his return Huntly obtained a summons against Moray and his wife, and had their own letters against him suspended.[42] Moray was once more paralysed into inaction, and his wife, who was in the north drumming up support for him, wrote warning that his neglect could seriously damage their cause.[43] Another worried kinsman wrote informing him of the activities of his enemies, urging him to 'strain every nerve for success in this present business' which would either establish his authority or ruin him.[44] It was the countess, however, who continued the legal struggle with Huntly, desperately trying to prevent him from having the authority of the law behind his actions in the locality.[45]

At court the king's return with his new wife did not interrupt the factional scheming. Bothwell tried, without success, to draw Maitland more closely to him by a bond of friendship, and then made another foray into the north to see the earl of Caithness whom he tried to draw into his alliance against the Gordons.[46] Huntly and Errol were meanwhile busy with their own dealings, and in the most important of these Huntly settled the question of Spynie Castle by granting it to the latest royal favourite and his own client, Alexander Lindsay, who paid his debts by giving the earl his bond of manrent, and recognising his rights to certain fruits of the bishopric which went with it.[47] Throughout the summer and autumn of 1590 both sides continued to strengthen their factions, and then on 7 December Maitland wrote that there was a 'broyll fallen out in the north', and that it had 'set the whole north in twoe partes, having taken armes on both sydis'.[48]

The roots of this outbreak of violence lay in the tension between the Gordons and the Grants. The Grants and their chief, Grant of Freuchie, were dependants of Huntly, but in 1587 one of Freuchie's kinsmen had been killed by the Gordons of Lesmoir, and another Grant was murdered by some of the outlaws in Huntly's employ 'be hinging of him be the bagstanes, binding of his heid and feitt together in the cruik, smuking of him to the deid'.[49] Huntly's failure to deal justly with the Grants' complaints left them bitter at this, and dissatisfied with the earl's lordship. The Lesmoir Gordons were again involved in persuading the Gordon widow of the late Grant of Ballindalloch to marry the brother of Gordon of Cluny, and to begin vying with John Grant, tutor of Ballindalloch, for control of the estates. Eventually, in October 1590, this led to the killing of a Gordon servant by the tutor who then appealed to his chief for protection, while the Gordons turned to Huntly for justice.[50]

Similar undercurrents of unease existed in Huntly's relationship with another north-east neighbour, Mackintosh of Dunnachtan. During the civil war the Mackintosh chief had joined the king's party against the Gordons, and had been rewarded for it, but he had also supported the 5th earl of Huntly against the Forbes.[51] In 1580 Mackintosh broke with his overlord and bonded with Atholl.[52] By 1583, however, he was in trouble for ravaging the surrounding countryside, and Moray was given a commission to oppress the clan,[53] and it may have been this which persuaded him to return to Huntly in 1586.[54] This soon brought unwanted interference in his affairs, and while the bond with Huntly was renewed in 1589, he quarrelled with the earl over the latter's building of a castle in Badenoch which was too close to his own lands, and which he obstructed by refusing to fulfil terms of vassalage in supplying men and materials.[55]

A third neighbour was John Campbell of Cawdor who by the spring of 1590 had defeated the rival Campbell lairds to assume control of the Argyll earldom. He was reputedly a client of Maitland's 'from whome he receaved instructions to inginder differences of warrs betuein Huntley and Murray', although there is little direct evidence of this.[56] Huntly had been backing the other Campbell lairds against Cawdor, having accepted bonds of manrent from Glenorchy and Lochnell, and Maitland certainly used these tactics elsewhere, but Cawdor's part in the politics of the north-east remains shadowy.[57]

On hearing that Huntly had responded to the appeal from the Gordons by using his shrieval authority to issue commissions against the tutor of Ballindalloch and seizing Ballindalloch house, Grant of Freuchie and Cawdor decided on collective action against him.[58] On 5 November, three days after Ballindalloch was taken, they met at Forres where they were joined by Mackintosh, Atholl, Moray, Lord Fraser and a number of other barons and lairds from Moray and Nairn. While the Dunbar lairds present argued against opposing Huntly, 'shewing how hard it was for any faction in these partis to resist Huntley', pressure was put on Atholl and Moray to assume the leadership of a new alliance against him, 'haveing at this tyme so great a partie, and being so weill freinded at court'.[59] They were hardly likely to refuse this, and a bond was drawn up amongst them all providing for mutual assistance, but not including the Dunbars, or Mackintosh who came to a separate agreement with Freuchie a week later.[60]

It was a further two weeks before Huntly responded with a raid at Baweny where he narrowly missed capturing his rivals who fled from there to Moray's castle at Darnaway.[61] Huntly paused to gather a few hundred more men, seized control of Elgin where he had the cathedral fortified, and arrived at Darnaway on 24 November.[62] His men approached the castle noisily, and began riding around it, shouting and letting off shots, and provoking a short exchange of fire in which Gordon of Cluny's brother was fatally wounded, 'shot in the mouthe throw the craig'.[63] Seeing that Moray would not surrender to the commission which he had from the privy council, and lacking the equipment to storm the castle, Huntly withdrew across the Spey, followed at a distance by a growing and increasingly confident force led by the Stewart earls.[64]

Sporadic fighting followed, but it was of a minor nature as both sides had received instructions from the king, and were hastening to obey them. Huntly's rapid retreat from Darnaway appears to have been in response to the receipt of letters cancelling his commission to arrest John Grant, ordering his forces to disperse, and commanding him to ward in St. Andrews. His rivals were also ordered to discharge their men and to ward in Perth.[65] By 30 November 1590 Huntly had reached Perth himself, and intended to go straight to court with his complaints, although the chancellor was sure that he would ward in St. Andrews and would face examination by the privy council. If his activities were found to be offensive, he 'will with all severitye be demeaned and used be his majestie as one who has most heighlye offended against his owne crowne and person'.[66] Maitland's letter to Lord Burghley was, however, intended to assure the English who were nervous of Huntly's imminent arrival, and there was little thought of punishment by James or his chancellor.[67] By the middle of December Huntly, Atholl and Moray were all in Edinburgh with substantial followings, where an attempt by the king to negotiate a quick settlement foundered due to the death of Cluny's brother, and the most that could be done was to demand caution from the principals involved in the Darnaway incident.[68]

Court politics once again intervened. Huntly's wife succeeded in having his caution suspended for fifteen days, which enraged the Stewarts who accused the privy council of partiality and of allowing Huntly the opportunity to take his revenge. The countess's brother, the duke of Lennox, also supported Huntly, but was persuaded to change sides after 'being sharpelie said to by Bothwell and wiselie advised by other freindes' that his first loyalty was to the Stewarts. Bothwell had 'taken part with Murray and Atholl before the King and the Council and in the streets', and had so packed Edinburgh with his friends and supporters that Huntly had to have an escort provided by the burgh magistrats when moving to and from court. For their part Atholl and Moray lobbied Bowes for English backing, which they got, and by mid-January James had received Elizabeth's advice on the matter. Following their local triumph the Stewarts were confident of further success, and their friends were boasting that Huntly 'shall hardlie remayne in his hous or contrye'.[69]

It was an empty boast. Since the beginning of the crisis in November, Chancellor Maitland had been worried that Glamis would be the one to achieve a settlement of the feud at a time when his own relations with the king were less warm than they had been for some time. He therefore approached Huntly himself, and the earl was only too glad to exploit the opportunity. Seeing the possibility of a reconciliation between his favourite magnate and his valuable chancellor, James encouraged them. Huntly appears to have received a remission for his treason in 1589, a bond of friendship was agreed by them at 'the King's express command' and was kept by James, Errol was reconciled with Maitland, and Huntly 'had great court and all doune at his plesour'.[70] Thus when the privy council debated the matter, his friends there carried the day, and it was agreed that he should be allowed home while Moray and Atholl were restrained at court, the chancellor having 'promysed to the said erle that advantage upon his enemy'.[71] Furthermore, while Atholl, Moray, Freuchie and a large number of other northern barons and lairds were exempted from all of Huntly's commissions on 20 January, their interpretation of the raid on Darnaway was rejected, and the officer who claimed that Huntly's commission had been suspended before that event was deprived of his post for falsely executing and endorsing his letters.[72] Huntly's alliance with the chancellor had paid off, and he kept up Maitland's gratitude by remaining friendly towards Glamis 'whereby Huntlay gayneth no little profitt betwixt them'.[73]

In contrast, the Stewarts were becoming frustrated by Huntly's freedom in the north where he had returned during January, and by the success of his friends at court.[74] A meeting with Bothwell at Kelso early in February brought no results, and they lost the support of Lennox whom the king tried to employ as a mediator, a part for which he had 'greater desire than power'.[75] Denied access to the king, Atholl and Moray were fed reports of Huntly's gathering strength in the north where a large number of lords assured him of their support, and where he acquired the bond of Cameron of Lochiel to attack Moray and his friends from the west.[76] They were also convinced of the king's partiality, and that he had granted Huntly a commission against them,[77] but when in mid-February they were finally permitted to leave court they still thought their alliance 'strong enough for Huntlay and all his forces in case the King shall stand indifferent betwixt them'.[78] Once in the north, they began to raise their forces at Forres, not far from Huntly's main strength which had been gathered around Spynie Castle and Elgin, and which had been ravaging the surrounding countryside.[79] No real fighting was recorded before the privy council's order of 15 March that Huntly should remain on the east bank of the Spey, Moray on the west bank of the Findhorn, and Atholl in the south. Both sides were again to find caution and come to Edinburgh within ten days to try once more to negotiate a settlement.[80] What brought about this decision is unknown, although it was probably due to a feeling that Huntly had had his chance to avenge the killing and dishonour at Darnaway, and the time had now come to calm the situation. Certainly that was the effect, and the principals returned to court where Huntly channelled his energies into the legal prosecution of John Gordon's killers.[81]

By then a more serious issue had overtaken court politics when on 15 April 1591 Bothwell was accused of conspiring against the king with a number of witches. From the start Bothwell insisted that it was all a plot to ruin him, and while there are good grounds for believing that Bothwell had an interest in sorcery, the entire episode looks deeply suspicious.[82] Whatever the explanation, Bothwell had been ensnared, and it was time for his friends and clients to start paying their dues. Up until March Bothwell had still been working in Atholl's and Moray's interests,[83] and on 27 May he wrote to Moray from imprisonment in Edinburgh Castle asking him to be present at his trial when he expected to prove his innocence.[84] Moray wrote his reply on 18 June, politely refusing, and on the same day he wrote to Maitland telling him of his decision, but offering a quite different excuse.[85] Three days later the chancellor visited Bothwell and suggested he might go into exile, a proposal the earl promised to consider, but that night he escaped from the castle with suspicious ease, thus completing his disgrace, and reducing himself to outlawry.

At the time no-one could know that Bothwell's fall would be permanent, and so its effects on the remainder of the Stewart faction were not immediate. In spite of his protestations to Bothwell about being unable to be in Edinburgh, Moray was in the burgh days after the earl's escape when he struck one of Huntly's servants in the tolbooth.[86] His friends even had some success at the end of the month when Grant of Freuchie persuaded the privy council that Huntly wanted 'na thing ellis bot the wrak and ruyne of the said complenar and his hous', and a commission Huntly held was suspended.[87] However, Huntly had realised the significance of Bothwell's fall immediately it occurred in April,[88] and in July he simultaneously launched a legal and an actual attack against Moray's Spey fishings.[89] A letter from one of Moray's servants at around the same time virtually accused him of neglect and incompetence. This man, John Leslie, had captured two of Lord Spynie's men who had been oppressing Moray's tenants, Spynie being a close friend of Huntly's, but he had been unable to have them executed because Moray had forgotten to leave the appropriate commission, and now the two were to be released on caution. Leslie told Moray that he was so bad at communicating that it was little wonder he was badly served, and he asked for a number of hagbutts to be sent north as they were in great need of them.[90]

Huntly needed no lessons in the responsibilities of lordship, and in July he was back at court trying to get his lieutenancy restored. While he was again 'a very great courtier', the king continued to follow the advice of those who said he would simply abuse this to crush Atholl and Moray, and the royal signature was withheld.[91] Huntly did, however, succeed in overturning the council's decision in Grant of Freuchie's favour.[92] The implications of Bothwell's removal from the court were now becoming more apparent, and early in September Atholl was warded after he was accused of harbouring the earl.[93] It was probably that association between Huntly's enemies and the rebel Bothwell which finally persuaded the king to give him back the lieutenancy of the north.[94]

During September and October of 1591 the feud in the north reached an unprecedented level of violence after Huntly's men initiated fresh attacks principally against the Grants and Mackintoshes. 'Blood is drawn dailly in the north', wrote Bowes, and 'More blood will be drawn unless the king prevent it', but James had no interest in preventing it, having accepted Huntly's offers, made in August, to serve the king against his rebels in return for the lieutenancy.[95] Scores of dead were claimed on both sides, and these may have been exaggerated, but in a claim made by Moray's son years later the losses sustained in just one raid by Huntly's MacDonnell clients from Lochaber were estimated at thirty Mackintosh dead, and the theft of five hundred cows, a thousand sheep and goats, and a hundred pairs of horses and mares.[96] Whatever the actual losses were, they were heavy, and by mid-October they had achieved their aim. Seeing that neither Atholl nor Moray could help them, Grant and Mackintosh sued for peace, and on 22 October they signed a bond entering into friendship with Huntly 'as thai war befoir'. During the following month a number of other northern barons and lairds scurried back into the Gordon fold, and the war for control of the north was over.[97] With Bothwell hiding as an outlaw, Atholl in disgrace, Moray isolated, and their northern allies all cowed into submission, the Stewart faction had been destroyed at court and in the countryside, and a commentator could write with confidence that 'Huntly rules all in the north, and over Moray'.[98]

The Stewarts' fortunes sank even lower whn on 27 December Bothwell attempted a coup at Holyrood in which he intended to kill Maitland and seize the king.[99] With even Lennox implicated, the Stewarts as a whole were suspected of collusion, and Moray's name was soon being mentioned along with Bothwell's,[100] his movements being secretive enough for his own servants not to know his whereabouts.[101] By January 1592 Moray was himself an outlaw for having reset Bothwell, but when a letter reached him from Lord Ochiltree towards the end of the month offering the chance of making his peace with the king and Huntly, he accepted it.[102]

Where the initiative for this came from is debatable, and Ochiltree's letter can either be seen as the first step in a sinister plot by the chancellor, or by Huntly, or by them both, to kill Moray, or as a genuine offer from the king alone, or with Maitland, to pacify the feud and restore Moray. The weight of the evidence seems to point to a plot. Huntly's motives are obvious, while the chancellor was even more dependent upon him since the Holyrood raid in which Moray was suspected of having played some part. The two therefore persuaded the king that Moray should be asked to come in and discuss the feud, and his kinsman, Lord Ochiltree, was used unsuspectingly to gain his confidence.[103] While this proceeded Huntly was also armed with a far-ranging commission to hunt down Bothwell and his supporters, and until 5 February he was busily engaged in that activity.[104] On the 7th he was back at court in Edinburgh, and that morning, as the king prepared to go hunting, he told him that he was going across the Forth to pursue one of Bothwell's friends. James appears to have had an idea of what was in Huntly's mind, but he rode out having given the earl no more than a nominal warning not to cause trouble. Balfour's suggestion that James was jealous of Moray's reputation with the queen is an unlikely motive, but, like Maitland, the king needed Huntly's support, and had little liking for Bothwellites.[105] Huntly left after the king, heading for Leith, but then turned off towards Queensferry where all the boats were under orders not to leave port, as they had been in all the Forth ports since 21 January in order to restrict the movements of the rebels.[106] Huntly's commission secured him a passage, and once across, he and his men headed straight for Donibristle, the home of Moray's mother, which lay east of Aberdour on the north shore of the Forth. When Moray refused to surrender himself, the Gordons laid siege to the house, and some fire was exchanged during which Captain John Gordon, brother to the laird of Gight, was wounded. A fire was then lit to smoke the defenders out, and Patrick Dunbar, the sheriff of Moray, and five other men finally broke out from one entrance while Moray escaped from another. Dunbar and the others were slain, and after a search along the shore Moray was also found and hacked to death, Huntly himself being reputedly made to fully implicate himself in the killing by striking a blow, thus inspiring the dying Moray to quip that 'You have spoilt a better face than your own'.[107]

By evening rumours of what had happened had reached Edinburgh, but the king refused to allow Lord Ochiltree to go and investigate, confined him to his quarters, and put a restriction on movements out of the burgh.[108] Huntly, meanwhile, had retired for the night to Inverkeithing which was only a few miles from Donibristle, and from there he sent Gordon of Buckie to inform the king of his success. However, Ochiltree heard of his presence in Edinburgh before he could see the king, and after gathering his own men, and some belonging to Lennox and Mar, he chased him out of the burgh and all the way back to Inverkeithing. Hearing Buckie's report, Huntly deserted the town, leaving behind the wounded Captain Gordon and his servant who were taken prisoner.[109] News of the murder now spread rapidly, and while the king was said to be 'highly offended', speculation was very soon rife on the subject of conspiracy, especially when within forty-eight hours news had arrived that Campbell of Cawdor had been 'slain in the north by the practice of Huntly' eight days before, thus adding to the growing anger and fear which soon forced the king to leave Edinburgh.[110]

The crown's reaction to the murder was one of official outrage and actual indifference. Huntly's commissions, including his lieutenancy, were cancelled on 8 February, and there was talk of pursuing him, but the king did nothing.[111] He even refused to see Moray's mother, denied her the right to carry his corpse in procession, and would not view the gruesome painting she had done of Moray in death.[112] The Stewarts had some immediate satisfaction when Lord Ochiltree, who felt his reputation had been compromised, seized the wounded Captain Gordon and his servant from the protection of Lord Spynie, and had them executed.[113] Such quick justice could not be visited on the other killers so easily, but 'all men are bent on revenge of this cruel murder', especially the Stewarts and their friends who had found a rallying cause, and who were already beginning to murmur about a plot.[114] Within a week of the murder both the king and his chancellor were being blamed by Moray's friends and by the populace who were being encouraged to see the event as a catholic conspiracy. Huntly's interpretation exacerbated the situation as he let it be known that the deed had been done under the king's commission, but when the pursuit of Huntly was postponed on 13 February on the grounds that a force could not be levied in time, and because the king wanted to continue his campaign against Bothwell, feelings began to run much higher. The earls of Atholl and Argyll declared that their men were ready to march, while other noblemen and the ministers and leading burgesses of Edinburgh put pressure on the king to go north. Instead James rode out of Edinburgh amidst popular demonstrations against himself and Maitland, with the royal guard in a mutinous mood over their pay, and headed west. Ochiltree then added to the anger by announcing that only the king, Maitland and himself knew Moray's whereabouts, which was as good as accusing the other two of plotting with Huntly.[115]

By going to Glasgow James hoped that tempers would cool in his absence, and that he would 'avoid the fury of the people',[116] but among the Stewarts the determination to have vengeance had been increased by the king's inactivity. Ochiltree crossed the Forth and met with Atholl, Montrose and the lairds of Grant, Mackintosh, Wemyss and other dependants of Atholl's who all agreed to a bond committing them to avenge Moray's death since 'this murthour was be law neglectit'. He then returned to Edinburgh and had friendly noblemen in the south subscribe it. The Stewart faction had been recreated, and when Ochiltree next saw the king he hinted in 'rough language' that he would 'embrace and refuse no friendship that wald assist and tak pairt in the revendge of that murthour', which was a thinly disguised threat to ally with Bothwell.[117] On 22 February James returned to Edinburgh, having failed to construct a convincing explanation of what had happened.[118] There he summoned the Edinburgh ministers Bruce, Rollock and Lindsay to instruct them to pacify the people, but it was they who appear to have done most of the talking, and James promised them justice. Two days later the king left the burgh again, leaving it as volatile as before with 'Many spitefull libels ... ' being ' ... cast in the streets ... where sundry banished men are now bold to lodge, and most men arm themselves ready for troubles'. Bruce and Rollock also rode with him to ensure that the promise was kept, and the part played by the presbyterian ministers throughout the crisis was one of astute manipulation out of which they hoped to gain concessions and enhanced influence.[119] Bothwell had also been encouraged by the reaction to Moray's murder, and 'may go where he pleases', for 'By this last deed he has got more favourers than he had 'if the[y] dorst otter there myndes' '.[120] He wrote to 'his loving brethren, the ministry and eldership of Edinburgh', setting out before them a list of Maitland's treasonable crimes, including his part in Moray's murder, and projected a picture of himself as another oppressed, protestant nobleman trapped in the chancellor's scheming.[121] A coalition of interests was thus forming for which Moray provided a symbol of unity, and whose diverse aims included vengeance on Huntly, a protestant crusade, and the restoration of Bothwell, all of which were in opposition to the king's own wishes.

Once out of Edinburgh, the king and his pro-Huntly advisers tried again to find a way of legitimising the murder without implicating James in the conspiracy.[122] The king had also been in touch with Huntly since the murder:

> Since your passing heirfra, I have beene in suche perrell of my life, as since I was borne I was never in the like, partlie by the grudging and tumults of the people, and partlie by the exclamatioun of the ministrie, whereby I was moved to dissemble. Alwise, I sall remaine constant. When yee come heere, come not by the ferreis; and if ye do, accompanie yourself, as yee respect your owne preservatioun. Yee sall write to the principall ministers that are heere, for thereby their anger will be greatlie pacified.[123]

James was clearly unconcerned about Moray's death, and hoped that Huntly could keep the church at bay by some public gesture. Huntly, however, was prepared to face his critics, and sent the master of Elphinstone to the king with an offer to stand trial. On 8 March the privy council, which was then sitting at Linlithgow where the king had moved the court, further postponed the raid which had been planned for the 10th.[124] This decision to face an examination by the king and privy council stemmed the flow of criticism the king had been enduring for the past month, but Huntly delayed entering himself in ward in Blackness, and instead caused another scare when he occupied Perth with a small army. The councillors, including Maitland who was now seeking to extricate himself from too close an association with the king's indulgence of Huntly, demanded tougher dealings with the earl, and he was warned to ward immediately.[125] Huntly entered Blackness between 10 and 12 March, and although those friends who had been present at Donibristle refused to obey the council's order, he took so many armed men with him that he could assume control of the castle. From there he conducted negotiations through Lennox who was again acting as a third party, but nothing came of them, and 'it is not known what to do with Huntly'.[126] On 18 March a proclamation was issued commanding Moray's kinsmen not to pursue Huntly as he had done nothing 'bot by hes Maistes Commissions, and sua wes nather airt nor pairt of the Murthour',[127] although when a deputation of commissioners was sent to him to get a written statement of its contents Huntly was evasive, and they left empty-handed.[128] After about a week in ward Huntly petitioned for caution, promised to appear before the justice-ayre of his own shire, and left Blackness 'expres aganis all justice and equitie, and in particular aganis the common lawis of Scotland'.[129]

On 22 March 1592 Huntly and the others who had been at Donibristle were denounced by the privy council, but it seems to have been little more than a formality which had to be gone through until surety was given.[130] For the Stewarts this was little satisfaction, and was less welcome than the good fortune a cousin of Moray's had when he intercepted Huntly's baggage en route to Blackness, and robbed it of 6,000 merks.[131] Atholl and Ochiltree were becoming increasingly restive, and in spite of orders to remain within their own bounds they held a meeting at Dunkeld which was attended by the young earl of Argyll and other friends, at which they decided to lobby for the holding of a convention of the nobility at which they could discuss how to punish Huntly.[132] However, in spite of this being welcomed by many privy councillors, and having the support of Mar, Morton and other less committed noblemen, Huntly's friends in the chamber, particularly Spynie and George Hume, were able to frustrate them.[133] The king responded by leaving Edinburgh, where he had returned at the beginning of April, making his way to Perth, and demanding Atholl's submission. The earl was persuaded by his friends to comply, and he spent two weeks in ward.[134] With his position at court as secure as ever, Huntly was able to pass the remainder of the spring at home, cowing any dissent among restless dependants and cementing friendships.[135]

For the king the most dangerous point of the crisis had passed, but below the surface deep resentments remained. Old Lady Doune, Moray's mother, had died cursing him, the General Assembly was preparing to petition for Huntly's punishment, the English lobby was fully backing the Stewarts, and even Chancellor Maitland was now on their side.[136] Maitland had kept a low profile since February, and at the end of March he had been asked to retire from court as his presence was a focus of discontent, but he retained his offices and his influence, and he had found that the best means of defending himself was to join the chorus of criticism of Huntly.[137] The king's own attitude, at least as revealed to Bowes, was that no assize could be found to try Huntly, and that no other means of prosecution existed.[138] His own subjects were less easily fobbed off, and at the parliament in June he was only able to carry through Bothwell's forfeiture, and ignore a supplication presented on behalf of Moray's young heir, by granting the presbyterians the 'Golden Act' which largely confirmed the gains they had made in church government since 1585.[139] While this placated the church, it served only to spur Bothwell to attempt another coup which was launched against Falkland on 27 June without success. In spite of his failure and losses Bothwell was gaining support as his treatment was contrasted with that of Huntly, and his propaganda made good use of his Stewart kinship and protestant sympathies.[140] James, of course, was furious, and embarked on another short campaign to hunt down the earl, dealing irritably with yet another deputation of ministers and burgesses who petitioned for Huntly's punishment and the reform of the chamber. He told them that Moray's origins were scarcely comparable with those of a man like the earl of Eglinton, murdered in feud in 1585, but which had aroused little passion.[141] A month later he was still saying that the killing of Moray had been 'done for a particular feud', and was excusable, but by then reports that Huntly had heard the mass and was encouraging catholicism in the north had been relayed south, and the king was forced to admit that he might have to take action against him.[142]

Huntly had spent the summer drumming up more support. He levied troops as though he were still the king's lieutenant,[143] and acquired more bonds from within the region and beyond it.[144] However, he also faced difficulties with the lairds of Cluny, Gight and Innermarky, who confronted him over his negotiations with the king while in Blackness when he had considered laying the blame for the murder on them. Huntly probably thought that he could do more good if he was cleared of the killing, but he had not discussed this with his friends who told the earl that they expected him to have them fully restored, or they would take their service elsewhere.[145] They were also unhappy with his offer to the king, made some time in July, to go into temporary exile, as they feared they would suffer without his protection. In contrast his court friends encouraged this, but the Stewarts and their allies saw no justice in Huntly simply visiting the continent at his own suggestion.[146]

By August Huntly was sure enough of his dependants to unleash the Camerons, MacDonnells and other clans under his control on the Mackintoshes and Grants. They and their friends retaliated with attacks on the lands of the Gordons themselves, and the fighting spread throughout the north-east as one bloody and violent episode ignited another. The Grant estate of Ballindalloch was ravaged, and eighteen Grants were thought to have been slain, while the Mackintosh barony of Pettie suffered from a devastating raid led by Gordon of Auchindoun, Huntly's uncle, in which as many as a thousand clansmen were said to have savagely slaughtered up to forty people, stripped the country of its livestock, and inflicted damage later estimated at 200,000 merks. The Gordons also suffered losses, even in Strathbogie itself, and a number of lairds were slain.[147] If Huntly meant to teach Grant of Freuchie and Mackintosh of Dunnachtan a lesson, he merely drove them closer to Atholl to whom they appealed for help. Atholl in turn appealed to the king for a commission, and in the light of Huntly's religious indiscretions the king gave him a powerful one. Armed with this, Atholl raised his own forces and rode for Darnaway, and while he had to turn back at the first attempt, narrowly avoiding capture, he soon established himself there, and was able to muster a threatening force with which to defend the Moray estates, and to try and turn the scales against Huntly. The fighting now escalated, spreading down through Badenoch into Lochaber as well as continuing in Moray and deep into the country east of the Spey. In effect the feud had become a regional civil war.[148]

It was November 1592 before the king realised that the conflict had 'sa brokin the cuntre, that grit numeris of honest and trew men ar in poynt of present wrak,[149] and on the 9th he gave the earl of Angus a commission of lieutenancy and judiciary over the warring clans, though not over the Gordons or any lowland kindreds, and instructed him to mediate between the earls. For a man with no experience of the highlands it was a difficult task to take on, and it was made no easier by the suspicion that Huntly's chamber friends had persuaded the king to appoint a catholic nobleman who was friendly to his cause.[150] Huntly responded favourably to Angus's intervention, agreed to ward in Aberdeen, then in his control, give caution for his dependants, and assure his enemies. On 28 November the king wrote to Angus telling him that peace would be best achieved by enlisting Huntly's assistance in suppressing the disorderly Mackintoshes, and that he should be deputised.[151] Two days later he wrote again informing Angus that the privy council was sending up assurances to be signed by both sides 'to draw on fast a conference, and in the end, a finall agreement'.[152] These were signed shortly afterwards, and some sort of peace was achieved between Huntly and Atholl, although fighting continued erratically among the clans into the middle of December.[153] On 3 January Huntly wrote to the king accusing Atholl of breaking the assurance, and asking for the restoration of his former authority. Huntly also displayed deep indignation that Atholl had been granted such wide-ranging powers from the king in the autumn, an 'honour that nevir was don to nain of his forbears'. He showed a passing regret for the fact that in 'ane civil contry' the 'puir pepill' should have had to suffer 'the war with sik extraordinar crualtie', but the real issue for him remained a philosophy of lordship which was violently critical of men who believed that obligations to lords were temporary. The reason for the war, he explained, was that 'I se thair is na mair for the present bot sik man sik maister', and to him that was utterly unacceptable.[154]

However, this had already been overshadowed by the discovery on 1 January 1593 of letters from Huntly, Errol, Angus and Auchindoun which implicated them in a plot to enlist Spanish help in overthrowing the protestant regime. On his arrival back at court on 3 January Angus made a report favourable to Huntly, and was then suddenly arrested, while Atholl was appointed king's commissioner for the north.[155] When news of the Spanish Blanks reached the others, they met in Aberdeen where Errol argued vehemently for an armed revolt, but as in 1589 Huntly was more cautious, and refused to countenance this, believing that there was more to be gained from playing for time. Errol accused him of being 'feeble' and left in a rage, but Huntly was right to predict that a revolt would have ensured their complete defeat.[156] At court his friends tried to have the order for them to ward postponed, but for once they failed, and Huntly agreed with the more militant Errol that they should disobey the command. Thus on 5 February 1593 the two earls and Auchindoun were denounced for treason.[157]

The king had decided on a show of strength which would serve as much to satisfy protestant and English opinion as it would to remind Huntly of his authority. Within the week he was in Aberdeen with a small army, the rebels having offered no resistance and retreated into the north. Over the next few weeks assurances of loyalty were taken from the surrounding lords and lairds, a justice court was held, and the government of the north was divided between the earls of Atholl and Marischal along with an impressive list of deputies which included many of Huntly's enemies, men like Grant, Mackintosh and Lord Forbes.[158] Yet the entire campaign was little more than a demonstration, and James had even tried to prevent the English ambassador accompanying him so that he would not report on its leniency.[159] A few of Huntly's cautioners were arrested for the non-payment of their surety,[160] but on 16 March the rebels were relaxed from the horn, and by April Marischal was being accused at court of being soft in the use of his authority.[161]

Atholl, of course, was less concerned about upsetting the Gordons. He now had ambitions to supplant Huntly in the north, and turned down a marriage alliance with the Gordons which was offered to him.[162] Huntly was also thought to have communicated with Bothwell, a particularly dangerous move as on his return home the king had turned again to pursuing the rebel earl, and had extracted from the nobility gathering at a convention at the beginning of May a promise to cooperate with him in this with all the diligence of their own 'particulair deidlie feidis aganis thair awin privat enemies'.[163] At court Huntly's friends were busy cultivating his interests, and were even canvassing for support among the Edinburgh crafts in order to gain him some popular backing.[164] In the north 'he has grown strong with a great party', justifying the decision not to fight in February, and during May there was further skirmishing. It was at this time that Huntly's reputation for bloodiness was enhanced when he captured one of Atholl's servants, hanged him, and then had 'his head, arms and legs to be cut off in his own presence at Strathbogy and to be set on poles'.[165] The affair of the Spanish Blanks and the subsequent royal raid on Aberdeen in the early part of 1593 had been little more than an interlude in the feud, and had no more than a superficial effect on the politics of the north.

When parliament met in July there were still those who hoped that the catholic earls might be forfeited, but the king needed Huntly's support and was negotiating a settlement with the church which would enforce no more than a short exile.[166] The claims of the Stewarts continued to be ignored, and parliament's only interest in Moray's murder was to administer the escheats of some of the lesser known killers. The 'noblemen and gentilmen of the Stewartis' were a sizeable faction to disregard, and were angered that 'thair blude was spilt without redres, and Bothuell lang baneist without any originall caus'. The king should have read the signs better when at the opening of parliament Atholl refused to ride with him. The return of Maitland at the end of the spring had also been arranged in the face of Lennox's opposition, the chancellor being too close to the Hamiltons who were the duke's rivals for the succession. On 24 July 1593 Lennox led the Stewarts in a dramatic coup at Holyrood at which they engineered 'the inbringing of Bothwell' and seized control of the king.[167] Hopes among the Stewarts of 'pryvate revenge' ran high,[168] but Bothwell was unable to hold onto the king without actually imprisoning him, and James was able to regain his freedom by degrees, particularly after he had detached Lennox from the others. Although Bothwell was acquitted of the charges of witchcraft for which he was originally arrested in 1591, the king's hatred of him was now so great, and the earl's distrust of James so deep, that when Bothwell was summoned before the privy council to answer for his treason he refused, and was once again denounced on 25 October.[169]

Meanwhile the earl of Argyll had begun to take a more active part in northern politics, although he was still only eighteen. At the end of June 1592 a meeting of his family's friends had taken place in Stirling where Cawdor's murder had been discussed. While a number of men were then under suspicion, the evidence pointed increasingly to Campbell of Ardkinglas, Cawdor's rival in the struggle to control the earldom. Argyll certainly knew enough by this time to feel very insecure, and he was unable to concern himself with the murder of his cousin Moray. In July 1592 Colquhoun of Luss was murdered by clansmen dependent on Argyll, presumably for having given a bond of manrent to Huntly, on 28 March 1593 an attempt was made to kill Ardkinglas, a number of lesser suspects were rounded up in April, and in September Argyll arrested the powerful Campbell laird of Glenorchy and the laird of Lawers.[170] By then Argyll had already decided to give more active support to Huntly's enemies, and at the beginning of August his men began making large raids into his territories. Once again all the north-east was locked in conflict, and in the 'daillie spilling of much bloode' the dead were now being numbered in hundreds.[171] Nor was it confined to the highland clans as Aberdeen was forcibly made to accept Huntly's terms, while fighting took place in Inverness which resulted in a Mackintosh victory and the burgh having to sign a bond promising to resist Huntly in future, or 'accept the deadly feud of the said Lachlan'.[172] As in 1592, the fighting continued through to the end of December, by which time Mackintosh had formally bonded with Argyll, who was taking over from Atholl as Huntly's major opponent.[173]

At court the success Bothwell had had in July persuaded even Maitland that Huntly should be restored.[174] The decision of the synod of Fife to excommunicate Huntly irritated the king, and he was determined to free himself from the presbyterian party, and from Bothwell and his friends.[175] On 5 October 1593 he made a sudden raid on Stirling to arrest Atholl, who fled.[176] After returning to Edinburgh, he left again on the 12th to conduct a border raid, but before joining up with the muster he was confronted at Fala by Huntly, Angus and Errol who humbly submitted to him. James accepted the submission, and agreed with them that they would be tried by assize, the implication seeming to be that they would suffer no more than a minimal punishment, but in the meantime they were to remain in open ward in Perth.[177] On 17 October a deputation from the church and the burghs angered the king even more by petitioning him for a fair trial in which the earls would not be improperly dealt with.[178] James wrote to Huntly reassuring him of his confidence in him, and telling him not 'to misinterprete my exterioure behavioure the last daye, seeing what ye did, ye did it not without my allowance, and that be your humilitie in the action itself, youre honouring of me serued to counteruaile the dishonouring of me be otheris before'. James told him there was much he wanted to discuss with him, but in the meantime:

> Alluayes assure yourself and the rest of youre marrouis that I am earnister to haue your daye of tryall to haulde forduart then yourselfis, that be your seruices thaireftir the tiranie of thir mutins may be repessit; for I protest before God in extremitie, I loue the religion thay outuardly profess, and hatis thaire presumptuouse and seditiouse behauioure, and for your pairt in particulaire I trou ye haue hadd proofe of my mynde towardis you at all tymes, and gif of my fauoure to you ye doubt, ye are the onlie man in Scotlande that doubtis thairof, sen all youre enemies will needis binde it on my bake.

The king added in a postscript: 'I hope to see you or this moneth be endit (gif ye use yourself weill,) in als guide estaite as ever ye was in'.[179] Clearly Huntly was not going to be punished, and James even instructed the bearer of this letter with advice for the earl to follow when examined. On 25 October Bothwell was denounced, and on the 31st a convention of estates met at Linlithgow which established a commission under Chancellor Maitland to investigate the catholic earls' treason. It sat in Edinburgh on 12 and 19 November, and on 26 November a convention of the estates met in Edinburgh and passed the 'Act of Abolition', by the terms of which the three earls along with Sir Patrick Gordon of Auchindoun and Sir James Chisholm of Cromlix were given until February 1594 to submit to the established religion, in which case their involvement with Spain would be forgiven, on condition it was never repeated, or they could go into exile, their lands being reserved for their heirs. They had also to give caution for their behaviour, entertain a minister in their houses, remove any Jesuits from their presence, and be responsible for the religion of their tenants. These points had to be enforced immediately, and a written decision on conformity had to be in the king's hands by 1 January.[180]

The king's very obvious plan to create a powerful catholic *politique* party around Huntly and the Humes, who were already established at court, aroused widespread fear. Argyll complained bitterly to Mar that he had allowed this to happen, presumably by not organising more effective opposition at court and in the privy council, the English predicted that Huntly would 'not only get courte againe, but also be greater than ever he was', and Andrew Melville accused James of favouring catholics.[181] Bothwell also tried to exploit this by posing as the protestant champion, but he had 'fallen into the deepest displeasure that may be had with his prince', and looked incapable of preventing Huntly's triumph.[182] However, John Ross, a presbyterian minister whose militant sermons had provoked the privy council into hauling him in for examination, had told his inquisitors that Huntly was 'sa far past in mischief, murther and apostasie' that he could not be forgiven, and in a sense he understood the earl better than the king.[183] By 1 January 1594 no communication had arrived from the three earls, or Auchindoun, and Errol at last had the rebellion Huntly had been putting off for so long.[184]

The king delayed until the 18th when a convention of the estates recognised their refusal to take advantage of the 'Act of Abolition'. He continued to drag his feet, and it was the end of the month before the earls were ordered to ward, and 8 March before they were forfeited. Even when the forfeiture was confirmed by parliament in May, the noblemen present 'suspendit thair vottis, becaus the intentions of the Catholic lords war nawayis clearlie provin judiciallie'.[185] This closing of ranks by the nobility, and the king's reluctance to act decisively arose from an unwillingness to become too firmly committed to the English-presbyterian interest which was still closely identified with Bothwell, and from an unwillingness to plunge Scotland into religious warfare. Bothwell's defeat at Leith at the beginning of April had revealed his power to be less threatening than had been assumed, but the strong links between him, the Stewarts, and England diverted attention from the catholic earls, allowing them even more time to prepare themselves.[186]

At the beginning of April the campaign against Huntly had an almost premature beginning as a private venture led by the earl of Argyll. Sporadic fighting had gone on during the spring in which Argyll's forces played a peripheral part.[187] However, on 6 May Argyll had interrogated John Oig, one of Cawdor's killers, and he had implicated the Campbell lairds of Glenorchy, Lochnell and Lawers, as well as confirming Huntly's part in the plot. According to Oig, the plotters had all signed a bond after the murders by which they bound themselves to one another's defence, although Ardkinglas had refused to sign it, having hoped to extricate himself from the whole business. For the Campbell lairds the issue was simply one of domestic clan politics, while for Huntly the removal of Cawdor eight days before Moray reduced the likelihood of Argyll's strength being allied to the Stewarts until their own house was in order. This was largely what had happened, but when Oig revealed his story, Argyll wanted to march immediately against Huntly, and was only persuaded to delay his plans by the earl of Mar.[188] He did continue to levy his men, Oig was executed, having been himself of little importance, a raid failed to capture MacAulay of Ardincaple in his home at the end of May, and a month later Ardkinglas was again questioned.[189] During his two interrogations on 21 and 28 June there were even more shocking revelations when he not only confirmed what Oig had said, but added Maitland's name to the plotters, and claimed that the conspiracy had actually failed as Argyll and his younger brother were also to have been killed, leaving Campbell of Lochnell, a client of Huntly's, to inherit the earldom. The laird of Glenorchy was also questioned on the 28th, but he was much less insecure than Ardkinglas, and simply denied everything, offering to prove his innocence in court. Three days later Ardkinglas retracted his confession, swearing that Glenorchy knew nothing about the murder and that the great contract was all a story he had invented to distract attention from his own participation in it. By 6 July Argyll and Glenorchy had been reconciled, and a few days after that two more of the murderers had been executed and another put to death.[190] The truth of the conspiracy was 'smothered' as too many of the political community were implicated, and when in a quite different case in the justice court in 1600 the prosecution cited Ardkinglas's trial in making a point of precedence, the crown was reluctant to release the papers of the trial for the defence to examine.[191] Clearly there had been a cover up of some sort, and the results of Argyll's investigations were to leave him determined to have vengeance on Huntly, and deeply embittered with his own kinsmen.[192]

The time allowed by all these diversions had not been wasted by the catholic lords. In April 1594 Spanish agents probably carrying gold had arrived, and in the second week of July a ship docked in Aberdeen with more money, messages and Jesuits. To their surprise they were arrested by the burgh authorities, but on 19 July Huntly, Errol, Angus and Auchindoun appeared outside the burgh and threatened it with 'ane perpetuall querrell' if they did not release their prisoners. The money was welcome as it allowed Huntly and Errol to supplement the service of their dependants, tenants and seasonal clansmen with paid soldiers, but it was Spanish troops that were looked for, not subsidies, and on 12 August Huntly and Errol wrote to Philip again pleading for support.[193] Without that support they were doomed, since the catholics in the south had either decided to opt for a *politique* solution or, like Angus, could not deliver their own followers to the cause. In effect the rebels could only count on Huntly, Errol and their friends and dependants in the north-east, with some additional support from those highland clans who fought for Huntly for reasons connected with local politics rather than the religious toleration which was the public aim of the rebels.[194]

On 15 July 1594 the king finally issued to Argyll, Atholl, Lord Forbes and a number of other men commissions of fire and sword against the rebels, and on 25

July these three received commissions of lieutenancy for the north. Musters were also proclaimed throughout the country from the end of August, after the festivities surrounding the baptism of Prince Henry were over.[195] James was still stalling, hoping no doubt that Huntly would change his mind, and there were strong English fears that all that was intended was a repeat of the 1593 campaign. They lobbied hard for the rebels to be dealt with 'without regard to feuds', but the entire operation was almost abandoned when Argyll threatened to withdraw due to diversionary tactics by some of Huntly's friends in the western isles, and his own distrust of his kinsmen.[196] Then on 17 August the privy council postponed the musters which were now to begin on 30 September, following the 'grite grudge and murmuring' of many people at being asked to abandon their harvests at a time of dearth, and because the king had not yet been able to raise the thousand paid soldiers who would form the core of the army.[197] This force was raised over the next few weeks by a number of loans and contributions,[198] while some additional propaganda was gained from the discovery of an agreement made between the catholic lords and Bothwell in August, a revelation which exploded Bothwell's carefully cultivated image as the protestant champion, and damaged Huntly's reputation with the king, but it had been an alliance formed of desperation not calculation.[199]

Towards the end of September Argyll marched east with an army estimated at between 6,000 and 12,000 men, most of whom were his own levies with large contingents from MacLean of Duart, the Mackintoshes and Grants, and from Atholl who declined to serve under Argyll himself, but sent the laird of Tullibardine in his place. They were almost entirely on foot and lightly armed, although some 1,500–2,000 carried firearms, and a large proportion had bows. Marching up into Badenoch, they besieged Ruthven Castle on 27 September, but the MacPhersons defending it refused to surrender, and Argyll continued on down Strathspey, crossing the river, and climbing up onto the high ground on the other side which he had to traverse in order to meet up with Lord Forbes and the 1,100 cavalry he had gathered in Mar. Keeping to such terrain was also necessary as long as Argyll was unprotected by cavalry. When Huntly and Errol heard of the imminent arrival of Argyll, they were at Strathbogie with only their own cavalry. Deciding that a victory was possible if Argyll could be engaged before he joined with Forbes, they made their way to Auchindoun, arriving there on 2 October, their horse being delayed by a small artillery train. Their own force was only about 1,500 strong, 200 of these being supplied by Errol, the rest being friends and dependants of Huntly, but they were all mounted and 'all weall borne gentlemen'. They also had with them five field pieces, and a company of paid soldiers who had been in Huntly's service for the last few years. On the morning of 3 October they set out to find Argyll, and around midday they stumbled upon him high up on the slopes of Ben Rinnes in Glenlivet. Two of the field pieces had been abandoned, the heavy, steep ground was against them, and the sun was in their faces, but Argyll's large army was disorganised and surprised, and the confusion was increased when Huntly's guns opened fire on them. Errol then led some 300 men in the vanguard in an almost suicidal charge up the slope into a hail of shot and arrows which claimed the life of Auchindoun and left Errol seriously wounded. The charge drove home, but after the initial shock Argyll's men rallied, and Errol was soon in danger of being surrounded. At that point Huntly's larger force of 1,200 braved the heavy firepower of the highlanders, and smashed into their flank. With most of his men unable to come to grips with the enemy, and being unable to match the better-armed horsemen, Argyll's army dissolved into an ill-disciplined rabble, and began to flee the field. A stout rearguard action by MacLean, and the nature of the ground which did not favour an effective pursuit, prevented a wholesale slaughter, but there was no doubt about the scale of the defeat. Argyll, who was led weeping from the battle, lost something in the region of 500 men, including Campbell of Lochnell, leaving his army shattered. On the other hand, while the catholics lost less than a score of dead, all their fatalities were landed men, and they suffered extremely badly from bullet and arrow wounds, and from the loss of a large number of horses, including Huntly's which was shot from under him. It was an astonishing victory, defying all the military science of the period, and one in which providence was considered to have intervened, but it left the best part of Huntly's army maimed for the rest of the campaign.[200]

The king, meanwhile, left Edinburgh on 4 October and received Argyll's news from the earl himself at Dundee three days later.[201] Argyll's own army, or part of it, did rendezvous with a contingent of Lord Forbes's force who were sent to try and rally it, but fighting broke out between them over some feud, and its only contribution to the remainder of the campaign was to oppress the neighbouring countryside regardless of loyalties.[202] The king himself reached Aberdeen on 12 October, unopposed by Huntly and the wounded Errol who had scattered their men and slipped into Sutherland, a decision which had again caused a quarrel between the two earls. Extremely bad weather favoured the rebels, and the king was largely confined to the burgh until the last week of the month. On 26 October he was at Terrisoul where the ministers and captains of the paid soldiers persuaded him to oppose the majority of the privy council and order the demolition of Strathbogie Castle, the castles of the other rebels having already been destroyed.[203] He returned to Aberdeen on 4 November, by which time the money to pay the soldiers was drying up, and while the ministers wanted to try and raise more to continue the campaign, the king left the burgh a week later, and was back in Edinburgh by the end of the month.[204]

Huntly's enemies had at last had some satisfaction, but the defeat he had acquiesced in was relatively superficial. Before he returned home, the king had left the duke of Lennox, Huntly's brother-in-law, as his lieutenant in the north with only 200 men to enforce his authority.[205] The English may have been convinced that James had made a decisive break with his catholic subjects, but in the north Lennox handed the forfeited estates over to the rebels' wives, protected and even pardoned many of the rebel lairds, and by the beginning of January 1595 was losing his men by desertion as Huntly resumed effective control of the region.[206] A bitter quarrel had meanwhile broken out between Atholl, who felt aggrieved at being passed over for the youthful earl of Argyll, and the latter, who was in disgrace after his defeat, and was now suspicious that a number of his kinsmen had betrayed him. They had found further cause for disagreement in the administration of the young earl of Moray's lands, and Moray himself was resentful of Atholl. Argyll's forces were also raiding into estates in the north-east, creating a desire there for the return of Huntly's protection.[207] By February the Gordons themselves had even recovered their confidence sufficiently to make raids of their own against the Forbes.[208]

Meanwhile the revelations of Bothwell's alliance with the catholic lords had left him 'as a man able to doe nothinge'.[209] During the early part of the new year further investigations produced more concrete evidence which resulted in the execution of a number of his lesser supporters, and the desertion of Lord Ochiltree, the last of the Stewart noblemen to remain loyal to him.[210] Angus, who had not been present at the battle of Glenlivet or Balrinnes, had written to Philip II since then asking once again for his help as 'we have no other hope than the aid of your Highness'. He was hunted in his own country, but narrowly avoided capture.[211] In the north Huntly openly met with Lennox, and offered to go into exile along with Errol. Lennox accepted, and on his return to court the privy council approved his decision in an act of approbation on 17 February.[212] Leaving their affairs in good order, the three catholic earls departed for the continent where they continued to scheme for Spanish aid with Bothwell, who had fled to Paris, and with the exiled Scottish catholic community. However, while there was another Spanish scare in Scotland later in the year, the truth soon dawned on the earls, as they were able to see for themselves the level of Spanish commitment to their cause.[213] Bothwell never returned home, but the others made their way back to Scotland during the summer of 1596 to a hostile reaction from the church. The king remained unwilling to persecute his catholic subjects, and during the next year he negotiated terms acceptable to himself, the church, and the rebel lords themselves under which they were fully restored in exchange for submitting to the established religion.[214] By 1608 Angus had changed his mind about this, and went into exile until his death three years later, while Huntly and Errol continued to be a thorn in the side of the church by practising catholicism, but as protagonists of the Counter Reformation in Scotland they were a spent force. Following the riot in Edinburgh in December 1596, the king had written to Huntly hoping to regain his service. He reminded the earl of 'how often I have incurred skaith and hazard for your cause', but warned him to make his peace with the church, 'or else if your conscience be so kittle as it cannot permit you', then his estates and titles would be protected for his family, and he should go abroad for good where he could 'look never to be a Scottishman again'. James made it clear that he wanted Huntly back, but there could be no more debate on the religious issue.[215] Huntly agreed, but took the occasion to remind the king that his offence was not so great anyway, and that 'the prins pairt to his subjects, suld be, as the fathers to the children, not be rigour to seik thair utter ruin, (albeit racelie thay have faillit,) bot be humiliation, to accept thair ammendment'.[216] A year later, in December 1597, having been accepted back into the communion of the church, it was reported that 'Huntly was never so great nor ever so much made of both with King and Queen'.[217] By 1599 he had been created a marquis.[218]

Laying the Scottish Counter Reformation to rest was easier than pacifying the feud between Huntly and his enemies. During Huntly's exile, in the summer of 1595, Lord St. Colme, the brother of the murdered earl of Moray, had captured one of the killers, Innes of Innermarky, and brought him to Edinburgh where he was tried and executed along with his servant.[219] At the beginning of 1597 the laird of Moncoffer was murdered for his part in Moray's murder by some others of his friends,[220] and in December of that year Lord St. Colme was discovered to be plotting Huntly's murder.[221] Argyll had also re-opened the Cawdor inquiry in July 1595 against the advice of his kinsmen. Ardkinglas and the widow of the executed John Oig were both examined, and again there were allegations about a contract involving Huntly and a number of Campbell lairds. Early in March 1596 Argyll had Ardkinglas arrested, and in the face of stiff opposition from the king, and from the Campbell lairds, he insisted on a formal trial by assize, but a series of postponements followed, and what actually happened 'in the grittest pannell that was in our dayis', as it was described by one lawyer in 1617, was never revealed, although Ardkinglas was set free, and continued to suffer harassment from his chief.[222] In the north the death of Atholl in 1595 in the midst of an ever more bitter quarrel with young Moray removed one of the principals of the feud, and while his heir, who was of a cadet branch of the family, did succeed in getting Mackintosh's bond of maintenance in 1597, he was a man of little significance.[223] A number of the warring clans made their own peace in 1598,[224] but Huntly's return brought many of them back to submit to his lordship.[225] In January 1598 Huntly wrote a letter to Sir Patrick Murray, a royal household servant, asking for his help in getting his commissions back. In a statement of his aims Huntly made it very clear that Gordon power would not be brushed aside as a result of his recent defeats, writing that

> . . . we craif na thing bot our awin plaice and sik as hes bein in all tymis past the custoum of our predicessouris, and that because nane in this partis mair or vill presum to minister justeis aganis ony spetiall heland clanis heir bot ve.[226]

In fact Huntly's power was to decline before his death in 1636, but it was a long, slow erosion caused by his persistent nonconformity, and was not a sudden result of what happened in the 1590s.

During Huntly's negotiations with the church the question of Moray's murder had been raised. Both in March 1596 and in May 1597 the General Assembly had insisted that as a condition of his restoration he should declare his repentance for the killing and offer assythment for it, but the king reserved for himself the details of settling the feud.[227] Throughout 1597 attempts were made to negotiate between Huntly and Argyll, but Argyll was obstructive and refused to grant anything more than annual assurances until Moray was of age. For his part Huntly wanted the feud buried as quickly as possible, and offered marriage and lands in assythment.[228] Throughout the following year there was a complete stalemate, although the church did appeal to have Moray's body buried, an act which would itself have a symbolic value in signifying the desire for reconciliation.[229] The king's enthusiasm for settling feuds received a new impetus with the Act anent Feuding in June 1598, and Huntly's willingness to negotiate may have helped him towards his marquisate ten months later, while the Stewarts and their friends were driven from court.[230] In the summer of 1600 the feud threatened to escalate when Huntly executed a servant of Crichton of Cluny who he thought had been sent to assassinate him, and throughout the remainder of the year Argyll continued to make any progress in the pacification of their quarrel impossible.[231]

From the autumn of 1601 the privy council began to deal more directly with the feud, royal mediation alone having failed. It was Moray himself who was now proving the most obstinate, resisting the king's appeals, the council's orders, and applying for a licence to go abroad so that he could avoid the issue.[232] At the end of March the king dined with both Huntly and Argyll when he asked them 'how can ye two, being two peers of my land, either do me good service or do your nation credit, being ready to cut one another's throat'? James reminded them that he might need to conquer England, a feat which would be impossible without his two strongest noblemen being reconciled. As Thomas Douglas told Cecil in his letter, such arguments made one think the king 'had neither wit nor judgement', but in luring his nobles into peace with the suggestion of rich rewards in England the king's strategy was not entirely without merit.[233] An attempt to begin arbitration in April was then frustrated by Moray who excused himself in order to seize Darnaway from Atholl who still held it in ward.[234] Real progress began to be made in May when it was agreed to begin mediation at St. Andrews on 8 July, and during the next three months the king and the other arbitrators devised the basis for a settlement.[235] A few minor threats to the peace were ironed out over the winter,[236] and on 22 February 1603 the agreement was completed 'as all men wonder'.[237] The details of the settlement were kept secret, although the marriages of Moray to Huntly's eldest daughter, and of Huntly's heir to Argyll's eldest daughter formed the heart of the agreement. Financial arrangements accompanied the marriage contracts which may have been intended to cover the question of compensation, although this may have been dealt with separately. Certainly there was no question of Huntly doing homage, or of any bonds of manrent being exchanged.[238] Except for a brief resurrection of the feud in 1616 by dependants of Huntly and Moray who disagreed over an interpretation of the settlement, the peace lasted.[239] Huntly and Argyll continued to snipe at one another over the control of clans in the central highlands, but the marriage alliance between them prevented more serious fighting between their kinsmen until their sons took opposite sides in the civil war, and highland politics again merged with wider political issues.

In the context of magnate politics this feud was essentially a successful one for the earl of Huntly. He had succeeded in reversing the damage done to Gordon power during the lifetimes of his father and grandfather, he had destroyed the opposition he faced from Moray, resisted the threat from Argyll, and in spite of all his treasons retained his close relationship with the king. At the same time, however, he had failed in his ambitions to permanently damage the power of the Campbells, although the hurt done was enough to poison the clan's politics for the duration of Argyll's life, and he sacrificed the possibilities of unparalleled authority in the north and influence at court for the ideals of the Counter Reformation. Therein lay his gravest mistake, and he consistently misunderstood the king's diplomatic posturing, mistaking it for doubts about his commitment to protestantism. He also put too much faith in Spanish help. That he survived those mistakes was due to his friendship with the king which, remarkably, survived all his indiscretions and disobedience. It was also due to the political need the king had for his power as a counterweight to the presbyterians, to Bothwell and the Stewarts, and to England, as a means of governing the north, and in helping him attain the English succession, the last of which James never thought of as inevitable. Ultimately Huntly's failure to restore catholicism to Scotland, and his refusal to accept the implications of that failure, at least in public, drove him from the centre of the stage, and saw his power eclipsed. His loyalty to that ideal was equalled only by his loyalty to the responsibilities of lordship and kinship which continued to guide his handling of local affairs for the remainder of his life. The real failure of this episode in Scottish politics was the earl of Moray, who never understood those responsibilities, and who paid dearly for his neglect.

At a more general level this feud demonstrates in detail the working of Scottish politics towards the end of the sixteenth century. To intervene in the localities the crown was clearly dependent upon local co-operation, and in the campaigns of 1589, 1593 and 1594 royal victories, won largely by default, had no more than a temporary effect upon the distribution of power in the locality. That was partly a matter of choice: James did not want Huntly crushed, but the choice was a narrow one given the level of dissent within the political community at such a decision, and the actual cost of a sustained campaign. Royal power was not easily exercised in a high-handed way, and the price to be paid could easily outweigh the advantages to be gained. For the politicians, whether they were magnates, courtiers or royal officials, resources of power and outlets for it had to be found both in the localities and at court. Most men could independently claim to have one or the other; thus Moray had his own local power, while Maitland's was based on his offices and his position at court. The chancellor, however, manipulated that power base to attach local clientage through which he influenced local affairs. Bothwell was even more successful in creating a faction based on the Stewart kinship, and on his usefulness to others as a manager of their affairs at court. Huntly bestrode both, dominating the chamber and having enormous local resources of his own, but effectively combining the two through his dependence on reliable subordinates like Spynie at court and Auchindoun in the locality. It was Huntly's alliance with Maitland which destroyed Bothwell and the Stewarts, and there is little doubt that it was on these two men that the king wanted to base his government, a desire frustrated by Huntly's catholicism and Maitland's death in 1595. Whatever the specific politics of these relationships, the interplay of court and locality provided much of their dynamic, and winning the game required success in both. The rules by which those politics were conducted were tough ones requiring tough men prepared to make full use of faction and feud in the pursuit of a whole range of ambitions ranging from the international diplomacy of the Counter Reformation to fishing rights on the River Spey. However, the fact that it was the king who emerged in the mid-1590s as the most powerful figure in Scotland was of enormous importance in creating a political context favourable to a sustained attack on feuding itself which, in association with the court's move to London in 1603, permanently altered the nature of Scottish politics.

## NOTES

1. See E. J. Cowan, 'Clanship, kinship and the Campbell acquisition of Islay', in *Scottish Historical Review*, lviii, 2, No. 166, 1979, quote from p. 140.

2. *Scots Peerage*, iv, pp. 534–535 and 539–540.

3. *Ibid.*, p. 541; *C.S.P., Scot.*, ix, p. 476; Moysie, *Memoirs*, p. 66.

4. *C.S.P., Scot.*, x, p. 3.

5. *Scots Peerage*, iv, p. 541; Moysie, *Memoirs*, p. 71; S.R.O., Gordon Castle Muniments, G.D., 44/13/4/8, for the vice-chamberlaincy.

6. *C.S.P., Scot.*, x, p. 84.

7. *Estimate*, p. 31.

8. *C.S.P., Scot.*, x, pp. 3 and 85.

9. *C.S.P., Scot.*, ix, p. 655.

10. For the strong convocations which always surrounded him see, for example, *C.S.P., Scot.*, xiii, Part 1, p. 395; Part 2, p. 961.

11. *Scots Peerage*, vi, pp. 316–317; S.R.O., Moray Muniments, N.R.A., 217/3/2/180, 217/2/3/239, 217/2/3/70.

12. *Historie*, p. 246.

13. S.R.O., Moray Muniments, N.R.A., 217/2/3/168, 217/2/3/260–268; Gordon, *Sutherland*, p. 214; *Historie*, p. 246.

14. *Historie*, p. 246. Oddly enough, in 1589 he was described as 'a papiste and freinde to the Erle of Huntly', quite remarkable for the man who was to die as a protestant martyr at Huntly's hands, *C.S.P., Scot.*, ix, pp. 666–667.

15. S.R.O., Gordon Castle Muniments, G.D., 44/1/1/3.

16. S.R.O., Moray Muniments, N.R.A., 217/2/3/176; S. R.O., R.D., 1/24/9.

17. *R.P.C.*, iv. pp. 86–87 and 100; *H.M. C.*, vi, Moray M.S., p. 650. Two of Moray's servants were killed by the Gordons at this time, W. Fraser, *The Chiefs of Grant*, Edinburgh, 1883, vol. iii, pp. 176–179.

18. S.R.O., Moray Muniments, N.R.A., 217/2/4/24.

19. *Estimate*, pp. 11 and 32.

20. Brown, 'Bonds of Manrent', appendix, p. 393, No. 2.

21. *Ibid.*, pp. 467ff. These were Munro of Foulis, MacAngus of Glengarry, Mackenzie of Kintail, MacLeod of Lewis, MacGregor of Glenstray, Drummond of Blair, Robertson of Struan, Dunbar of Cumnock who was also sheriff of Moray, Donald Gorm of Sleat, Grant of Freuchie, Rattray of Craighall, Menzies of Pitfodells, the provost of Aberdeen, Menzies of that Ilk, Scott of Abbotshall and James Beaton, fiar in Malgund. Even more importantly, in April 1587 Archibald Campbell of Lochnell, Argyll's cousin, gave Huntly his bond, and in the following year the most powerful of the Campbell cadets, Duncan Campbell of Glenorchy, followed him, although in both allegiance to Argyll was excepted. A bond of friendship was also made with the earl of Orkney in 1587.

22. *C.S.P., Scot.*, x, pp. 276-277.

23. *R.P.C.*, iv, pp. 121, 131, 149-150 and 210; *C.B.P.*, i, p. 259; Gordon, *Sutherland*, p. 208; S.R.O., Gordon Castle Muniments, G.D., 44/13/2/1.

24. *C.S.P., Span.*, iii, p. 580; *C.B.P.*, i, p. 236; Birrel, 'Diary', p. 24. In October 1587 catholic agents were intercepted at Leith en route to see him, Moysie, *Memoirs*, p. 65. See, too, *C.S.P., Scot.*, ix.

25. *C.B.P.*, i, pp. 308-309 and 321-322; *C.S.P., Span.*, iv, pp. 227-228. Huntly tried to introduce his Jesuit uncle to the king, Moysie, *Memoirs*, p. 66, and had been in communication with Parma, *C.S.P., Span.*, iv, p. 197.

26. *C.S.P., Span.*, iv, pp. 224-225.

27. *Ibid.*, p. 10; Spottiswoode, *History*, ii, p. 392. The fact that Huntly subscribed the Confession of Faith may have ensured that Maxwell continued to receive most of the subsidy, *Ibid.*, p. 390.

28. Huntly was in charge of all the shires of Cromartie, Nairn, Elgin, Forres, Banff, Aberdeen and Inverness, excluding the region between the waters of Inverness and the Spey, *R.P.C.*, iv, p. 307. Communication with Spain continued throughout the summer, *C.B.P.*, i, pp. 328-329; *C.S. P., Span.*, iv, p. 361, but by September Huntly was becoming impatient, *Ibid.*, pp. 429-430, and by October Parma was expressing to Mendoza his regret at the frustration of all their well-laid plans, *Ibid.*, pp. 455-456.

29. *C.S.P., Scot.*, ix, pp. 682ff; x, pp. 1 and 4; *C.B.P.*, i, pp. 335-336; Spottiswoode, *History*, ii, pp. 390-391; Moysie, *Memoirs*, p. 72; Calderwood, *History*, v, pp. 6-36. These letters were dated January 1589 and had been preceded by communication with Spain in November 1588 reaffirming their commitment, *C.S.P., Span.*, iv, pp. 478-479. James himself was also in communication with Spain at the time.

30. *C.S.P., Scot.*, x, pp. 4ff; *C.B.P.*, i, pp. 335-336; Moysie, *Memoirs*, p. 75.

31. Lee, *John Maitland of Thirlestane*, Chapter 8, 'Huntly's Rebellion'; *C.S.P., Scot.*, x, pp. 17, 24-25, 27, 31, 42, 54, 62 and 69; *R.P.C.*. iv, pp. 367, 371, 373 and 375; *C.B.P.*, i, p. 337; Spottiswoode, *History*, ii, pp. 392-395; Moysie, *Memoirs*, pp. 73-76. There is a lot more material on this but these references will convey the essence of the rebellion.

32. *C.S.P., Scot.*, x, pp. 54 and 83-85; *R.P.C.*, iv, p. 821; Spottiswoode, *History*, ii, pp. 397-398; Moysie, *Memoirs*, pp. 76-77. During the rebellion Fowler reported that all the king's servants were Huntly's friends, *C.S.P., Scot.*, x, p. 17, and he was back in favour by July, *Ibid.*, p. 127.

33. *C.S.P., Scot.*, x, pp. 83-85; *R.P.C.*, iv, pp. 387, 405 and 501; Spottiswoode, *History*, pp. 397-399; Moysie, *Memoirs*, pp. 76-77; Balfour, 'Annales', i, p. 386. A report on the rebellion and on how to avoid a repetition of it was ignored, *R.P.C.*, iv, pp. 825-826.

34. S.R.O., Moray Muniments, N.R.A., 217/2/3/230, 217/2/3/227, 217/2/3/229, 217/2/3/232.

35. Ibid., N.R.A., 217/2/3/236, 217/2/3/217.

36. Brown, 'Bonds of Manrent', appendix, p. 459, No. 90, p. 470, No. 79.

37. *C.S.P., Scot.*, x, p. 202; S.R.O., Moray Muniments, N.R.A., 217/2/3/280.

38. *C.S.P., Scot.*, ix, pp. 538, 676 and 678. This had been encouraged by Maitland, *Ibid.*, p. 680.

39. See the king's declaration for the order of government, *R.P.C.*, iv, pp. 423-427; Spottiswoode, *History*, ii, p. 404.

40. For the commercial transactions between them, S.R.O., Moray Muniments, N.R.A., 217/2/3/2, 217/2/3/3, 217/2/3/66. On Bothwell's mediations, *C.S.P., Scot.*, x, pp. 184, 191, 196, 253, 259, 264 and 279; *R.P.C.*, iv, pp. 493-494; Gordon, *Sutherland*, p. 200.

41. *C.S.P., Scot.*, x, pp. 277 and 839; S.R.O., Moray Muniments, N.R.A., 217/2/3/285, 217/2/3/295, 217/2/3/274.

42. S.R.O., Moray Muniments, N.R.A., 217/2/3/257, 217/2/3/287–288; *R.P.C.*, iv, p. 496.

43. S.R.O., Moray Muniments, N.R.A., 217/2/3/255.

44. Ibid., N.R.A., 217/2/3/304.

45. Ibid., N.R. A., 217/2/3/292.

46. *C.S.P., Scot.*, x, pp. 351–352, 368 and 392.

47. *Ibid.*, pp. 277, 352 and 410; Brown, 'Bonds of Manrent', appendix, p. 470, No. 80; S.R.O., Moray Muniments, N.R.A., 217/2/3/270.

48. *C.S.P., Scot.*, x, p. 431.

49. Gordon, *Sutherland,* p. 214; Fraser, *Chiefs of Grant,* iii, p. 178.

50. Gordon, *Sutherland,* p. 214; Spottiswoode, *History,* ii, p. 410.

51. Mar gifted him lands from the Moray bishopric, S.R.O., Fraser-Mackintosh Collection, G.D., 128/32/2/15; Morton granted him the barony of Dunnchattan directly from the crown rather than indirectly from Huntly, S.R.O., Mackintosh of Mackintosh Muniments, G.D., 176/104; against the Forbes, S.R.O., Moray Muniments, N.R.A., 217/2/3/65.

52. Brown, 'Bonds of Manrent', appendix, p. 393, No. 2; he also bonded with Campbell of Cawdor in 1581, p. 544, No. 68; and was granted the ward and non-entry of Huntly's lands, S.R.O., Mackintosh Muniments, G.D., 176/123.

53. *Spalding Miscellany,* ii, pp. 83–84; S.R.O., Mackintosh Muniments, G.D., 176/123.

54. Brown, 'Bonds of Manrent', p. 470, No. 78.

55. S.R.O., Airlie Muniments, G.D., 16/34/5; Gordon, *Sutherland,* p. 214. Mackintosh also allied with Lord Lovat in 1588, S.R.O., Fraser-Mackintosh Collection, G.D., 128/31/2/30.

56. *Historie,* pp. 246–247; Gordon, *Sutherland,* p. 214.

57. The killing of both Cawdor and Moray within eight days of one another, and some of the evidence from the trial of those responsible for the former, certainly suggest that Cawdor was more involved in the politics of the region than appears.

58. Gordon, *Sutherland,* p. 215.

59. *Ibid.,* and Spottiswoode, *History,* ii, p. 410.

60. Brown, 'Bonds of Manrent', appendix, p. 54, No. 92 and No. 93. The signatories to the bond of 5 November were Atholl, Moray, Lord Fraser, Grant of Freuchie, Campbell of Cawdor, Stewart of Grandtully, Grant of Rochiemurchus, Sutherland of Duffus and Grant of Belliston.

61. *C.S.P., Scot.*, x, p. 425.

62. *Ibid.*, p. 428; S.R.O., Moray Muniments, N.R.A., 217/2/3/296.

63. *C.S.P., Scot.*, x, p. 462; Moysie, *Memoirs,* p. 85; Melville, *Memoirs,* p. 406; *Historie,* pp. 246–247; Gordon, *Sutherland,* p. 215.

64. *C.S.P., Scot.*, x, pp. 428 and 433; *R.P.C.*, iv, p. 548.

65. *C.S.P., Scot.*, x, pp. 428–429, 431 and 433.

66. *Ibid.*, p. 431.

67. *Ibid.*, p. 435.

68. *Ibid.*, p. 437; Melville, *Memoirs,* p. 405; Moysie, *Memoirs,* p. 85.

69. *C.S.P., Scot.*, x, pp. 437, 442–443 and 447.

70. *Ibid.*, pp. 354–355, 423–424, 434, 442–443, 437 and 439; Moysie, *Memoirs,* p. 85. Maitland claimed that he was forced into this accommodation because of his isolation, but was 'ever ready to endure their feuds if he be accompanied with the rest of his fellows', *C.S.P., Scot.*, x, p. 443.

71. *C.S.P., Scot.*, x, p. 450; Melville, *Memoirs,* pp. 406–407.

72. Fraser, *Chiefs of Grant,* iii, pp. 176–179; *R.P.C.*, iv, kpp. 569–570.

73. *C.S.P., Scot.*, x, p. 469.

74. *Ibid.*, p. 456; Melville, *Memoirs*, p. 407.

75. *C.S.P., Scot.*, x, pp. 456 and 462.

76. Among those who assured Huntly of their support were Lord Spynie and the laird of Innermarky, one of whose friends was whipped by a servant of Moray's. For this and other support, *C.S.P., Scot.*, x, pp. 452, 454, 456 and 462; Brown, 'Bonds of Manrent', appendix, p. 470, No. 81; S.R.O., Moray Muniments, N.R.A., 217/2/3/309. Huntly also enlisted in his employment Captain Thomas Kerr and fifty mounted soldiers, *C.S.P., Scot.*, x, p. 497. In contrast Moray could only add the support of Dunbar of Boighall, S.R.O., Moray Muniments, N.R.A., 217/2/3/330.

77. He did have a commission against a William Grant, *R.P.C.*, iv, p. 832, and *C.S.P., Scot.*, x, p. 460.

78. *C.S.P., Scot.*, x, p. 469.

79. *Ibid.*, p. 469; *C.B.P.*, i, p. 376.

80. *R.P.C.*, iv, p. 597.

81. S.R.O., Moray Muniments, N.R.A., 217/2/3/272, 217/2/3/323, 217/2/3/314, 217/2/3/346; *R.P.C.*, iv, p. 626.

82. For a discussion of Bothwell's interest in necromancy, see E. J. Cowan, 'The Darker Vision of the Scottish Renaissance: The Devil and Francis Stewart', in I. B. Cowan and D. Shaw (eds.), *The Renaissance and Reformation in Scotland*, Edinburgh, 1983, pp. 125–140. Also Lee, *John Maitland of Thirlestane*, pp. 230–231. Details can be found in *C.S.P., Scot.*, x and R.P.C., iv. For Melville's comments, *Memoirs*, pp. 395–397.

83. *C.S.P., Scot.*, x, pp. 456 and 482.

84. S.R.O., Moray Muniments, N.R.A. 217/2/3/251.

85. Ibid., N.R.A., 217/2/3/252, 217/2/3/254.

86. *C.S.P., Scot.*, x, p. 452.

87. *R.P.C.*, iv, pp. 646–647.

88. *C.S.P., Scot.*, x, p. 507.

89. *Ibid.*, p. 541; S.R.O., Moray Muniments, N.R.A., 217/2/3/155.

90. Ibid., N.R.A., 217/2/3/327.

91. *C.S.P., Scot.*, x, pp. 541, 547 and 557.

92. *R.P.C.*, iv, pp. 663–664.

93. *C.S.P., Scot.*, x, pp. 557, 569 and 571–572.

94. *Ibid.*, p. 572.

95. *Ibid.*, pp. 557 and 572.

96. *Ibid.*, pp. 572 and 474; S.R.O., Moray Muniments, N.R.A., 217/2/4/180.

97. *C.S.P., Scot.*, x, p. 593; Fraser, *Chiefs of Grant*, iii, p. 159; Brown, 'Bonds of Manrent', appendix, p. 470, No. 83. Atholl made a belated attempt to maintain these men by taking up their case before the council but by then they had already made their peace with Huntly, S.R.O., 'Moray Muniments, N.R.A., 217/2/3/347.

98. *C.S.P., Scot.*, x, p. 601.

99. Lee, *John Maitland of Thirlestane*, p. 235.

100. *C.S.P., Scot.*, x, pp. 611 and 617; *C.B.P.*, i, pp. 390–391.

101. S.R.O., Moray Muniments, N.R.A., 217/2/3/356.

102. Spottiswoode, *History*, ii, p. 419; S.R.O., Moray Muniments, N.R.A., 217/2/3/356 and 217/2/3/361, for a summons by Huntly against one of Moray's servants.

103. *C.S.P., Scot.*, x, pp. 619 and 639–640; *Historie*, p. 247; Gordon, *Sutherland*, p. 216; Moysie, *Memoirs*, p. 88; Melville, *Memoirs*, p. 407; Spottiswoode, *History*, ii, p. 419; Balfour, 'Annales', i, p. 390; Calderwood, *History*, v, pp. 144–146. The wider implications

of the conspiracy are discussed at a later stage. See also Lee, *John Maitland of Thirlestane*, pp. 237–242; Gregory, *History of the Western Highlands and Islands*, pp. 244–259; D. H. Willson, *King James VI and I*, London, 1956, pp. 107*108*.

104. *C.S.P., Scot.*, x, p. 632; Moysie, *Memoirs*, p. 88; Spottiswoode, *History*, ii, p. 419; Balfour, 'Annales', i, p. 390; Melville, *Memoirs*, p. 407.

105. *C.S.P., Scot.*, x, p. 633; Moysie, *Memoirs*, pp. 88–89; Gordon, *Sutherland*, p. 216; Balfour, 'Annales', i, p. 390.

106. *R.P.C.*, iv, pp. 718–719. The *Historie*, pp. 247–248, claims the ferries were laid up in preparation for the murder.

107. Versions on the attack differ. Only Gordon says that Huntly asked for a surrender, and that Captain Gordon was shot first. He also relates that the house was fired and then stormed, and that the earl was killed by Gight and Cluny in revenge for the death of their brothers. Moray's mother was also said to be in the house, and her kinsmen later claimed that the experience killed her, and she did indeed die a few months later. Gordon, *Sutherland*, p. 216; Moysie, *Memoirs*, pp. 88–89; *Historie*, pp. 247–248; Pitcairn, *Criminal Trials*, i, Part 2, pp. 357–358; *C.S.P., Scot.*, x, pp. 633–636; Birrel, 'Diary', pp. 26–27; Spottiswoode, *History*, ii, p. 419; *Spalding Miscellany*, ii, 'The Chronicle of Aberdeen', p. 66; S.R.O., Moray Muniments, N.R.A., 217/2/4/58.

108. *C.S.P., Scot.*, x, pp. 635–636 and 639–640; Moysie, *Memoirs*, pp. 88–89.

109. *C.S.P., Scot.*, x, p. 641; Moysie, *Memoirs*, p. 89.

110. *C.S.P., Scot.*, x, pp. 633–634 and 636.

111. *R.P.C.*, iv, p. 725; *C.S.P., Scot.* , x, p. 636.

112. *C.S.P., Scot.*, x, p. 641; Moysie, *Memoirs*, pp. 90–91, who claims that James went hunting the next day and only Lord Hamilton would accompany him; Calderwood, *History*, v, p. 146; Spottiswoode, *History*, ii, p. 420.

113. *C.S.P., Scot.*, x, p. 641; Moysie, *Memoirs*, pp. 90–91; Gordon, *Sutherland*, p. 216.

114. *C.S.P., Scot.*, x, p. 636.

115. *Ibid.*, pp. 637–638; Moysie, *Memoirs*, p. 91; Calderwood, *History*, v, pp. 144–146; Spottiswoode, *History*, ii, p. 420.

116. *C.S.P., Scot.*, x, p. 116.

117. *Ibid.*, pp. 661 and 639–641; Moysie, *Memoirs*, pp. 92–93. It was said that, before making his attempted escape from Donibristle, Moray had told his sister to see that Lord Ochiltree avenged him, and he in turn had taken an oath to 'yield the like reward to some of them' or die in the attempt. Lady Doune apparently took three bullets from Moray's body, and gave them to friends who promised to return them to the killers, *C.S.P., Scot.*, x, p. 641.

118. *Ibid.*, p. 641; Calderwood, *History*, v, p. 147. A captured servant of Bothwell's was tortured to try and persuade him to say that Moray had been at the Holyrood raid.

119. Calderwood, *History*, v, p. 147; *C.S.P., Scot.*, x, p. 645.

120. *C.S.P., Scot.*, x, p. 648.

121. Calderwood, *History*, v, pp. 150–156.

122. *C.S.P., Scot.*, x, p. 643.

123. Calderwood, *History*, v, pp. 146–147.

124. *C.S.P., Scot.*, x, p. 643; *R.P.C.*, iv, p. 735.

125. *C.S.P., Scot.*, x, pp. 650–653; Calderwood, *History*, v, p. 148; Moysie, *Memoirs*, p. 92.

126. *C.S.P., Scot.*, x, pp. 654–655; *C.B.P.*, i, p. 391; *Historie*, p. 248; Moysie, *Memoirs*, p. 92; Calderwood, *History*, v, p. 149.

127. Pitcairn, *Criminal Trials*, i, Part 2, p. 358.

128. *C.S.P., Scot.*, x, p. 658.

129. *Historie*, p. 248; Moysie, *Memoirs*, p. 92; Calderwood, *History*, v, p. 149.

130. *R.P.C.*, iv, pp. 734–735.

131. *C.S.P., Scot.*, x, pp. 654 and 657; *C.B.P.* , i, p. 391. This Robert Stewart was a younger son of Lord Innermeith. He later tried to kill Huntly.

132. *C.S.P., Scot.* , x, pp. 644, 655–657, 663–664 and 666.

133. *C.S.P., Scot.*, x, pp. 655, 658 and 663. Lord Spynie had already initiated proceedings against Moray's heir over the old question of the bishopric, and was very soon at feud with his family in his own right, S.R.O., Moray Muniments, N.R.A., 217/2/3/349, 217/2/4/13.

134. *C.S.P., Scot.*, x, pp. 668, 670 and 674; he remained in ward for two weeks, and was freed on 7 May.

135. *Ibid.*, pp. 679 and 686.

136. *C.S.P., Scot.*, x, pp. 679, 681 and 684; Calderwood, *History*, v, p. 149.

137. Lee, *John Maitland of Thirlestane*, pp. 248ff; *C.S.P., Scot.*, x, p. 697.

138. *C.S.P., Scot.*, x, p. 693.

139. S.R.O., Moray Muniments, N.R. A., 217/2/4/58. Moray's unburied body was still lying in Leith kirk at this time, W. Scot, *An Apologetical Narration of the State and Government of the Kirk of Scotland Since the Reformation*, Wodrow Society, Edinburgh, 1846, p. 59.

140. *C.S.P., Scot.*, x, pp. 697, 707ff, 775–776; Spottiswoode, *History*, ii, pp. 421–422; Ochiltree was certainly involved in plotting the raid, Melville, *Memoirs*, p. 407; see also *C.B.P.* for this period and Lee, *John Maitland of Thirlestane*, pp. 252–253.

141. *C.S.P., Scot.*, x, pp. 745–746.

142. *Ibid.*, pp. 782 and 792; Birrel, 'Diary', p. 28.

143. *C.S.P., Scot.*, x, pp. 701 and 705.

144. Brown, 'Bonds of Manrent', appendix, p. 471. Cameron of Lochiel repeated his bond, while Dunbar of Blair and Colquhoun of Luss gave their manrent.

145. *C.S.P., Scot.*, x, pp. 655, 719–720 and 729–730.

146. *Ibid.*, pp. 705, 741–742, 748 and 760.

147. This may have been sparked off by the execution of two of Mackintosh's younger sons by the earl of Caithness acting in Huntly's interests, *C.S.P., Scot.*, x, p. 645. For the fighting, see *Ibid.*, pp. 811–812, 815 and 817; Gordon, *Sutherland*, pp. 217–218; Moysie, *Memoirs*, pp. 98 and 161; Spottiswoode, *History*, ii, pp. 424–425; S.R.O., Moray Muniments, N.R.A., 217/2/4/180; S.R.O., Mackintosh Muniments, G. D., 176/240; *R.P.C.*, x, p. 466. There was also trouble in Aberdeen where Huntly appeared in force to ensure his candidate was elected provost in the face of competition from Lord Forbes, *C.S.P., Scot.*, x, pp. 784 and 801.

148. *C.S.P., Scot.*, x, pp. 801–802, 811–812 and 817; Moysie, *Memoirs*, p. 98.

149. Fraser, *Chiefs of Grant*, ii, p. 3.

150. *R.P.C.*, v, pp. 19–20. The king also wrote to men like Grant of Freuchie asking them to co-operate with Angus: Fraser, *Chiefs of Grant*, ii, pp. 3–4. Some suspected that Huntly himself suggested Angus, *C.S.P., Scot.*, x, p. 815; *Historie*, p. 259.

151. *C.S.P., Scot.*, x, p. 820; W. Fraser, *The Douglas Book: Memoirs of the House of Douglas and Angus*, Edinburgh, 1885, iv, p. 37, No. 31.

152. Fraser, *The Douglas Book*, iv, pp. 37–38, No. 32.

153. *C.S.P., Scot.*, x, p. 820; though the murderers of Moray were exempt from the assurance which was to be nullified if Huntly sheltered or protected them, something he continued to do, *C.S. P., Scot.*, x, p. 822. The level of the fighting still remained very fierce, *C.S.P., Scot.*, x, pp. 821 and 824.

154. *Spalding Miscellany*, i, 'The Straloch Papers', pp. 5–6.

155. *C.S.P., Scot.*, x, pp. 828–830; xi, pp. 15–19 and following; *R.P.C.*, v, pp. 33–36; Moysie, *Memoirs*, p. 101; Melville, *Diary*, p. 205; Calderwood, *History*, v. pp. 192–221; *Historie*, p. 260. Angus did not remain a prisoner, and 'rycht craftelie he escapit furth of preason'. See, too, in connection with him, Fraser, *The Douglas Book*, iv, pp. 188–189; Spottiswoode, *History*, ii, pp. 425–427.

156. *C.S.P., Scot.*, x, pp. 34–35.

157. *Ibid.*, pp. 35, 37 and 40–41; *R.P.C.*, v, p. 42.

158. *R.P.C.*, v, pp. 43–44, 46–47 and 49–51; *C.S.P., Scot.*, xi, pp. 66–67, 68 and 72–73.

159. *C.S.P., Scot.*, xi, p. 48.

160. *Ibid.*, pp. 77–78; Fraser, *Chiefs of Grant*, iii, p. 184, No. 162.

161. *R.P.C.*, v, pp. 53–54; *C.S.P., Scot.*, xi, pp. 80–83.

162. *C.S.P., Scot.*, xi, pp. 82–84 and 89.

163. *R.P.C.*, v, p. 72; *C.S.P., Scot.*, x, pp. 82–83 and 89.

164. *C.S.P., Scot.*, xi, p. 91.

165. *C.B.P.*, i, p. 462; *C.S.P., Scot.*, xi, p. 91.

166. Moysie, *Memoirs*, p. 102; *A.P.S.*, iv, p. 15.

167. Moysie, *Memoirs*, pp. 102–103; *Historie*, p. 270; *C.S.P., Scot.*, xi, pp. 130ff and 145; *C.B.P.*, i, pp. 477–481; Spottiswoode, *History*, ii, pp. 433–434; Lee, *John Maitland of Thirlestane*, pp. 261–265, has a fuller account of the details of the coup.

168. *C.S.P., Scot.*, xi, p. 145; *C. B.P.*, i, p. 481.

169. *C.B.P.*, i, pp. 488–490, 493–494 and 508; Spottiswoode, *History*, ii, pp. 435–437; *R.P.C.*, v, pp. 100–101.

170. *C.S.P., Scot.*, x, pp. 684 and 705; xi, pp. 99–100, 102–103 and 170; *R.P.C.*, iv, p. 756; v, pp. 68–69; Moysie, *Memoirs*, p. 162; *Historie*, p. 248; W. Fraser, *The Chiefs of Colquhoun*, Edinburgh, 1869, i, pp. 156–157; Brown, 'Bonds of Manrent', appendix, p. 388, No. 64; Cowan, 'Clanship, kinship and the Campbell acquisition of Islay', p. 141.

171. *C.S.P., Scot.*, xi, pp. 137, 139, 143, 151–153 and 160; *C.B.P.*, i, pp. 487, 493, 494 and 497. Huntly was said to have attempted to have Mackintosh murdered, *C.S.P., Scot.*, xi, pp. 165–166. He was also reputed to have captured two of Atholl's cooks, and 'burnt them both, sending the Earl's word that he had left two roasts for them', *Ibid.*

172. *C.S.P., Scot.*, xi, pp. 162 and 179; Gregory, *History of the Western Highlands*, p. 254; S.R.O., Mackintosh Muniments, G.D., 176/162.

173. *C.S.P. Scot.*, xi, pp. 251 and 261; S.R.O., Mackintosh Muniments, G.D., 176/164.

174. *C.B.P.*, i, p. 498.

175. *C.S.P., Scot.*, xi, p. 181; Spottiswoode, *History*, ii, pp. 437–440; Calderwood, *History*, v, pp. 261–268.

176. *C.S.P., Scot.*, xi, pp. 191, 193 and 210; Moysie, *Memoirs*, p. 105; *Historie*, pp. 281–282.

177. Calderwood, *History*, v, pp. 269–270; Moysie, *Memoirs*, pp. 105–106; Melville, *Diary*, p. 209; Melville, *Memoirs*, pp. 283–284; Spottiswoode, *History*, ii, pp. 438–440; *C.B.P.*, i, p. 506. There were rumours that the king had seen the earls privately during the summer, *Ibid.*, pp. 475 and 496.

178. *R.P.C.*, v, pp. 101–103; Calderwood, *History*, pp. 270–271; Moysie, *Memoirs*, pp. 106–107; Melville, *Diary*, p. 209; Spottiswoode, *History*, ii, pp. 439–441; *C.S.P., Scot.*, xi, pp. 203–205; Melville, *Memoirs*, pp. 284–291.

179. *Spalding Miscellany*, iii, 'Gordon Letters', pp. 213–214. This letter is undated, but appears to belong to this period.

180. *R.P.C.*, v, pp. 103–109; Melville, *Diary*, p. 209; Moysie, *Memoirs*, pp. 108–109;

Melville, *Memoirs*, pp. 291–295; Spottiswoode, *History*, ii, pp. 441–445; Calderwood, *History*, v, pp. 271–280.

181. *C.S.P., Scot.*, xi, pp. 199, 200, 217, 250 and 245; *C.B.P.*, i, p. 497; Melville, *Diary*, p. 210.

182. *C.B.P.*, i, pp. 510 and 514.

183. *Historie*, p. 321.

184. *C.S.P., Scot.*, xi, p. 260.

185. *R.P.C.*, v, pp. 116, 130, 134 and 140; *A.P.S.*, iv, pp. 55–56; *Historie*, pp. 327–328 and 330.

186. *C.S.P., Scot.*, xi, pp. 304–306, 344 and 374; *C.B.P.*, i, pp. 530 and 539; Moysie, *Memoirs*, pp. 113–116; *Historie*, pp. 301–302; Spottiswoode, *History*, ii, p. 448; *R.P.C.*, v, pp. 141, and 143–144.

187. *R.P.C.*, v p. 134; *C.S.P., Scot.*, xi, pp. 282, 288–294 and 277.

188. *C.S.P., Scot.*, xi, pp. 331 and 338; *Warrender Papers*, S.H.S., Third Series, Edinburgh, 1932, No. 19, ii, pp. 246–251; *Historie*, p. 248.

189. *C.S.P., Scot.*, xi, p. 344.

190. *Highland Papers*, S.H.S., Second Series, Edinburgh, 1914, No. 5, i, pp. 175–190; *C.S.P., Scot.*, xi, pp. 370 and 376. Argyll was hereditary justice general.

191. *C.S.P., Scot.*, x, p. 376; Pitcairn, *Criminal Trials*, ii, pp. 120–121.

192. See Cowan, 'Clanship, kinship and the Campbell acquisition of Islay', for his comments on the effects of this on the Campbells.

193. *R.P.C.*, v, p. 145; *C.S.P., Scot.*, xi, pp. 364 and 385; *C.B.P.*, i, pp. 470 and 474; Spottiswoode, *History*, ii, p. 458; *Historie*, pp. 328 and 331; Fraser, *The Douglas Book*, iv, p. 374, No. 334; Moysie, *Memoirs*, p. 118; *C.S.P., Span.*, iv, p. 613.

194. There appears, however, to have been some reluctance to become involved in the campaign by men who thought 'bloodshed ane unfitting mean to work any man's conversion', and the religious issue forced a number of northern catholics into Huntly's camp, *The Spottiswoode Miscellany*, Spottiswoode Society, Edinburgh, 1844–45, i, 'Battle of Balrinnes', p. 261.

195. *H.M.C.*, iv, 'Argyll M.S.', p. 488, No. 292; *R.P.C.*, v, pp. 157–159.

196. *C.S.P., Scot.*, xi, pp. 389–390, 398, 400, 403, 408, 417, 419, 422 and 432; Spottiswoode, *History*, ii, p. 458.

197. *R.P.C.*, v, pp. 163–164.

198. *Ibid.*, pp. 167 and 170–172; Moysie, *Memoirs*, p. 119.

199. *R.P.C.*, v, pp. 173–175. Suspicions of this first arose in July, *C.B.P.*, i, p. 342.

200. *Spottiswoode Miscellany*, i, 'Battle of Balrinnes', pp. 261–270; *C.S.P., Scot.*, xi, pp. 348–354 and 456–460; Calderwood, *History*, v, pp. 348–354; Moysie, *Memoirs*, pp. 119–121; *Historie*, pp. 338–343; Gordon, *Sutherland*, pp. 226–229; Spottiswoode, *History*, ii, pp. 458–460; Balfour, 'Annales', i, pp. 396–397; Birrel, 'Diary', p. 33; Melville, *Diary*, p. 213; *R.P.C.*, v, pp. 175–176; *C.S.P., Span.*, iv, pp. 590–591.

201. *R.P.C.*, v, p. 179.

202. *C.S.P., Scot.*, xi, pp. 476 and 486–487; Spottiswoode, *History*, ii, p. 460; Gordon, *Sutherland*, p. 229–320; *R.P.C.*, v, p. 190.

203. R.P.C., v, pp. 180–185, for acts while in Aberdeen; Melville, *Diary*, p. 214; Spottiswoode, *History*, ii, p. 460.

204. *R.P.C.*, v, pp. 187–190. Strathbogie has been delivered to Sir John Gordon of Pitlurg on 12 October in the king's name in an obvious attempt to avoid this, *Spalding Miscellany*, i, 'The Straloch Papers', p. 9. See also *R.P.C.*, v, p. 189; Birrel, 'Diary', p. 30; Melville, *Diary*, pp. 215–216; *C.S.P., Scot.*, xi, pp. 464–466.

205. *R.P.C.*, v, pp. 187–188 and 192; Moysie, *Memoirs*, p. 120.

206. *C.S.P., Scot.*, xi, p. 512; *C.B.P.*, i, p. 551; ii, p. 15; *Historie*, p. 347; Moysie, *Memoirs*, p. 124; Melville, *Diary*, p. 215; Spottiswoode, *History*, ii, p. 460, is the only source to praise Lennox's administration of the north.

207. *R.P.C.*, v, p. 190; *C.S.P., Scot.*, xi, pp. 476, 486, 496, 500–501, 506–507, 509 and 523.

208. *C.S.P., Scot.*, xi, p. 529.

209. *C.B.P.*, i, p. 549.

210. *C.S.P., Scot.*, x, pp. 496 and 525; Moysie, *Memoirs*, pp. 121 and 163; Spottiswoode, *History*, ii, p. 457; Calderwood, *History*, v, pp. 359–361 and 363–365; *R.P.C.*, v, pp. 205–207.

211. *C.S.P., Span.*, iv, pp. 613–614; Moysie, *Memoirs*, 122–123.

212. *R.P. C.*, v, pp. 207–208; Spottiswoode, *History*, ii, p. 460.

213. *R.P.C.*, v, pp. 328–331; *C.S.P., Span.*, iv, pp. 616–617 and 632; Moysie, *Memoirs*, pp. 122–123; *Historie*, p. 344, says that Huntly went to Germany; Spottiswoode, *History*, iii, p. 3; Birrel, 'Diary', p. 42.

214. *R.P.C.*, v, p. 328; *B.U.K.*, iii, pp. 897–98; *C.S.P., Scot.*, xii, pp. 429 and 500; xiii, Part 1, p. 56; xiii, Part 1, p. 132; *Spalding Miscellany*, i, p. 10; Melville, *Diary*, pp. 243–244; Moysie, *Memoirs*, p. 127; Spottiswoode, *History*, iii, pp. 7–9, 13–14, 47–48 and 54–55; Birrel, 'Diary', pp. 38 and 42; Calderwood, *History*, v, pp. 437–438, 441–446, 449–450, 455 and 655; *A.P.S.*, iv, pp. 123–124.

215. Spottiswoode, *History*, iii, pp. 47–48.

216. *Analecta Scotica*, (ed.) J. Maidment, Edinburgh, 1834–37, i, pp. 102–103. This letter is only dated December.

217. *C.S.P., Scot.*, xiii, Part 1, p. 132.

218. S.R.O., G.D., 44/13/2/4.

219. *Historie*, pp. 347–348; *C.S.P., Scot.*, xi, p. 643; Birrel, 'Diary', p. 34; S.R.O., Moray Muniments, N.R.A., 217/2/4/93.

220. Moncoffer's murder re-opened old sores with Lord Spynie who duelled with Crichton of Cluny over it. He was also continuing the struggle with the earl of Moray over the bishopric, *C.S.P., Scot.*, xii, pp. 439, 453 and 466; S.R.O., Moray Muniments, N.R.A., 217/2/4/13.

221. *C.S.P., Scot.*, xiii, Part 1, p. 141.

222. For the confessions, *Highland Papers*, i, pp. 190–194 and 159–171. On the trial and other aspects of the affair, Pitcairn, *Criminal Trials*, i, Part 2, pp. 363 and 391–392; *C.S.P., Scot.*, xi, p. 633; xii, pp. 157, 161–162 and 168; *Highland Papers*, i, pp. 152–159; Birrel, 'Diary', p. 37. The 1617 comment is found in Pitcairn, *Criminal Trials*, iii, p. 423, and the harassment of Ardkinglas in *R.P.C.*, v, pp. 322–323 and 407.

223. Brown, 'Bonds of Manrent', appendix, p. 551, No. 104; before his death a rift had opened up between Atholl and young Moray which was continued by Atholl's successor, and concerned their control of Moray's ward and marriage, *A.P.S.*, iv, p. 6; *R.P.C.*, vi, p. 383; *Historie*, p. 281; *C.S.P., Scot.*, xiii, Part 2, p. 969.

224. Brown, 'Bonds of Manrent', appendix, p. 497, No. 5, between Mackintosh and Cameron, and p. 478, No. 9, between Grant and MacAngus.

225. Gordon, *Sutherland*, p. 280; Brown, 'Bonds of Manrent', appendix, pp. 471–473, No. 87–96. Mackintosh appears to have bonded with Huntly and Moray, p. 551, No. 104, and had resumed commercial business with Huntly during the summer of 1597, S.R.O., Mackintosh Muniments, G.D., 176/180.

226. *Warrender Papers*, ii, pp. 353–356.

227. *B.U.K.*, iii, p. 897–98 and 922; Spottiswoode, *History*, iii, pp. 54–55, 61 and 62.

228. *C.S.P., Scot.*, xii, pp. 427 and 500; xiii, Part 1, pp. 72, 97, 128 and 135.

229. *R.P.C.*, v, p. 444.

230. *C.S.P., Scot.*, xiii, Part 1, pp. 395, 398, 422, 435, 494 and 497; S.R.O., Gordon Castle Muniments, G.D., 44/13/2/4.

231. *C.S.P., Scot.*, xiii, Part 2, pp. 667, 728, 730, 739, 754 and 777, and Lord Doune was warded for refusing to co-operate.

232. *R.P.C.*, vi, pp. 290, 296, 347 and 351; *C.S.P., Scot.*, xiii, Part 2, pp. 895, 916 and 940.

233. *C.S.P., Scot.*, xiii, Part 2, pp. 961, 978 and 1015.

234. *R.P.C.*, vi, p. 372; *C.S.P., Scot.*, xiii, Part 2, p. 969; and see S.R.O., Moray Muniments, N.R.A., 217/2/4/153, 217/2/4/244; *R.P.C.*, vi, pp. 383 and 545.

235. *R.P.C.*, vi, p. 378; *C.S.P., Scot.*, xiii, Part 2, pp. 978, 992, 1015, 1022–1023, 1029 and 1047.

236. *C.S.P., Scot.*, xiii, Part 2, pp. 1081 and 1089.

237. *R.P.C.*, x, p. 660; Birrel, 'Diary', p. 58 and Balfour, 'Annales', i, p. 411, date this at 13 February; Calderwood, *History*, vi, p. 205, claims it was the 23rd; and Nicolson, *C.S.P., Scot.*, xiii, Part 2, p. 1106, suggests 1 February, although on the 9th he says arbitration is almost completed, pp. 1106 and 1110.

238. *C.S.P., Scot.*, xiii, Part 2, p. 1106. For Huntly's offers made before April 1599, see S.R. O., Forbes Collection, G.D., 52/70, for a memorandum of claims made by Moray in 1602, S.R.O., Moray Muniments, G.D., 217/2/4/179, and his answers to Huntly's reply to these, G.D., 217/2/4/180. The minutes of the contract of marriage between Huntly's son and Argyll's daughter are in S.R.O., Gordon Castle Muniments, G.D., 44/33/2, and also on the marriages, Gordon, *Sutherland*, p. 208.

239. *R.P.C.*, x, pp. 466 and 660.

*Part Three: Uprooting the Feud*

# 7

# *Ideology — Christians and Gentlemen*

Peace had always been an integral part of the teaching and mission of the Christian church,[1] and it has long been recognised that the reformed church in Scotland had a deep concern for the violence in Scottish society.[2] The medieval church had also acted as a peacemaker by taking on a traditional mediating role in local communities, and by making peace an essential condition of full admission to its sacramental life. At particular times and in particular places it also provided the initiative for peace movements, some of which were successful. Peace did not become universal, but some feuds were pacified, some were made less destructive, and the prohibition of their prosecution on Sundays did receive a degree of acceptance.[3] Peace was not simply a desirable condition between men which was derived from a sense of self-preservation, but was itself sanctified. As John Bossy puts it, 'the rituals of social peace had acquired in the common understanding an intrinsic holiness', and it was that holiness which ought, in an ideal world, to characterise the normal relations between people living in a Christian community.[4]

The Reformation revitalised the Christian faith throughout western Europe in both catholic and protestant countries, and that revitalisation included a renewed attack on private violence. The Council of Trent repeated the church's long-standing opposition to duelling, and it has been effectively argued that the greatest obstacle to the Tridentine reformers was neither backsliding nor protestant resistance, 'but the internal articulations of a society in which kinship was a more important social bond and feud, in however conventionalised a form, a flourishing social activity'.[5] One practical effect of this was that feuding kindreds found it impossible to attend church together to celebrate the mass, and, for example, when Alessandro Sauli was sent from Cardinal Borromeo's Milan to Corsica to be its bishop, he found it necessary to establish confraternities devoted to eliminating feuds before he could begin his reforming mission.[6] Such a function was a common one for confraternities like the Nome di Dio in Bologna which was begun in 1566–67 to compose differences between conflicting parties, and to settle lawsuits before they ended up in court.[7] The emphasis here was less an ethical one than one of religious observance, its impetus coming from the obligation to facilitate attendance at mass, and submission to the confession. In a feuding society the former was practically impossible, or at the least highly dangerous, and the latter implied what Bossy has rightly called 'unilateral disarmament'.[8] Of course, the post-Tridentine catholic church was, in practice, less than wholly committed to social peace, and the Venetian clergy contributed substantially to the rise of private violence in that state during this period.[9] Yet while the Reformation may have shattered 'the covenant of peace' which bound Christendom together as a religious community, the renewal and self-examination it inspired resulted in

184

greater efforts to promote communal peace within both catholic and protestant Europe.[10]

This point is important if one is to avoid the obviously tempting but simplistic explanation of the disappearance of private violence as the result of protestant ideology in the hands of a rising middle class.[11] Even the suggestion that a protestant society was more likely to be successful in reducing private violence is a tenuous one which fails to convince.[12] Whether this essentially Weberian thesis is correct or not, Calvinism was fiercely critical of private violence and the ideology which sustained it. The reformed church in Scotland was unquestionably Calvinist in its theology and structure, and it would be surprising to find that the powerful influence this Genevan form of Christian thought had on the Scottish church, and ultimately on Scottish society, did not affect thinking on such an important issue. The Calvinist censure of private violence gave a new militancy to the church's traditional peacemaking role in Scotland, and found little resistance at an ideological level from a governing elite already disturbed by renaissance re-evaluations of the honour society, while in the crown the church secured an ally whose enthusiasm sprang from the desire to make the cause of peace a statement of its own credibility.

Evangelical zeal, not patient suffering, characterised the church's attitude to the violence in Scottish society. The Calvinist ministry could not really have approved of the old laird of Kilravock who, in answer to the king's question about how he could bear to live in such a turbulent locality, answered that 'They were the best neighbours he could have, for they made him thrice a day to go to God on his knees, when perhaps otherwise he would not have gone once'.[13] Kilravock was jesting, but in 1576 the General Assembly was in a more serious mood when it discussed feuding. Alarmed by Morton's failure to face the issue, it lamented a kingdom 'miserably divided in factions and deedly feed'. Its principal concern, however, was the same as that of the Tridentine reformers. Feud was so widespread and divisive that

> the parishioners, for fear and suspicioun which they have of others, dar not resort to their parish kirks, to hear the word of unity preached, nor to recieve the sacraments and seals of their salvation; quherof riseth a shamefull and insufferable slander to the Kirk of God, and his true religion within this realme ... [14]

This complaint was to be a persistent one, and the 1598 'Act Anent Feuds' was to some extent directly due to this specific grievance the church lobby kept before the crown.[15] More immediately the 1576 assembly decided to appoint visitors in various localities to 'endeavour themselves, and travell with parties, to reduce them to a Christian unitye and brotherly concord, as becometh the brethern and members of Jesus Christ'.[16] How successful these visitors were, if in fact they did anything, is unknown, but while the thinking behind this new campaign was traditional to the church, the campaign itself was more sustained than before, and its ideological thrust grew increasingly more hostile to feud and the social bonds which maintained it.

It was, however, 1581 before the General Assembly returned to the problem when attention was drawn to the disruptive effects feuding was having on parish life. Committees of local barons, gentlemen and ministers had been appointed to oversee parish reorganisation, but were being hampered by 'deidit feidis, grudgeis, variances and occasiouns of displeasours amangis thame'.[17] The assembly encouraged ministers to co-operate with local magistrates in persuading contending parties to assure one another, emphasising once again the church's mediating role in local communities.[18] Later in the year the assembly commissioned William Christeson to go and tell the king of 'the great division, and deadly feeds in all quarters of the realme, to the great hinderance not only of religion, but of the common wealth; desiring his Grace to authorise some Commissioners of the kirk, as they shall direct, for repairing thereof'.[19] David Lindsay and John Durie were also asked to petition the king about the 'great feeds and disorders in all the countrie, and to desire order to be put there to', and they too were to offer the church's services 'to treat amity and reconciliatione betwixt parties'.[20] Such appeals brought no immediate response from the crown, but in 1590 the king told the General Assembly that they had a mutual interest in promoting good rule.[21] That partnership was to be a fairly fruitful one as the crown slowly began to come to grips with private violence. A commission of ministers and other men were made responsible for 'taking up of deidlie feeds among professors',[22] the 1595 act designed to pacify feuds allowed the presbyteries a share in dealing with less important cases,[23] and in 1596 ministers who met for 'taking up of deadly feuds, and the like' were exempted from the prohibitions on public gatherings.[24] There is little surviving evidence of the kind of work the church performed in this capacity, although in Aberdeenshire it was credited with some successes,[25] and its greatest achievements lay in influencing opinion rather than in taking a formal part in the procedures of peace.

This ideological battle was largely fought from the pulpit, and about this the king was much less happy. In 1596 he told the church that in return for less public exposure of the crown's inadequacy in enforcing peace, 'his chamber doore suld be made patent to the meanest minister in Scotland'.[26] Yet while many ministers were not willing to offend the king, and were deferential to local noblemen, there was among the ministry astonishing confidence in the Word of God, which even in the mouth of 'the silliest and wikest bodie in the warld, will slaie and kill the starckest man that gangis on eirth'.[27] The assurance this gave, especially to ministers in somewhere like Edinburgh where they were less exposed to the power of local lords, allowed fundamental challenges to be made in a public manner about the very basis of a feuding society. Of course, God's Word was not perceived in magical terms, and Robert Rollock, the principal of Edinburgh University, warned his students that 'the conscience of a miserable malefactor will be so senseless, that it will nowise be moved by the preaching'. Such men would 'disdain and scorn' preaching, would claim that the minister did simply ' "prate and rail what he pleaseth" ', and 'after preaching, will go out merrily to his dinner, and there curse and swear and blaspheme God's name, and thereafter go to his bed as a beast, or a senseless sow'.[28] Such language was all very well when directed at the lower orders, but Rollock was arming his students to attack the men who ruled Scottish society, it was they who were being held up for ridicule as mindless pigs who wallowed in their own degeneracy.

In his *Institutes of the Christian Religion* John Calvin clearly opposed any breach of the sixth commandment by private men.[29] Calvin criticised those who thought that treating all men charitably was only for monks and others under special vows,[30] and condemned human pride as a 'disease' which 'begets in all men a furious passion for revenge, whenever they are in the least troubled'.[31] Justice was not the prerogative of the private man, but of God: 'Vengeance is mine; I will repay, saith the Lord', and consequently to take revenge was to deprive God of his right; it was to usurp the place of God. Commenting on *Romans*, he insisted that 'it is not lawful to usurp the office of God, it is not lawful to revenge; for we thus anticipate the judgement of God who will have this office removed for himself'.[32] This was primarily a theological, not an ethical or political principle, but in Scotland all three inspired vehement censures of vengeance. Robert Bruce, the Edinburgh minister, followed Calvin in exhorting men to leave judgement to God, proclaiming that 'There is nothing quhereunto nature bends the self mair nor to rankour and envie; and there is nothing quheirin nature places her honour mair gluckedly nor in private revengement'.[33] Bruce's 'nature' was that of the fallen man, and James Melville agreed that 'subtill revenge is nocht Christian', and saw 'all revenge as devillrie, and namelie, serpentine'. Melville, however, admitted that revenge was nevertheless 'maist neidfull to be market, it is sa in use in the warld in this our age, and esteimed a mean point of prudence'.[34] Charles Ferme, the principal of Fraserburgh College, was another to stress the sinfulness of vengeance in his own *Logical Analysis of the Epistle of Paul to the Romans*, describing it as 'the usual and daily practice of the natural man and the world who know not Jehovah'.[35] King James advised his son in *Basilikon Doron* not to tolerate any 'unlawfull things, as revenge, lust or suche like', putting vengeance in a context which was clearly concerned with divine law, and which saw it as a sin and not simply a crime.[36] The privy council picked up a second strand of criticism when it vilified revenge as 'ane forme maist baistlie and detaistable, and incredible to be in the persone of ane ressonable man'.[37] The reason the councillors had in mind had in some respects roots of a different kind, but the two strands of thought were closely related. What, after all, could be more unreasonable than to choose damnation?

It was the usurpation of divine authority which was, however, at the heart of the church's condemnation of vengeance. Rollock was scornful of

> these men of this land, who, in no measure, are patient, but are aye revenging — those who will do two wrongs for one, — (he will glory that he hath slain two for one, and he will brag of his foul murder, and say, 'I have one slain, he hath two'; he hath better than his own;) — it is impossible, I say, that these men cannot have God before their eyes; they look not to God, because in suffering injuries, they leave not the revenge to God, and so their damnation shall not be so much for the wrongs, as because they usurped the office of the Judge, and gave him not vengeance to whom it belongeth.[38]

That divine vengeance had an eschatological significance, as in Napier's vocabulary in *A Plaine Discovery of the Whole Revelation*,[39] and there was a duality of meaning in Rollock's stipulation to 'commit vengeance unto him who judges justly',[40] or to 'put the revenge in the hand of the Judge'.[41] Here Rollock was both expecting providential judgement, and looking forward to the punishment which would follow God's final judgement. There was a stern warning for the man 'who strkes with the sword at his own hand, whom the lord hath not armed to strike, he shall be stricken with the sword. It is a dangerous matter to slay, if the Lord put not the sword into thine hand'.[42] The implication there was clear: violence could be legitimated by God, and justice, or vengeance, could be done by those on whom God had conferred rightful authority.

The poet and minister, Alexander Hume, in 'Ane Briefe Treatise of Conscience', advised his readers to 'remit thy vengeance therof to God, and crave justice of the Magistrat'.[43] Rollock expressed this principle in the Calvinist language of a calling. He warned the ordinary man to 'look that thou go not beyond the bounds of thy calling', and asked, 'Shalt thou, that art a private man strike with a sword? Is that thy calling?'[44] Clearly it was not, that was the business of the secular, and Godly, magistrate. There was, however, a danger in this of seeking a kind of vicarious vengeance as Alexander Hume hinted at in his poem 'To His Sorrowfull Saull, Consolation', when he wrote that 'The Hiest judge he will revenge thy wrang'.[45] Neither God nor the civil magistrate was in the business of effecting vengeance by proxy, and Calvin himself had argued that it was 'superfluous to make a distinction here between public and private revenge', as 'he who, with a malevolent mind and desirous of revenge, seeks the help of a magistrate, has no more excuse than when he devises means for self revenge'.[46] Nor would he have sympathised with Hume's 'Consolation' if by that he meant satisfaction, for in assuming that attitude 'we do not make God so much our judge as the executioner of our depraved passion'.[47] Here there was no room at all for the moral of *The Atheists Tragedy*, that 'patience is the honest man's revenge',[48] but where the magistrate had been authorised 'to avenge the afflictions of the pious at the command of God' he was unable 'to afflict nor hurt'.[49] Rollock, therefore, was careful to distinguish between the obligation 'to commit vengeance to God', and the desire 'to lay a vengeance to a wicked man' by wishing God to do one's revenging,[50] and the king also understood the distinction, recommending that enemies of the crown be treated 'without using any persuasion of revenge'.[51] James had been tempted, since 'I have ever thought it the dewtie of a worthy Prince, rather with a pike, than a penne to write his just revenge', but while there had been exceptions, such as with Bothwell, he had tried to avoid this, 'wishing all men to juge of my future projects, according to my by-past actions'.[52] Yet while the man who was a king could not prosecute vengeance, the king who was a magistrate could, since 'the sword is gevin you by God not onely to revenge upon your owne subjects the wrongs committed amongst themselves'.[53] Here, of course, was a theology to which the crown was very receptive, and which could form the basis of its own political ideology. Thus in 1609 the privy council proclaimed that the crown was 'in nothing more wronged than by the presumption of any private subject in preissing to tak revenge of injureis done to thame at thair awne handis as gif the authoritie of a magistrat wer to no purpois'. Private vengeance was not only anathema to God, but had become the 'utter enemeis to owre crowne and estaite'.[54]

Propaganda of this nature was likely to be understood in 1609, by which time the civil magistracy was successfully containing private violence, but only two decades before it was those magistrates themselves who were most severely condemned by the church. In 1588 Robert Bruce told his Edinburgh congregation of nobles, crown officials, lawyers, rich burgesses, and possibly even the king himself that

> There is no example or proclamation of judgement that will make them leave off from burning, slaying, and murder. This is not looked to by the Counsell, and he who should punish this overseeth it. Ane thay that are inferior magistrates overseeth it, so that this land is overwhelmed with sin that it cannot be discharged until the great God himself do it.[55]

Here Bruce was less concerned with the General Assembly's complaint that feuding disrupted parish life, or with the theological implications of private vengeance, than with charging the entire political community with collective irresponsibility and sinful negligence in their governing. The implications of such unrestrained preaching alarmed the king, but the ministers defied him, and especially in the years between 1585 and 1596 they used their freedom in Edinburgh to expose the governing elite to withering attacks from their pulpits. In 1592 Walter Balcanquhal accused the king and his nobles of failing in their duty, and threatened them with the fate of the Regent Morton who had 'als great place in this realme as anie subject among you'.[56] Rollock similarly spurned all deference in a sermon in which he wished that 'our bloody men, whether they be noblemen, lords, earls, barons, or others, had been beheaded long since'. To him 'it is a marvel that plague followeth not after plague continually, till this land be purged of this blood that crieth continually in the streets'.[57] Like Jeremiah, Bruce had 'many things to lament', and he was in no doubt that the responsibility lay with 'our great men of this countrey' who were 'running headlong to banish the spark of life that is left in them'.[58] In Scotland, observed Rollock, men appeared to strive to commit evil deeds of murder and oppression with no thought for eternal life,[59] while Bruce drew conclusions of a wider social import, claiming that 'this country is heavily diseased ... so long as thir floods of iniquitie quhilk flow from the great men remains'.[60] The very men who, as lesser magistrates, John Knox had encouraged a generation earlier to take up the sword 'geven unto zow by God, for maintenance of the innocent, and for punishment of malefactors'[61] were now being accused of equating their own desires with what was lawful, and consequently, 'there is a heavy judgement hanging over this country'.[62] What was surprising to Bruce was that judgement had not yet taken place:

> To come to this particular, the Lord is not risen as yet in this countrey, suppose he hath sitten long. And why hath he sitten but to see gif his enemies will repent? And hath this taken effect? No; for he hath not greater enemies in no part than the great

men in this country, where the Word is so clearly uttered. So that the greater the knowledge be the greater is the contempt, and the greater the contempt be the heavier must be the judgement that abideth them. Now, in all this time of the Lord's sitting what are they doing? They are burning and scalding, slaying and murdering, and using all kinds of oppression, and raging so as there were not a king in Israel.[63]

The sting in the tail was reserved for the king, but it was the nobility to whom Bruce was addressing himself, and to whom the church was looking for a responsible lead in reducing the violence in their society.

Earlier in the century the theologian and historian John Major had written that nobility was 'naught but a windy thing of human ancestry. True nobility was the consequence of virtue, not ancestry'.[64] That, of course, was not an original idea, but it was being heard more loudly than before, and when Rollock preached that 'The nobilitie of the King is bot dung in respect of the leist drop of the blude of Christ', the thinking behind it may have been orthodox enough, but it popularised the criticism to which nobility was being subjected.[65] The king would have been as uncomfortable as any other nobleman with this kind of language, yet he too was a critic of the level of violence 'especially by the greatest ranks of subjects in the land'.[66] James was unhesitatingly conservative in his regard for the nobility as 'virtue followeth oftest noble blood', and it was the nobility who 'must be your arms and executors of your laws'.[67] However, that conservatism did not blind the king to their failings:

> The naturall sicknesse that I have perceived this estate subject to in my time, hath beene, a fectlesse arogant conceit of their greatnes and power; drinking in with their very nourish-milk, that their honour stood in committing three points of iniquitie: to thrall by oppression, the meaner sort that dwelleth neare them: to maintaine their servants and dependars in any wrong, although they be not answerable to the lawes, (for any body will maintain his man in a right cause) and for anie displeasure, that they apprehend to be done unto them by their neighbours, to tak up a plaine feid against him, and (without respect to God, King or commonweale) to bang it out bravely, hee and all his kinne, against him and all his: yea they will thinke the King farre in their common, in-case they agree to grant an assurance to a short day, for keeping of the peace: where, by their naturall dewtie, they are oblished to obey the law, and keepe the peace all the daies of their life, upon the perill of their verie craigges.[68]

Like the ministers, the king was not attacking the nobility because they were powerful, nor did he want to see that power reduced, but both were attacking the abuse of that power, and seeking to persuade individual noblemen to reform their behaviour. James was criticising a mistaken concept of honour and loyalty, and the violence of the bloodfeud; he had no intention of emasculating his most useful servants.

The nobility were, however, out of step with the church's and the king's thinking on how they ought to behave in a Christian and civil society. James wrote that they were suffering from a 'naturall sickness', and Bruce spoke in terms of a 'disease', analogies shared with the Danish crown, Christian III having called feud 'a general plague in the Kingdom', and James's brother-in-law having continued to hold this view.[69] This malaise was also commented on by Sir James Melville of Halhill who was concerned that the nobility 'hald na reull, they schaw na sound exemple',[70] while Sir Richard Maitland wrote in 'Satire on the Age' that honour and nobility were both in danger because of that lack of example expected from the leaders of Scottish society.[71] Instead of offering wise counsel, and being examples of virtuous living, they were the 'profane men' who surrounded the king,[72] the 'condemned men sitting in sic occupations, without onie thocht of thair damnatioun'.[73] In 1589 Bruce preached to a large noble congregation whom he invited to evaluate their moral, and, by implication, their political worth. The challenge this time was a personal one: 'Be ye in the rank of great men, ye ought to take tent to your consciences; speciallie, in respect that the Lord has placed you in ane great calling.'[74] That calling was not merely to serve their own and their kinsmen's interests, but to be active participants in government, to be Godly magistrates. As Williamson has rightly argued, such preaching actually underwrote the political structures of Scottish society,[75] but that did not make the exercise any less painful. Rollock was striking raw nerves when he asked, 'Art thou a King? Art thou a Councillor? Art thou a Minister? Gif I see not gude deidis in thy awin calling, al thy wordis is bot winde'.[76] James Melville was also worried that the nobility 'neglects and castes af thair publict callings', and defined these 'to be consallours to their King, fathers of the peiple, and defendars and meanteiners of the Kirk'. However, instead they preferred to live 'as privat men', being satisfied to 'keipe that quhilk thair fathers has left them, and tak thair pastyme and pleasur', and 'to sit at hame for their ease and pastyme, as thouche thay war born for their awin bellie lyk beasts'.[77] Like the previous generation of reforming ministers, these men were not interested in social upheaval, but they wanted social and moral change, and they wanted the nobility to lead the way towards it by fulfilling their God-appointed role in society, a role which the ministers had interpreted and were determined to encourage.

As a judge it is not surprising that Sir Richard Maitland saw the excess of violence as a result of the lack of justice and the poverty of the law. To him it was these conditions in society 'Quhilk causis of blude the greit effusion (For na man sparis now to slay)'.[78] The ministers, however, understood the problem as arising from the human response to God's divine law. As the writer of the *Historie* wrote when condemning the laird of Johnstone's slaughter of Lord Maxwell in 1594, whatever excuses Johnstone could offer, he had 'not respectit the law of God, that hes expresslie forbidden all kynd of slaughter',[79] and it was that disobedience which was the real issue. Why was it that the noblemen who were called to govern by example 'play the oppressours and bangsters'?[80] Bruce answered that: 'Thir oppressions . . . would not burst out in sick ane high measure, gif they had advised weill their consciences'.[81] Human sin was at the root of Scotland's violent society. What would become of them, Rollock asked, since 'We are fallen now to such shameful murder, as was never heard among Turks'?[82] Bruce's rhetorical questioning was in the same vein: 'What shall murder never cease? Shall never this ravishing cease? Shall never these oppressions cease? But shall the ears of the judges, magistrates and pastors, perpetually be grieved?'[83] The sin which generated this violence inspired Calderwood to portray an apocalyptic picture of 'the sonne slaying the father, the one brother the other, and brother sonnes killing eache other, theeves spoiling and oppressing, and men daylie ravishing women'.[84] Calderwood was reporting this long after it was supposed to have been true, and his intention was to show what effect the preaching of the gospel had had, but such language was also resonant with undertones of the Apocalypse, and it was in a context of expectation that much of this preaching took place. In 1581 there was no certainty that judgement would not strike as Balcanquhal lashed the nobility and the courtiers for 'the oppressiouns, the cruelteis, and all the rest of the vices that are into your courts'.[85] There is almost a hint of despair in Rollock's preaching that the sinners cannot be brought to repentance, that they had gone too far down the road to damnation to be saved:

> Fy upon foul butchers! who are more meet to be butchers dogs than men. What care they to wash their hands in innocent blood? But I say to thee, if ever thou gettest grace it is a wonder; fy upon the butchers of Scotland! ... When will these bloody men leave off the shedding of innocent blood, in this bloody and barbarous nation?[86]

Rollock's assertion that 'Of all nations it is the most barbarous and bloody'[87] was one which was deeply offensive to many Scots who were quick to distance themselves from the barbaric highlands. The Edinburgh bailie, Richard Abercromby, told the privy council in a complaint about oppression he had suffered on his estates close to the burgh that such behaviour was particularly offensive 'in a cuntrie quhilk sould be peciabill, sa neir the seat of justice, and sould rather gif exampill to the far Hielandis and Bordouris, quhair sic forme of unquheit is usit'.[88] The idea that feuding was not civilised was a powerful one, and was particularly likely to inspire the crown to take actions to protect its image and that of the kingdom before the outside world. To the king and his councillors feud thus became something 'odious to God and reprotchefull to that natioun'.[89] This national embarrassment could not be described by other than the most hostile language; it was 'that monster itself', 'that auld monster of deidlie feid', that 'detestable monster', 'that auld barbaritie', 'that mischeavous weid', 'this poisounable hearbe', 'a devilische forme'.[90] This was the vocabulary of a civil and a Godly government whose sensitivity had been aroused by the belief that 'their barbarous name is unknowen to anie other nation',[91] and which was determined to prove its own respectability by its commitment to 'roote out these barbarous feidis', and 'all sic customis, faschiouns and behaviouris as did in ony wayis smell of barbaritie and revenges'.[92] There was, of course, a propagandist value in this for the crown, but it did nevertheless reflect a feeling that if Scotland was to be counted among the civilised nations of Europe, and if it was to be seen to be among the elect, its people would have to learn to behave with 'comeliness and decencie that is requirit in a civill and weill governit peopil'.[93]

In spite of the language he and his servants used, the king's considered solution was cautiously to advise the enforcement of the law, beginning with those closest to him. Thus, 'ye shall make all your reformations to beginne at your elbow, and so by degrees to flow to the extremities of the land'.[94] He was not expecting conversion, but he did hope for education. In some respects so did Rollock, but he was less concerned with the political repercussions implicit in attacking the feud. While he could ask 'quhat regaird has God for persons?',[95] the crown could not possibly consider allowing such language to escape from the narrower theological context of God's final judgement. Damnation, therefore, remained the church's business, not the crown's. Rollock was contemptuous of such conservatism in the distribution of punishment, and asked, 'what damnation shall these murderers get who oppress the innocent man?'[96] None was the answer, if by that was meant an earthly punishment, but, said Rollock, 'I denounce a heavy damnation against thee; let the king, the magistrates, and all the world, wink at thee, the hand of the Lord shall light on thee'.[97] Such unilateral announcements of God's will created tension between the church and the crown, which disliked being exposed so publicly. In 1602 the king briefly imprisoned Henry Blyth, the minister of the Canongate kirk, after he preached a fierce sermon denouncing the crown's slowness in responding to a fatal encounter between the Lindsays and Ogilvies after a service in Holyrood kirk on that same day,[98] while in 1598 the decision by Haddington presbytery to go ahead and excommunicate Lord Hume for a murder annoyed the king as 'the Kirk must be satisfied also towards Lord Hume'.[99] Stirling presbytery had almost gone as far as that only a few years before when David Forrester was murdered by the Bruces, and Patrick Simpson, the minister of Stirling, did denounce the killers from his pulpit.[100] Yet the strain between church and crown which surfaced on such occasions did not destroy the growing awarenesss that they shared the same ambition, and the disagreement was largely a tactical one.

There was no argument over the ultimate fate of the unrepentant, or about the nature of their sin. Bruce uncompromisingly told his congregation that 'out of question ye shall see their end miserable; ye sall see them spectacles of the judgement of God'.[101] Rollock was equally determined to imprint in the minds of his listeners that what they were facing was not simply crime, but sin of the most wicked kind:

> Thou wilt come out and stick a man in sight of the sun; so, that murder shall not so much be laid against the charge as contemning of God, who shined before thee when as thou slewest that man.[102]

James Melville wrote to his patron, the earl of Angus, telling him that the violent crimes in this country were 'crying to the heavinnes for just vengeance from the righteous God',[103] and some men saw providence acting in events like the ruin of the earl of Caithness, which Sir Robert Gordon interpreted as divine punishment.[104] Yet other unjust men went unpunished, and the ultimate deterrent which lay at the heart of evangelical protestant preaching was in the judgement which followed death. Rollock threatened a bloodfeud with God himself. 'Take on one and take on all,' he warned, for 'if thou takest on the blood of one servant of God, thou shalt take on all the innocent blood from Abel to that man whom thou hast slain'.[105] Here was a kindred able to match that of the greatest lord! Yet such a man was not without hope, for in Christ's redemptive act was God's offer of peace. The cross was a divinely appointed assythment in which Christ had paid the price of God's justice. The theology here is conventional, as is the language it is expressed in, but the social context made it all the more potent. Thus in his sermons on Christ's Passion Rollock repeatedly speaks of blood, reminding his listeners that there is 'No remission without blood', a concept which would have required no explanation in a feuding society.[106] The murderer was 'but dead, if thee get no relief in the Mediator; without satisfaction for thy sins thou shalt never see heaven'.[107] God's holy justice 'requireth our blood', his wrath 'cannot be satiate without blood', but had been 'satiate by the only blood of Christ'.[108] Freedom from condemnation and peace with God came only when 'Ane man is justified by the blud of Jesus Christ'.[109] Such grace came free, but as John Davidson preached, 'the suddane appearance of the conversioun of great men, long inbred with evill doing, is not to be straight credited, without notable signes of repentance'.[110] That repentance was man's part of the bargain, and as long as it remained real God's forgiveness was on offer.[111]

The Scottish clergy had a pessimistic enough belief about human nature not to expect social peace simply to flow from men's personal conversions. Rollock thought that no man could 'make his peace effectual',[112] and Ferme believed peace among men to be impossible, counselling non-resistance to violence.[113] Alexander Hume appealed to his readers not to be in conflict with any man because of the damage it would do to their own conscience,[114] but piety of this nature was not the way towards a Godly society, not for a church which had so enthusiastically inherited a partnership with Caesar. Bruce envisioned a crusade, with 'God striking a man inwardly in his conscience with the feeling of his guiltiness, and the prince striking him upon the craig with the sword outwardly'. In taking up the sword in such a cause the prince was bound to succeed, since 'this is not the work of nature; it is the work of his calling; and walking in his calling, he must ever prosper ... '[115] Yet, as Rollock knew very well, 'to put power in the hands of a natural man, is as much as to put the sword in the hands of a mad man'.[116] In James VI the ministers recognised a magistrate who was neglectful rather than evil, who only required someone to 'stir up the motion which God has given him in some measure',[117] someone not afraid 'to tak Kingis and Princes be the lug'.[118] To some extent the ministers themselves filled that role. Davidson commented that 'I looke not for anie great good thing at his hand, till he repent him of his sinnes',[119] and in 1591 'admonished him of neglect of justice, carelesse appointing of the magistrates of justice, placing unfit men in offices, granting remissiouns'.[120] Bruce complained that James 'went not about in person to execute justice yeerlie, as Samuell did',[121] John Craig told him that his problems with Bothwell were a providential judgement on his failure to respond to pleas for justice,[122] and John Ross went as far as to tell James 'That blude sould put an end to him; that is to say, the puneischement and jugement of innocent bludeshed unpuneist, out of all questioun, sould persew him and hunt him to his death'.[123] Ross was, however, among the more extreme of the clergy, and was forced to apologise for his remarks, and Bruce was fairly confident that the king could be inspired to 'go forward in that work which he has already begun'.[124] Bruce's political realism forced him to conclude that such inspiration, or stirring up, would 'be done by you, my lords, who are about him', by those noblemen who were themselves exercising their power responsibly in their calling, both as lords functioning within traditional roles and as the inferior and Godly magistracy to whom Knox and Buchanan had both appealed.[125] Were they to fulfil those expectations and support the king in his own calling, then it would be as easy to 'remedy the oppression of his subjects, as it is to take his repast when he is hungry'.[126]

This enthusiasm for a reformed nobility contrasted sharply with attitudes to the court. There was little doubt that a minister like James Melville had the court in mind when he wrote of the 'Debauchit men, godless flatterers, wha haid sauld themselves in body and conscience to do anie thing for warldlie preferment'.[127] To him it was a 'godles and wicked' place, a nest of 'unthankfull flatterers', a rabble of 'prodigall spenders'.[128] Rollock shared in this distaste for the irresponsibility and evil the court stimulated, condemning the men 'who fling their heads in the air, and make their boasts of their evil deeds'.[129] This view of the worldly court was a persistent one in reformed thinking, but it was also a fairly long-standing theme of late medieval poetry, and Alexander Hume's satirical treatment of the court in 'Ane Epistle to Maister Gilbert Mont-creife' was drawn from commonly held Renaissance ideas about court life rather than from particular experience of the Scottish example.[130] Similar attitudes are present in Maitland's poems 'Na Kyndness at Court Without Siller' and 'The laird of Lethingtounis Counsale to his Sone beand in the court',[131] in John Stewart of Baldynneis's sonnet 'Of Ambitious Men',[132] and in the anonymous 'Suppois I war in court most be'.[133] Alexander Montgomery's own disappointments at court certainly soured his taste for it, as was clear from 'Ane Inventione Against Fortun; Conteining ane Admonitione to his Friends at Court', and in 'The Oppositione of the Court to Conscience':[134]

> The Court and Conscience wallis not weill;
> These tua can nevir weill accord.
> Qua leivis in Court and halds him leill,
> Lang or that lyf mak him a lord;
> And conscience stenzies if he steill:
> So Court and Conscience walis not weill.[135]

Virtue and wisdom were of little use in this environment, themes repeated by Hume and Melville of Halhill who argued that royal service should not be at the mercy of 'favour of surname, kin, frend or allia, bot for sufficiency, vertue, and loyalte'.[136] The king himself knew very well that the counsel he got was heavily compromised by private obligations, 'for when anie man's particular cometh in questioun, then the partiallitie may be seen'.[137]

Good counsel, it was widely believed, was most likely to come from noblemen who had obligations of their own, but also had a degree of wealth and power not to be so easily corrupted. Yet Hume was critical of the fact that

> How ignorant and inexpert they be,
> Upon the privie counsell men be chused
> Or else the King and councill ar abused.[138]

The point Hume was making was not that noblemen should be excluded, but the relatively conventional one that they should be qualified for the job, and in this Melville agreed, suggesting that offices should be reserved for 'the wysest of them'.[139] By that he did not mean that they had to be trained lawyers, and the followers of the earl of Angus were quick to disagree with him when he refused to grasp the chancellorship in 1585 because 'it required skill in the lawes, and more learning than hee had'. Angus had in fact attended St. Andrews University, and had been at ease in the company of Sir Philip Sidney and James Melville, but he simply did not want the position. The exchange, recorded by Hume of Godscroft, is, nevertheless, an interesting one, even if it reveals more of Hume's ideas than of the Douglases. They told Angus that 'learning does not alwayes the turne, knowledge of the customes of the Countrey is more requisite, and is onely required in Counsell'.[140] This honest wisdom, based on noble blood, experience of and familiarity with ruling, and sound common sense, was the basis of good counsel, not the worldly flattery of courtiers. It was not, however, exclusive to noblemen, and lesser men could aspire to high office if they gave such service. Chancellor Maitland was one who did, but Bruce did warn him that 'people have great expectations of new raised men', and condemned them quickly for their faults, as did God.[141]

Although a Calvinist himself, the king was of the belief that 'the most part of your people will ever naturally favour justice'.[142] Enforcing that justice was his business, his calling, as 'God hath made me a King and a judge to judge righteous judgement'.[143] However, James's concept of justice was not a legalistic one, and while he thought it his duty to 'put the lawes to due execution',[144] he added the cautionary note that a king should 'Use justice, but with some moderation as it turnes not in Tyrannie: otherwaies *summum ius*, is *summa iniuria*'.[145] Thus, for example, he might remit a killing where he believed a reputable man had slain some rogues in self-defence, even if he had no evidence to prove his innocence. It was obvious that such a man should not suffer, because 'lawes are ordained as rules of vertuous and sociall living, and not to be snares to trap your good subjects: and therefore the law must be interpreted according to the meaning, and not the literal sense thereof: *Nam ratio est anima legis*'.[146] Hume of Godscroft believed that the Regent Morton had ruled according to similar principles, and at the very least his description indicates how he thought Morton ought to have administered the law. He had employed

> a just moderation and tempering of justice with lenitie; punishing some (lest impunity might breed contempt of the law) punishing the fewest and in the general sort, lest too much rigour might drive them to despaire, and to force them to desperate courses, and to stirre up new commotions. He knew the nature of his countrey-men, how they cannot easily endure to have their lives touched, or their blood medled withall, and how hard it is to over-master them by the strong hand, and a violent way, but farre more easie to be overcome and gained by fair meanes; and therefore out of his wisedome hee made choyce of this, as the best way for his purpose of settling Peace.[147]

Hume's trust in noble wisdom is again evident, but so is his preference for a form of justice which was not an objective code. At the root of this attitude, and of the research by Balfour, Skene and Craig into the history of Scottish law was a basic mistrust of law as an instrument of political control, and one of Hume's complaints about the earl of Arran was that 'if there was not Law for it, it was all one, hee caused make a Law to serve his ends', or that the law was 'the cloake of their oppression'.[148] Sir Richard Maitland betrayed similar prejudices in his poem 'The Evills of new-found Lawis' which he thought were being manipulated by those in power.[149] This did not mean that 'the severitie of Justice'[150] should always be laid aside, and in 1604 the privy council condemned private assurances 'as gif the law did [not] astrict ony man to Keip his Majesties peice'.[151] The king would not have been in disagreement with that, but he was no more prepared to be compromised in his freedom by the law than he was by private privileges. James's concept of justice remained a conservative one, and instead he would 'mixe Justice with Mercie, punishing or sparing, as ye shall find the crime to have bene wilfully or rashly committed, and according to the by-past behaviour of the committer'.[152]

This subjective interpretation of law was highly vulnerable to abuse, but it was not just its abuses which were being questioned. Rollock disliked the power this gave to kings for quite the opposite reason that James was attracted to it. He did agree that one should not be rash in judging capital crimes, or in making crimes capital, and that kings and judges should, like any other man, 'be loath to put out that life that God hath put in'.[153] However, 'if the crime be capital and deadly, the prince hath no power to hold his hand back from execution, and to forgive'.[154] Rollock's magistrate was the prisoner of the law, and his conceptualisation of justice was Deuteronomic: 'Thine eye shall not spare the murderer, neither look upon him with a pitiful eye' was the text of his sermon.[155] This depersonalisation of justice was common to reformed thought, and in Denmark the church had encountered a feuding society with the warning that 'we do not condemn thee, but thine own deeds, and the holy law'.[156] Rollock therefore distinguished between crimes which only 'by the lawes of princes are made capital', and which 'upon just considerations, the prince hath power to dispense with', and those 'that are capital by natural law', which no prince could remit.[157] On this subject this unusually 'mylde and meeke man' could become very heated, threatening that 'the King of heaven will not have any to usurp his authority',[158] and comparing remissions to the setting free of Barabbas.[159] However, he was not alone, and Henry Blyth was another who publicly and specifically criticised the king for being so indulgent towards murderers and killers.[160] What Rollock and other ministers wanted was a more rigid adherence to the letter of the law, and more laws. In the lawyers trained in Roman civil law they found pragmatic allies. They too were frustrated by the lack of written law. According to Craig, 'with us there is the greatest scarcity of written laws and naturally in several matters we follow the Civil Law'.[161] John Leslie, the former bishop of Ross and session judge, made much the same point:

this far to the lawis of the Realme we are astricted, gif ony cummirsum or tribulisum cause fal out, as eft chances, quhilke can nocht be agreit be our cuntrey lawis, incontinent quhatevir is thocht necessar to pacify this contraversie, is cited out of the Roman lawis.[162]

That influence grew increasingly throughout the seventeenth century, as did the church's interpretation of law, and between them they gradually displaced and discredited the less formal justice of the king, and of feudal magistrates.[163]

The corruption and abuses of the courts inspired commoner complaints. Scottish poets of the fifteenth and sixteenth centuries had a healthy tradition of satirising judges and their courts, as in Robert Henryson's 'The Scheip and the Doig', or William Dunbar's 'Certane Ballattis agane the vyce in sessioun Court and all estaites'.[164] Maitland, who was himself a judge of the court of session, continued in that vein, particularly in his 'Complaint aganis the lang Law sutes' where he was critical of the fact that litigation was taking so long that barons were leaving unfinished cases to their heirs, and poorer men were being ruined. If the law was so obstructive:

> Then everie wicked man at his awin hand
> sall him revenge as he sall think it best
> Ilk bangeister and limmer on this land
> with frie brydill sall doe quhat pleis thame best.[165]

Alexander Hume was even more damning. The courts were too tied up with technicalities, 'Ane house ov'rlaid with proces sa misguided,/That sum to[o] late, sum never was decided,' the poor were exploited 'ane hundreth divers wayes', an advocate was unlikely to be helpful to his client 'Unles his hand annointed be with mair', 'skaffing clarks' would also seek ways to add expenses, 'In everie point they will be slack and lang', and agents were equally avaricious. To Hume all associated with the law were

> As sanguisugs [bloodsuckers] quhilk finds the feeding gud,
> Cleaves to the skin quhile they be full of blud,
> Quhile all the vaines be bludles, dry and tume.
> Na uther wayes the simple they consume.

Such justice naturally favoured the rich and powerful who could pay for it with their money, or their influence. In fact justice was for sale:

> Sum senators als weill as skaffing scribes,
> Are blinded oft with blinding buds and bribes,
> And mair respects the persone nor the cause,
> And finds for divers persones divers lawes,
> Our civill, cannon, and municipall,
> Suld equallie be ministred till all.[166]

Montgomery, who had had his own bitter experience of the court of session, shared Hume's pessimism about the justice of the courts. In his sonnet 'To the Lords of the Session' he wrote:

My Lords, late lads, nou leidars of our lawis,
Except your gouns, some hes not worth a grote.
Your colblak conscience all the countrey knauis;
How can ye live, except ye sell your vote?[167]

To what extent this lack of respect — and here one is again confronted by a conventional poetic theme — for the lawcourts and their judges was shared by less literate people is, of course, unknown, and the rise in litigation among those who could afford it shows their confidence in the likelihood of success as much as it does their belief in the justice of the system.

Equally objectionable to those who wanted to see a more objective law was partiality. In conformity with other reformed thinkers like Heinrich Bullinger, who demanded magistrates who 'swerves from the path of justice neither because of partiality, fear nor bribes',[168] Bruce encouraged the nobility and other men in public office to 'cast away your affections', to 'bury them under your feet', and 'let justice strike indifferently where it should strike'.[169] Rollock also warned magistrates to 'take heed of thie heart, and to the affections thereof'.[170] Secular commentators were becoming equally uncomfortable with this aspect of Scottish life. Maitland wanted judges to enforce the law 'Without favour freindship or feid',[171] and the writer of the *Historie* believed it was the duty of princes and magistrates 'equallie to do justice to all men, ever having respect to the caus, and not to the persone; for give a juge sall have mair respect to freyndship then to the equitie of the caus, the jugement is corruptitt'.[172] The king wrote that lesser judges were 'being caried away eyther with feade or favour',[173] and was, in principle, of the opinion that justice was not there so that a prince could 'reward your friends, or seeke to crosse your enemies'.[174] As Rollock said, it was indeed 'no small thing to be a judge',[175] for in accepting such a responsibility men were being asked to renounce their friends, and deal fairly with their enemies; to set aside family and feud. The fact that this did not occur was to Rollock 'a corruption sometime of the judgement of Scotland',[176] and as the king pointed out, it was unlikely to be reformed as long as the greater part of the administration of criminal law lay in private hands. It was these courts which were 'the greatest hinderance to the execution of our lawes in this countrie'.[177] This was not because Scottish magistrates were not interested in justice and were intrinsically irresponsible, for they were quite capable of being able to 'judge uprightly in general; but come to the particular, to kinfolks, friends, and alliances, this man or that man with his bud, O there the judgement is perverted'.[178] Here was the crux of the matter, 'for while a Turk may judge uprightly in general', it required a man of the highest Christian integrity to judge equitably in every case, and too many Scottish judges, both noblemen and those trained as lawyers, had too many obligations which compromised their integrity.[179] The king thought that justices of the peace might at least solve the problem of the franchise courts, but had to admit that 'I know no present remedie, but by taking the sharper account of them [the heritable judges] in their Offices; using all punishment against the slothfull, that the Law will permit: and ever as they vaike, for any offences committed of them, dispone of them never heritably again'.[180] James, however, was himself too subjectively involved in dispensing personal justice himself to be able to turn his back on it, and, as Rollock had perceived, the problem was not simply an administrative or political one, but had far deeper implications.

To Rollock and other ministers the favouring of 'particular' interests over objective moral choices was sinful. Alexander Hume singled out 'Judges maist unjust' as among those with most to fear from God's judgement.[181] Rollock thought judges must be free of all emotions, or affections, and counselled that even when faced with 'the wickedest in the world, yet seek not the destruction of the creature, but hate its crime, and look that thine affections slay not the man, but look that justice slay him'.[182] Nor would he allow the judge to take any vicarious pleasure in his sentencing of the guilty, for punishment was a solemn and public affair which could not be done in private since 'if there be good justice, the judgement must be before the people' who 'have their own right and interest in judgement seats'.[183] The king may have had some reservations about the people's rights in punishment, but he agreed that even for the prince it was not 'for satisfying any particular passions of yours, under colour therof'.[184] He too was responsible to God who saw any hidden motives, and if these were false, 'how justly that ever the offender deserve it, ye are guiltie of murther before God'.[185] As for the innocent, it was not enough to set them free, and Rollock demanded that their innocence should be publicly proclaimed 'albeit that the whole world should speak against it'.[186]

Few would have argued with the principle that the innocent ought to be protected: it was the protection of the guilty which caused greater debate. This was a society of mutual obligations, and those bonds were essentially sociable, not anarchic. Sir Thomas Craig believed that

> no safer or stronger guarantee for the permanence of amicable and loyal relations among the members of a civil society could be imagined than the feudal oath of fealty.[187]

According to him, 'Its principles are founded on the ideas of gratitude and ingratitude',[188] but it was the manner in which those principles operated in relations among kinsmen, and between lords and men, which had so corrupted the justice of the law. Maitland's complaint that 'Affectioun blinds us sae long, / All equitie is put away',[189] possibly betrayed a hint of his own guilt as a less than impartial judge, while Hume was more direct in accusing judges: 'They mon shaw favour to their awin dependers,/Quhat sa they be persewers or defenders'.[190] The king blamed the high level of crime on the fact that 'all men set themselves more for freendes then for justice and obedience to the lawe'. This was a corruption, said James, so inbred in Scottish society that 'bearnes sucke [it] at the pap'. Whatever crime a man committed, his friends would save him 'by feade or favour', by corrupting the courts, or by any other means within their power.[191] Bruce joined the king in subjecting the roots of Scottish society to critical scrutiny, and ended up attacking its fundamental power structures:

let no community of name, ally, proximity of blood, or whatsoever it be, move you to pervert justice, but let every man be answered according to the merit of his cause. Except these affections that accompany great men be removed, no question, ye must pervert that place. Let no thief pass because he is your servant, nor the murderer because he is your kinsmen, nor the oppressor because he is your dependar: Therefore in time lay them aside, and let the execution declare that no man is spared for feed or favor.[192]

The sermon in which Bruce made this plea was specifically directed to the large noble presence in his congregation who must have been unhappy with this redefinition of good lordship. In effect Bruce was asking them to be bad lords in the sense in which lordship was then understood. Rollock reiterated this, attacking the thinking which reasoned that if an accused man 'be a kinsman or a friend, they will say this man is no murderer, howbeit he be as great a murderer as Barabbas was'.[193] As for the followers of these noblemen, he scornfully called them 'silly ignorant bodies, who think the commandment and will of their masters will excuse them'.[194] Building on ground already softened by the humanist criticism of Major earlier in the century, the church was thus driving a wedge between lord and man, appealing to the individual conscience under the discipline of the preached Word of God as the arbiter of a man's actions.[195] Earthly lordship was limited, and no obligations to a temporal lord would excuse a man for his crimes. At God's judgement 'Na butie, blude, nor riches sall remeid, / But welth and wit, friends, force, and all sall faill'.[196] Hume was not advocating doing away with lordship, and other poets continued to praise other aspects of it. Thus in a sonnet 'To The Erle of Caithnes', William Fowler encouraged him

> to keip in justice all his pepill still,
> and baith with love and feare to governe thame,
> to save the poore anes, and to punish ill,
> and with great valeur purches glore and fame
> for to decore his house and noble name.[197]

Neither Bruce nor Rollock would have disagreed with that, but the politicisation of conscience they were fomenting did in the long term erode lord-man relationships. As Rollock said: 'Indeed ane man will gif thee gaine for honoring him in thy lifetime, bot quhen thou is lying in thy deathbed, can thou get advantage out of the hand of ane man?'[198]

The Reformation also forced lay people to question their family loyalties, and to place greater emphasis on the chosen community of the church. Calvin's reminder that 'we are bidden to honor our parents only in the lord'[199] emphasised the generational confrontations that confessional differences created. Theodore Beza's description of his conversion is also revealing in its implications for the ideology of the family: 'I burst assunder every chain, collected my efforts, forsook at once my native land, my kinsmen, my friends, that I might follow after Christ'.[200] Clearly the church did not want to undermine the family as a social institution, but both catholics and protestants demanded an ideological commitment to the faith before the family. The latter was reinforced within the community of faith in the condemnation of illicit sexual behaviour, the major preoccupation of the lower courts of the church,[201] and in the encouragement of traditional patterns of familial authority, as when Rollock criticised 'our lords and gentlemen' who 'think it enough to take off their hats, and to bow their knees to them [parents]. Stands the honour of thy parents in a ceremony?'[202] That was sufficient to preserve the family as an organic social unit, but, in common with much of the rest of Europe, it was not enough to guarantee the same level of political potency for kinship.[203]

The Gospel itself was essentially critical of any human relationships which obscured its truth. Bruce preached that Christ himself turned his back on the 'carnal band' which joined him to his own family, proclaiming that 'These are my mother and brethern quha heares the word of God and dois it'.[204] Jesus had taught that 'it is not that carnall conjunction that I reverance', but 'the spiritual conjunction' created by a unity of faith, obedience, and the presence of the Holy Spirit.[205] If Christ thought so little of 'the band of blood, running throwe a race', then so should the church in which men were united 'not by ane carnall band of blood or allya', but 'be ane spirituall band'.[206] Here was a kinship of a much higher nature. Rollock enthused that 'Thair was never sic sibnes betwixt twa thingis in the warld, as is betwixt the God of glorie and ane eirthlit man'.[207] He pointed out that while 'Thou will count thy sibnes with this man, and that man, gif thou be joined with him in blude or alliance ... all conjunctions amang men, ar bot ane pendicle of that quhilk is betwixt God and man'.[208] Hume even conceived of eternal life as a place of liberty where he was set 'Furth of the bands of flesh where thou art bound',[209] but Rollock, like Bruce, was more interested in emphasising different bonds than none at all, and told his listeners that 'Fra time thou enters in the Kirk of Christ, thou enters in bandes'.[210] Calvin had taught this too, admitting that while 'the condition of humanity requires that there be more duties in common between those who are more nearly connected by the ties of relationship, or friendship or neighbourhood', yet 'the whole human race, without exception are to be embraced with one feeling of charity'.[211] Hume similarly asked of men, 'Are they not all Adam's suns?', but he was equally interested in arguing that the recognition of man's common humanity was in itself reasonable. It was

> ... the force of reassone suld maintein,
> The binding band quhilk lastinglie hes bein,
> Be nature knit, ordoned till indure,
> Mens amitie and friendship to make sure.

And:

> Upon this earth as in a cietie wide,
> Like citizens we dwell and dois abide:
> And nature hes preferd us to the beasts,
> Be prenting reason deiplie in our breasts.[212]

To Hume it was irrational to allow society to be divided by particular interests — 'Particulair gaine dois sa man's reasone blinde'[213] — as such thinking created conflict among those with far greater bonds of affinity than those lesser bonds which set one group apart from another. Such irrationality retarded the recognition of nationality, and the evolution of the state:

> If this be trew quhilk trulie I report,
> How mekill mair sall love and lautie stand
> Amang the pepill native of a land,
> Quhilk dois imbrace, obey, and onely knaw,
> A kirk, a King, a language and a law.[214]

Craig explained the origin of communities in the necessary joining together of families as a means of defence, and the growth of the state as the result of the process by which the bonds between kinsmen were replaced by those between citizens:

> To the force of these circumstances the extention of amicable and social relations beyond the limits of kinship and dependancy is due: and from it also sprang the root (firmly planted in natural instinct) from which, in time, the wider relation of common citizenship was developed.[215]

The crown had its own reasons for being enthusiastic about such thinking, none of which was particularly original, but which had a greater impact than before when placed alongside the church's teachings. The king himself, in his own words, 'must be of no surname nor kinne, but equall to all honest men'. James, therefore, advised that royal servants should be dismissed if they continued to put loyalties to kinsmen before those to the crown, for 'it becommeth you not to bee followed with partiall or factious servants'.[216] This concern over the whole question of the legitimacy of kinship obligations belies Sir Richard Maitland's nostalgic poetry lamenting the passing of true kindness.[217] Maitland was premature, and while men like Robert Lindsay of Dunrod might write in specific instances that 'na kyndnes standis with zow quhar proffet may be haid',[218] Scottish kinship remained a very powerful social and political bond; hence the criticism. Its undermining by church and state in the seventeenth century was a long-term process, but the intellectual erosion had begun long before that transformation of loyalties was complete.

Honour too was being re-evaluated. Of course, debate on what was honourable had always interested chivalrous society, and the humanist emphasis on virtue, education and self-restraint was only building on a long-established tradition.[219] In 'The Palice of Honour' Gavin Douglas had identified honour with those of the warrior society, the 'most valiant folk', but he had hinted that others with quite different qualifications might enter into it.[220] Before him William Dunbar had been concerned that honour was in decay, another well-established tradition, and one continued by Maitland whose hankering for the good old days infects almost all his verse.[221] This idea that men were less honourable than before ran parallel to a growing discomfort with what that honour actually was like in practice. The writer of the anonymous 'Why Sould Nocht Allane Honorit Be' had as his hero a man who lacked all the martial skills, but 'He is bening, courtas and gude, / And servis us of daily fude, / And that with liberalitie'.[222] Why indeed should such a man not be honoured? Sir James Melville of Halhill, who was everything a renaissance courtier was expected to be, quoted an unknown Scottish poet, probably himself, to indicate his understanding of honour:

> Think ye that honour consistis in vain weidis,
> Or noblenes in outward braggis and bruitis?
> Gentilnes is kythed be noble deidis,
> As kyndly trees ar knawen be ther fruitis.[223]

In Scotland such criticism was far less popularly accepted than in England where honour was by the later sixteenth century much more clearly identified with gentlemanly conduct and service of the state.[224] Yet while the latter remained fairly muted, the former was gaining ground in court and noble society. In 1567 Robert Sempill had written in 'Ane Exhortatioun To The Lordis' of nobility as 'gentilnes', and of honourable warfare as 'gentill war',[225] and it was this kind of language, and the thinking which inspired it, which threatened the violent honour of the feud from within noble society. In Montgomery's 'The Cherrie and the Slae' it is Courage who asks 'What canst thou losse when honour lives', but it is Reason who has to bring discipline and clear thinking into the debate, thus providing a solution to the problem confronting the poet.[226] Melville also contrasts these qualities, and was critical of men who thought themselves honourable when 'Will is your gyd', while 'to raissoun ye gif na plaice', and he advised the king that the man 'subject unto raissoun' was stronger than other men.[227] The king, of course, needed no such advice, and shared Melville's view of honour, but few noblemen were as well educated as James was, and their honour was in fact resistant to education. After his period at St. Andrews University the 8th earl of Angus moved to the court at the age of fifteen where a private tutor tried to teach him Latin, logic and rhetoric, 'but with such successe as is customable to youth and to Nobilitie'. Hume of Godscroft, who was Angus's secretary, said that the earl came to regret this, and spent his exile in England educating himself, but to Hume such resistance was understandable among nobles: 'nature, counsell, and example drawing them rather to the exercises of the body, which are more agreeable to their inclination, and are esteemed more proper for their place'. To the nobility, learning was 'too base', and learned men were thought 'pedantick and of a mean spirit':

> Nay most men do accompt the studie and knowledge of them prejudiciall, hurtfull, and no small let and impediment to politick activenesse, and that it doth abate the courage of the minde and vigour of action, which is requisite for their charge and calling of being States-men and Warriours.[228]

Changing that attitude would bring about a transformation in ideas about honour, and with it a change to more civil behaviour. Thus, MacLean of Duart was seen by one commentator as a man who rose above his barbaric neighbours because his 'educatioun was civile', and he was 'broucht up in the gude lawis and manners of Scotland from his yowth'.[229] In Montgomery's poem, 'A Cartell Of The Thre Ventrous Knichts', it was concluded that ' . . . Honour is that only pearle of pryce',[230] and Fowler wrote in his dedication of his translation of *The Triumphs of*

*Petrarch* that 'Noble harts and generous high aspyring mynds' did place honour above any other code of moral behaviour,[231] but the honour they were extolling was quite different from that of the bloodfeud.

King James exposed the customs and behaviour of a martial and feuding society to examination in the light of this civil honour. In 1613 he and the earl of Southampton wrote the preface to a proclamation against duelling in England in which they ridiculed 'Cavillers' who were simply pleasing 'the vulgar taste', not gentlemanly society which ought to abhor such behaviour. Furthermore, duelling undermined God's law and that of the civil magistracy, and there could be no toleration of a code of honour which transformed 'consideration into passion, reason into appetite, and men into beasts', sending young men out into the field 'as soone as they can hold a Sword in their hand'.[232] These ideas were not new to James, or due to any particular influences in the English court. There Francis Bacon wrote in the following year that duelling was 'a kind of satanical illusion and apparition of honour; against honour, religion, against law, against moral virtue',[233] but in *Basilikon Doron* the king had expressed the view that the duel was 'committing the quarrel, as it were, to a lot; whereof there is no warrant in the Scripture, since the abrogating of the olde lawe'. He was, as one might expect, even more horrified at the idea of a sovereign submitting to a trial of arms, thus entrusting 'the safetie or wrecke of the whole common-weale' to its outcome.[234] James's condemnation of duelling, like that of feud, did not mean that he wished entirely to strip the nobility of their military ethos, and he was prepared to permit weapons at court which were 'knightly and honourable', by which 'I meane rapier-swordes, and daggers', not 'tuilyesome weapons' which, if worn at court, 'betokens confusion in the country'.[235] In particular he connected feuding with the widespread carrying of 'Gunnes and traiterous Pistolets', and was determined to regard 'all such as weare and use them, as brigands and cut-throats'.[236] Nor was it honourable to wear armour, especially when, as was common in Scotland, it was worn beneath the clothes. Appearing armed had less to do with defence than with intimidation, and when concealed hid evil intentions. Honest men 'should be ashamed to beare the outward badge, not resembling the thing they are not', besides which, he added, armour was a dangerous defence against shot. As for those who disagreed with him, they had no answers to his objections, and 'I knowe none but the olde Scots fashion; which if it be wrong, is no more to be allowed for ancientnesse, then the olde Masse is, which also our forefathers used'.[237] Underlying all this was a belief on James's part that the prominence of weapons, and the level of violence, reflected on his rule, as he said it 'betokens confusion in the country', and therefore dishonoured the king. James moved slowly on this path, but by 1621 he had completely turned his back on the honour culture of his younger days, proclaiming that he, the king, was 'the fountaine of all honoure'.[238]

Robert Rollock, however, scorned the whole idea of earthly honour, and subjected it to an even more radical criticism than that of the poets or the king. It was 'The warldlie man that huntis efter the honour of the warld', who 'desyres to be estemed of, to be had in admiratioun, and to be in gude grace'. He 'wald be accountit of be men', and would have 'the Prince accounting of him above all courtiours'.[239] Like St. Thomas Aquinas, Rollock argued that such honour was merely transient:

> Bot anis lay him doun in his bed, and let death seaze on him, thair he layis doun his honour; and gif ze tel him of the honour quhilk he was seiking, he will spit at it.[240]

In contrast to this, those who are godly during their lives will receive honour in heaven.[241] Here was an honour which all men could aspire to, and which was not the preserve of the nobility. They were accused of living according to a false sense of honour which 'will not let God be honourit' should it conflict with their personal honour. They would rather sin than be disgraced, or 'esteimed a fuill'.[242] This separation of martial honour, or chivalrous honour, from Christianity was clearly appreciated by those faced with the choice, as Lord Sanquhar admitted at his trial.[243] As long as the older chivalrous honour survived — and it did for a very long time — a dichotomy existed which demanded difficult moral choices. The problem of how to be an obedient, lawful subject, a Christian, and a gentleman all at once was not easy to resolve.[244] It was a dilemma which the clergy, however, did not have to face, and their redefinition of honour placed them high in the new honour hierarchy, and to some extent explains their social progress during the seventeenth century.[245]

What Rollock was doing was directing men's gaze from earth to heaven, and of course it is difficult to measure the effect of such preaching, and easy to be cynical about the likely response to it. Yet this was a society in which the word of the church did matter, and in which salvation was an issue. Thus, while it is unlikely that Rollock and other ministers succeeded in radically altering how people lived their lives in the short term, they probably did sow enough disquiet to bring about change over a longer period. In the seventeenth century men were no more saintly than those of the previous century, but they may have sinned differently, and as a consequence society was reshaped. Rollock told those who heard him preach that 'All thir outwarldlie thingis, as kindred, nobilitie, beautie, wisdome, warldlie eloquence, riches, honour, with all the rest of thir things quhilk man has in admiratioun is nathing',[246] and that their 'vain glorying' was nothing less than 'ane kind of blasphemie' in which, in another metaphor borrowed from the feud, 'thou spuilyies God of his glory'.[247] At death 'Their drinking, their hawking, their hunting, their caroling, their dicing, and other pastimes, will not then bring comfort or true peace to the soul'.[248] Nor did wealth and possessions bring any permanent security, and those 'that takis greit plesour in zour chartouris' were warned that 'thou is ane futile quha thinkis that thou hes ane inheritence in eirth'.[249] The New Testament was far more valuable than 'the testaments of their fathers', and 'albeit thou get earldoms, and kingdoms, and great possessions left to thee by the testaments of thy forefathers', judgement would fall heavily upon them 'if thou gettest not this testament'.[250] Men could choose to ignore this as impractical, and many clearly did, but at least in their pursuit of earthly wealth and security they could employ means less likely to incur divine wrath. The bloodless conflict of the courtroom did not inspire the same condemnation as the feud, even if the same avaricious and competitive instincts were its inspiration. Perhaps a more fundamental change took place as a result of the church's emphasis on individual guilt and conscience. Not only was an inheritance worthless in God's eyes, but 'the leist spark of regeneratioun is worth all the genealogies that can be in this warld'.[251] The world of the bloodfeud was being turned upside down as the corporate society of kinsmen, friends, dependants, and ancestors was replaced with the awful isolation of the individual sinner standing before the judgement of God. In this new world men inherited nothing from their parents, not even their feuds, and 'they get through them and their birth a poison and pest with their flesh, whereby they are made the children of wrath, and shall get hell for their inheritance'.[252]

## NOTES

1. See, for example, Bossy, 'Blood and Baptism', pp. 139–142, and for medieval Scotland, Lord Cooper of Culross, 'From David I to Bruce, 1124–1329', in *Introduction To Scottish Legal History*, pp. 9 and 11, and Grant, *Independence and Nationhood* pp. 116–117.

2. T. C. Smout, *A History of the Scottish People, 1560-1830*, Fontana/Collins, 1981, p. 101; Wormald, *Court, Kirk and Community*, p. 94; and Williamson, *Scottish National Consciousness In The Age of James VI*, pp. 72–73.

3. Bloch, *Feudal Society*, pp. 412–420; Duby, *The Chivalrous Society*, Chapter 8, 'Laity and the Peace of God'. See Keen, *Chivalry*, pp. 94–97, for the church's opposition to tournaments, and pp. 234–235 for opposition to private war. For the Russian Orthodox experience, D. H. Kaiser, *The Growth of the Law in Medieval Russia*, Princeton, 1980, p. 16.

4. J. Bossy, 'Holiness and Society', in *Past and Present*, 75, 1977, pp. 130–135.

5. J. Bossy, 'The Counter Reformation and the People of Catholic Europe', in *Past and Present*, 47, 1970, pp. 55–56.

6. *Ibid.*

7. Paoli Prodi, *Il Cardinale Gabreli Poleotti*, Rome, 1959 and 1967, ii, pp. 189–191. I owe this reference to Mr. Chris Black of the Modern History Department in the University of Glasgow.

8. Bossy, 'The Counter Reformation and the People of Catholic Europe', p. 56.

9. Wright, 'Venetian Law and Order: A Myth?', pp. 19ff.

10. Bossy, 'Holiness and Society', p. 134.

11. See, for example, Smout, *A History of the Scottish People*, pp. 100–101.

12. Macfarlane, *The Origins of English Individualism*, pp. 50–51; Stone, *The Crisis of the Aristocracy*, p. 21; James, 'English Politics and the Concept of Honour', pp. 45ff.

13. Chambers, *Domestic Annals*, i, p. 287.

14. *B.U.K.*, i, pp. 216–217. For a discussion of how the protestant church in Wurttemberg dealt with this problem, see 'Communion and Community: The refusal to attend the Lord's Supper in the sixteenth century', in D. W. Sabean, *Power In The Blood, Popular culture and village discourse in early modern Germany*, Cambridge, 1984.

15. *C.S.P., Scot.*, xiii, Part 1, p. 322.

16. *B.U.K.*, i, pp. 216–217.

17. *B.U.K.*, ii, pp. 520–521. For an example of this, see *Stirling Presbytery Records*, 1581-7, (ed.) Kirk, p. 246, where one party is excused attendance before the presbytery in an adultery case because of the danger to him of feud.

18. *B.U.K.*, ii, pp. 520–521.

19. *Ibid.*, p. 530.

20. *Ibid.*, p. 544.

21. Calderwood, *History*, v, pp. 105–106.

22. *Ibid.*, p. 178.

23. *R.P.C.*, v, pp. 248–249.

24. *B.U.K.*, iii, pp. 874–875; Spottiswoode, *History*, iii, p. 53; Calderwood, *History*, v, pp. 410–411.

25. Spottiswoode, *History*, iii, p. 62. Some attempt was made to link feuding with catholicism, *Spalding Miscellany, ii, 'The Woodrow M.S.'*, pp. 151–152.

26. Calderwood, *History*, v, p. 397.

27. Rollock, *Works*, i, p. 243 on '2 Corinthians 10'.

28. *Ibid.*, p. 521 on 'John III'.

29. J. Calvin, *Institutes of the Christian Religion*, (tr.) H. H. Beveridge, Edinburgh, 1863, i, p. 539.

30. *Ibid.*, pp. 359–360.

31. *Ibid.*

32. J. Calvin, *Commentaries on the Epistle of Paul the Apostle to the Romans*, (tr.) J. Owen, Edinburgh, 1849, pp. 473–474.

33. *Sermons of The Rev. Robert Bruce*, (ed.) W. Cunningham, Wodrow Society, 6, Edinburgh, 1843, p. 146, on 'The Fifth Upon The Sacraments'.

34. Melville, *Diary*, p. 16.

35. C. Ferme, *Logical Analysis of the Epistle of Paul to the Romans*, Wodrow Society, Edinburgh, 1850, pp. 283–284.

36. *Basilikon Doron*, p. 20.

37. *R.P.C.*, vi, p. 596.

38. Rollock, *Works*, ii, p. 173, on 'Of the Passion of Christ'.

39. Napier, *A Plaine Discovery of the Whole Revelation*, e.g. pp. 112–113 and 122–123.

40. Rollock, *Works*, ii, p. 178, on 'Of the Passion of Christ'.

41. *Ibid.*, p. 176.

42. *Ibid.*, pp. 36–37. Luther had also upheld this principle, see Broude, 'Revenge and Revenge Tragedy in Renaissance England', p. 51.

43. *The Poems of Alexander Hume*, (ed.) A. Lawson, Scot., Text Soc., 48, Edinburgh, 1902, appendix A, 'A Briefe Treatise of Conscience', p. 119. This was written in 1593.

44. Rollock, *Works*, ii, pp. 34–35, on 'Of the Passion of Christ'.

45. Hume, *Poems*, p. 35.

46. Calvin, *Romans*, pp. 473–474.

47. *Ibid.*

48. Quoted in Broude, 'Revenge and Revenge Tragedy in Renaissance England', p. 56, and see pp. 47–54.

49. Calvin, *Institutes*, ii, pp. 459–460. Also see *Ibid.*, p. 667; *Romans*, pp. 471–477; *Commentaries on the Book of Genesis*, (tr.) J. King, Edinburgh, 1847, i, pp. 206–208.

50. Rollock, *Works*, ii, p. 177, on 'Of the Passion of Christ'.

51. *Basilikon Doron*, p. 9.

52. *Ibid.*

53. *Ibid.*, p. 28.

54. *R.P.C.*, viii, p. 343.

55. Bruce, *Sermons*, pp. 321–322, on 'The Second Sermon Upon Psalm LXXVI'.

56. Calderwood, *History*, v, p. 161.

57. Rollock, *Works*, i, p. 505, on 'Luke VII'.

58. Bruce, *Sermons*, p. 108, on 'The Fourth Upon The Sacraments'.

59. Rollock, *Works*, ii, p. 386, on 'Of the Resurrection of Christ'.

60. Bruce, *Sermons*, p. 171, on 'The First Upon Isaiah'.

61. *The Works of John Knox*, (ed.) D. Laing, Wodrow Society, Edinburgh, 1846–64, iv, p. 482.

62. Bruce, *Sermons*, p. 171, on 'The First Upon Isaiah'.

63. Bruce, *Sermons*, pp. 313–314, on 'The Fourth Sermon Upon Isaiah'.

64. Quoted in Williamson, *Scottish National Consciousness In The Age of James VI*, p. 98.

65. Rollock, *Works*, i, p. 355, on '2 Corinthians 5'.

66. *Basilikon Doron*, p. 21.

67. *Ibid.*, p. 25.

68. *Ibid.*, pp. 24–25.

69. Philpotts, *Kindred and Clan*, pp. 82–84 and 101.

70. Melville, *Memoirs*, p. 269.

71. *The Penguin Book of Scottish Verse*, (ed.) Scott, p. 180.

72. Rollock, *Works*, ii, p. 432, on 'Of the Resurrection of Christ'.

73. *Ibid.*, pp. 376–368, on '1 Corinthians 2'.

74. Bruce, *Sermons*, p. 143, on 'The Fifth Upon the Sacraments'.

75. Williamson, *Scottish National Consciousness In The Age of James VI*, p. 135, where he argues that it was the Jacobean bishops who unsettled it.

76. Rollock, *Works*, i, p. 375, on '1 Corinthians 2'.

77. Melville, *Diary*, pp. 130–131.

78. *The Penguin Book of Scottish Verse*, (ed.) Scott, p. 180.

79. *Historie*, p. 300.

80. Melville, *Diary*, pp. 131 and 271.

81. Bruce, *Sermons*, p. 143, on 'The Fifth Upon The Sacraments'.

82. Rollock, *Works*, ii, p. 371, on 'Of the Resurrection of Christ'.

83. Bruce, *Sermons*, pp. 395–396, on 'A Sermon Upon Heb. XII v 1'.

84. Calderwood, *History*, v, p. 359.

85. *Ibid.*, iii, p. 776.

86. Rollock, *Works*, ii, p. 143, on 'Of the Passion of Christ'.

87. *Ibid.*

88. *R.P.C.*, iii, pp. 109–112.

89. *R.P.C.*, viii, p. 621.

90. *R.P.C.*, vi, p. 594; viii, pp. 591, 171 and 621.

91. *Basilikon Doron*, p. 25.

92. *Ibid.*

93. R.P.C., vi, p. 594.

94. *Basilikon Doron*, p. 25.

95. Rollock, *Works*, i, p. 396, on '2 Corinthians 4'.

96. *Ibid.*, ii, p. 37, on 'Of the Passion of Christ'.

97. *Ibid.*

98. *C.S.P., Scot.*, xiii, Part 2, pp. 1028–1029.

99. *C.S.P., Scot.*, xiii, Part 1, p. 214.

100. *C.S.P., Scot.*, xii, p. 114; *Select Biographies*, (ed.) W. K. Tweedie, Wodrow Society, Edinburgh, 1845, i, p. 78.

101. Bruce, *Sermons*, p. 143, on 'The Fifth Upon The Sacraments'.

102. Rollock, *Works* ii, p. 371, on 'Of the Resurrection of Christ'.
103. Melville, *Diary*, p. 131.
104. Gordon, *Sutherland*, p. 340.
105. Rollock, *Works*, ii, p. 143, on 'Of the Passion of Christ'.
106. *Ibid.*, p. 175.
107. *Ibid.*, p. 461, on 'Of the Resurrection of Christ'.
108. *Ibid.*, p. 282, on 'Of the Passion of Christ'.
109. *Ibid.*, i, p. 44, on 'Titus 3'.
110. Calderwood, *History*, v, p. 338.
111. Bruce, *Sermons*, p. 188, on 'The Second Upon Isaiah'.
112. Rollock, *Works*, ii, p. 489, on 'Of the Resurrection of Christ'.
113. Ferme, *Logical Analysis*, pp. 281 and 285.
114. Hume, *Poems*, p. 119, appendix A, 'Ane Briefe Treatise of Conscience'.
115. Bruce, *Sermons*, p. 395, on 'A Sermon Upon Heb. XII v 1'. Here Bruce was challenging the king to be Godly not only for his own good, but because the spiritual and moral state of the nation in some measure flowed from that. See, for the roots of this, Mason, 'Kingship and Commonweal', Chapter 7 on 'From Virtue to Godliness: The Later Works of Sir David Lindsay'.
116. Rollock, *Works*, ii, p. 116, on 'Of the Passion of Christ'.
117. Bruce, *Sermons*, pp. 395–396, on 'A Sermon Upon Heb. XII v 1'.
118. Rollock, *Works*, i, p. 414, on '2 Corinthians 10'.
119. Calderwood, *History*, v, p. 338.
120. *Ibid.*, p. 140.
121. *Ibid.*, p. 172.
122. *Ibid.*, pp. 142–143.
123. *Historie*, p. 322.
124. Bruce, *Sermons*, p. 396, on 'A Sermon Upon Heb. XII v 1'.
125. *Ibid.*, pp. 395–396. For the development of the idea of an inferior magistracy in Scottish political thought, see Mason, 'Kingship and Commonweal', pp. 286–302. The importance of the lesser magistrates in underwriting church discipline is discussed in B. Lenman, 'The Limits of Godly Discipline in the Early Modern Period with Particular Reference to England and Scotland', in K. von Greyerz (ed.), *Religion and Society in Early Modern Europe 1500–1800*, London, 1984, pp. 124–145.
126. Bruce, *Sermons*,p. 396, on 'A Sermon Upon Heb. XII v 1'.
127. Melville, *Diary*, p. 131.
128. *Ibid.*
129. Hume, *Poems*, pp. 76–77; Rollock, *Works*, i, p. 497, on 'Luke VII'.
130. Hume, *Poems*, pp. 76–77.
131. *Maitland Quarto M.S.*, pp. 16b–18b; *Scottish Poetry of the Sixteenth Century*, (ed.) Eyre-Todd, p. 205.
132. *Poems of John Stewart of Baldynneis*, (ed.) T. Crockett, Scot. Text Soc., New Series, 5, Edinburgh, 1913, p. 155.
133. *Bannatyne M.S.*, ii, p. 233.
134. Montgomerie, *Poems*, pp. 129–131.
135. *Ibid.*, p. 128.
136. Melville, *Memoirs*, p. 304.
137. Calderwood, *History*, v, p. 140.
138. Hume, *Poems*, p. 76. Similar criticism of a lack of education among the nobility had been levelled before by, for example, Major and Buchanan, see Mason, 'Kingship and Commonweal', pp. 47–48 and 394.

139. Melville, *Memoirs*, pp. 385–386.
140. Hume, *History*, pp. 429–430.
141. Calderwood, *History*, v, p. 170.
142. *Basilikon Doron*, p. 20.
143. *C.S.P., Scot.*, x, p. 524.
144. *Basilikon Doron*, p. 25.
145. *Ibid.*, pp. 37–38.
146. *Ibid.*
147. Hume, *History*, p. 331.
148. *Ibid.*, pp. 390 and 364.
149. *Maitland Quarto M.S.*, pp. 80b–81.
150. *Basilikon Doron*, p. 20.
151. *R.P.C.*, vi, p. 595.
152. *Basilikon Doron*, p. 20.
153. Rollock, *Works*, ii, p. 87, on 'Of the Passion of Christ'.
154. *Ibid.*
155. *Ibid.*, pp. 88–89.
156. Philpotts, *Kindred and Clan*, p. 110.
157. Rollock, *Works*, ii, pp. 88–89, on 'Of the Passion of Christ'.
158. Calderwood, *History*, v, p. 339; Rollock, *Works*, ii, p. 89, on 'Of the Passion of Christ'.
159. Calderwood, *History*, v, p. 359.
160. For example, when Lord Glamis received a remission for killing his own servant, *C.S.P., Scot.*, xiii, Part 2, p. 884, and Birrel, 'Diary', p. 56.
161. Quoted in Stein, 'The Influence of Roman Law On The Law Of Scotland', p. 219.
162. Ibid., p. 216.
163. See Stein's 'The Influence of Roman Law On The Law Of Scotland'.
164. For Henryson, see R. Lyall, 'Politics and Poetry in Fifteenth and Sixteenth Century Scotland', in *Scottish Literary Journal*, iii, 1976, pp. 6–10; for Dunbar, *Bannatyne M.S.*, ii, pp. 145–147.
165. *Maitland Quarto M.S.*, pp. 81–82b.
166. Hume, *Poems*, pp. 73–74.
167. Montgomery, *Poems*, p. 99.
168. J. Wayne Baker, *Heinrich Bullinger and the Covenant: The Other Reformed Tradition*, Ohio University Press, 1980, pp. 117–118. Knox too had separated the power wielded by an inferior magistrate from the man who held the office, Mason, 'Kingship and Commonweal', p. 300.
169. Bruce, *Sermons*, p. 355, on 'A Sermon on 2 Tim. 11 v 22'.
170. Rollock, *Works*, ii, p. 107, on 'Of the Passion of Christ'.
171. *Maitland Quarto M.S.*, pp. 80b–81.
172. *Historie*, pp. 245–246.
173. *C.S.P., Scot.*, x, p. 524.
174. *Basilikon Doron*, p. 22.
175. Rollock, *Works*, i, p. 77, on 'Of the Passion of Christ'.
176. *Ibid.*
177. *Basilikon Doron*, p. 26.
178. Rollock, *Works*, i, p. 505, on 'Luke VII'.
179. *Ibid.*
180. *Basilikon Doron*, p. 26.
181. Hume, *Poems*, p. 39.

182. Rollock, *Works*, ii, p. 75, on 'Of the Passion of Christ'.

183. *Ibid.*, pp. 179–180.

184. *Basilikon Doron*, p. 22.

185. *Ibid.*

186. Rollock, *Works*, ii, p. 89, on 'Of the Passion of Christ'.

187. Craig, *Jus Feudale*, i, p. x.

188. *Ibid.*

189. *The Penguin Book of Scottish Verse*, p. 179.

190. Hume, *Poems*, p. 74.

191. *C.S.P., Scot.*, x, pp. 523–524.

192. Bruce, *Sermons*, p. 355, on 'A Sermon on '2 Tim. 11 v 22'.

193. Rollock, *Works*, ii, p. 107, on 'Of the Passion of Christ'.

194. *Ibid.*, ii, p. 97.

195. Major quite specifically attacked the close bonds between lords and their men because they intensified feuding, see Mason, 'Kingship and Commonweal, pp. 129–130. Also Kelley, *The Beginnings of Ideology*, pp. 60–63.

196. Hume, *Poems*, p. 38.

197. *The Works of William Fowler*, (eds.) H. W. Meikle (vols. i–iii), J. Craigie and J. Purves (vol. iii), Scot. Text Soc., New Series, 6, Third Series, 7 and 13, Edinburgh, 1914, 1936, 1939, i, p. 256.

198. Rollock, *Works*, i, p. 427, on 'Philippians 1'.

199. Quoted in Kelley, *The Beginnings of Ideology*, p. 77. The church had always intruded itself into kinship relations, and had enormously influenced the development of the family in Europe, see Goody, *The development of the family and marriage in Europe*. Its disintegrating effect was especially felt prior to or in the early stages of the establishment of reform movements, p. 89–90.

200. Kelley, *The Beginnings of Ideology*, p. 56.

201. See, for example, *Stirling Presbytery Records, 1581–1587*, (ed.) Kirk.

202. Rollock, *Works*, i, p. 210, on 'Of the Passion of Christ'.

203. Kelley, *The Beginnings of Ideology*, pp. 53–87, calls this 'a kind of sublimation of blood into belief'; and Williamson, *Scottish National Consciousness In The Age Of James VI*, pp. 69–70, writes that 'Grace emerged as the means whereby natural man (with his traditional ties) could be transformed into Christian man (with altogether new political loyalties)'.

204. Bruce, *Sermons*, p. 67, on 'Upon the Lord's Supper in Particular'.

205. *Ibid.*

206. *Ibid.*, p. 66.

207. Rollock, *Works*, i, p. 386, on '1 Corinthians 2'.

208. *Ibid.*

209. Hume, *Poems*, pp. 35–36.

210. Rollock, *Works*, i, p. 348, on '2 Corinthians 5'.

211. Calvin, *Institutes*, p. 539.

212. Hume, *Poems*, pp. 69–70.

213. *Ibid.*, p. 72.

214. *Ibid.*, p. 70.

215. Craig, *Jus Feudale*, i, p. 2.

216. *Basilikon Doron*, pp. 22–23.

217. See, for example, *Maitland Quarto M.S.*, 'Advyce to Kyndnes', pp. 35–36b; 'On the Warldis Ingratitude', pp. 82b–83b; 'Na Kyndnes at Court Without Siller', pp. 30–30b.

218. Fraser, *Pollok*, ii, pp. 154–155, No. 152.

219. See James, *English Politics and the Concept of Honour*, pp. 59–60; and for Scotland, Mason, Kingship and Commonweal, see Part 1 on Chivalry and Citizenship.

220. See James, *English Politics and the Concept of Honour*, p. 4.

221. *Bannatyne M.S.*, ii, pp. 159–160; and *Maitland Quarto M.S.*

222. *The Penguin Book of Scottish Verse*, pp. 192–194.

223. Melville, *Memoirs*, p. 272.

224. See James, *English Politics and the Concept of Honour*, pp. 22–28. Mason has argued that the chivalric values of the Scottish nobilityhad been no more than superficially dented by humanist criticism: Kingship and Commonweal, p. 67. In fact writers like Boece had underlined the chivalric code, pp. 106–107.

225. *Satirical Poems Of The Time Of The Reformation* (ed.) J. Cranstoun, Scot. Text Soc., 20.24, 28.30, Edinburgh, 1889–91, 1892–93, i, p. 49.

226. *A Choice of Scottish Verse, 1560–1660*, (ed.) Jack, p. 57.

227. Melville, *Memoirs*, pp. 270 and 382.

228. Hume, *History*, pp. 360–361.

229. *Historie*, p. 219. By this time the association between highlanders and barbarism was becoming more pronounced in contrast to views held earlier in the century by Boece, Bellenden and even Buchanan that the highlanders were untainted with decadence and had retained their natural virtue, see Mason, Kingship and Commonweal, pp. 89–90 and 407–409.

230. Montgomerie, *Poems*, p. 213.

231. Fowler, *Works*, i, p. 15. The dedication was to Jean Fleming, Lady Thirlestane, dated 1587.

232. J. F. Larkin and P. L. Hughes, *Stewart Royal Proclamations, James I*, Oxford, 1973, pp. 302–308.

233. Quoted in Hale, 'Sixteenth Century Explanations of War and Violence', p. 11.

234. *Basilikon Doron*, p. 28.

235. *Ibid.*, p. 46.

236. *Ibid.*, p. 25.

237. *Ibid.*, p. 46.

238. Quoted in James, *English Politics and the Concept of Honour*, p. 8.

239. Rollock, *Works*, i, p. 331, on '2 Corinthians 5'.

240. *Ibid.*, i, p. 332.

241. *Ibid.*, ii, p. 300, on 'Of the Passion of Christ'.

242. *Ibid.*, i, p. 346, on '2 Corinthians 5'.

243. See James, *English Politics and the Concept of Honour*, p. 14.

244. Bacon wrote that 'By the law and right of arms, he that putteth up an injurie shall be degraded of honor and nobilities and he that revengeth himselfe of it, shall by the civill law incurre a capital punishment', quoted in Broude, 'Revenge and Revenge Tragedy in Renaissance England', p. 52.

245. Rollock insisted that ministers had honour conferred on them, and that to try and take it away was sacrilege, *Works*, i, p. 344, on '2 Corinthians 5'. James has already pointed this out for Caroline England, *English Politics and the Concept of Honour*, p. 75.

246. Rollock, *Works*, i, p. 355 on '2 Corinthians 5'; and ii, p. 629, on 'Of the Resurrection of Christ'.

247. *Ibid.*, i, p. 344–345, on '2 Corinthians 5'.

248. *Ibid.*, i, p. 521, on 'John III'.

249. *Ibid.*, i, p. 319, on '2 Corinthians 5'.

250. *Ibid.*, ii, p. 254, on 'Of the Passion of Christ'.
251. *Ibid.*, i, p. 355, on '2 Corinthians 5'.
252. *Ibid.*, p. 523, on 'John III'.

# 8

# *Personnel — Magistrates and Servants*

The contrasting reputation James VI has had among Scottish and English historians has in recent years been less pronounced, and the apparent paradox of his kingship is now closer to being understood.[1] Yet James did not have to wait until he had become King of England before he found his kingship under attack, and some of the fiercest criticism he ever had to suffer came from his fellow-countrymen before 1603. Much of that grew out of the debate over the fate of the reformed church in which James was an active participant, and which was never really resolved even at his death. However, James's achievement in bringing greater peace to Scottish society during his lifetime was loudly acclaimed at the time, and has rarely been seriously questioned since. But in the 1580s and 1590s it was, and this king who presided over the most dramatic reduction in violence in Scottish history was being widely criticised for doing nothing about it.

The loudest critics were the clergy, and their efforts to stir up the king's conscience have already been described. English intelligence was no more flattering than the outspoken presbyterian ministers, and reported 'his careless guiding and government' which permitted 'such murders and havoc amongst his subjects who should be preserved under his protection'.[2] The loyal courtier Melville of Halhill wrote that in selling remissions the king had 'his God offendit, for spairing to do justice upoun sic bludy tirrantis',[3] and the author of the *Historie* believed that 'when negligence has so overcum him, he lousis the brydill to all mischeif in his cuntrie'.[4] John Ross told James 'That he would crave God that his words war fewar, and his deidis war in greater nomber'.[5] All of this highlighted genuine areas of weakness in the young king; James was careless, he did sell remissions easily, he was an erratic worker, and he did make promises he could not keep, while prematurely applauding his own achievements. Fortunately, James was given the time to learn from his mistakes, and was surrounded by highly talented advisers and councillors who helped make his government so successful. In dealing with law and order the king came to show a very sustained interest in particular policies, to have a grasp of detail, and to meet most of his critics' early objections. The exception was probably remissions which sprang partly from a need for money, but more importantly from James's preference for peace rather than punishment. In 1599 he was very honest about what was often a youthful naiveté when 'I thought (by being gracious at the beginning) to win all mens hearts to a loving and willing obedience, I by the contrary found, the disorder of the countrie, and the loss of my thankes to be all my reward'. This 'overdeare bought experience' had taught him that too much clemency allowed offences to grow 'to such heapes', and contempt of royal authority to become so great that when an attempt was made to enforce justice, 'the number of them to be punished, would exceed the innocent; and ye would be troubled to resolve whom-at to begin'.[6] Yet

215

in spite of this confession the king never lost his impetuous desire to forgive, and while the privy council itself was not opposed to remissions, it had to continue reminding James of 'our humble opinionis concerning remissionis'.[7]

In 1579 the twelve-year-old king wrote to the earl of Eglinton and Lord Boyd asking them to make their peace with one another, and while another hand probably lay behind this, it was in this personal capacity that James would do most of his peacemaking.[8] Initially James greatly underestimated the difficulty with which peace could be made, a common enough assumption among the young. Following the Stirling coup in 1585, he thought that his nobility could be prevailed upon to forget about all the faction fighting and feuding which had dominated their politics for years simply by agreeing to unite behind the crown.[9] A year later Randolph wrote of his 'readiness to compose matters that might trouble his peace, though with some disadvantage'.[10] In 1587 his idealism was taken even further in the great banquet he held for his nobles, and which embraced both the Christian love-feast and the feasting of rival warriors in heroic and barbarian cultures:

> At this conventioun the King maid ane harang to his nobellitie and estaites, declairing, that seing he was now come to his perfect aige of twentie ane yeiris compleit, hafing mony wechtie effaires to be advysit, thocht it best first to reconceill his nobellitie, quhairin his Majestie had teane no small travell, and to such poynt as all sould tend to the pleasour of God, his Majesties standing, the weill of the countrie, and thair awin ease and tranquilletie; protesting befoir God that he loved nothing so mikle as ane perfyt unioun and reconciliatioun amangis his nobellety in hairtes and gif ony sould seime obstinat, that the remnant of his nobiletie sould hald hand to the repressing of thame, and the first brekkaris of that happie unioun persewit be all extremitie.[11]

Here the theatricals and the symbolism might have been right, but the substance was entirely lacking. Until the nobility themselves had been persuaded that peace and order were in their interests too, and until James was prepared to work at the problem, such public demonstrations were meaningless.

It was another eight years before James returned to the bloodfeuds. Roger Aston thought that he simply wanted a quiet life after the strains of dealing with Bothwell and Huntly, so that 'he may have hunting and hawking, which are his chief delights'.[12] However, the king's objections to feuding ran deeper, and in 1595 he summoned all his nobles who were at feud to Edinburgh where he attempted to either reconcile them or put them under assurance.[13] The death of Chancellor Maitland may have been one reason for this sudden burst of activity, as

> During the life of the late Chancellor his Majesty thought all well governed. Now he begins to think other ways, minding by using of his laws to make great profit to himself and contentment to his people; which order if it be protected shall 'effectuat' both.[14]

Throughout the winter of 1595-96 the king was 'so resolute to all agreement of feuds against this time as they adventure to excuse but not deny their coming'. Furthermore, 'As to the horners the King is severe therein and begins to reign and rule like himself'.[15] Then, as happened so often with James, he ran out of steam, and the campaign collapsed, it being too dependent upon his own involvement in it to succeed without him.

Two years later, in 1598, the king's own officials complained that James was neglecting affairs, and making it impossible for them to perform their responsibilities properly. In particular he had abandoned his own work to go hunting with the duke of Holstein, his brother-in-law. However, swapping notes with Holstein may have been a worthwhile exercise, the Danish crown being more experienced than his own in pacifying feuds.[16] In the summer of 1598 James returned to the problem, having decided to make the feuds a major issue at a convention of the estates planned for the end of June. He and his councillors drew on the example of parliament's settlement of the Gordon-Forbes feud, between 1578 and 1581, and on traditional pacification procedures, but the final legislation was very much a reflection of the king's own ideas. In 1604 the privy council drew attention to the fact that the 1598 act had been constructed from 'certane articles pennit be his Majesties awin self for removing of the saidis feidis'.[17] In 1598 James was more determined to follow this up than he had been three years earlier, and in the following months it was reported that 'The King hastens all agreement of feuds', that 'The King is hastening to agree all other feuds by all possible means or at least to get them under assurance', and that 'The King labours these agreements at all hands'.[18] Much of the motivation for this came from James's fear that he would have to fight for the English succession, and that he would need a united nobility with which to do it.[19]

However, interest did not wane after 1603. Within a year a new act had been passed which incorporated within it ideas James had expressed five years earlier in *Basilikon Doron.*[20] Both Spottiswoode and the privy council itself state that the king wrote to them ordering that a new act be passed which would put less influence on assurances as they implied that the subject had a right to feud. The new act duly incorporated the king's thinking.[21] Much the same happened in 1609 when James wrote to the council expressing his concern that some feuds were still causing difficulties, and ordering that they stop allowing assurances at all as they 'retene the memorie of that monster itselff, and makis you by accepting any suche conditioun to seame to gif allowance thairto'. The letter was written on 29 July 1609, and on 6 August the privy council published a new proclamation which basically reiterated the king's words to them.[22] Elsewhere Spottiswoode wrote that James 'was ever seriously commending to the council the removing of the barbarous feuds'.[23]

The king's commitment to ending feuding went beyond creating policy, and he consistently involved himself in the more traditional role for a king of mediator. In 1589 he composed a feud between Huntly and Marischal,[24] in 1591 he intervened in the internal Kerr feud,[25] and in 1599 he brought the lairds of Drumlanrig and Johnstone to agreement.[26] At a convention in 1602 he persuaded Lord Ochiltree and Lord Loudoun to submit their feud,[27] and at the same time took up the dispute between Lennox and Argyll which involved him in their affairs from February through to May, in which month he spent two whole days on this feud alone.[28]

Even minor feuds like that between the laird of Abercairny and John Gibson received remarkably detailed attention from the king.[29] This was the king acting as a feudal overlord, living and working among his vassals, and persuading them towards just peace settlements. It was the kind of government to which the Scottish nobles responded, and in which James was at his best.

Much of this disappeared in 1603 when James departed for London, but even from that distance he continued to fulfil this role where possible. In 1605 he wrote to the privy council demanding information on the Douglas-Stewart feud, and in 1608 he again asked for details following Lord Torthorwald's murder.[30] In 1606 he gave specific instructions regarding Gilbert Gray of Bandirrane who had slaughtered the master of Oliphant,[31] and a year later he told the council how to handle the feud between the earl of Mar and Colquhoun of Luss.[32] Also in 1607, he expressed his anger at the murder by the laird of Lochinvar of one of his own servants, and shortly afterwards Lochinvar was charged with the crime.[33] In 1608 his instructions for the treatment of a feud between the Forbes family and Irvine of Drum were acted upon immediately the letter was received, and the council even picked up some of his phraseology in the process.[34] In the following year he told the council to ensure that no feud broke out between two Scott lairds after he had received information from one of them, and in 1614 he was still showing an interest in this quarrel.[35] In 1609 it was he who insisted on the execution of Lord Doune's son for killing a man in a feud,[36] and on Lord Maxwell's death three years later for another feud killing.[37] However, in 1611 he seemed to run out of patience when commenting on yet another feud, and he told the privy council to stop bothering him with questions of this nature since they ought to know by now how to handle a feud.[38] Thirteen years after the 1598 act he was entitled to his outburst.

While the union of 1603 reduced the king's personal involvement in mediation, it did not end his interest in feuding, and it was only from about 1610 that it began to wane, although by then the problem itself was very much in decline. When James did return home in 1617, he found himself playing the old role of overlord in pacifying a feud between Huntly and Errol who had fallen out following some bloodshed between their followers.[39] Whether it is in this, or in the flow of letters between James, his councillors and those involved in the Crawford-Edzell feud,[40] one finds a king with a very clear grasp of detail, and a major influence in directing policy. The achievement, which James was not slow to claim for himself, was a real one, even if it had taken a lot of prompting to force the king to recognise that feuding could not be wished away; that must be worked for with patience and determination.

Obviously the king did not do all this alone, and neither the campaign against feuding in particular nor against violence in general could have been successful without the co-operation of other powerful interests within the kingdom. Clearly the church was a close ally, indeed it was the inspiration behind the whole commitment to better law and order. Yet while the church and the crown were a persuasive authority, very little could have been achieved without the nobility. The more traditional early modern picture of a declining nobility being ground between absolutist monarchies and a progressive middle class is looking increasingly unconvincing. Both in France and in England the success of the nobility in adapting to changes taking place around them, and of drawing into their ranks rising social groups ensured that aristocratic power was far from spent. Elsewhere, such as in Spain or in Poland, noble power was in fact increasing in relation to the crown or other status groups.[41] In Scotland, too, there was little serious challenge to the nobility although, as we saw, there was considerable debate over how they exercised their power. The changes which resulted from that debate certainly altered the nobility, and the nature of that change has yet to be fully investigated, but it is a mistake to see in this the culmination of the crown-magnate struggle which formed the bedrock of Scottish political history from the fourteenth to the sixteenth centuries.[42] James VI was certainly not anti-noble, quite the contrary. His problem was that 'noblemen forbear Court and Council, unless for their own particulars, when the occasions force them'.[43] What James wanted, and needed if his policies were to succeed, was a working nobility who would give him their counsel in making policy and their co-operation in enforcing it. Without either, his government could not be effective.[44] In maintaining a high aristocratic profile in government James was not entirely successful, but enough noblemen did continue to give him this kind of service to carry through the changes which would have been impossible without them.

John Erskine, 7th earl of Mar, was eight years older than the king, but the two were brought up together at Stirling Castle, of which his family had the keepership. Mar appears to have been more influenced than James was by their tutor, George Buchanan, and he was an early enthusiast of the militant protestants — his father had been regent in 1571-72 — who made his first political act in 1578 when he helped Morton regain control of the young king. He survived Morton's fall in 1580, but was excluded from government by Lennox and Arran. This and his religious beliefs made him a prominent figure in the Ruthven faction which itself formed the government in 1582-83, and while he again survived its overthrow, his part in the failed coup against Arran in 1584 resulted in exile. A year later he returned with the exiled lords, was admitted to the privy council, had Stirling Castle restored to him, and over the next decade became a prominent member of the court who prevented his sympathies for the presbyterians and for Bothwell leading him into conflict with the king. From 1592 he was being tipped as the next chancellor, and these expectations were enhanced when he was given custody of Prince Henry in 1594. Mar had been present at the 1587 peace banquet, and was regularly in attendance at council meetings at the time of the 1595 initiative against feuds, but his extremely keen sense of honour, and his involvement in a feud with the Livingstons which grew out of rivalry with Maitland, and from the queen's jealousy, resulted in his leading the opposition to the 1598 act. That may have cost him the chancellorship, but he remained on the reconstituted privy council, and showed a high attendance throughout the winter and early spring of 1598-99 when the act began to be enforced. Thereafter his attendance remained high, and he was one of the lords of the articles in 1600 when the 'Act Anent Feuding' received statutory authority from parliament. His relationship with the king also remained close; he helped rescue James from the Edinburgh mob in 1597, was one of those who frustrated the Gowrie conspiracy in 1600, and was sent on embassy to London in 1601 where he made a favourable impression on Elizabeth. In 1603 he accompanied James south, being created a Knight of the Garter and being admitted to the English privy council. This did not mark an end of his work in Scotland, however, and over the next few years he fulfilled a number of commissions before becoming lord treasurer in 1616. A year later he returned to Scotland permanently, apparently for health reasons, and he continued to perform his duties as treasurer until his retiral in 1630. He died four years later after a lifetime of political activity, and, after 1585, loyal service to the king with whom he remained a close friend.[45]

John Graham, 3rd earl of Montrose, was of an older generation than Mar and the king. He had sided with the king's party during the civil war, and entered the Regent Lennox's privy council in 1571. He played an important part in negotiating and enforcing the Pacification of Perth, but by 1578 had fallen out with Morton, joining the faction which opposed him. Three years later he had a central role in bringing Morton to the scaffold, and in 1583 he became a close ally of Arran, ensuring that Gowrie was executed in 1584. His loyalty was rewarded with an appointment as an extraordinary lord of session, with Gowrie's old office as treasurer, and with a share in the forfeited Ruthven estates. Most of this was lost in 1585 when the exiled lords returned, but he was lucky to escape with no more dire consequences than bloodfeuds arising from the above executions. While he was allowed to retain his seat on the privy council as part of the 1585 compromise, he was effectively excluded from power, and was implicated in the 1589 rebellion against the men who had defeated him four years before. However, in 1591 he was re-admitted to the court of session, serving there until 1596, and his loyalty throughout the turbulent troubles with Bothwell and Huntly brought his talents once again into royal service. His privy council attendance steadily grew, and in 1598 he was surprisingly appointed president of the council, becoming chancellor in 1599 at the age of fifty-one. It was an office he filled quietly, but he did bring great experience and the dignity of his status to it. From 1599–1604 he presided over a period of intense anti-feud activity, particularly the pacification of a great many feuds among the nobility, an achievement which would have been much more difficult under a chancellor who was not a nobleman. Like Mar he had feuds of his own, especially with Errol in the 1590s, but he was always sympathetic to strong royal government, and clearly shared Arran's more extreme ideas about how royal authority ought to be enforced.[46]

No other earls gave this level of service in the royal administration, but that was not necessarily the best kind of service noblemen could offer. Mar's role as a close companion of the king was at least as important as his formal duties in bureaucratic offices, and so too were his and Montrose's responsibilities as powerful local magistrates and lords. Archibald Douglas, 8th earl of Angus, died in 1588 when aged only thirty-three, but he could easily have attained the heights of royal confidence and office-holding enjoyed by Mar and Montrose had he lived longer.

He was also an even greater power than they were locally. Like Mar he had a strict protestant education, though in Morton's household, being the regent's nephew, and at St. Andrews University. In 1574, at the age of nineteen, he was appointed lieutenant of the entire borders, adding to this the west wardenry in 1577. During the last two years of Morton's domination of Scottish politics he became his uncle's principal ally, and not surprisingly he was forfeited in 1581 following his fall. He was in exile in England in 1581–82 and again in 1583–85, and there he applied himself to widening his education, and befriended the presbyterian exiles to whom he came to epitomise the Godly magistrate. In 1585 he was one of the leaders of the Stirling coup, but following its success he refused to be considered for the chancellorship, and

> professed that he delighted as much to hunt out a theefe, as others did to hunt a haire; and that it was as natural to him, as any other pastime or exercise is to another man.[47]

While he did attend the privy council fairly regularly, it was on the borders that he continued to do his best work before dying of consumption three years later.[48]

Lord John Hamilton was the effective head of the defeated Marian party from 1575, and it was because of this and his family's feud with the Douglases that he was driven into exile in England in 1579. He too returned in 1585, but was no more willing than Angus to fill royal offices. Already in his later forties, Hamilton became the elder statesman of the Scottish court, defeat and exile having tempered his taste for political adventure. His loyalty was probably the greatest service he gave, in recognition of which James helped him to rebuild the lost Hamilton fortune, and in 1599 raised him to marquis. However, while he had little interest in the privy council, Hamilton did some useful policing on the borders, and was usually present at parliaments and conventions, including that of 1598.[49]

In contrast, Ludovick Stewart, 2nd duke of Lennox, was a generation younger than the king, but he too represented a potentially divisive figure in that he was the king's heir until the birth of Prince Henry. Although nominal offices and gifts were showered on him throughout his early years, it was not until the crisis with Bothwell that he began to exercise any power on his own. By remaining loyal to the king he divided the Stewarts, and was the chief beneficiary of Bothwell's ruin. However, in 1593 he briefly joined the Stewarts and helped Bothwell in his only successful coup, thus making it plain how important a figure he was. A year later he played a major part in the royal campaign against his brother-in-law, Huntly. From 1594–1603 his attendance at the privy council was respectable, and following his lieutenancy in the north in 1594 he held further lieutenancies in the highlands and islands in 1598 and 1599. In 1601 he headed an important embassy to France and in 1603 he accompanied James south, becoming a naturalised Englishman — by birth he was French — and continuing to be a dominant court figure. In fact after his arrival in Scotland in 1583 Lennox probably spent more time at court than any other nobleman, and had among his many offices that of lord high chamberlain which gave him enormous influence within the king's chamber. Lennox had feuds with Montrose and Argyll, but was never too deeply implicated in any violence, he attended the 1598 convention, and he was among the king's most intimate advisers and servants in Scotland for over a decade before the union.[50]

Less intense service was rendered at a distance by Archibald Campbell, 7th earl of Argyll, who recovered from his humiliation at Glenlivet to play an essential role in crushing the MacGregors, and in putting down the MacDonald rebellion in 1614–15. Although nominated to the privy council in 1598, he rarely attended, and he was never on good terms with the king. However, his work in the highlands, for which he received a series of commissions of lieutenancy and justiciary, was significant, even if it was always self-interested. He also retained his hereditary office of justice-general.[51]

John Kennedy, 5th earl of Cassillis, was entangled in a whole web of local feuds, and one doubts if his attendance at the 1598 convention would have been to support the feuding legislation. He did, however, put in an erratic attendance at the privy council, served for a very short time as treasurer, and was nominated to the new council in 1610.[52] Most of the remaining earls confined their responsibilities to local affairs.

Andrew Stewart, 3rd Lord Ochiltree, came to prominence after Bothwell's fall in 1591, when his own feud with the earl made him of particular use to the king. Moray's murder forced him to change sides, but the king later persuaded Ochiltree to abandon Bothwell for good. From 1591 he was a privy councillor, and was re-appointed in 1598 when he also attended the convention of the estates which legislated against feuding. He was at various times first lord of the bedchamber, governor of Edinburgh Castle, and keeper of ordnance, but his most enduring work was done as lieutenant of the western isles in 1608 when he was responsible for the capture of the island chiefs which led to their recognition of the Iona Statutes a year later. After 1610 Ochiltree began to shift his interests to Ireland where the king had rewarded him with lands for his years of loyal service.[53]

One identifiable group of noblemen who gave good service to James were men who themselves had been Marians, or whose families had been. Lord Hamilton was the most important of these, but there were a number of others. John Fleming, 6th Lord Fleming, had himself fought for the queen during the civil war. In 1579 he was admitted to the household, and in 1583 was appointed one of the ushers. In 1590 Fleming went on embassy to Denmark, but it was not until 1598 that he received a seat on the privy council. He was present at the 1587 banquet, the 1598 convention, and sat on about half the privy council meetings during the months immediately after the 'Act Anent Feuds' was passed. Thereafter his attendance was never very high, but in 1603 he became earl of Wigton in recognition of his long years of service. A number of important commissions were filled by him over the next few years, including bringing the Cunningham–Montgomery feud to a peaceful conclusion, but while he was re-appointed to the privy council in 1610, his involvement in public affairs began to decline, and he died in 1619.[54]

Another man who had ended up on the losing side in 1573 was Alexander Livingston, 7th Lord Livingston. Taken prisoner in 1571, he remained a political suspect throughout the Morton regency, but like Fleming was introduced into the king's chamber after Morton's temporary eclipse in 1578. In 1581 he sat on the assize which convicted Morton, but a year later was forced into exile along with the fallen Lennox. He returned in 1583 with the young Ludovick Stewart, was rewarded with some of Mar's forfeited properties, and in 1584 helped frustrate Mar's coup at Stirling. This rivalry with Mar continued into the 1590s when it thrust Livingston into the centre of court intrigue. In 1592 he succeeded his father as Lord Livingston, and began to show an interest in the work of the privy council which he also joined in that year. He was appointed to the reconstituted council in 1598, attending the convention that year, and remained a fairly regular councillor until 1603. Livingston was also appointed to the commission to try the catholic earls in 1593, to the tax commission in 1594, and was granted custody of the king's daughters, Elizabeth and Mary, all of which brought him the reward of the earldom of Linlithgow in 1600. Further rewards and responsibilities followed, and it was only in the last year of his life, in 1621, that he crossed the king by voting against the Five Articles of Perth.[55]

The Elphinstone family followed a similar pattern of exclusion from power in the 1570s followed by restoration after 1578. A year earlier the 3rd Lord Elphinstone made over his estates to his son and heir Alexander, having recognised that he was unfit to rule them himself. In 1580 Alexander Elphinstone, then aged twenty-eight, was invited to court where he was created an ordinary gentleman of the chamber, and joined Lennox's faction. In 1584 he sat on the assize which condemned Gowrie, but he did not emerge from the chamber until 1599 when he became a privy councillor. He too attended the 1598 convention, and was regular in attending council meetings over the following years when he became an extraordinary lord of session, and served as treasurer from 1599–1601. Thereafter his frequency in attendance became less consistent, but he carried out a number of other commissions, and was appointed to the new council in 1610. A bitter legal dispute with Mar increasingly demanded his attention, but he lost this in 1626, and died a very old man some ten or twenty years later, there being some uncertainty about the date.[56]

Robert Seton, 6th Lord Seton, came from a family with strong Marian loyalties. He was admitted to the privy council in 1589, and served as a commissioner of taxation and auditor of exchequer in the years which followed. He was present at the 1587 banquet, the 1598 convention, was a lord of the articles in 1600, and continued to attend council until his death in 1603, by which time he had been created earl of Winton.[57]

Alexander Hume, 6th Lord Hume, was restored to his father's titles in 1578, but soon gained a reputation for feuding and violence which made him an unlikely candidate for royal favour. In fact his feuding with Bothwell was put to good use, and he was richly rewarded from the spoils of the earl's fall. Hume was more comfortable at the court or in the field than in administration, but he was admitted to the privy council in 1597, and was entrusted with delicate missions abroad in 1599 and 1602. Having travelled south in 1603, he quickly returned as lieutenant of the entire borders on both the English and Scottish sides. In 1603 he became earl of Home, and received many other favours during the remainder of his life which was largely spent at court with the king until his death in 1619.[58]

Younger sons of noblemen had always sought means of advancement from the crown, either through the court and royal household, or in administration, which in medieval Scotland normally meant a career in the church. James Elphinstone, brother of the above Lord Elphinstone, was educated in law on the continent before returning to practise in Edinburgh. There his brilliance was not long in being recognised, and he was appointed to the session as an ordinary lord in 1587. From 1589 he was employed by the privy council to advise them in affairs of state where expertise in foreign languages was necessary, particularly French and Latin. His services were also put to use by the queen whose household he helped to manage, and it was largely as a result of his and his colleagues' success there that he was made a member of the Octavian government in 1596. By this time James was also using him to conduct secret correspondence with the catholic powers of Europe, and in 1598 he was appointed secretary of state, being knighted soon afterwards. In 1603 he became Lord Balmerino, was granted estates in Fife, and keepership of Holyroodhouse. Two years later he succeeded Chancellor Dunfermline as president of the court of session, and had now reached the peak of his career. Although his main interests were in foreign affairs and in civil law, Balmerino was a major figure in the government during the crucial years when a policy dealing with feuding was formulated. In 1608, however, his career was cut short when the king sacrificed him to save his own reputation which was seriously threatened by revelations about James's earlier relations with the papacy. Balmerino was sentenced to death for treason, but was permitted to live in exile on his own estates.[59]

A similar career was followed by Lord Seton's younger brother, Alexander Seton. He studied at the Jesuit college in Rome, becoming renowned for his knowledge of Greek, Latin, architecture and mathematics, and in 1571 impressed the pope with a Latin oration while still only sixteen. He then moved to France where he studied civil and canon law, having decided to pursue a secular career back in Scotland. He came to the bar in 1577, but it was as an attendant of his father on his embassy to Henry III in 1583 that he first served the crown. Two years later he joined the privy council, becoming an extraordinary lord of session in 1586, and an ordinary lord in 1588. In 1593 he became president of the court of session, having achieved an unrivalled reputation among his colleagues as the most brilliant civil lawyer in the country. He was also a skilled financial administrator whose work in managing the queen's estates at Dunfermline made him a prominent Octavian in 1596. He was created Lord Fyvie in 1597. His attendance at council meetings was only surpassed by Chancellor Montrose between 1598 and 1604, and his reward was the chancellorship itself in 1604, and the earldom of Dunfermline a year later. While he showed a degree of deference to Dunbar until 1611, and at times seemed to lack confidence in his own power, he was the most important figure in the royal administration until his death in 1622. It is inconceivable, therefore, that he was not an influential figure in shaping royal policy and enforcing it, and the confidence the king had in him, his legal expertise, and his noble connections were essential in contributing to his success.[60]

Unlike Balmerino and Dunfermline, Alexander Lindsay, fourth son of the 10th earl of Crawford, made his way into royal service through the court. He appeared there in the 1580s, probably as a client of Huntly's, and following Huntly's loss of favour in 1589 he became the king's favourite in the chamber. That year he fleetingly held the captaincy of the guard, but he did retain the vice-chamberlaincy, and in 1590 became Lord Spynie. Two years later he served as a lord of the articles and joined the privy council, but that was the height of his success, and later in the year Colonel Stewart accused him of treason, a charge of which he was cleared, but which still lost him the king's confidence. He did, however, continue to serve as a councillor and courtier, being present at the 1598 convention, but was involved in a number of feuds of his own, and in 1607 he was shot dead in Edinburgh by a member of a rival branch of the Lindsay kindred.[61]

Thomas Lyon was a bitter enemy of Spynie and of the Lindsays. He owed his emergence in public affairs to the killing of his brother, Lord Glamis, in 1578 in a fight with the Lindsays in Stirling. As the 8th Lord Glamis was only a child, Thomas, who became master and tutor of Glamis, now became the head of this rich, protestant family. Although the Lyons had been among Morton's friends, the master of Glamis had already deserted him by the time of his execution. However, he remained committed to the same political tradition as his brother, and in 1582 was one of the leaders of the Ruthven Raid. In 1583 he was forfeited, but returned from exile to attempt a coup with Mar at Stirling in 1584. Failure drove him back into exile, but in 1585 he came home as a senior member of the exiled lords, was re-admitted to the privy council — he had served from 1582 to 1583 — held the captaincy of the guard from 1585 to 1588, and was treasurer from 1585 to 1596. Glamis was also an extraordinary lord of session from 1588 to 1591, and a full member of the court until 1598, and he was one of the most regular councillors until his retiral from public office in 1598 due to illness. Though nearly always outmanoeuvred by Maitland whose office he wanted, and only ever rewarded with a knighthood in 1590, Glamis was one of the most important politicians and court managers of the decade following the successful raid on Stirling in 1585. While few major advances were made in reducing violence during this period, the political successes the king had were the base on which later achievements were built, and Glamis had a significant share in attaining those. He lived on in retirement until 1608, his last years having been embittered by a row with his nephew.[62]

Among the baronage, that body of men who formed the untitled nobility, there were few who played very important roles in royal government during this period, although there were many whose local co-operation made that government possible. Kenneth Mackenzie of Kintail, the chief of the powerful Mackenzie clan, successfully expanded his territories in the north-west by making himself of use to the king. He made the effort to understand how the law could be put to good use, was invited to take a seat on the privy council in 1596, and became a client of Chancellor Dunfermline. He attended the 1598 convention, served on many crown commissions, attended council meetings when in the south, and in 1609, two years before his death, was created Lord Kintail.[63]

On the borders a number of baronial families were just as astute in judging when it was time to give up their rieving, becoming responsible for enforcing the king's peace instead. Among these the Kerrs of Cessford, the Scotts of Buccleuch and the Johnstones of that Ilk were the most successful, although their service was essentially local and self-interested. John Carmichael of that Ilk was the chief of a much less significant border kindred than any of these, but he had a record of service to the crown from the 1570s when Morton first recruited him. His political loyalties forced him to flee in 1581, and again in 1583 after the fall of the Ruthven regime in which he had a lesser part. However, in 1585 he came home with the other exiles, and attached himself to Maitland's clientage. He was knighted three years later, admitted to the privy council, and appointed warden of the west march. In 1589 he was sent on embassy to Denmark, and in 1590 undertook another diplomatic mission to England. In 1598 he was re-appointed to the west wardenry, it having been recovered by the Maxwells and Johnstones in the interval, but in 1600 was murdered by a party of Armstrongs while conducting his duties.[64]

Local service by men of this status with their own kindreds and dependencies behind them, and with local offices already, had always been exploited by the crown, and it was a common route to nobility and even greater local power. Equally traditional was advancement through service in the royal household. Robert Melville of Murdocairny was a younger son of Melville of Raith, a minor Fife laird, who first found employment in the household of Mary of Guise, then with Henry III in France, and then Queen Mary. Mary brought Melville onto her privy council in 1562, and used him on diplomatic missions, and he remained loyal to her until the end of the war, being captured at Edinburgh in 1573. Forced into retirement throughout the Morton regency, he was recalled to court in 1579 with so many other Marians. He was knighted in 1581, and became Gowrie's depute in the treasurer's office. However, he had no sympathy for the Ruthven faction, and helped James escape from them in 1583. This brought him admission to the privy council, and his latent diplomatic skills were again put to use over the succeeding years. In 1589 he became vice-chancellor during Maitland's absence in Denmark, held a number of commissions on the borders, went on another English embassy in 1593, became an extraordinary lord of session in 1594, and that year assisted Lennox in administering the north after the defeat of the catholic earls. By 1595 Melville was the most assiduous councillor in attendance in spite of his sixty-eight years, and he continued to make regular appearances until 1600 when illness began to affect his work. He briefly lost the treasurer depute's office to the Octavians, but received it back in 1598. Melville was present at the 1598 convention, and while he resigned his place on the council and the session in 1600-01, he continued to make irregular appearances until 1604, and was re-appointed in 1610. Six years later he was at last rewarded with the title of Lord Melville, and he died in 1621 on the Fife estates which his career had earned him. Melville was no old family retainer kept on by James for sentimental reasons, he had to work hard to get where he did, and it was not done overnight, but involved him in over sixty years of personal service to the king, his mother and his grandmother.[65]

His younger brother, James Melville of Halhill, followed a very similar career pattern in Guise, Valois and Stewart households, in diplomacy, as a supporter of Mary in the civil war, and in retirement under Morton. He was recalled to court in 1580, becoming a gentleman of the bedchamber, and being involved in the fringes of court politics for the next twenty years. James knighted him in 1590, but did not bring him onto the council until 1600 where he served until 1603. He declined to follow the court to London, preferring to retire to his estates and write his *Memoirs*.[66]

Traditionally one of the most sinister figures of the Jacobean court, William Stewart, a younger son of the laird of Galston, was perhaps a generation younger than the Melvilles. He began his career as a soldier in the employment of the Prince of Orange, becoming a captain in 1575, and a colonel by 1580, by which time he had a reputation which interested Spain in recruiting him. In 1581 he went back to Scotland, and was patronised by the earl of Gowrie who had him appointed captain of the guard on the success of the Ruthven Raid. Colonel Stewart was then sent on embassy to England, and on his return deserted Gowrie, helping James escape, and allying himself to Arran, another former soldier. This service saw him appointed to the privy council, and awarded the lands of Pittenweem in Fife. A year later he brought Gowrie in for trial and subsequent execution, and was instrumental in foiling the Stirling coup. Not surprisingly he lost his offices in 1585, but was soon engaged in secret business for the king on the continent which continued to maintain him in royal employment for the next decade or more. Less clandestine was his part in arranging the king's marriage, a service for which he was knighted in 1590. In 1596 he had a commission of lieutenancy for the highlands and islands, he sat on the committee which considered the colonisation of the isles in 1598, and sat on the council of war in 1602. He rarely attended privy council meetings, and was largely a specialist in secret diplomacy and military affairs, but he was an important crown servant for twenty years.[67]

Walter Stewart was the eldest son of Stewart of Minto, the provost of Glasgow and a laird of some significance in that locality. Like Mar he was brought up with the king at Stirling, and it was as one of the King's companions that he was appointed a gentleman of the newly formed chamber in 1580, and was granted the priory of Blantyre. In 1582 he became a privy councillor and lord privy seal, an extremely useful office for a man whose power base lay in the chamber. Over the next fifteen years he survived the vagaries of political life, remaining completely loyal to the king, and becoming a close friend of Lennox, the dominant figure in the chamber. After Maitland's death he demonstrated that he also had administrative skills, and Blantyre was credited with persuading the king to put more effort into enforcing law and order. He was a member of the Octavian government, an extraordinary member of the court of session from 1596, and for a while held all the financial offices of lord treasurer, comptroller and collector. He was a very influential figure at the time of the 1595 initiative against feuding, was present at the 1598 convention, and held the treasurer's office in the months immediately following enforcement. He temporarily lost favour in 1599, and while regaining the king's confidence, did not recover all his offices. In 1600 he sat as one of the lords of the articles in the parliament which confirmed the 1598 legislation. Although still essentially a courtier, he held other government commissions after the union, was re-appointed to the court of session in 1610, and became justice of the peace for Lanarkshire and Renfrewshire. His rewards came in lands around Glasgow, and the title of Lord Blantyre in 1609, eight years before his death.[68]

By far the most successful of the king's household was George Hume. He was the younger son of one of the Hume families on the east march who was introduced to the court as a youth in the early 1580s by his chief, Lord Hume. He became a gentleman of the bedchamber, and accompanied the king to Denmark in 1589. On his return James knighted him and made him master of the wardrobe, and Hume began to purchase his own estates on the borders. As Bothwell had murdered his brother some years before, Hume was quick to make himself useful to the king in the campaign against the earl. From 1593 he was a privy councillor, but he remained largely a chamber figure, being described as of the 'cubicular courtier' party which opposed the Octavians. He attended the 1598 convention, his attendance at privy council became more regular, and in 1601 he replaced Elphinstone as treasurer. During the next two years he earned a reputation for dealing toughly with horned men, and became one of the hardest-working members of the privy council. In 1603, however, James took him to London where Hume was admitted to the English privy council and, more importantly, where he added the keepership of the great wardrobe to his Scottish household office. He was created Baron Home in 1604, and a year later earl of Dunbar. In 1606 he returned to Scotland to oversee the king's ecclesiastical policy, and until his death in 1611 he had greater influence with the king than Dunfermline had, largely because he continued to travel as often as possible back to London to protect his power base. Described as a man of 'deep wits' and 'few words', Dunbar was a ruthless figure who saw that royal policy was enforced, and he never really outgrew the role of a household servant who was unquestionably obedient to his master. Yet that obedience ensured that he was less patient than others in enforcing the king's peace, particularly on the borders, and his dominance during the period when private violence was largely curbed was crucial.[69]

David Murray entered royal service at much the same time as Dunbar, being the younger son of a minor Perthshire laird. He was appointed cup-bearer to the king, and master of the stables in 1584, but he remained a fairly insignificant household figure until 1599 when he was given a seat on the privy council, and was appointed comptroller and steward of the stewartry of Fife. He had been knighted during the previous year. His part in saving the king during the Gowrie Conspiracy of 1600 brought him a share of the forfeited Ruthven estates, and ensured that his fortune was made. He held a number of lesser financial offices, and was increasingly used by the king in his dealings with the church, but from 1603–11 he was also captain of the horse guard. His privy council attendance was relatively high, and in 1610 he was appointed to the reconstituted council. At a local level he exercised a number of commissions for the peace in Perthshire, Fife, Kinross and the stewartries of Menteith, Strathearn and Fife, in which regions the king richly rewarded him with estates. This former cup-bearer was created Lord Scone in 1604 and Viscount Stormont in 1621. It is unlikely that he was a great initiator of royal policy, but like Dunbar he saw that it was enforced, and as captain of the horse guard he was active in enforcing the peace, especially on the borders.[70]

Mark Kerr was son and heir to the commendator of Newbattle, and was appointed a gentleman of the bedchamber in 1580. A year later he became master of requests and joined the privy council, in 1584 he succeeded his father as an extraordinary judge of the court of session, and in 1591 he was created Lord Newbattle in recognition of his service and his wealth. Newbattle was an active councillor throughout the 1590s, serving on a number of committees, was present at the 1598 convention, and sat as a lord of the articles in 1600. In 1606, three years before his death, he was created earl of Lothian.[71]

Appointed to the bedchamber at the same time as Newbattle was William Stewart, a younger son of the laird of Traquair. He became governor of Dumbarton Castle in 1582, and a privy counsellor in 1584. In 1591 he succeeded his brother as laird of Traquair, and was knighted two years later when the king also gifted him lands. While never a very committed councillor, he was a man who could be counted on to give good service, and was probably invited to the 1598 convention for that reason.[72]

William Cranstoun was the son of a minor laird from the eastern marches. After 1603 he was put in command of the mounted guards on the borders where he brutally enforced a rough form of justice. In 1605 he became keeper of Lochmaben Castle and deputy lieutenant of the borders, serving largely under Dunbar whom he succeeded as lieutenant in 1611. Two years previously he had been created Lord Cranstoun, and in 1611 his influence on the borders was further enhanced when he was appointed a justice of the middle shires, and was admitted to the privy council. Cranstoun was a tough, ruthless borderer, like Dunbar, whose service was essentially confined to that region, and who had a major impact on the lawlessness that had for so long characterised it.[73]

More immediately distinctive, and more obviously qualified to claim to be a *noblesse de robe* because of their profession, were the lawyers who rose to positions of power and to the peerage through royal service. Lawyers had always served the crown, but they had usually been churchmen trained essentially as canon and civil lawyers. Since the earlier part of the sixteenth century more and more secular lawyers had achieved success, and the lawyer class, which, because of its freedom from clerical restraints was able to become dynastic, rose in status and wealth.[74] During his minority James was served by a number of lawyers some of whom, like Robert Pitcairn, Mark Kerr and Adam Bothwell, were all intending to follow careers as churchmen before the Reformation forced them to look to the crown to make use of their training and skills.[75]

By the minority of James VI a number of legal families had established themselves firmly at the top layer of their profession where they had greater opportunity of access to royal patronage. In 1578 Lewis Bellenden of Auchinoul inherited the office of justice clerk from his father while only twenty-five. A year later he joined the privy council and was knighted shortly afterwards. Although a committed member of the Ruthven faction, he was not persecuted by Arran on its fall, and in 1584 was allowed to succeed to Sir Richard Maitland of Lethington's place as one of the ordinary lords of the court of session. Within the year he was working closely with John Maitland of Thirlestane to undermine Arran, and he plotted with the exiled lords while in London on diplomatic business. In 1589 he was sent to Denmark as an ambassador, and was a hard-working administrator, councillor and judge at the time of his early death in 1591.[76]

John Maitland of Thirlestane shared a similar background to Bellenden in that his family had already pushed its way into the political elite. He was educated at Haddington Grammar School, St. Andrews University, and then in France where he completed his training in the law. He was granted the commendatorship of Coldingham abbey by the crown, became lord privy seal in 1567 when his father resigned it in his favour, and a year later became a judge of the court of session. Maitland was very much in his elder brother's shadow until 1573 when he died following the capture of Edinburgh Castle. Having been closely associated with Lethington's Marian politics, Maitland was forced to spend the next five years in open ward as a political suspect. He returned to court at the end of the regency, was re-admitted to the court of session in 1581, became a privy councillor in 1583, was knighted and appointed secretary of state in 1584, and was a key figure in the Arran administration, although he had no political loyalties to Arran himself. On the return of the exiled lords he became vice-chancellor and keeper of the great seal, and in 1587 was promoted to the chancellorship itself, a position he held until his death in 1595. Maitland never dominated the privy council as much as is often thought, he was always an outsider among the king's intimates in the chamber, and was insecure among the nobility, but his shrewd handling of his rivals and of the king's affairs allowed James to surmount the crisis created by his difficulties with Bothwell and Huntly. Except in the 1587 parliament Maitland made few contributions to better law and order, feud and faction being too important to him as political tools, and it is difficult to estimate whether he could see beyond the political jungle he competed in so astutely.[77]

The Maitlands and Bellendens were among the elite legal families, and were able to operate their own patronage network within the legal profession. Alexander Hay came from a minor Wigtownshire family, and succeeded in attaching himself to William Maitland of Lethington's clientage; in 1564 Lethington was instrumental in getting him appointed clerk to the privy council. Hay was sufficiently non-political himself to survive the civil war unscathed, continuing in his office, becoming director of chancery in 1577, clerk register to the privy council and an ordinary lord of session in 1579, sitting on a string of government commissions, acting as an arbiter in the Gordon–Forbes feud, and remaining a very regular figure at the privy council until his death in 1594.[78]

Sir Richard Cockburn of Clerkington was another Maitland protégé, but this time of John Maitland, his uncle, who ensured that Clerkington succeeded him as secretary of state in 1591, and that he was appointed a lord of the court of session. Clerkington held onto his office for only a year after Maitland's death, but exchanged it for that of lord privy seal in 1596. Never of any significant political weight, Clerkington appears to have been a dedicated administrator who continued as a privy councillor, a judge of the course of session and as lord privy seal until 1626.[79]

Less is known of Sir John Cockburn of Ormiston who succeeded his own father to a seat on the court of session in 1588, having been in practice for some time before then. Maitland patronage probably secured for him the lord justice clerk's office on Bellenden's death in 1591. Ormiston also failed to acquire any great political reputation, but he was a hard-working councillor, was justice clerk throughout the period when private violence was attacked, attending the 1598 convention, and was nominated to the reconstituted council in 1610.[80]

A contemporary rather than a client of Maitland's was Alexander Colville, another younger son of Fife origins. He became commendator of Culross in 1567, sided with the king's party during the war, and was appointed by Morton to the session in 1575. Four years later he took his seat on the privy council, and, apart from a brief hiatus in 1585, was an active councillor until 1590, after which his attendance declined until his death seven years later. Colville was appointed to a commission to examine the law in 1578, and he collected the decisions of the court of session from 1570 to 1584.[81]

John Skene belonged to this same generation of lawyers. The sixth son of a minor Aberdeenshire laird, he was educated in the burgh school, at King's College, and at St. Andrews University where he took his degree. After a year's teaching in St. Mary's, Skene went to Scandinavia and then on to Paris to complete his legal studies, returning to Scotland to practise as an advocate in 1575. Recognising his talents, Morton commissioned him to write a digest of Scottish law along with Sir James Balfour of Pittendreich, but the project was abandoned at Morton's fall. In spite of the king's remark that 'ther were many better lawyers', he was appointed to accompany the earl Marischal's embassy to Denmark in 1589 where his linguistic expertise was very valuable. Skene served on a number of committees concerning the welfare of the church, and participated for the prosecution in the witch trials. In 1591 he was knighted and sent off on embassy to the Netherlands; in 1592 he was commissioned to have the major acts of parliament reprinted, a work completed in 1597; in 1594 he was appointed clerk register and an ordinary lord of session; and in 1596 he was a member of the Octavian government. Always a very reliable councillor with a high rate of attendance until shortly before his death in 1611, he brought a wide knowledge of Scottish law, and some financial skills, to the council table. He also published editions of *De Verborum Significatione, Regiam Majestatem* and *Quoniam Attachiamenta*.[82]

Like Skene, Edward Bruce was a first-generation lawyer whose own abilities brought him to the attention of the crown. He was the younger son of a Clackmannanshire family who made a name for himself in the commissary court. Rewards soon came by way of the commendatorship of Kinloss, a place on the court of session, and as a depute to the justice general. From 1594 he began to be employed on diplomatic missions, and from 1596 to 1603 he sat on the privy council, during which time he also attended parliament and any conventions. However, in 1603 Lord Kinloss, as he now was, departed for England where he became a naturalised Englishman, took a seat on the English privy council, became master of the rolls, and was awarded an M.A. by Oxford University.[83]

Of all the lawyers who served James VI, however, the most dramatically successful was Thomas Hamilton. He was born in 1563 the eldest son of a burgess of Edinburgh who himself practised law, and he began his education at Edinburgh High School. From there he was sent to Paris where he was tutored by his uncle and the rector of the university, John Hamilton. In 1587 he was admitted as an advocate in Scotland, and within five years his energy and brilliance had projected him to a seat on the court of session as an ordinary lord, and in 1593 onto the privy council. At the same time he was appointed along with Skene to the law commission. In 1596 he was one of the figures behind the establishment of the Octavian government, and was appointed lord advocate, an office he wielded with enormous effect until 1612. He attended the 1598 convention, and more than anyone else was responsible for enforcing much of the criminal legislation passed during the crucial years when he was advocate. He was knighted in 1603 and became lord clerk register in 1612, but exchanged this for the secretaryship of state within a few months, and in 1616 became lord president of the court of session. He was amply rewarded by the king for his service, becoming Lord Binning in 1613, earl of Melrose in 1619, a title which he exchanged for earl of Haddington in 1627, and he received many gifts and grants which together with his profits from office made him an extremely rich man. Although less trusted by Charles I than by his father, Hamilton became lord privy seal in 1627, and continued in crown service until his death ten years later. As one of the sharpest lawyers of his day, Hamilton's practical skills and his knowledge certainly made an important contribution to the evolution and the implementation of royal policy in the area of private violence and other criminal behaviour.[84]

Too much can be made of the rise of the legal profession in early modern Scotland, and of the supposed creation of a *noblesse de robe* which sided with the crown, its patron, against the older nobility.[85] Much more could usefully be said about how they co-operated with the nobility, about the 'complex symbiosis based on mutual needs and services' which Harding found in France, and which makes more sense than a 'robe-sword polarity'.[86] Jonathan Dewald has also concluded from his analysis of the *parlementaires* of Rouen that 'we do better to understand *noblesse de robe* and *noblesse d'épée* as components of a single, reasonably cohesive landed elite, rather than by seeing France as dominated by a pair of fundamentally hostile elites'.[87] If that doubt exists for France, this concept of a divided nobility is even less convincing in Scotland where it is quite meaningless to make this artificial distinction. At least in France contemporaries were aware that differences did exist, and social and political tensions were recognised, although these may have been subsequently exaggerated by historians. In Scotland the distinction was scarcely noticed by contemporaries, and men like the earl of Mar and Thomas Hamilton worked alongside one another without any obvious strain which might have arisen from a robe-sword conflict of aims, or from social prejudice. There is no question that the Scottish crown was successful in attracting to its service, through the inducement of places on the court of session, royal offices, commendatorships and titles, the best of the legal profession. Yet the crown had always employed church-trained lawyers, and the careers of men like Adam Bothwell show a continuity in patterns of employment which the Reformation only mildly dislocated. A number of these men, however, came from families already established in the law outside the church, and the Maitlands and Bellendens were already on the inside of the governing elite by the end of the civil war. Others were pushing their way through for the first time, making themselves useful to the king, and doing much of the tedious administration that no-one else would do. A great deal more will have to be known about their social and political connections before their full impact on government can be evaluated, but it is clear even from this brief analysis that the legal profession represented no more than a minority interest in the government of Scotland, at least until a decade after union, by which time the major achievements in the area of law and order had been completed. Even if one includes Dunfermline and Balmerino whose social origins were quite different from the rest, the lawyers remain only one amongst a number of powerful and overlapping interest groups present in government. Nor were lawyers necessarily any more interested in law and order, or in social peace, than other men, and the case of Lord Justice Clerk Ormiston being disciplined by the privy council for feuding with the earl of Linlithgow is a useful reminder of that fact.[88] Certainly, with the exception of Thomas Hamilton, they were less favoured by the king in terms of titles, offices and other rewards when compared to members of the nobility or household servants. There is little doubt that these highly educated men, with their vast knowledge of civil and criminal law, did influence the way in which bloodfeuds and other forms of social violence were handled by the crown in the important years between 1595 and 1609, but one has to beware of exaggerating that influence, or of putting too much emphasis on their professional distinctiveness when social origins, religion, and place in the patronage network might be equally important. Nor is it very useful to see them as creating tension and division within the governing elite, except perhaps in the very short term — it was the employment of bishops in the royal administration, not of lawyers, which finally aroused the wrath of the nobility — and their integration into that elite led not to a decline in noble influence, but to their own aristocratisation.[89]

Those men who rose up through the royal household and chamber were following a form of service which was as old as kingship itself. The king's personal servants and companions were often his most trusted advisers, and too much concentration on administrative institutions at the expense of relationships has often obscured that. The earl of Arran reputedly said 'that it was an ordinary thing in all ages for meane men to rise to great fortunes; and that therefore it ought not either to be wondered at, or to be envied', and he was, of course, quite right.[90] Men like Dunbar, Scone, Blantyre and Melville had always been able to attain wealth and power simply through good service. It was certainly not a·quick route to either, and — at least while in Scotland — James never promoted his servants too hastily, while some never emerged from obscurity at all. For those clever enough, like Dunbar, or those who held on long enough, like Melville, the rewards could be extremely worthwhile, but in almost every case complete loyalty was expected, and the underlying master–servant relationship never altered. Many of these men had social origins similar to those of the lawyers, among the lesser landowning families of the kingdom, but on the whole they were less well educated in the formal sense than either the lawyers or the nobility. What specific contribution they made was probably more at the level of executing policy than conceiving it, but here too one has to avoid making too crude generalisations. Most of these men spent their lives at court, growing up with the noblemen there, and with the king, and they would have moved easily into office and into the peerage. Hume of Godscroft wrote of the Regent Morton that 'When he was a serving-man, he was industrious, carefull and faithfull; when he came to an estate, and was a Noblemen, he behaved himself as if he had been bred such from his infancie'.[91] Much the same could be said of the king's other servants.

The emphasis laid on crown-noble tensions has often obscured the level of co-operation between the two, and in James VI's reign the defeat of Bothwell and Huntly has been mistakenly interpreted as a victory over the 'noble class', as has been the elimination of bloodfeuds, and the curbing of violence. The enormous service given to the king by his nobles has been greatly under-estimated, or prematurely dismissed. In the long term, James only restored crown-noble relations to the sort of balance of power which existed under his grandfather, and he did it with the help of the majority of his nobles. Those nobles who did serve the king were not some new 'service nobility', except in so far as noblemen had always served their kings, and they fulfilled the role the king expected and wanted them to, that of his chief advisers and magistrates. After 1603 they did begin to reduce their commitment to governing in Edinburgh, but their flocking to London says more about their determination to hold onto their power by maintaining open access to the king than about any profound alterations in the structure of power in Scotland. Furthermore, their local power remained almost entirely intact. On the question of violence it is puzzling to imagine that the nobility had any vested interest in anarchy and bloodshed, or that they were less responsive to humanist and Calvinist criticisms than other status groups. Most noblemen were at feud, but that does not mean that they wanted feuding, and it was the obligations of honour *and* the desire for peace which had involved them as lords in a continual round of breaking and making the peace. The solution which they finally hammered out in co-operation with the king recognised the need to maintain honour and to make peace. Without the nobility adding their counsel, and without their local co-operation, the bloodfeud and other forms of private violence could not have been eliminated. It was their lead in response to increased criticism, and not their defeat, which allowed change to take place, and the conservatism of that change was clearly designed to protect their interests and their power.

That conservatism extended to the king himself who had no desire to undermine his most effective servants. James was by nature a peacemaker, but his early negligence and carelessness earned him the extreme disapproval of the church, and it was the doubts about his commitment to his 'calling' that stung him into action. Political difficulties before 1595–96 hampered any real attempt to come to grips with the problem of violence, and only after a stable political base had been laid could the question of law and order be faced with the sustained determination it required. While a high political ideology may have attracted James intellectually, he was in practice a pragmatist, and the connection between a self-conscious absolutism and peace was rarely stressed. Royal justice and the letter of the law were always less important to him than the achievement of peace itself, and therein James's thinking was medieval rather than absolutist. His personal involvement was considerable, whether he was personally mediating as an overlord, writing detailed instructions from London, or initiating policy. James was very proud of his achievement in uprooting bloodfeuds, but while he had every right to be, the achievement was not all his, and it was the calibre of his servants, whatever their political or social backgrounds, which put that achievement within his grasp.

## NOTES

1. Willson, *James VI and I*, was very much in the tradition of Anthony Weldon whose own views can be found in *James I by his Contemporaries*, (ed.) R. Ashton, London, 1969. Smith (ed.), *The Reign of James VI and I, is more balanced, while Donaldson is far from hostile to him in James V–VII.* At the fore of James's admirers is Wormald, see *Court, Kirk and Community*, and her important article, 'James VI and I: Two Kings or One?', in *History*, 68, 1983, pp. 187–209, which is the best explanation to date of why James succeeded in Scotland, but appeared to fail in England.

2. *C.S.P., Scot.*, x, p. 573.

3. Melville, *Memoirs*, p. 391.

4. *Historie*, p. 246.

5. *Ibid.*, p. 322.

6. *Basilikon Doron*, p. 20.

7. *Melrose*, ii, p. 402.

8. Fraser, *Memorials of the Montgomeries*, i, p. 169.

9. Spottiswoode, *History*, ii, p. 333.

10. *Estimate*, p. 48.

11. Moysie, *Memoirs*, pp. 63–64, and see also Balfour, 'Annales', i, p. 385 and Birrel, 'Diary', p. 24.

12. *C.S.P., Scot.*, xi, p. 589.

13. *Historie*, p. 365.

14. *C.S.P., Scot.*, xii, p. 99.

15. *Ibid.*, p. 136.

16. *C.S.P., Scot.*, xiii, Part 1, pp. 214–215.

17. *R.P.C.*, vi, pp. 594–596, and also *C.S.P., Scot.*, xiii, Part 1, p. 288, for his preparations for the convention.

18. *C.S.P., Scot.*, xiii, Part 1, pp. 419, 422 and 577. See, too, Spottiswoode, *History*, iii, p. 164–165.

19. See, for example, above, p. 171.

20. *Basilikon Doron*, pp. 24–25.

21. *R.P.C.*, vi, p. 595; Spottiswoode, *History*, iii, pp. 164–165.

22. *R.P.C.*, viii, pp. 591–592.

23. Spottiswoode, *History*, iii, p. 190.

24. *C.S.P., Scot.*, x, p. 6.

25. *Ibid.*, pp. 544 and 588–589.

26. *Ibid.*, xiii, Part 1, p. 579.

27. *Ibid.*, Part 2, p. 940.

28. *Ibid.*, pp. 940, 961, 962 and 977.

29. *H.M.C.*, iii, 'Abercairny M.S.', p. 419.

30. *Melrose*, i, p. 7; *R.P.C.*, viii, pp. 543 and 809.

31. Pitcairn, *Criminal Trials*, ii, pp. 514–515.

32. *R.P.C.*, vii, p. 528.

33. *Ibid.*, pp. 435 and 540–541.

34. *Ibid.*, viii, p. 540.

35. *Ibid.*, pp. 588–589; S.R.O., Elibank Papers, G.D., 32/1/8.

36. *R.P.C.*, viii, pp. 602 and 610; Pitcairn, *Criminal Trials*, iii, pp. 74–76.

37. Pitcairn, *Criminal Trials*, iii, pp. 50–52; *R.P.C.*, x, p. 44.

38. *R.P.C.*, ix, pp. 602 and 622. Two years earlier this irritation had already begun to show, *Ibid.*, viii, pp. 391–392.

39. Gordon, *Sutherland*, pp. 340–342; Balfour 'Annales', ii, p. 68; *R.P.C.* , x, pp. 594–595.

40. See *R.P.C.*, vii and viii.

41. For France, see Harding, *Anatomy of a Power Elite*, and J. Dewald, *The Formation of a Provincial Nobility, The Magistrates of the Parlement of Rouen, 1449–1610*, Princeton, 1980. In England aristocratic power has recently been shown to be remarkably resilient, L. Stone and J. C. F. Stone, *An Open Elite? England 1540–1880*, Oxford, 1984, and J. Cannon, *Aristocratic Century: The peerage of eighteenth century England*, Cambridge, 1984. On Spain, see Lynch, *Spain Under the Hapsburgs*, pp. 140–148, and H. Kamen, *Spain 1469–1714: A Society in Conflict*, London, 1983, pp. 153–157. For Poland, Davies, *God's Playground*, i, pp. 321–372. This theme is also discussed by Powis, *Aristocracy*, pp. 43–62, where he too argues against the idea of decline or defeat, and similar points are made in H. Kamen, *European Society, 1500–1700*, London, 1984, pp. 91–119.

42. This is most forcefully argued by Lee in *John Maitland of Thirlestane* and *Government by Pen.*

43. *C.S.P., Scot.*, xiii, Part 2, p. 618.

44. This is convincingly argued by Wormald, *Court, Kirk and Community*, pp. 51–52, and Brown, 'Scottish Politics, 1567–1625', in Smith (ed.), *The Reign of James VI and I*, p. 26. See, too, her debate with Lee in M. Lee, 'James VI and the aristocracy', in *Scotia: American–Canadian Journal of Scottish Studies*, 1, 1977, pp. 18–23, and Wormald's reply to his criticisms in *Scotia*, 2, 1978, pp. 70–76. The point that noblemen were so crucial to royal government was first made by K. B. MacFarlane in *The Nobility of Later Medieval England*, Oxford, 1973, see p. 161.

45. In all of the short biographical notes which follow I have limited references to a minimum, as to attempt to list them all would be tedious. Further information about all these men can be found in many of the primary sources in the Bibliography, and any evaluation of them is based on a much wider reading than is suggested by my notes. For Mar, *Scots Peerage*, v, pp. 615–621; *Dictionary of National Biography*, (ed.) L. Stephen and others, London, 1855–1912, xvii, pp. 422–426. He is first linked with the

chancellorship in 1592, *C.S.P., Scot.*, x, pp. 776 and 777–778, and speculation continues until 1599.

46. *Scots Peerage*, v, pp. 231–237; *D.N.B.*, xii, pp. 333–335; G. Brunton and D. Haig, *An Historical Account of the Senators of the College of Justice from its Institution in MDXXXII*, Edinburgh, 1832, pp. 188–191.

47. Hume, *History*, p. 430.

48. *Scots Peerage*, i, pp. 194–196; *D.N.B.*, xv, pp. 281–284.

49. *Scots Peerage*, iv, pp. 370–372; *D.N.B.*, xxiv, pp. 192–195.

50. *Scots Peerage*, v, pp. 356–357; *D.N.B.*, lv, pp. 107–108.

51. *Scots Peerage*, i, pp. 346–349; *D.N.B.*, viii, pp. 318–319.

52. *Scots Peerage*, ii, pp. 475–477.

53. *Scots Peerage*, vi, pp. 516–517; *D.N.B.*, liv, p. 272.

54. *Scots Peerage*, viii, pp. 545–547; *D.N.B.*, xix, p. 278.

55. *Scots Peerage*, v, pp. 443–445; *D.N.B.*, xxxiii, pp. 383–384.

56. *Scots Peerage*, iii, pp. 536–538; *D.N.B.*, xvii, p. 314; Brunton, *Senators*, pp. 242–243.

57. *Scots Peerage*, viii, pp. 590–591.

58. *Scots Peerage*, iv, pp. 462–465; *D.N.B.*, xxvii, pp. 223–225.

59. *Scots Peerage*, i, pp. 554–562; *D.N.B.*, xxii, pp. 322–323; Brunton, *Senators*, pp. 206–212.

60. *Scots Peerage*, iii, pp. 369–372; *D.N.B.*, li, pp. 261–264; Brunton, *Senators*, pp. 198–202; M. Lee, 'King James' Popish Chancellor', in Cowan and Shaw (eds.), *Renaissance and Reformation in Scotland*, pp. 170–82.

61. *Scots Peerage*, viii, pp. 95–101; *D.N.B.*, xxxiii, pp. 280–281.

62. *Scots Peerage*, viii, pp. 284–287; *D.N.B.*, xxxv, pp. 351–353.

63. *Scots Peerage*, vii, pp. 503–504.

64. *D.N.B.*, ix, p. 130.

65. *Scots Peerage*, vi, pp. 96–99; *D.N.B.*, xxxvii, pp. 245–246; Brunton, *Senators*, pp. 227–230.

66. *Scots Peerage*, vi, pp. 90–91; *D.N.B.*, xxxvii, pp. 240–241.

67. *Scots Peerage*, vii, pp. 64–68; *D.N.B.*, liv, pp. 362–364.

68. *Scots Peerage*, ii, pp. 81–83; *D.N.B.*, liv, pp. 359–360; Brunton, *Senators*, pp. 225–226.

69. *Scots Peerage*, iii, pp. 286–288; *D.N.B.*, xxvii, pp. 230–232.

70. *Scots Peerage*, viii, pp. 191–196; *D.N.B.*, xxxix, pp. 353–355.

71. *Scots Peerage*, v, pp. 455–456.

72. *Scots Peerage*, viii, pp. 400–401.

73. *Scots Peerage*, ii, pp. 592–593.

74. Donaldson, 'The Legal Profession in Scottish Society in the Sixteenth and Seventeenth Centuries', in *Juridical Review*; J. Durkan, 'The Early Scottish Notary', in Cowan and Shaw (eds), *Renaissance and Reformation in Scotland*, pp. 22–40.

75. For Pitcairn, see *D.N.B.*, xlv, pp. 322–333; Brunton, *Senators*, pp. 139–140. For Bothwell, see *Scots Peerage*, v, pp. 428–430; *D.N.B.*, v, pp. 444–446; Brunton, *Senators*, pp. 119–122; D. Shaw, 'Adam Bothwell, a Conserver of the Renaissance in Scotland', in Cowan and Shaw (eds.), *Renaissance and Reformation in Scotland*, pp. 141–169. For Kerr, see *Scots Peerage*, v, pp. 453–454; Brunton, *Senators*, p. 147.

76. *Scots Peerage*, ii, pp. 68–70; *D.N.B.*, iv, p. 188; Brunton, *Senators*, pp. 194–196.

77. *Scots Peerage*, v, pp. 298–301; *D.N.B.*, xxxiv, pp. 357–360; Brunton, *Senators*, pp. 140–46; Lee, *John Maitland of Thirlestane*.

78. *D.N.B.*, xxv, p. 250; Brunton, *Senators*, pp. 175–176.

79. Brunton, *Senators*, pp. 219–220; *C.S.P., Scot.*, x, p. 507.

80. Brunton, *Senators*, pp. 216–217.

81. *D.N.B.*, xi, p. 418; *Scots Peerage*, ii, pp. 553–556.

82. *D.N.B.*, lii, pp. 336–338; Brunton, *Senators*, pp. 230–234; A. L. Murray, 'Sir John Skene and the Exchequer, 1594–1612', in *Stair Society Miscellany*, i, 26, Edinburgh, 1971, pp. 125–155.

83. *Scots Peerage*, iii, pp. 474–476; *D.N.B.*, vii, p. 96; Brunton, *Senators*, pp. 238–240.

84. *Scots Peerage*, iv, pp. 309–314; *D.N.B.*, xxiv, pp. 208–211; Brunton, *Senators*, pp. 221–225.

85. Donaldson, *James V–VII*, pp. 216–221, has emphasised the king's 'preference for reliance on men of middle-class origins and an intention to make service, rather than birth, the path to advancement'. Apart from the problems in using class terminology in this context, Donaldson has missed the obvious point that what James preferred was men of birth who were also reliable. R. Mitchison, *Lordship to Patronage, Scotland 1603–1745*, London, 1983, pp. 10–11, follows a similar argument in suggesting that James created 'a new nobility of service' which 'had characteristics which marked it off from the older nobility'. This fails to take account of the fact that the older nobility were changing themselves, and that service had always been an integral part of noblemen's relations with the crown. Lee, *John Maitland of Thirlestane* and *Government by Pen*, gives the credit in controlling the nobility to Chancellor Maitland and 'the lesser gentry'. See, too, his criticisms of Wormald's revision of this thesis, 'James VI and the aristocracy', *Scotia*, 1, 1977, pp. 18–23, and her reply in *Scotia*, 2, 1978, pp. 70–76. However, Wormald has also tended to see a division within the political elite between lawyer-administrators and noblemen which has led her to accept the French concepts of *noblesse d'épée* and *noblesse de robe* as valid for Scotland, *Lords and Men*, p. 162, and 'Bloodfeud, Kindred and Government', pp. 90–97.

86. R. R. Harding, 'Aristocrats and Lawyers in French Provincial Government, 1559–1648: From Governors to Commissars', in Malament (ed.), *After the Reformation*, pp. 100 and 96. See, too, Harding, *Anatomy of a Power Elite*, p. 190, 'the construction of the absolutist state coincided with a tightening of the bonds between the old patrimonial elites and the very class of lawyers that were introducing bureaucratic procedures into local government'.

87. Dewald, *The Formation of a Provincial Nobility*, p. 309.

88. *R.P.C.*, ix, pp. 240 and 242.

89. Marriage gives some indication of this integration. Thus Thomas Hamilton was able to marry his son and heir to a daughter of the earl of Mar, and four of his own daughters were also married into noble houses, *Scots Peerage*, iv, pp. 314–315. In the long term what was happening was the 'aristocratizing of the higher middle strata' in society, V. G. Kiernan, *State and Society in Europe, 1550–1650*, Oxford, 1980, p. 10.

90. Hume, *History*, p. 391.

91. *Ibid.*, p. 357.

# 9

# Legislation — Custom and Law

Sixteenth-century governments were not interventionist in the manner of modern governments, and even in more centralised states than Scotland the greater part of governing was a local concern. Law itself was rarely innovative, and the interest of men like Skene and Balfour in editing old laws reflected 'a continual turning back' in search of an authority derived from antiquity.[1] Yet earlier in the Middle Ages attempts had been made to limit the effects of the bloodfeud,[2] and those concerned about it could not simply wait for it to disappear. There was no inevitable decline of the bloodfeud in early modern society, and in contemporary Venice magistrates were facing an increase in feuding as their ability to control the *terraferma* from the city of Venice slipped out of their hands.[3] Throughout the 1590s much of the debate on law and order within Scotland had concerned the question of how the crown could satisfy those critics who were urging the king to enforce civil peace, and at the same time avoid alarming a very widespread community of interests which believed that the state's freedom to act was limited by private rights, privileges and traditions. The legislation of the Jacobean period responded to that problem with a programme — a term which is only meaningful in the unconscious sense — which did innovate, and did increase the degree to which the crown interfered in private rights, but its philosophy was a conservative one, and in practice it made compromises in order to get the job done. Social peace, not state building, was the ambition which inspired it.[4]

The framework on which a more effective means of ending feuds was built already existed in private arbitration. When in 1578 the politically sensitive Gordon-Forbes feud was brought to the attention of parliament, it was agreed to appoint a commission of eight arbitrators to negotiate the issues between the two families, and this was approved by parliament in the following year. Six months later nothing had been achieved, and the privy council asked the Gordons and Forbes to appoint their own arbitrators with the proviso that if they failed to arrive at a solution a committee of privy councillors would replace them. This appears to have been what happened, and in 1581 parliament approved the king's right to act as oversman.[5] Here private arbitration remained the basic principle upon which peace was founded, but the crown was granted the authority to pressurise men into negotiations, and the authority to persuade them to compromise before their right to private arbitration was superseded by the crown's responsibility to maintain the peace, that is by imposing a settlement. It was this *ad hoc* arrangement, approved by noble-dominated parliaments during the royal minority, which was later to form the basis of more comprehensive legislation towards the end of the century.

In 1582 the Lennox-Arran privy council made a serious attempt to tackle the law and order issue. Justiciary courts were to be held throughout the kingdom, and attention was drawn to feuding in the west of Scotland, where Lennox and Arran had most of their own lands. Widespread disorder was blamed on 'sindre deidlie feidis, grudgeis and displeasures standing betuix sindre gret personis, thair freindis and partakers, throw bloodsheid and uther inconvenientis happinit amangis thame'. The participants in eight separate feuds were, therefore, ordered to assure one another before a certain date.[6] This initiative was sunk by the Ruthven Raid a few weeks later, but at a convention in February 1583 the new regime persuaded a large number of the nobility to

> assure eache one others, to be unhurt, unharmed, molested, persued, or in anie wise invaded, ather for old feed or new, otherwise than by ordinar course of law and justice; nather sall we, nor anie that we may lett, make provocatioun of trouble, displeasure, or tumult, in word, deid or countenance . . .

It was agreed that within forty days they would submit their feuds to the king who, with the advice of the privy council, would appoint arbitrators for them.[7] Once again nothing came of this measure, and its aims may have been more political than social, but it did contain a voluntary surrender to the crown of the right to arbitrate.

Throughout the 1580s feuding increased, and the king's naively idealistic attempt in 1587 to reverse this trend was a complete failure. A discussion within the government in the spring of that year did raise the possibility of enforcing a royal decreet 'gif parteis having discension not eslie to be reconcelit will not subject thame selfis and kynnisfolk commandit to obey the chargeis of tua newtrall persones', but this was far too extreme.[8] What did emerge was a grand banquet of the nobility at which they renounced their feuds in a spirit of goodwill, festivity and, no doubt, drunkenness:

> Upon the xv day of Mai, the King maid the banchet to all his nobiletie, at ewin in Halyroudhouse, quhair the King maid thame, efter drinking of many scolis ane to ane uther, and made thame efter supper, quho utherwayis had beine at great fead, tak twa and twa be handis, and pas from Halyroudhouse to the merket croce of Edinburgh, quhair the provost and baillies had prepaired ane table and desert for his Majestie, at the quhilk theare was great mirthe and joy, with sik ane great number of pepill as the lyke had not beine seine befoir.[9]

The sentiments were the right ones for celebrating peace, but they had not been preceded by the hard bargaining to give them more than a superficial meaning. Two months later, in July, parliament passed an 'Act for Universal Concord Among the King's Lieges' which was equally lacking in substance.[10] Until the political environment was more stable, there was really nothing that could be done, and it was a despairing privy council which wrote in 1591 of the 'multitude of deidlie feidis' in which men 'tak their privat revenge and advantage of utheris, disdaining to seik remeid be the ordinair forme of law and justice, without fear of God or reverance of his authoritie'.[11]

By 1595, with both Bothwell and Huntly defeated, the king was more confident of his authority, and more realistic than he had been in 1587. Using as an excuse, or reason, the threat from Spain, a convention of the nobility meeting in November recognised the unacceptable level feuding had reached, and allowed the king to mediate the more important ones, and to imprison those who refused to co-operate. Lesser feuds were to be settled by sheriffs working alongside local barons and presbyteries. This act was essentially an emergency measure, being 'provided upon the resisting of foreign enemies', and as such it had limited implications. The privy council did summon the principals of seven feuds to assure one another and submit to arbitration, but the order was largely ignored, except for the signing of a few assurances. A committee of two noblemen, two councillors and two ministers was appointed to administer the work, but they are not heard of again either.[12]

In May 1598 it was observed that 'almost all feuds in Scotland are renewed so dangerously as this country was not under such appearance of trouble these 20 years'. So bad had the situation become, and so frustrated were royal officials with the king's erratic attention to the problem, that some were said to have threatened to resign. In response to this the nobility were informed that feuding would be discussed at a convention of the estates planned for June, and the king plunged himself into a bout of work in preparation for it.[13] The convention met on 29 June 1598 in Holyroodhouse, the king having spent the last days beforehand putting the finishing touches to the proposed act, and trying to mediate between some noblemen who threatened to obstruct the legislation in order to protect their particular interests.[14] Bureaucracy and lordship were fused in kingship, while noblemen were faced with reconciling their private loyalties with their public responsibilities.

A convention of the estates was always more likely to be amenable to crown management than parliament, since it could be called at shorter notice, and its composition was less rigidly fixed. At this one there were nine officers of state present, the commissioners of five burghs, three bishops, and five men who had been awarded the temporalities of pre-Reformation abbacies for their service to the crown. These twenty-three men (two burgh commissioners for Edinburgh) would almost certainly have backed any legislation initiated by the crown, with perhaps one or two exceptions. The remaining twenty-five — one duke, seven earls, ten lords and seven barons — required more sensitive handling if they were to be persuaded to support the crown. Of these, Lords Fleming, Seton, Fyvie (the future Chancellor Dunfermline), Newbattle, and Elphinstone all made careers out of crown service, as did Sir George Hume (the future Treasurer Dunbar), and the barons of Edzell and Traquair. These, too, were unlikely to oppose the king. What opposition there was would have come from among the duke of Lennox and Lord Hamilton, the earls of Angus, Errol, Marischal, Cassillis, Glencairn, Mar and Sutherland, Lords Maxwell, Livingston, Spynie, and Ochiltree, the barons of Kintail and Tullibardine, and possibly from the less important barons of Dudhope and Roslin. Most of this last group had at the time, or had had in the recent past, feuds of their own. In fact opposition to the proposed act was led by the earl of Mar who was resisting any royal interference in his feud with Lord Livingston, who was also present at the convention. That opposition was very important, not because it was likely to command a majority of the votes of the convention, but because without the backing of a substantial number of the nobility the legislation could never be effectively enforced. The king 'made many long and pithy harangues for persuading agreements amongst them all to regaird his services and good', but Mar remained stubborn, forcing a vote so that 'by plurality of votes it passed'. It was not the unanimous reception the king had hoped for, and it would have to be tested in practice, but the 'Act Anent Removing and Extinguishing of Deidlie Feuds' had become law.[15]

The act decreed that those parties presently at feud were to be charged to appear before the king and the privy council where they had to submit their feuds to two or three friends on either side (on some occasions a written submission would be accepted). In the submission they would, as was customary, list their grievances and claims against the other party. The arbitrators would be named by the parties, not by the crown, and the practice of naming an excess number from whom the other side could choose those to whom it had no objections was also continued. This arbitration committee had thirty days in which to reach agreement, or they could elect one of their number as oversman, granting to him the power to draw up a binding settlement still within the original thirty days. If neither a compromise nor an oversman could be agreed on, the committee had to set out in writing their points of disagreement which were to be submitted to the king who at this point became oversman himself. If the arbitrators failed to make this submission to the king, abandoned the proceedings, or allowed them to drag on beyond the time permitted, they were each to be fined £1,000. Once the business was in the king's hands he, or privy councillors or judges appointed by him, would deliver a decreet arbitral against which there was no appeal, and which would be registered by the crown with the status of an act of the privy council. The act was thus very conservative in substance, adopting forms and principles already long established. The only difference it made was in insisting on a mandatory submission of the feud to arbitration, and in allowing that process a finite period in which to work before the crown imposed a solution of its own.[16]

Feud was divided into three categories by the act: where there had been no slaughter, where there had been slaughter on both sides, and where there had been slaughter on only one side. In the first case the act was to be implemented in full in the hope that it could prevent an escalation of the situation. In the second case, where private revenge had already introduced the blood-justice of the feud, private assythment was to be agreed by both parties rather than each prosecuting the other in court. In effect this meant that the great majority of existing feuds were being left in private hands. Only where a killing had taken place on one side, and vengeance had not yet taken its course, did the crown reserve to itself the right to intervene, as

> ... the pairtie grevit can not refuis in resoun to submit in maner foirsaid all querrell he can beir to ony persoun Innocent. Justice being maid patent to him aganis the giltie.[17]

In this case justice was to be provided by the law, not by kindreds or lords. When punishment was meted out, the quarrel was to cease. The king's right to pursue in his own action was reserved should the offended party decide not to pursue,[18] and where a private settlement was reached it could be set aside should new evidence appear at a later date. Great emphasis was laid on the offended party not seeking revenge from innocent kinsmen, and on kinsmen not protecting the guilty in an effort to make slaughter a crime which was isolated from the responsibilities of the kindred to either the victim or the criminal.[19] While there was, therefore, some increase in the importance of the third party — the crown — in dealing with cases of slaughter, the main emphasis of the act was still on private arbitration and privately initiated prosecutions.

The act, which was enforced with some success between 1598 and 1603, was ratified in parliament in 1600 without opposition.[20] The need to present a united front towards England as James's succession to the English throne grew more imminent, and the prospects of a share in that rich inheritance for those favoured by the king, resulted in many of the more significant noble feuds being either settled or assured by 1603. Without serious noble opposition the king felt more confident of extending royal powers over the settlement process. The privy council act of 5 January 1604 arose from the king's dissatisfaction with the progress of the campaign as a whole, and from both a practical and an ideological objection to assurances which were 'rather ane fosterar nor removear of the same [feuds]', implying a 'grant and confessioun of ane feid and querrell'. In future a party with a complaint was to bring it to the privy council who would judge its legitimacy, warn the offended party not to seek private revenge, and if necessary bind one or both parties to keep the peace. It would also guarantee that the complaint would be dealt with by pursuing the offender, and by ensuring that the king did not grant a remission or respite. The council would also ask the offended party if they had 'ony querrell grudge or inimitie againis the kin, freindis or surname of the offendour being innocent and saikles of the deid committit', and if they failed to satisfy the council on this they could be imprisoned and fined 'greit and huge sowmes'.[21] Since 1598 a more hostile attitude to feuding had developed, and the fact that this was simply passed as an act of the privy council suggests that opposition to this kind of interference in private affairs had diminished. Yet it was only the offensive aspects of kin responsibilities which were being attacked, not those which contributed to keeping the peace, and the thinking behind this act was not assertive absolutism, in spite of its language. Essentially the king was simply fulfilling his responsibilities as a peacemaker, a traditional role, in a society which had recognised the need to allow him greater powers in order to achieve a level of peace demanded by a higher degree of expectancy, and had been shaken by the long years of violence and instability it had had to endure.

This conservatism is even more apparent in the enforcement of the feud legislation. After 1598 the privy council did make a more systematic attempt to deal with feuding, and the instances of assurances being renewed suggest that records were being kept in the advocate's or treasurer's office of the progress of the peacemaking. Yet there was little urgency in the work, and even after 1604 assurances continued to be used. Between 1599 and 1607 Lord Maxwell and John Crichton of Crawfordston renewed their assurances at periodic intervals.[22] Quarrels over the interpretation of assurances continued to be submitted to the privy council,[23] and it used its authority to enforce broken assurances rather than trying to undermine them.[24] Behind this lay a feeling that personal honour was often more likely to achieve results than strict application of the law. However, cautions to keep the peace were in greater use after 1604, particularly after 1609 when justices of the peace were introduced, and in the long term they replaced private assurances.[25] The acquiescence of the nobility in this largely accounted for its success as more pressure could be put on lesser men, and any refusal to cooperate in this early stage of the pacification process was likely to bring automatic denunciation and horning, which by this time was more effective for most of the kingdom.[26]

Flexibility also characterised the privy council's attitude to arbitration and prosecution. In 1613 the 2nd Lord Torthorwald was denounced for refusing to come to a private settlement of his family's feud with the Ochiltree Stewarts, one of whom had murdered his father a few years before.[27] Here the killer was isolated from the rest of his kindred,[28] just as Andrew Haitlie was in 1607 when he would not submit his feud with James Home of Eccles.[29] This commitment to a private agreement in the Torthorwald-Ochiltree case was maintained in spite of the fact that the 1st Lord Torthorwald's murder in 1608 interrupted negotiations which the privy council had already got under way. The council had even resisted the king's desire to prosecute Torthorwald in 1605 for the murder of Captain James Stewart in 1596, and told him that Torthorwald was involved in 'friendlie dealing' with the Stewarts. It was their hope that 'be the amicable dresse of the wyse freindis on ather syde, this mater salbe sua handlit, as your maiestie sall heir no farder thairof'.[30] In 1613 Lord Ochiltree and the 2nd Lord Torthorwald 'wer reconcilled by the Lordes, hartily chapen hands, and mutually embracing one ane another'.[31] This preference for the justice of the feud rather than that of the courts was characteristic of crown policy and thinking at this time. In 1609 the king condemned the 'malicious and revengefull heate' of one Edinburgh burgess who was pursuing another at law for mutilating him in a fight, and in 1617 the two men were finally reconciled before the privy council when the offender did homage and begged for forgiveness of his victim.[32] When John Spottiswoode of that Ilk expressed his regret at killing his friend Mathew Sinclair of Longformacus in a quarrel when 'the devill, taking advantage, made me [an] instrument of that lamentable and wicked deid', he offered both assythment and homage, but Sinclair's brothers refused, and demanded that 'his Maiesteis lawis may have course in the said meter of the punischement of the nocent, and comforte of the innocent'. The privy council, however, pressed for a private arbitration.[33] In 1619 when the council were faced with resolving a feud between the Kings of Barracht and the laird of Meldrum, they decided that it had imposed its own bloody justice, and that

> it will be more agreeable to the contentment of the pairtye, and will procure more assured peace to the said James and his freindis, that your maiestie sall grant ane pardoun for the slaughter, nor that the mater salbe broght to publict contestatioun and audience at the consaill table.[34]

In another case, a last-minute reconciliation 'under the aix' between two families brought about a stay of execution in 1620, and this was followed by the privy council recommending to the king that he set aside the judgement of the assize.[35] The law did not suddenly become a harsh code of punishment in the early seventeenth century, and the crown continued to be more interested in peace, and in bringing parties to 'perfyte freindship and reconciliatioune'[36] than in imposing the letter of the law. In early modern Scotland, as elsewhere, adjudication did not necessarily exclude arbitration.[37] There were, of course, instances when prosecution did bypass arbitration, as in 1618 when James Stewart, the son of Stewart of Kilpatrick, was charged with having conceived a deadly feud against Andrew Cunningham and of murdering him on Arran in May 1618. Stewart admitted his guilt, and offered compensation, but the crown was looking for an example, and the king insisted on his execution.[38]

The principle of arbitration, though governed by the guidelines of the 1598 and 1604 legislation, remained the same as before. In the case of the feud between Haitlie of Mellirstanes and Home of Eccles they were 'reconceilled by a committee from the consaill table',[39] but when in 1600 John Lundy of that Ilk and Andrew Murray of Balvaird did make a direct submission of their feud to the king, arbitrators were named who were not crown officials, but local men who understood the specific problem.[40] Good lordship continued to be important, as in 1617 when a feud between the Gordons and Forbes was settled largely by the king personally mediating between Huntly and Errol during his Scottish progress.[41] In 1619 it was the earls of Perth and Glencairn who wrote to the privy council accusing them of negligence in allowing the Buchanan-MacFarlane feud to break out again, and of ignoring their advice.[42] Nor did the rights of the kindred disappear. In 1606 Lord Roxburghe made peace with Kerr of Ancrum, but the latter's younger brothers reserved their right, and that of any other member of the kindred, to pursue Roxburghe in any cause for which they had not received satisfaction.[43] Roxburghe and Ancrum, who were kinsmen themselves, may have thought that they could come to an arrangement over the murder by Roxburghe of the latter's father, but without including the kindred it was a peace based on fragile security. The best peace still had to include the agreement of neighbours, lords and kinsmen if it was to endure.

The settlements themselves also reflected a continuity with the earlier period. In 1616 the Lindsay kindred patched up the feud between the Crawford and Edzell branches with the laird of Edzell swearing that the killing of Lord Spynie in 1607 had not been deliberate (he had been trying to kill the earl of Crawford), but occurred 'most unhappilie upone mere accident and suddantie'. He agreed to pay 8,000 merks to Spynie's heir, and to sell him some land, while the latter forgave Edzell, gave him a letter of slains, and received him into his 'amity and freindship'.[44] In 1622 the privy council itself delivered a decreet arbitral in settlement of a feud between the laird of Lekkie on the one side and Dunrod and Calderwood on the other, granting Lekkie lands in assythment, and decreeing that his daughter should be married to Calderwood's heir.[45] Nor was it just the compensatory aspects of the settlements which survived. In 1602 it was the privy council which decided that John Neilson, a tailor burgess of Dumfries, had not offered sufficient assythment to two burgh officers whom he had tried to shoot, and he was ordered to increase his offer of assythment, and make public amends at the burgh market place by craving pardon, offering the sword by the point, and doing homage while barefoot and wearing nothing but his sark.[46] By 1616 the importance of such a ceremony was still recognised by the council, which decreed that James Ramsay of Priorletham was to go on his knees before Sir John Wemyss of Wemyss in St. Andrews kirk, and there admit his fault and beg forgiveness.[47] The contempt the laird of Lekky showed for the offer of homage made to him in 1622 arose not from a disregard for the meaning of that act, but from the fact that insufficient assythment accompanied it.[48] As in Schleswig, where acts of 1558 and 1636 drove a wedge between the justice of the kindreds and the jurisdiction of the law, there was no immediate break with assythment which in the former lasted until 1649, and in the latter had an even longer life.[49]

Obstacles to settlements did exist. Minorities delayed the pacification of a number of feuds, including some of the major noble ones.[50] Some men still refused to consider making peace because they wanted vengeance,[51] or attempted to stir up old hatreds after peace had been made,[52] and the peacemaking itself was dogged by the 'shiftis and protracting' of men who had not suddenly lost their sense of honour.[53] That feuding was driven from lowland Scotland by the end of the king's reign was not simply due to the acts of 1598 and 1604, but to a whole range of legislation associated with creating a more peaceful society. The crown's growing ability to ensure that settlements were made and kept was what gave the arbitrated peace a permanence which had formerly been impossible. When in 1604 two Turnbull lairds were found to have failed to pay a woman for the notorious slaughter of eight of her brothers, a warrant was issued for their arrest, but their crime was the non-payment of the 2,000 merks, not the killings.[54] In 1617 Leslie of Audcraig told the privy council that he could not pay the Leiths of Harthill the 3,500 merks agreed upon for the slaughter of one of their kinsmen. The council's reaction was not to scrap the settlement and impose a punishment, but to persuade the Leiths to accept 2,000 merks within a limited time and forego the outstanding amount.[55] Jacobean government had not given up on the medieval understanding of justice as peace.

In a kingdom like Scotland where no standing army existed, and where the crown could not afford to pay for an army when one was required, it was necessary to have an armed population. Arms were also a sign of status, symbolising the authority and honour of their wearer. It was expected, therefore, that men would own and wear arms appropriate to their status, and that they would be able to play their part in the kingdom's defence. In spite of the survival of a military ethos, however, the high cost of arms caused quite a degree of resistance to meeting the minimum requirements made by the crown on individuals. Wappinschaws were held throughout the country in 1574, 1584, 1596, 1598 and 1599 in order that sheriffs could inspect the level of armed preparedness in their localities, but these were highly unpopular. In 1574 the privy council noted that many men were turning up with weapons borrowed from neighbours, and they were given eight months in which to satisfactorily equip themselves. Ten years later little had changed, and in 1596 in the midst of the king's preparations for resisting Spanish invasions and enforcing his claim to the English crown, attendance was still low. A 'sluggishness and cairlessness' was in evidence, caused by 'the not exercise of armour this lang tyme begune'. In 1599 the wappinschaws were simply abandoned through lack of public interest.[56]

This slackness in attitudes to weaponry is worth remembering when discussing what was, in spite of it, an armed society. Yet the crown's concern that men should own the requisite weaponry was matched by a desire to see those weapons used in a controlled manner. Above all there were worries about the dangers of handguns, a favourite weapon of those engaged in feuds. Gun control, the king wrote in *Basilikon Doron,* was one means of securing the abolition of feuds.[57] As early as 1567 draconian legislation had been passed by the first parliament of the reign, making amputation of the right hand the punishment for firing, or even wearing a pistol without authorisation.[58] In 1574 parliament decided that such severity was counter-productive because no-one would enforce the act, and punishment was reserved for those who actually shot at someone, whether they hit them or not. Death was decreed for those who killed with a gun, and fines were to be imposed on those who wore firearms without a licence.[59] However, the law continued to be widely ignored in spite of repeated proclamations from the privy council.[60] In 1579 parliament further criticised the harshness of the punishments, and allowed magistrates greater discretionary powers of enforcement, a measure which did result in a few prosecutions.[61]

The worst offenders continued to be many of those noblemen who sat in parliament making these laws, and who were expected to see them implemented. Twelve years passed before in 1591 the privy council granted powers to any liege to make a form of citizen's arrest of any person he saw wearing, bearing, or firing guns without a licence.[62] This was a typical Scottish solution, pushing the issue back into private hands, but it was equally ineffective, and was highly likely to cause violent quarrels if anyone did try to enforce it. Two years later the privy council complained that

> wicked men, holden in deidlie feid and malice, for their privat revenge, sall, be shuitting of hagbutis or pistollettis, touking outragious countenance or reprochefull speichis, do quhat lyis in thame to entir noblemen or gentlemen in blude . . .

The association with feuding was clearly being made, but the council did nothing more than order a search of Edinburgh for illegally owned guns.[63] Guns provoked more trouble in burghs than elsewhere, and even a minor burgh like Peebles had provided its magistrates with laws of its own to try and tackle the problem,[64] but without more persistent effort from the government little could be achieved.

In 1595, the same year in which an attempt was made to restrain feuding itself, the privy council abandoned the thinking of the previous twenty years, and in effect revived the 1567 act. Dismemberment returned as the universal punishment for all firearms offences in conjunction with fines, imprisonment, and the confiscation of the weapons. This, explained the council, was because 'the murthour committit in Scotland was sa far owt of all measure and mearcie, be the treasonable use of pistols and small gunnis'.[65] To demonstrate its resolve the government ordered that three men arrested in Edinburgh for illegally wearing guns on the day the act was passed should be prosecuted under it. In fact they were released on the scaffold, the point having been made.[66] Later that year the category of those liable to suffer mutilation was extended.[67] Hand in hand with this renewed confidence in severity came an attempt at prevention. Condemnation of the gun as an instrument of 'revenge of particular quarrellis and privat grudgeis' in 1596 was followed by a declaration that the crown intended to abolish handguns altogether. A minimum size of pistol was established, and craftsmen who broke the law were to be executed.[68] While this did give the privy council a more vulnerable type of offender on whom they could vent their wrath, further proclamations later in the year suggest that this law was no more paid attention to than previous ones.[69]

If enforcement of gun control in England, which began in 1514, created policing problems, Scotland was likely to prove even more difficult.[70] Coercion was one solution, and in 1597 two men who came into the king's will during their trial were banished for life simply for wearing guns without licences.[71] In that same year Perth burgh magistrates were summoned to 'byde tryal' when David Edmonstone of the Wowmet was shot dead within their jurisdiction.[72] Most of this reflected a policy which chose to make a few strategic examples rather than attempting to vigorously enforce the law. Occasionally its full rigours were applied, as when George Porteous had his hand cut off before being beheaded for shooting Adam Bothwell dead the day before.[73] Yet there were few such cases, and the government's intention was clearly to persuade the majority of men to leave their guns at home by a discretionary use of its powers.

Controlling the market seemed an obvious solution, and the 1596 act was followed two years later by another from the privy council which limited gun size to 'an elne in the rotch' as a minimum size, while also outlawing certain types of handguns.[74] Yet as long as there was a demand such guns would continue to be produced or imported, and at a convention that summer the nobility were persuaded to give an undertaking to see that the firearms legislation was enforced among their followers and within their jurisdictions.[75] In 1600, as an accompaniment to the ratification of the 'Act Anent Feuds', parliament criticised the circumvention of the law by legal technicalities, and authorised the lord advocate and the treasurer to co-ordinate prosecutions. In future this could be done either through the privy council or the justice courts. If offenders were tried and found guilty by the former they could be warded, have their moveables escheated, and be fined as the council thought fit. The justice court, however, would punish under the provisions of the 1595 act. Finally, all existing gun licences were cancelled, and new ones were only to be issued by the king and the privy council.[76] This allowed the crown a greater degree of flexibility as the privy council was less easily entangled by clever lawyers than the court of justiciary, but there was a further attraction in the revenue-raising potential of the act, a potential which had been brought to notice a few months before when the master of Ogilvy had agreed to pay a £5,000 fine to avoid criminal prosecution for his use of firearms in an incident with Lord Spynie.[77]

This 1600 act remained the basis of all future efforts to control firearms.[78] In 1601 the making of petards was outlawed,[79] and in 1603 sheriffs were threatened with the pains of the law themselves if they failed to uphold it in their localities.[80] By 1608 proclamations were only concerned with offences in the north, an indication that elsewhere the campaign was having some effect.[81] Assizes could still refuse to convict if they thought the punishment too extreme, but dismemberment was occasionally enforced 'to the terrour of all utheris to offend in the lyke soirt'.[82] Instances of breaking the gun laws are recorded in the 1620s, and in the highlands gun control was much later in becoming a reality, but the large-scale shoot-outs and the casual use of guns were eradicated from most of the rest of Scotland during the first decade of the seventeenth century. That was the same period when the greatest advances were made against feuding, and the connection between the two, which was made by contemporaries, appears to have been a justifiable one. Whether the decline of feuding made men more willing to go out without their guns, or whether the successful enforcement of gun control reduced the level of violence in society cannot really be ascertained, and there is probably some truth in both these propositions.

If guns were a recent problem, private combats, or duels, had a long history of dubious legitimacy in the eyes of medieval kings. Since the thirteenth century trial by combat had been in decline in Scotland, although it continued under licence.[83] While the Italian duel did not become as widely popular in Scotland as in some other European states, it did make some impact in the later decades of the sixteenth century. In 1580 the privy council pointed out that private combats were only lawful when 'na uther triall is to be had', and that the sending of 'ony infamous libellis or utheris, or to appoint or keip trystis for the combat' was a criminal offence.[84] This noble-dominated council had little thought of securing a monopoly of violence for the state, and they were simply worried about the potential impact this form of continental violence might have. Twenty years later, in April 1600, the privy council were scathing about those who saw an excuse for duelling 'upoun everie licht occassioun, quhairupoun mony deidlie feidis and uther inconvenientis hes oft fallin oute'.[85] Shortly before this the king had signalled his intention to get tough on this issue when he pressed for the execution of an Edinburgh burgess who had killed a fellow burgess in a private combat,[86] although it was not until November that parliament made death the penalty for unlicensed duelling itself.[87] In that same year John Wilson, also of lowly status, fought a duel, and 'being tane with het bluid, was execute at the flesh stocks where he had slain the man the night before'.[88] For the governing elite itself prevention rather than punishment was the only acceptable cure, and in 1602 the earl of Argyll and the duke of Lennox were committed to their chambers for challenging one another,[89] while in 1608 the master of Caithness and the commendator of Melrose and their seconds were warded for arranging a duel before being reconciled by the privy council.[90] Fortunately the publicity with which such men liked to announce their intentions allowed the privy council to act before many of the duels actually took place.

In contrast tuilyies (fights) broke out spontaneously, and were particularly associated with places where men congregated in numbers. When parliament met it was common for the privy council to order that no-one 'tak upoun hand to invaid molest or persew utheris, or gif provocatioun or displeasour be word, deid or countenance, owther for auld feid or new'.[91] To break the peace of parliament was treasonable, but it was broken, and violent incidents were not unusual in the ante-rooms of the privy council itself, or in the courts as rivals met one another before a hearing.[92] In 1593 parliament made it treasonable and a crime of *lèse majesté* to hurt, strike, or slay anyone in the parliament house, in the court of session, before the king, or in the council rooms while it was in session. Even if the incident took place before any of the king's deputies, or senior officials, a £100 fine was to be levied, and striking a judge was to be punished with death.[93] This act was passed in the context of an affair the previous day when two lords of the articles had exchanged blows, although it was not simply a response to one incident.[94]

Such legislation also reflected the king's desire to give the crown greater dignity, and to distance it from private violence. This made it particularly important that Edinburgh should be made more peaceful, and on the same day as the above act was passed, the burgh magistrates were granted greater policing powers.[95] In 1597 all inhabitants of burghs were ordered to assist their magistrates in 'redding and stoppin all tuilyeis' since so many offenders were escaping.[96] Of course, many of the offenders were native to the burgh themselves, and it would be a mistake to see them as victims of violence imported by the nobility and their followers. In 1600 the 'frequent tuilyeis' of Edinburgh and the Canongate were still allowing men to 'revenge thair particular querrelis', and all arms were banned within a mile of wherever the king happened to be.[97] Peace within the verge, that area of approximately four square miles within which the king resided, had been the responsibility of the Edinburgh magistrates since they had made an agreement with the constable earlier in the century, but the status of the men who so often broke it made enforcement difficult.[98]

That enforcement could be strict, but it only became effective when the court left Edinburgh. In 1601 John Dundas of Newliston was charged with having struck another gentleman in the rooms next to where the king was sitting in session with the lords of council and session. Dundas was lucky to be excused the assize, and to be punished with a fine.[99] Lesser men could expect little mercy, and in 1603 Walter Graham was scourged from the Castle Hill to the Nethir Bow, had his right hand cut off, and was banished for life after he struck a minister near to the tolbooth while the privy council was sitting.[100] By 1611, however, distance had given the king confidence, and when the earl of Lothian became involved in an affray he wrote to the privy council telling them that an earl and a councillor ought to know better, and ordered him to be fined £10,000. The council replied that this was far too severe, and persuaded the king to mitigate the fine, although he did tell them they were too soft![101] That, of course, was easy for James to write from the distance of London, but distance was what helped the crown aspire to that dignity which laws so often fell short of. The removal of the court took much of the tension out of Edinburgh, the potential for tuilyies was reduced, and as a corresponding decrease in feuding took place the mentality which often provoked them began to disappear.

Kings in Scotland had been trying to restrict the size of noble retinues and convocations since the fifteenth century.[102] To a degree this reflected their own insecurity in the face of such visible power, but these large followings were also the cause of friction as rival groups met, or were the means by which existing quarrels were pursued. In 1579 and 1581 insecure minority governments tried to limit the size of retinues in what was largely a political move to protect their own vulnerability.[103] In 1583 retinues were limited to sixteen for an earl, eight for a lord, and six for a baron or knight, and in 1590 these were further reduced to twelve, eight and five respectively, with the additional condition that they be unarmed.[104] This act was extremely unpopular, and unrealistic, and a year later the numbers were increased to twenty-four for an earl, sixteen for a lord, and ten for a baron or knight. It was again decreed that they should be unarmed, that licences should be sought before entering Edinburgh, and that lords would be held responsible for any crimes committed by those in their retinues.[105] This too appears to have been widely disregarded as lords continued to turn up at court with far greater numbers of men than were permitted, and royal insecurity often encouraged friendly noblemen to provide additional protection.

Convocations, usually associated with lords levying their forces within their localities, were a threat to local peace, and could be raised in preparation for wider political employment. In 1587 the privy council attacked those who raised mercenary companies, ostensibly for service abroad, but in fact 'to assist some subjects of this realme in thair particulair querrelis aganis utheris, to the raising and intertenying of civile seditioun, insurrectioun and uproare within the cuntrey'.[106] In spite of this both Lord Maxwell and the earl of Huntly are known to have maintained bands of paid soldiers, and Chancellor Maitland was said to 'keep a great train to save his life from his enemies'.[107] More commonly lords used dependants and servants in local disputes, 'chieflie for leding of the teinds this present seasoun of the yeir quhairupoun hes followit and dalie is liklie to follow sindry deidlie feidis and utheris greit inconvenientis'.[108] This habit, however, was a long time in dying, and the act of 1590 was repeated in 1591 and 1595, while in 1610 the king was still having to remind his councillors of 'how odious these convocationis be unto us, as savoreing of that auld barbaritie which wes the roote of all deidlie feidis'.[109]

The failure of the retinue legislation of 1591 resulted in a new attempt being made in 1600. Numbers were once more reduced to twelve for an earl, eight for a lord and four for a baron or knight, and a loophole was closed which had allowed a lord, for example, to be accompanied by eight barons or knights each with four servants, thus multiplying his retinue without breaking the letter of the law.[110] In 1606 the privy council decreed in a more assertive mood that in future those who appeared before them with excessive retinues would automatically lose the case if they were the pursuer, and be denounced and arrested if they were the defender.[111]

Yet resistance to such limitations on the status of great men, some of whom were themselves councillors, proved deep-rooted. In 1610 the king wrote to the privy council complaining that 'it wald seame rather that thair apperance war not so muche ether for obedience or cleiring thameselvis' as 'to imprent in thair waik hairtit adversarie some feir of thair parteis grite freindship and upoun terrour to enforce him to relinquische his just persute'. He advised them to make more use of the 1579 act's postponing technique as the best discouragement of the practice since long stays in Edinburgh for lords and their followers would prove very costly. The council responded with another act along these lines, and this began to have some effect.[112] As with gun control, there was an interdependence between feuding and convocations or retinues since the practical need for them declined along with feuding, just as feuds were less likely to be stimulated as large bands of armed men became a rare occurrence.

Those bonds which existed between lord and man were encouraged where the relationship could be seen to be a stabilising influence in society. In 1585 bonding among noblemen had been discouraged for narrow political reasons,[113] but the general band, under which lords recognised their responsibility for those men who lived on their lands, was popular with the crown.[114] However, it had its critics, like Forbes of Tolquhane, who objected to being lumped together with the rest of his surname, and having to answer for broken men who, through no fault of his, were living within his bounds. It was, he said, peaceful men like himself who ended up paying fines for the crimes of these outlaws, and he poured scorn on this 'maist pernicious and dangerous practique'.[115] The general band was rarely used outside the highland zone, and one Lennox landowner complained that he should not have to observe it since none of his men 'speik with the Irishe tung, but onlie sic landed pecable men as speikis onlie Scottis language'.[116] The earl of Orkney was equally determined not to be included in the band as his islands were a 'civile cuntrey'.[117] It was an unpopular measure, but the fact that it reinforced local obligations and authority was in its favour, and the general band enjoyed a modest degree of success.

In all these measures lords were being asked to alter their behaviour and habits, but the crown was also in need of some reform if it was to be more effective in enforcing the peace. One old thorn was that of respites and remissions. In 1584 the Arran government passed an act against the granting of respites or remissions for capital offences for three years since the practice was thought to encourage slaughters. Those already held were nullified unless a letter of slains could also be produced.[118] As usual good intent was insufficient, and those with a hand in dispensing court patronage continued to exploit the mercy market. Acts of 1585 and 1587 passed equally unnoticed.[119] The difficulties this created in a feuding society were obvious. In 1591 Hay of Gourdie, whose son had been killed by a man who had since obtained a seven-year respite, reminded the privy council of the dangers involved in continuing with the practice. Not only was it unlawful, but

gif thay salbe frustrat of justice undir pretens of the said pretendit respett purchest of his Majestie privatlie, and be suppressing of the treuth aganis a publict law, and his

Majestie solempne vow and promeis, it sall discourage all men to seik redres be way of justice heirefter, bot rather to seik thair privat revenge at thair maist advantage, quhen thai sall find it mekle mair easie to gett ane respett nor to summond and mak voyage to Edinburgh.[120]

Within two months of receiving this complaint the privy council responded with a new act. It was decided that all those who held respites or remissions would be called to account and must give caution, but that their lives would be guaranteed by the crown. Having given caution, they would then be obliged to 'mak assythment and satisfaction to the saidis kin and freindis' under the council's supervision. The privy council would also determine whether the king had an interest in the case, and would impose a fine where appropriate.[121] Thus the irregularly obtained respites and remissions were to be recognised, and justice would be done, not through the courts, but by the kindreds. Parliament ratified the act six months later, and instructed the treasurer, advocate and justice clerk to compile a list of those holding respites or remissions, and review their position in the light of the new legislation.[122] This act, which was repeated in 1593, was specifically allied to the problem of the feuds, and it too reflected the government's conservative instincts in placing the emphasis on reconciliation rather than punishment.[123]

While there continued to be exceptions, this 1591 act had some success. In 1605 James Gledstanes was brought before the justice court for a murder he had committed forty-four years before, in 1561, but having produced his respite he was ordered to give caution that he would satisfy the injured party and get a letter of slains from him.[124] In 1612 William Murray turned up at his trial for slaughter with a remission he had acquired earlier in the year, but which had only been passed under the privy seal. The judge declared the remission null, but since Murray had a letter of slains from the dead man's kindred, the judge ordered him to satisfy two younger sons who had been neglected by the assythment, and to get the remission passed under the great seal.[125] In both these cases the principle of satisfying the kindred was seen as the essential component of justice by the court, not the king's mercy which was largely secondary. The privy council shared this view, and in 1612 they granted a remission to Alexander Scott for the slaughter of a collier on the grounds that the dead man's kindred had accepted assythment which, in the council's view, was more helpful to the family than punishment would have been.[126] Even when prosecution had got under way the crown usually preferred to allow a privately agreed settlement to interrupt the proceedings, and would set aside the law for the sake of communal peace.[127] This underlines the fact that the place of the family in pursuing justice did not disappear during the Jacobean period under the onslaught of criminal law. In fact the latter protected it by formally recognising kin responsibilities. In 1621 the privy council recommended that remissions be granted in a case brought before them, but only after both sides had found caution to behave, and as a prelude to negotiating peace, because 'it may be certanelie expectit, mutuall revengeis wilbe huntit for on aither syde'.[128] The privy council's job was to prevent that revenge being exacted, and remissions and respites did that by protecting the guilty from blood justice. It was not the privy council's business, or that of the courts, to tell the kindreds what the price of peace should be, and assythment remained a private business between them. Not all slaughters were dealt with in this way, and some were decided at law, but there was no fundamental changeover to punitive and public justice.

For those men who were subject to criminal prosecution, and who tried to evade it, horning remained the crown's principal weapon. The utter confusion which surrounded the laws governing the status of outlaws was highlighted in a case in 1600 between the crown and Robert Auchmowtie who was tried for killing an Edinburgh burgess in a private combat. Auchmowtie's lawyer fought a clever defence which exploited this confusion to the full, and which inspired the lord advocate to heights of erudition and rhetoric in maintaining the king's case. However, the king and his advocate wanted a conviction, and a royal warrant was finally produced condemning the 'verry frivolous subterfugeis' of the defence, and demanding that the assize produce a verdict. Anticipating the worst, Auchmowtie asked to be taken into the king's will, but this was refused, the assize convicted him, and he was later executed.[129] That verdict did not reflect any decision on the debatable status of Auchmowtie's victim at the time of his death, and the question of whether Wauchope was a horned man or not remained open. From the evidence of the long and learned argument between advocate Hamilton and the defence lawyer it was clear that no-one really knew what horning meant.[130]

Parliament had tried to tidy up the law in 1567,[131] but this was interrupted by the civil war, and it was not until 1573 that the privy council returned to the problem with an order to sheriffs to co-operate more with the treasurer by publishing lists of horned men within their jurisdictions.[132] Six years later parliament again complained that scant regard was paid to letters of horning, and further efforts were made to oil the bureaucratic wheels by increasing the supervisory powers of crown officers over local officials.[133] Of course, the underlying defect in such legislation was that the public interest which those men who sat in parliament recognised quickly suffered when it clashed with their private interests. However, the 'double think' persisted, and in 1584 an 'Act Anent the Better Execution of Decreets' was passed,[134] while the 'Act Anent Slaughter and Troubling Made by Parties in Persute and Defence of Their Actions' revived legislation of 1555.[135] The first of these dealt again with the administration of the law, but the latter was concerned with the more fundamental question of whether private persons could kill outlaws without themselves breaking the criminal law. Traditionally outlawry had very often meant that the outlaw was fair game for other men, but most early modern states were aware of the dangers inherent in this, and when Venice experimented with an explicitly permissive law in 1531–32, the violence which followed forced it to be abandoned.[136] By the 1584 act an outlaw who wounded or slew his pursuer could be further pursued by the victim or his kindred by an irreducible act of horning. However, if the outlaw was slain, his heir and kinsmen were to be absolved of any responsibility for the original crime, and the affair was never to be raised again. Outlaws could, therefore, be slain, whether they were guilty of the original charge or not, but only by the party which was pursuing them.[137] This act was given a trial period of seven years, lapsed between 1591 and 1594, and was then given perpetual status in 1594.[138]

In 1586 the privy council attempted to clarify the distribution of the profits arising from hornings. They decreed that all of a rebel's property and goods were to be seized, while the rebels were to be warded and stripped of any offices they held.[139] A year later it was decided that all escheats were to fall to the crown, not to private persons as had been happening,[140] and later in 1588 a loophole was closed by which rebels made over their property to kinsmen to avoid its confiscation.[141] Acts in 1588, 1590, 1591 and 1593 all tried to improve on the administration of horning,[142] but the most effective measure arose from the earl of Bothwell's rebellion. The 1592 'Act for Punishment of Resettars of Traitors and Rebells' made those who protected rebels liable to the same punishment as the rebels themselves, thus denying outlaws the protection which had so often made their condition tolerable.[143] In 1595 the privy council ordered that a list of resetters be compiled,[144] and in the same year sheriffs and their deputies were again asked to compile lists of horned men so that the crown could keep a central register.[145] Parliament added two more acts in 1597 and 1600 which made minor improvements to the working of the law,[146] and in 1598 and 1601 the privy council were heavily critical of sheriffs and stewards for their laxity in enforcement.[147] Revenue was probably as important as law and order in giving impetus to such legislation, and the role of the treasurer in its enforcement was crucial.[148] Yet while all this did make outlawry a more meaningful condition, and rebels were more likely to be brought to justice, horning was still a less than clear process. In 1611 the heir to the laird of Drumlanrig was so well defended by his lawyer's exploitation of legal technicalities that the crown agreed to free him on condition that the records of his trial would not be registered, they 'being so dangerous' that they could not be permitted to establish a principle likely to bring the whole edifice toppling down.[149]

Preventive measures were just as important in keeping the peace, and lawburrows, or caution, was intended to anticipate violence between parties by binding one or both to observe the peace. In 1579 parliament divided the pains of lawburrows between the offended party and the crown in an attempt to recoup something out of the system by putting the onus of enforcement in private hands.[150] This idea had been suggested ten years earlier, at the 1567 parliament, but had not been enacted.[151] In 1581 the scope of the law was widened to include intended bodily harm on the principal, his kindred, tenants or servants.[152] Over the next decade there was a substantial growth in the use of cautions, and in 1593 parliament increased the minimum amount of surety since what was being currently asked for was so small as to be meaningless.[153] A year later money was also the issue when attention was drawn to the number of people who were coming to private agreements with their pursuers, and were thus defrauding the crown of its share of the pains. The clerk register was therefore asked to hand in a monthly list of cautions to the treasurer and advocate to allow them to oversee enforcement.[154] In 1597 further tightening of the financial aspects of the law took place.[155]

For the crown the lack of local means of enforcement was a frustration it had to live with. Some independence from the network of private policing and courts was achieved with the creation of a royal guard. This was formally done by parliament in 1584,[156] but before 1603 the major function of the guard was to provide the king with some security. However, in 1603 money was made available to transform the guard into a mobile policing force who were put under the command of Sir David Murray, later Lord Scone.[157] The guard were employed on a variety of missions such as when they were sent to arrest some of the notorious Elliot family and bring them in for trial and execution, which they did with the loss of one man.[158] The king had his doubts about the effectiveness of this guard 'who at oure greate coist ar interteined',[159] and in 1611 they were prematurely disbanded, largely for financial reasons.[160] They had made a major contribution to policing in the borders in particular, and their removal did see some revival of disorder in the region, but no attempt was made to develop the principle of an independent force elsewhere, and they were not restored after 1611.[161]

The crown did have at its disposal a body of royal officers whose job it was to deliver royal letters, such as letters of horning, in localities. In 1585 it was discovered that there was widespread corruption among them with many false letters being executed, and a number were deprived of their positions. A list of legitimately commissioned officers was to be drawn up, and given to the ubiquitous treasurer along with the names of their sponsors, while similar exercises were to be performed by sheriffs, stewards and bailies for their jurisdictions. All complaints about any royal officer were to be made to the privy council who would investigate them, and would also ensure that the officers were sufficiently paid to reduce the likelihood of their accepting bribes.[162] Two years later further efforts were made to raise the standards of the officers,[163] and in 1592 parliament passed an act against deforcement, thus enhancing the dignity of their office.[164] Those who continued to exploit their position could be severely punished, and William Strachan, a royal messenger who forged and executed letters in the king's name, was very fortunate to escape with only a scourging and the loss of his job.[165]

It was much less easy to do anything about the higher officials responsible for enforcing the criminal law. In 1567 parliament had expressed concern at the wisdom of granting more heritable offices, especially judicial ones, but the practice was too tied up with the spoils of political life for anything to be done about it.[166] The poor reputation of some sheriffs did arouse occasional criticism, such as in 1599 when the sheriffs of Roxburgh, Berwick, Selkirk and Peebles were all charged to answer for their neglect before the privy council.[167] In 1600 a commission dominated by noblemen was established to investigate whether sheriffs and other local magistrates might be helped to better execute their offices, and the sheriffs themselves were ordered to attend a convention of the nobility to discuss the problems they encountered, and to offer advice on possible solutions.[168] Yet as the king himself had recognised, without attacking the fundamental heritability of the offices nothing could really be achieved, and the privy council could only protest from the sidelines.[169] In 1617 the possibility of purchasing those rights was examined, but the idea was abandoned due to the prohibitive costs, and in 1625 the crown only had the right to nominate sheriffs annually in eight shires.[170]

In the central criminal court the justice generalship was also hereditary, but the evolution of the lord advocate's office had a substantial impact upon the crown's role in criminal law. As early as 1579 the privy council had instructed the lord advocate and the treasurer to pursue 'all slauchters, convocations and utheris odious crymes' even when private parties declined to do so.[171] In that same year parliament recognised the advocate's discretionary powers in deciding whether private pursuits were groundless or worthy,[172] in 1582 deputes were first appointed,[173] and in 1587 the privacy of criminal prosecution was further eroded by parliament empowering the advocate and treasurer to 'persew slaughter and utheris crimes although the parties be silent or wald utherwayis privilie agree'.[174] This did not result in an immediate changeover from party prosecution to the dominance of the third party, but it did represent a shift in legal thinking which allowed the crown greater freedom to manoeuvre, and it had far-reaching implications for the future which may not have been anticipated at the time.[175] Private prosecution survived the reign, but the growth in the lord advocate's office, especially under Sir Thomas Hamilton who gave it enormous prestige, and the appointment of a solicitor general in 1591, and a procurator general in 1621 reduced the dependence on private parties, and increased the efficiency and independence of the crown.[176]

It would, however, be a mistake to see this as part of an intense centralising process. In 1587 parliament revived the sitting of justice ayres in localities in order to take justice out of Edinburgh where it was both costly and protracted. This response to demands for the local exercise of royal justice was not backed with the funding necessary to make it work, and the justice ayres were greatly circumscribed by the rights of local courts.[177] The lack of accountability of those who held heritable jurisdictions was made into something of a scapegoat by the crown which blamed 'the slouth of magistratis in not suppressing the first feidis'.[178] This accusation in the preamble to an act of 1609 establishing English-style justices and commissioners of the peace was an attempt to shift the blame from the crown itself, and to justify this new tier of local justice. These justices were to 'prevent all sic occasionis as may breid truble and violence amangis his mateis subiectis', and the men given this responsibility were to be crown appointees holding commissions to deal with breaches of the peace, disorderly gatherings, weapons offences, and any possible confrontation or dispute which could lead to violence.[179] Thus in 1611 the justice of the peace of the sheriffdom of Fife brought Sir David Carnegy of Kynnaird and Bruce of Earlshall before the privy council 'upoun supisitioun of some contraversie betuix thame'.[180] Over the next few years their powers were reinforced by additional legislation,[181] but they were squeezed between the existing franchise courts and the assertive church courts, and consequently made little impact upon local law and order. As a preventive authority they were probably of less significance than the establishment of a register of sasines in 1617 which helped direct many more local disputes into the court of session,[182] and they were established too late to be instrumental in reducing violent feuding. The level of local peace secured before 1609 suggests that in fact the hereditary courts and the leaders of local society did a far better job in co-operating with the crown in establishing peace than crown propaganda has led one to believe.

The transformation from a society which resolved its disputes in private bloodfeuds and agreements to one which had them decided by the pleading of lawyers before judges of the crown was not a sudden one, and it was one which had only begun during the Jacobean period. Feuding may have been under control by 1625, but it was only temporarily contained in the highlands, and the principles of private justice continued to be recognised in the courts into the 1640s.[183] Councillors might argue that 'the doing and ministring of justice is the speciall grund quhairupoun his Hienes croun standis and dependis',[184] but that justice was still equated with peace, not with an objective and punitive law enforced by royal judges. Resistance to making use of the courts continued to be inspired by the same disincentives of cost and time as before, and these may even have become more of an obstacle as fees and legal complexities both grew. Yet in spite of that the Earl Marischal had a point when he wrote to the earl of Errol asking him if they could settle their differences 'nocht be the law or truble quhilk is the cummour custome of the cuntrie in maiteris of less wecht'.[185] For Marischal, 'truble' — the feud — was as unacceptable as going to law, but as far as he could see, men were willing to do both for the slightest of reasons. Sir Robert Gordon suggested that litigation was gradually replacing feuding when he related how two highland clans had had their feud pacified by mediation, and 'have continued in peace and quietnes, without oppin hostilitie; bot they have had actions of law the one against the other'.[186] The effectiveness of this newly sharpened weapon was demonstrated by Mackenzie of Kintail who after years of fighting with the Glengarry MacDonnells finally achieved the territorial expansion he had coveted by exploiting his Edinburgh connections and his own knowledge of the law: 'Thus doe the tryb of Clanheinzie become greit in these pairts, still incroaching upon thir nighbours, who are unacquented with the lawes of thir kingdome'.[187] In that context, which was both an intellectual one and a political one, there was less and less toleration of the older form of competition. The case of the burning of Lord Forbes's corn at Sanset in 1615 in Caithness demonstrated that change. The burning was ordered by the earl of Caithness who was annoyed at the intrusion by Lord Forbes, who had recently bought the lands, into his sphere of influence. If Sir Robert Gordon is to be believed, Caithness had difficulty getting the job done, and was told by the Clan Gunn that 'ther wes such justice executed in Scotland that they culd have no saiff place of restrait after the cryme wes committed', and they cited the fates of the MacGregors and MacDonalds to emphasise the point.[188] However, a number of them finally agreed to take on the work, and the burning went ahead. Lord Forbes, with the help of Sir Robert himself, took Caithness to court, having gathered sufficient evidence to make a very persuasive case against him, and the earl agreed to make substantial compensation to avoid prosecution.

To his surprise the king insisted on pushing ahead in his own interest, the offence being a reasonable one, and Caithness only escaped forfeiture by resigning in perpetuity the sheriffdom and justiciary of Caithness, handing the Sanset incendiaries over for execution, providing a house and lands for the bishop of Caithness, and agreeing to satisfy his many creditors, as surety for which his sons were warded. The power of the Sinclair family in Caithness was thus broken over the burning of some cornfields, something which would have been quite inconceivable a few decades before, particularly so far north.[189]

The successful attack on private violence and the confinement of feuding to the less governable parts of the highlands was one of the major achievements of Jacobean government. Yet it would be wrong to place it wholly within the context of government. Certainly the crown was responsible for the practical business of making and enforcing laws which curbed violence and reduced the likelihood of feuding in the future. It also benefited in that violence moved closer to being a state monopoly, and power was enhanced at the centre at the expense of the localities. It would, however, be an over-simplification to see the decline of feuding as only the obverse side of state building, as a victim of early absolutism, and as nothing more than that. At the ideological level we have seen that what most concerned the church was creating a society prepared to meet the apocalypse. Fear of divine judgement and a desire to live out Christ's teachings in a godly community was what inspired the feud's most vocal and public critics. Among the governing classes, especially the nobility, the impact of that ideology was all the greater because the ideas which sustained the feud had already been softened by the Renaissance. In pushing the crown towards its own ideal the church made it possible for James VI to further his own ambitions. In fact the church positively encouraged him to seize greater power which he would exercise under God. It would therefore be inappropriate to restrict an evaluation of the campaign against feuding to the crown alone. The achievement was one made by Scottish society rather than by an institution within that society. More accurately it was the elite of that society who set themselves against private violence. The ministers of the church, the nobility, the king and the royal officials were all involved, drawing on a synthesis of ideas in which the emphasis may have varied, but which led to the same conclusion that violent feuding had to go. Whatever the vision of individuals or of groups within that elite was, the actual result satisfied all of them in some measure. The crown was left more powerful than ever before because that was the price men were prepared to pay for greater peace. As a by-product of that the lawyers were able to grow in status as more and more business was brought to the courts. The church was also able to increase its authority, although in some respects the removal of feuding was an effect of the church's already enhanced influence in society. By helping create a more peaceful society in which the sinfulness of crime was becoming more widely recognised, the church could point to the greater godliness of that society as a sign of Scotland's elect status. Finally, Scotland moved closer to being a civil society, thus fulfilling a long and often frustrated tradition of humanist aspirations.

Yet the translation of those ideas into legislation and its enforcement was not a straightforward one. Pragmatism rather than principles was what shaped the particular direction of the campaign, and the government put its efforts into making and keeping the peace rather than punishing criminals or sinners. Such an approach was in part a product of realism, but it also derived from the intrinsic conservatism of the personnel of government. James VI and his servants were prepared to make a number of innovations, but those were modest, and stopped well short of any revolution in government. The king himself essentially saw his role as a peacekeeper in medieval terms, and there is little evidence of radical thinking among his councillors. Even if there had been, the nobility would never have permitted laws to be passed or enforced which were an explicit threat to their power. The road to the elimination of private violence had therefore to respect a great array of other entrenched rights and privileges, such as hereditary franchise courts, which often stood in the way of more dramatic change. That political limitation aside, Scottish parliaments and privy councils saw no need to go further than they did. Peace was achieved, and if much of the bloodfeud's own principles were taken over by the law, and much of the socio-political framework within which feuds operated remained intact, so much the better. The long-term effects of the disappearance of feuding may have been more complex and more far-reaching than was intended, but in the short term Scottish society simply became less violent. Whether it actually became more just is less easily answered. Private justice continued to operate for some time, but was gradually eroded by the attraction of waging war in the courts, and by the growing belief that justice did not deal in compromises, only in right and wrong. Certainly more people turned to the law for justice, but whether the quality of that justice was any better than that hammered out between kindreds and lords in the bloodfeud is debatable.

## NOTES

1. J. C. H. Paton, 'The Dark Age, 1329–1532', in *Introduction to Scottish Legal History*, p. 20.

2. Cooper, 'From David I to Bruce', in *Introduction to Scottish Legal History*, p. 13.

3. Wright, 'Venetian Law and Order: A Myth?', p. 200. Lenman and Parker, 'State, Community and the Criminal Law in Early Modern Europe', in Gatrell, Lenman and Parker (eds.), *Crime and the Law*, pp. 23–27, emphasise that throughout Europe 'community law' was being forced aside by 'state law'.

4. The most extreme case for the conscious construction of an early absolutist state is made by M. Lee, *John Maitland of Thirlestane* and M. Lee, *Government By Pen, Scotland Under James VI and I*, Illinois University Press, 1980.

5. *A.P.S.*, iii, pp. 112–114, 164–165 and 230–231; *R.P.C.*, iii, p. 278.

6. *R.P.C.*, iii, pp. 500–503.

7. Calderwood, *History*, iii, pp. 700–702.

8. *C.S.P., Scot.*, ix, p. 398.

9. Moysie, *Memoirs*, p. 63. See also, Balfour, 'Annales', i, p. 385; Birrel, 'Diary', p. 24; Calderwood, *History*, iv, pp. 613–614.

10. *A.P.S.,* iii, p. 458.

11. *R.P.C.,* iv, p. 686.

12. *C.S.P., Scot.,* xii, pp. 73 and 87; *R.P.C.,* v, pp. 248–249.

13. *C.S.P. Scot.,* xii, Part 1, p. 214.

14. *Ibid.,* pp. 228–229.

15. *A.P.S.,* iv, pp. 158–159; *C.S.P., Scot.,* xii, Part 1, pp. 228–229.

16. *A.P.S.,* iv, pp. 158–159.

17. *Ibid.,* pp. 158–159. According to Balfour, *Practicks,* ii, p. 513, this principle was already established in Scots law.

18. The lord advocate's right to pursue for the king's interest had been enshrined in parliamentary acts of 1579 and 1587, *A.P.S.,* iii, pp. 144 and 458.

19. *A.P.S.,* iv, pp. 158–159.

20. *A.P.S.,* iv, pp. 233–235. There was no opposition to the act in 1600, its passage being managed by the lords of the articles.

21. *R.P.C.,* vi, pp. 594–596.

22. *Ibid.,* p. 44; *R.P.C.,* vii, pp. 295–296 and 738.

23. For example, see Gordon of Lochinvar's assurance with Vaus of Longcastle and Stewart of Dunduff which was broken when he killed the latter, *R.P.C.,* v, pp. 467 and 555–556; vi, pp. 266–267.

24. *R.P.C.,* vi, pp. 307–308 and 365; viii, p. 61.

25. *R.P.C.,* xi, pp. 417 and 452.

26. For example, see the denunciation of Leslie of Wardes in 1596, *R.P.C.,* v, p. 272, and Innes of Crombie in 1622, *R.P.C.,* xiii, p. 477.

27. *R.P.C.,* ix, p. 541.

28. *R.P.C.,* viii, pp. 144, 215 and 543.

29. *R.P.C.,* vii, pp. 391–392.

30. *Melrose,* i, p. 7.

31. *R.P.C.,* x, p. 45; Balfour, 'Annales', ii, p. 42.

32. *R.P.C.,* viii, p. 621; xi, pp. 202 and 318; Pitcairn, *Criminal Trials,* iii, p. 58.

33. *Spottiswoode Miscellany,* i, 'Murder of Mathew Sinclair', pp. 23–28; *R.P.C.,* ix, pp. 602–603 and 622.

34. *Melrose,* i, pp. 326–327.

35. *Ibid.,* i, pp. 353–355 and 357–358.

36. *R.P.C.,* vii, p. 183.

37. See S. Roberts, 'The Study of Dispute: Anthropological Perspectives', in Bossy (ed.), *Disputes and Settlements,* pp. 16–17.

38. Pitcairn, *Criminal Trials,* iii, pp. 440–441.

39. Balfour, 'Annales', ii, p. 21.

40. *R.P.C.,* vi, p. 83.

41. *R.P.C.,* xi, pp. 206, 224 and 225; Balfour, 'Annales', ii, p. 68; *Melrose,* i, p. 296; Gordon, *Sutherland,* pp. 341–342.

42. *R.P.C.,* xi, pp. 634–635 and 552; xiii, pp. 801, 375, 423, 441 and 493; Fraser, *Chiefs of Grant,* ii, p. 42; Pitcairn, *Criminal Trials,* iii, p. 545; S.R.O., Mar and Kellie, G.D., 124/6/64.

43. *R.P.C.,* vii, p. 272.

44. S.R.O., Inventory of Scottish Muniments at Haigh, i, box D, 6/Nov/1616.

45. *R.P.C.,* xiii, pp. 112–114.

46. *R.P.C.,* vi, p. 472.

47. *R.P.C.,* x, p. 452.

48. *R.P.C.*, xiii, pp. 745–746.
49. Philpotts, *Kindred and Clan*, pp. 104 ff. and 124–125.
50. For example, *R.P.C.*, xi, pp. 171–172.
51. *Ibid.*, pp. 337–338.
52. *Ibid.*, p. 385.
53. *R.P.C.*, xiii, p. 441.
54. S.R.O., Airlie Muniments, G.D., 16/683/41/127.
55. *R.P.C.*, xi, pp. 193–194 and 248.
56. *A.P.S.*, iii, pp. 91–92 and 676–677; v, pp. 266–267, 446–447 and 551. Permission not to attend was given if men had deadly feuds, *Ibid.*, p. 282.
57. *Basilikon Doron*, p. 25.
58. *A.P.S.*, iii, pp. 112–114, 164–165 and 230–231; *R.P.C.*, iii, p. 278.
59. *A.P.S.*, iii, pp. 84–85.
60. *R.P.C.*, ii, pp. 681–683; iii, pp. 105 and 175.
61. *A.P.S.*, iii, p. 146; *R.P.C.*, iii, p. 327; Pitcairn, *Criminal Trials*, i, Part 2, pp. 98–100.
62. *R.P.C.*, iv, p. 597.
63. *R.P.C.*, v, p. 90.
64. R. Renwick, *The Burgh of Peebles, 1604–1652*, Peebles, 1911, p. 10.
65. *R.P.C.*, v, p. 204.
66. *Historie*, p. 355.
67. *R.P.C.*, v, p. 247.
68. *R.P.C.*, v, pp. 274–275.
69. *Ibid.*, p. 322.
70. Williams, *The Tudor Regime*, pp. 236–237; Smith, *The Emergence of a Nation State*, p. 189; and for France, Kelley, *The Beginnings of Ideology*, pp. 196–197.
71. Pitcairn, *Criminal Trials*, ii, pp. 22–23.
72. Birrel, 'Diary', p. 41.
73. *Ibid.*, p. 51.
74. *R.P.C.*, v, pp. 437–438.
75. *A.P.S.*, iv, p. 164.
76. *Ibid.*, p. 228. For an example of a sixteenth-century gun licence, see that given to Lord Ruthven, the treasurer, in 1580, Pitcairn, *Criminal Trials*, i, Part 2, p. 91.
77. Pitcairn, *Criminal Trials*, ii, p. 145; *R.P.C.*, vi, pp. 201–202.
78. *R.P.C.*, vi, p. 258.
79. *Ibid.*, p. 491.
80. *Ibid.*, pp. 585–586.
81. *R.P.C.*, viii, p. 37.
82. *Ibid.*, pp. 602–603.
83. D. M. Walker, 'Evidence', in *Introduction to Scottish Legal History*, pp. 302–303; J. Neilson, *Trial By Combat*, Glasgow, 1890; Sellar, 'Courtesy, Battle and the Brieve of Right', in *Stair Miscellany II*, pp. 1–12. See too 'The Order of Combats', in *Spalding Miscellany*, ii, pp. 383–90.
84. *R.P.C.*, iii, p. 333.
85. *R.P.C.*, vi, pp. 97–98. The problem of duelling was nothing like as serious as it was in France where Henry IV began in 1602 to try and control it by encouraging provincial lieutenants to mediate between parties before the duel took place. However, noble resistance was very strong, and the duel remained firmly entrenched in spite of repeated efforts to outlaw it, M. Greengrass, *France in the Age of Henri IV, The Struggle for Stability*, New York, 1984, p. 183.

86. Pitcairn, *Criminal Trials,* ii, pp. 112–124.
87. *A.P.S.,* iv, p. 230.
88. Birrel, 'Diary', p. 49.
89. *C.S.P., Scot.,* xiii, Part 2, p. 961.
90. *R.P.C.,* viii, pp. 128 and 131.
91. *R.P.C.,* ii, p. 222.
92. The killing of Lord Glamis in 1578 and the attack on the earl of Glencairn in 1606 took place in this context, see above, pp. 124–125 and 96.
93. *A.P.S.,* iv, p. 22.
94. *C.S.P., Scot.,* xi, p. 129.
95. *A.P.S.,* iv, pp. 28–29.
96. *R.P.C.,* v, p. 403.
97. *R.P.C.,* vi, pp. 77–78.
98. W. C. Dickinson, 'Courts of Special Jurisdictions', in *Introduction to Scottish Legal History,* p. 396.
99. Pitcairn, *Criminal Trials,* ii, pp. 358–359.
100. *Ibid.,* pp. 416–417.
101. *R.P.C.,* ix, pp. 606–607, 609 and 610–611.
102. Balfour, *Practicks,* ii, pp. 533–534.
103. *R.P.C.,* iii, pp. 173 and 487.
104. *C.S.P., Scot.,* vi, p. 515; Calderwood, *History,* iii, p. 730; *A.P.S.,* iii, p. 301.
105. *R.P.C.,* iv, p. 572.
106. *Ibid.,* pp. 211–212.
107. For Maitland, see *C.S.P., Scot.,* x, p. 19.
108. *R.P.C.,* iv, pp. 513–514 and 660; v, p. 229.
109. *R.P.C.,* viii, p. 611. An act of 1612 extended the punishments reserved for illegal convocations to those who even planned to hold them, *R.P.C.,* ix, p. 370.
110. *R.P.C.,* vi, p. 169.
111. *R.P.C.,* vii, p. 288.
112. *R.P.C.,* viii, pp. 622–623 and 450.
113. *A.P.S.,* iii, pp. 376–377.
114. For example, see *R.P.C.,* iv, pp. 787–788; vi, pp. 45–46; *A.P.S.,* iv, pp. 41 and 140; Balfour, *Practicks,* ii, pp. 375–376.
115. *R.P.C.,* iv, p. 356, and see *R.P.C.,* v, pp. 249–250, 260–261, 279–280 and 283–284.
116. *R.P.C.,* v, pp. 260–261.
117. *Ibid.,* p. 436.
118. *A.P.S.,* iii, p. 298, repeated two years later, *R.P.C.,* iv, pp. 103–104.
119. *A.P.S.,* iii, p. 457.
120. *R.P.C.,* iv, pp. 680–682.
121. *R.P.C.,* iv, p. 695.
122. *A.P.S.,* iii, p. 575.
123. *A.P.S.,* iv, pp. 18–19.
124. Pitcairn, *Criminal Trials,* ii, p. 472.
125. *Ibid.,* iii, pp. 234–235.
126. *R.P.C.,* ix, pp. 337–338.
127. For example, Pitcairn, *Criminal Trials,* ii, p. 539, and see note 3 on that page.
128. *Melrose,* i, p. 402.
129. Pitcairn, *Criminal Trials,* ii, pp. 112–124.
130. See Balfour, *Practicks,* ii, pp. 557–561.

131. *A.P.S.*, iii, p. 44.

132. *R.P.C.*, ii, pp. 304–305.

133. *A.P.S.*, iii, pp. 142–143.

134. *Ibid.*, pp. 300 and 303.

135. *Ibid.*, pp. 299–300.

136. G. Cozzi, 'Authority and the Law in Renaissance Venice', in J. R. Hale (ed.), *Renaissance Venice*, London, 1974, pp. 294 and 319.

137. *A.P.S.*, iii, pp. 299–300.

138. *A.P.S.*, iv, p. 69.

139. *R.P.C.*, iv, pp. 70–71.

140. *Ibid.*, pp. 219–220. See, too, the 1567 act, *A.P.S.*, iii, p. 32.

141. *R.P.C.*, iv, p. 235.

142. *A.P.S.*, iii, pp. 524–525; iv, p. 42; *R.P.C.*, iv, pp. 490 and 590–591.

143. *A.P.S.*, iii, pp. 574–575.

144. *R.P.C.*, v, p. 247.

145. *Ibid.*, p. 234. Private persons were also asked to contribute names.

146. *A.P.S.*, iv, pp. 139–140 and 230–231.

147. *R.P.C.*, v, p. 440; vi, p. 329.

148. Sir George Hume in particular was 'very strict in his office for the King', *C.S.P., Scot.*, xiii, Part 2, p. 916.

149. Pitcairn, *Criminal Trials*, iii, pp. 212–218.

150. *A.P.S.*, iii, p. 144.

151. *Ibid.*, p. 41.

152. *Ibid.*, pp. 222–223.

153. *A.P.S.*, iv, p. 18.

154. *R.P.C.*, v, p. 130.

155. *A.P.S.*, iv, p. 140.

156. *A.P.S.*, iii, p. 298. This was staffed by forty men and was paid for from the fruits of small benefices.

157. *R.P.C.*, vi, pp. 581–582.

158. Pitcairn, *Criminal Trials*, ii, pp. 559–560.

159. *R.P.C.*, vii, p. 541.

160. *R.P.C.*, ix, p. 161.

161. Some were re-employed as debt collectors, *R.P.C.*, ix, p. 213.

162. *R.P.C.*, iii, pp. 720–721.

163. *A.P.S.*, iii, pp. 449–450.

164. *Ibid.*, pp. 577–578. During this period the lyon king of arms assumed greater control over royal messengers and heralds.

165. Pitcairn, *Criminal Trials*, ii, p. 455.

166. *A.P.S.*, iii, p. 39.

167. *R.P.C.*, vi, pp. 56–57. Criticism of sheriffs was not new, Milne, 'The Sheriff Court Before the Sixteenth Century' and Malcolm, 'The Sheriff Court: Sixteenth Century and Later', in *Introduction to Scottish Legal History*, pp. 350–55 and 356–62.

168. *R.P.C.*, vi, pp. 68–69.

169. *Ibid.*, pp. 584 and 590–592.

170. *A.P.S.*, vi, pp. 449–450, and for an earlier attempt in 1613, *R.P.C.*, x, pp. 20–21. Also Malcolm, 'The Sheriff Court: The Sixteenth Century and Later', in *Introduction to Scottish Legal History*, pp. 356–62. In 1747, when heritable jurisdictions were abolished, only ten of the thirty-three shrieval and stewartry jurisdictions were in the hands of the crown.

171. *R.P.C.,* iii, p. 173.

172. *A.P.S.,* iii, p. 144.

173. Smith, 'The Transition to Modern Law, 1532-1660', in *Introduction to Scottish Legal History,* p. 40.

174. *A.P.S.,* iii, p. 458.

175. Smith, 'The Transition to Modern Law, 1532-1660', in *Introduction to Scottish Legal History,* pp. 25-45.

176. For these offices, see Smith, 'Criminal Procedure', in *Introduction to Scottish Legal History,* pp. 434-437.

177. *A.P.S.,* iii, pp. 458-461, and see *R.P.C.,* iii, p. 500.

178. *A.P.S.,* iv, pp. 434-435.

179. *Ibid.*

180. *R.P.C.,* ix, p. 206.

181. *Ibid.,* pp. 220-226, 409-411 and 525-526.

182. Smith, 'The Transition to Modern Law, 1532-1660', in *Introduction to Scottish Legal History,* pp. 33 and 40, and Malcolm, 'The Sheriff Court: The Sixteenth Century and After', in *Introduction to Scottish Legal History,* p. 357.

183. For cases in which assythment was ordered by the justice court in 1640 and 1648, see *Selected Justiciary Cases, 1624-50,* (ed.) G. A. Gillon, Stair Society, 16, Edinburgh, 1953, i, pp. 306-308, and *Selected Justiciary Cases, 1624-50,* (ed.) J. I. Smith, Stair Society, 27, Edinburgh, 1974, iii, pp. 765-768.

184. *R.P.C.,* vi, pp. 233-234.

185. *Spalding Miscellany,* ii, 'Erroll Papers', p. 286.

186. Gordon, *Sutherland,* p. 245.

187. *Ibid.,* p. 248.

188. *Ibid.,* p. 332.

189. *Ibid.,* pp. 329-340; *R.P.C.,* x, p. 844.

# Conclusion

Language which is over-used runs the risk of becoming commonplace, even meaningless, and that has possibly been the fate of 'crisis' in the vocabulary of early modern historians. Yet whatever the current stage of the 'General Crisis' debate,[1] the concept and, for want of a better word, the term 'crisis' remain useful. A strong case has been made by Maurice Lee for excluding Scotland from a European-wide crisis in the seventeenth century, and for interpreting the Scottish revolution which began in 1637 as nothing more than the consequences of government incompetence and mismanagement.[2] However, in the sixteenth century it is much more difficult to avoid the language of crisis in a Scottish context. Writing towards the close of the century, the poet and minister, Alexander Hume, lamented 'These cursed times, this wors nor irone age',[3] and while his perspective may have been coloured by his theology, the description is far from inaccurate. There may have been no European crisis in the sixteenth century, although there does appear to have been crisis in France which bears a close resemblance to the Scottish experience,[4] but from the early 1540s until the later 1590s political conditions in Scotland were chronically unstable. Whether Scottish society as a whole was in crisis or not cannot be argued here, but an accelerating price rise which either ruined landlords on fixed rents, or created social tension where rents were increased; a growing population within the landed community scrambling to grab their share of a highly volatile land market; the shifting of wealth within that community while status and office often remained static; and a high incidence of plague, food shortages, and adverse weather, were the background against which political and religious upheaval took place. On top of all that, the twin pillars on which the late medieval Scottish kingdom rested, the Stewart monarchy and the Catholic Church, both collapsed. In the case of the latter the collapse was permanent, and the repercussions of the Reformation were felt long after 1559–60 in the continuing division of catholic and protestant, in the debate over church–state relations within the protestant community, and in the efforts of the new church to mould society to resemble the vision of its leaders. Unlike the old church, the monarchy did survive and recovered, but not before it had suffered a series of humiliating defeats, and not for more than half a century after James V's death in 1542. Religious disunity and crown weakness coupled with the socio-economic problems facing the landed community created strains which a feuding society was ill-equipped to cope with, and it fragmented into endemic feuding and violence.

That relationship between instability or crisis in the kingdom at large and feuding is not entirely a clear one. Fifteenth-century Scotland had also been a feuding society, but it was not disturbed to this extent by private violence, and the justice of the bloodfeud was able to maintain an equilibrium of war and peace within communities. Then the feud was not something very different from its

266

sixteenth-century version; what had changed were the conditions in which it found itself. The socio-economic environment was more favourable, there was no Reformation, and a succession of strong kings were able to reverse any apparent slide towards instability as they emerged from their minorities.[5] The question of whether feuds created or intensified instability, or whether instability exacerbated feuding, was one which worried Frenchmen during the Wars of Religion, and opinion varied then, as it does now among historians.[6] Such a complex problem cannot be easily resolved. A feuding society was not necessarily one in which violence was as prevalent as it was in late sixteenth-century Scotland or France, but in adverse conditions it was more likely to find that violence would become uncontrollable. That in turn generated further instability, and a cycle of tension and violence was created which was difficult to escape from. The modern state is also capable of becoming sucked into similar circumstances, but there the violence is expressed in a different form. This is not to detract from the basic violence of the bloodfeud, and its underlying bloodiness hardly needs to be emphasised again, but a feuding society did not have to be as violent as this one clearly was, and some of that must be explained by factors other than the bloodfeud itself.

The general political instability was intimately tied up with the fortunes of the crown, and with the religious question. The Marian minority, which effectively lasted from 1542 to 1561, began amidst defeat in war with England. Further disastrous defeats followed in the 1540s before French intervention pushed the English out, and reduced Scotland to the level of a French client state. During that decade protestantism also began to stir in Scotland, and by 1559 had sufficiently divided the political community to bring on a civil war which was won by the Anglophile protestant party. This Reformation was a defeat for the crown as well as the church, and the incompetent personal rule of Mary from 1561 to 1567 did little to restore royal authority. Rebellions in 1562 and 1565 were effectively crushed, but in 1567 Mary was herself forced to abdicate, and then fled to England a year later, after her escape and another short episode of civil war. A more earnest civil war broke out in 1570–73, and was ended, as in 1560, by English intervention. Peace was then maintained until 1578 when James's minority was brought to a premature end, and there followed sixteen years of coups and rebellions which were inspired by a mixture of religion and faction, in which feuds played the part of both cause and effect. In the thirty-six years between 1559 and 1594, only twelve years were not marred by actual civil war, rebellion, or a coup, and only 1563–64 and 1574–77 could reasonably be described as peaceful interludes.[7] Scotland had experienced nothing like this kind of sustained political conflict within the political community since the early fourteenth century, and while these events may have been too untidy to amount to what could be called the Scottish Wars of Religion — and in France the issues were not always religious either — the most meaningful comparison is with France. There the scale of warfare may have been greatly magnified, but the chronology was much the same, and the religious division, royal weakness, powerful particularist interests, intense factionalism, foreign intervention and manipulation, and feuding, were all very similar.[8]

In becoming so endemic and so violent the bloodfeud was much more difficult to defend against its critics. The return to political stability in the later 1590s, and the association of feud with instability, resulted in there being much less resistance to change than might have been expected. This backlash against the violence of recent years coincided with growing humanist influences, the church's strident opposition, the king's personal aspirations, and the rising status of the legal profession. The opportunity itself was created by political events, in particular the defeat of the catholic earls in 1594–95 and Bothwell's flight into what proved to be permanent exile. It is tempting to put these in the context of the crown crushing over-mighty magnates, but that is too crude a description. It was not because Huntly was an over-mighty magnate that James opposed him — in fact he was positively encouraged by the king to make use of his enormous power — but because he was an advocate of Counter Reformation. His and Errol's defeat was the last act in the religious struggle that had run through Scottish politics since the 1550s. After that, Scottish catholics opted for a *politique* course, or they left the country. Bothwell's exile was a personal victory for the king, and for Chancellor Maitland, which has to be seen in the context of feud and faction, not of crown and nobility. Maitland's opportune death shortly afterwards removed another of the major factional figures from the scene, and James's own willingness to rule above party and faction by having an open court, and in welcoming into government any of his nobility who wanted to be there, further reduced the political temperature. Court politics were slowly toned down to the level of petty faction, and were gradually divorced from local feuds as James's personal control of the court increased. One reason for that was the king's success in turning the eyes of his nobility to the south. James had no war to fight, and thus lacked what was often a unifying cause and a means of redirecting militaristic energies elsewhere, but by 1603 his nobility were as united behind the crown as they had been at the time of James IV's Flodden campaign in 1513, and for much the same reasons. James treated them as they expected to be treated, and he was leading them towards rich plunder. Once out of Scotland, the possibility of reversing the return to stability grew increasingly remote, although this can be exaggerated, and it remained more dependent on James's good management and good health than on the simple fact that he resided in London. That may have given the king 'a new immunity to established methods of pressure',[9] but the point was that James gave little cause for such methods to be employed. When his heir did, in 1637, and for reasons which were in large part associated with isolation from those pressures, the nobility were still able to seize control of both church and state.

  Without the political stability that was achieved from the late 1590s until the mid-1630s it would not have been possible to tackle the problem that feuding had become. The will to do something about it was not confined to the king and what is often identified as middle-class status groups, that is the lairds, lawyers, ministers, crown officials and burgesses. Much more politically important was the attitude of the nobility who had no interest whatsoever in prolonging violence, and who, like their French counterparts, were fully prepared to work with the king in finding a more acceptable level of peace. That, after all, was their responsibility as lords, magistrates and royal councillors. Unlike the French nobility, they were not inspired by the fear of popular revolt, but the preaching of the protestant ministry was just as anarchic in its implications for them as the Crocquant revolt of 1595 was for the French. In removing the cause of such public denunciations the nobility stemmed the flow of criticism, and they were able to have their revenge in standing by when the king closed the mouths of their presbyterian critics after 1596. In pricking the consciences of the nobility so effectively, the ministers did succeed in their aim of instilling in noblemen a greater awareness of their calling to be godly magistrates, but they also loosened the bonds between magnate and minister which had given them so much freedom in the first place. However, it would be a mistake to put too much emphasis on aristocratic fear of the church's ideology, or at least of where that ideology might lead. As a political elite, stability was in the nobility's interests, and a broad psychological reaction against the kind of conflict which had generated such social and political violence was not an uncommon one. The comparatively restrained conduct of politics which followed the ending of the Bruce–Balliol civil war in the mid-fourteenth century,[10] and which characterised elite politics after 1660, was clearly influenced by the instability and violence which had gone before. In France the excesses of the Wars of Religion, and the recurrent threat of popular revolt, prepared the way for the acceptance of Bourbon absolutism,[11] while on an even grander scale T. K. Rabb has argued that the continental warfare and havoc of the seventeenth century, particularly in the Thirty Years War, was the background against which European states and their elites retreated into the stability and security of the *ancien régime*.[12]

What is certainly clear from the Scottish evidence is that there was no coercion involved in persuading noblemen to stop feuding. Coercion was employed in individual cases, and Lord Maxwell was executed in 1613, but the level of coercion employed was kept within the limits agreed by the political community. The crown by itself did not have the power to exceed those limits. This raises the obvious question of the relationship between the reduction in private violence and the acquisition of a state monopoly of violence, a relationship which is closely bound up with state building.[13] In the context of the Wars of Religion Jean Bodin drew attention to the fairly self-evident point that 'In matters of state it can be taken as an unquestionable rule that he who is master of the armed forces is master of the state'.[14] Force is power, and the more force that is in local and private hands, the less powerful is the state. In fact if the centre lacks the force to impose its will on particularist interests, in other words if it does not have a monopoly of force, it is debatable if 'state' can meaningfully be used to describe it.[15] This process has been described in both Bourbon France and Tudor England where a number of reasons for its occurrence have been identified, but where war and the creation of armed forces directly financed by the state provide the major explanation for this fundamental change.[16] However, in France a state monopoly was not achieved until the personal reign of Louis XIV,[17] and M. E. James has cast some doubt on Lawrence Stone's assertion that a royal monopoly of violence was the Tudor monarchy's 'greatest triumph'.[18] James agreed that 'the kind of society in which the traditional politics of violence were practised' disappeared in Tudor and early

Stuart England, but what did not change was 'the weakness and uncertain operation of the order-keeping forces at the disposal of the state'. Without external sanctions the state had to rely to a considerable extent on 'the effective internalisation of obedience'.[19] In a European context Henry Kamen has made the similar point that 'consent rather than coercion was the basis on which the power of the emergent state came to rest'.[20] This certainly describes the Scottish experience more accurately than a state monopoly of violence which put the crown in a position to coerce the nobility.[21] The distribution of force in Scotland was still largely under the control of the nobility after the 1590s. What was different was their unwillingness to use it, and that is explained in terms of ideology, psychology and the desire for political stability. Four decades of peace was what largely demilitarised the Scottish nobility and their dependants, not royal power, and when the need for force arose again after 1637 there was what could be called a coercive vacuum in the state. The crown had no means of coercion at all, and the military potency of the nobility had declined to a very modest level indeed. Much of the success of the Covenanters was due to the greater speed with which they faced up to this situation, and created a new machinery of enforcement.[22]

This lack of power which was exposed in the crown in the 1630s does not mean that nothing had changed over the previous forty years. The limitation of the legitimate right to employ violence to the crown and to the inferior magistrates acting in their public capacity was largely achieved under James VI. Legitimate violence was monopolised even if the actual means of applying force was not. In itself this did potentially strengthen the power of the state, but the apparent reduction in particularist power without any real increase in state power was a manifestation of what has been called a 'contradiction in early absolutism'.[23] Thus the victims of the state's growing coercive authority were witches, vagrants, broken clans, and others so weak that any resistance was unlikely to test that authority beyond its capacity to enforce. An effective machinery of state coercion was only really created by the Covenanters in the 1640s, and the closest seventeenth-century Scotland came to a state monopoly of violence was that enjoyed by the Cromwellian army in 1651–60. Not until 1746, with the defeat of the Jacobite clans, was a permanent monopoly established, and the eighteenth-century British state which achieved it was very much an instrument of aristocratic power.

The decline of private violence and feuding during the first decade of the seventeenth century was, therefore, only the beginning of a very gradual accumulation of state power which in the first three decades of the century was based almost entirely on noble consent. For the nobility and the predominantly landed classes as a whole this was also the beginning of what Jim Sharpe has called in England a 'retreat into respectability'. Sharpe rightly argues that this was a much longer and more complicated transformation than is often recognised, and that aristocratic violence was still a problem in the eighteenth century, even if it had become less public.[24] That, however, was largely a social or criminal matter, not a political one. In rejecting the use of private violence in politics from the 1590s, the Scottish nobility were conforming to a European pattern of what

Anderson described as a 'slow conversion ... to the necessary form of its own political power, despite and against most of its previous experience and instincts'.[25] That conversion ensured their continuing domination of Scottish society, and, except for a brief hiatus in the middle years of the century, their retention of political power. Until the seventeenth-century nobility are subjected to analysis, one cannot know to what extent their long-term success, particularly after 1660, was based on the widespread acceptance of aristocratic ideals, rather than on more tangible power, but certainly before 1637 there is little evidence that they were in eclipse, in spite of economic difficulties, and of Charles I's efforts to undercut their political power.

How that power was exercised had altered as the feuding society began to crumble. Long years of domestic peace throughout lowland Scotland were almost bound to change habits and loosen ties of dependence.[26] Without the threat of violence the bloodfeud was destined to wither because the society which upheld it was defined in relationships which bound men together in love and fear. Love itself was not enough, and without the collective fear which the violence of feud inspired, the bonds ceased to be as important. Possibly the very instability and violence of much of the sixteenth century had intensified Scottish lordship and kinship at a time when economic and social developments were threatening to undermine them. With the return to peace, time caught up with the feud, and the church hastened the process, demanding allegiance to a quite different kindred and a different Lord. The lords themselves were partly responsible for these changes as they began adjusting to a London-centred court where cash rather than manpower was necessary,[27] and as they sought to cope with the effects of the price rise on their estates by more aggressive management.[28] There was little sentiment among the nobility for the past. Yet just how far the dissolution or metamorphosis of the feuding society had gone by the 1630s is uncertain, and without further research one cannot know how important the mid-century quagmire was in swallowing up what remained. Kinsman and lord were not redundant concepts, but they were not the same as they had been, and both were seeking new roles in a society without the bloodfeud. Of course, the transformation was not an even one throughout Scotland. In the years before the revolution the old marquis of Huntly was still presiding over the feuds of his kinsmen and dependants in the north-east, and in the highlands the feud survived into the eighteenth century. There feud had only been superficially attacked before 1625, its social roots remained largely intact, and peace rested on extremely fragile foundations. The mid-century convulsions resulted in an increase in highland feuding which was largely unchecked by Restoration governments whose attention was concentrated on problems further south. However, even in the highlands the feud was in the long term being divorced from lordship, becoming more of an extension of banditry, and by the later seventeenth century it had declined into an entirely corrupt form of the bloodfeud.[29] That association with the 'barbaric' highlands tainted the reputation of feud, contributing to the stereotype which was already evolving in the late seventeenth century. By then, of course, there was no-one left alive to explain that feud was not just about senseless slaughter. The earl of Mar had died in 1634, Huntly in 1636 and the earl of Argyll in 1638. These were the last of the old lords, men who had exercised powerful lordship as their ancestors had before them. Their sons had to exercise power according to a new set of rules, and in a sense their passing marked the close of the feuding society.

In law, the justice of the feud lasted another decade. The principles of assythment which had been protected by the conservative reforms of the Jacobean period were not abolished until 1649. In 1649 a parliament controlled by the church at the height of its power finally succeeded in equating crime with sin, and in imposing on the state the obligation to punish. In future there would be no compensation, no compromise, and no peace. The heirs of Bruce and Rollock had fulfilled their vision of a merciless state, blindly cutting a bloody swathe through the ranks of sinners. Law had defeated custom, and it was the church militant which had pushed it forward to victory.[30] If the one dominant force to shape the fledgling Scottish state in the seventeenth century was the aristocracy and aristocratic values, the other was undoubtedly the Calvinist reformation.[31] Those two periodically clashed, at other times they ran in harness. In the area of justice the latter triumphed over lordship, imposing on it the role of godly magistrate, but noble control of the franchise courts remained unchallenged until 1747, and the lawyers' acceptance of aristocratic ideals ensured that the law became just as powerful a tool for protecting entrenched rights and privileges as armed force had been. In many ways law became a much more effective instrument of oppression than lordship had been, and with the declining sense of responsibility among noblemen for their tenants and former dependants it had to be.

The justice of the feud cannot be idealised, but while there were good and bad lords just as there were good and bad lawyers, the chances were that the sixteenth-century lord was more accessible than the seventeenth-century lawyer. In its rough violence the feud was often able to provide a form of just desserts, and in assythment it provided a solution that was usually satisfactory to everyone, unlike criminal prosecution or litigation which generally favoured one side and left the other embittered. The justice of law was likely to be more distant, more technical, more of a professional monopoly than a community concern, more expensive, and, as its powers to punish grew, more bloody. That perhaps is to contrast the best of the bloodfeud with the worst of the law, and in choosing the latter, James VI, his nobility, the lawyers, and the church were retreating from a recent experience of feuding at its most anarchic. The stability they sought, and the vision they may each have anticipated, lay in a future without feuds. That in itself was to seek a break with the past which earlier ages could not have comprehended. This was a legacy of the Reformation, for as the king wrote when commenting on the wearing of armour and arms at court, if the mass could be abolished, then no custom was sacrosanct, no matter how ancient its history.[32] Men were learning that their society need not simply be inherited and passed on intact, but could be changed and shaped according to their ideals and aspirations. James himself conveyed this discovery to his privy council when he told them that

> For our pairt . . . we haif found one reule infallible, which is that the mater of feadis is not eternall, bot may be removed and not transmitted to posteritie.[33]

## NOTES

1. There is extensive literature available on this subject, but see, for example, T. Aston (ed.), *Crisis in Europe, 1560–1660*, London, 1965, and G. Parker and L. M. Smith (eds.), *The General Crisis of the Seventeenth Century*, London, 1978. For the most recent contribution to the debate, see P. Clark (ed.), *The European Crisis of the 1590s*, London, 1985.

2. M. Lee, 'Scotland and the 'General Crisis' of the Seventeenth Century', in *S.H.R.*, 63, 1984, pp.136–154. See, too, D. Stevenson, *The Scottish Revolution*, 1637–1644, Newton Abbot, 1973.

3. Hume, *Poems*, p.78.

4. J. H. M. Salmon, *Society in Crisis, France in the Sixteenth Century*, London, 1975, makes particular use of this theme. However, the instability of the Wars of Religion is also given prominence by Harding, *Anatomy of a Power Elite*, and Greengrass, *France in the Age of Henri IV*. See, too, P. J. Coveney (ed.), *France in Crisis, 1620–1675*, London, 1977.

5. Wormald, 'Bloodfeud, Kindred and Government in Early Modern Scotland'; Brown, 'The Exercise of Power', in Brown (ed.), *Scottish Society in the Fifteenth Century*; Grant, *Independence and Nationhood*, pp. 120–143 and 171–199.

6. Harding, *Anatomy of a Power Elite*, p.79, for the views of Bodin and others. Harding himself argues that 'Sixteenth-century society was vertically articulated, and governors owed much of their ability to direct obedience to their sprawling kinship and clientage connections. In the wake of the Reformation and the royal bankruptcy these networks of personal loyalties proved unreliable and uncontrollable. This was a major cause of the civil wars. Military indiscipline and the rise of private violence were also manifestations of the crisis', p.214 and also pp.71–78. See too Greengrass, *France in the Age of Henri IV*, pp.176–177; Kelley, *The Beginnings of Ideology*, p.201.

7. The chronology of this makes depressing reading. There was civil war in 1559–60 in which both French and English forces participated, Huntly's rebellion in 1562, Moray's rebellion in 1565, civil war in 1567 and 1568 when Mary was defeated, further civil war in 1570–73 with English intervention in 1572–73, the Stirling coup which ended the Morton regency in 1578 and narrowly avoided renewal of civil war later in the year, the campaign against the Hamiltons in 1579, Morton's execution and the fall of the Douglases in 1581, coups every year from 1582–85, Maxwell's rebellion in 1584–85, the campaign against Maxwell in 1587 and his rebellion in 1588, the Brig O'Dee rebellion in 1589, Bothwell's rebellion of 1591–94, the campaign against Huntly in 1593, and the rebellion of the catholic earls in 1594–95.

8. The most useful comparison with Scotland is Harding, *Anatomy of a Power Elite*.

9. Mitchison, *Lordship to Patronage*, p.48.

10. Grant, *Independence and Nationhood*, p.199.

11. Salmon, *Society in Crisis*, p.291. In England the Tudor fear of popular revolt also encouraged stability within the social elite, James, *English Politics and the Concept of Honour*, pp.32–43.

12. T. K. Rabb, *The Struggle for Stability in Early Modern Europe*, New York, 1975, pp.116–146. See, too, J. Strayer, *On the Medieval Origins of the Modern State*, Princeton, 1970, pp.90–91, and Powis, *Aristocracy*, pp.58–59, where doubts are raised about the idea that noblemen had anything to gain from uncontrolled private violence.

13. For the theoretical basis of this, see N. Elias, *The Civilising Process, Volume 2, State Formation and Civilisation*, Oxford, 1982. Elias's mechanistic explanations are often crude, and his use of historical evidence can be clumsy, but the broad process he describes

provides a useful frame of reference in which to debate the decline of private violence and the growth of state power.

14. Quoted in H. A. Lloyd, *The State, France, and the Sixteenth Century*, London, 1985, p.157.

15. In using 'state' in the context of seventeenth-century Scotland I am using the term in the imprecise and anachronistic sense. The French usage had a more exact definition, and was a contemporary term, Lloyd, *The State, France and the Sixteenth Century*, pp.146–168. This specific point about state violence is made by Bodin, *Ibid.*, pp.157–158.

16. For France, see, for example, D. Parker, *The Making of French Absolutism*, London, 1983, pp.59–64. On England, see Stone, *The Crisis of the Aristocracy*, pp.96–134, and Williams, *The Tudor Regime*, pp. 109–126 and 235–241. V. G. Kiernan argues that war was 'an organic need' for the evolving states of western Europe, and helped persuade the nobility 'to give up its suicidal feuds', see 'State and Nation in Western Europe', *Past and Present*, 31, 1965, p.31.

17. Greengrass, *France in the Age of Henri IV*, pp.183–184.

18. Stone, *The Crisis of the Aristocracy*, p.97. 'The greatest triumph of the Tudors was the ultimately successful assertion of a royal monopoly of violence both public and private, an achievement which profoundly altered not only the nature of politics, but also the quality of daily life.'

19. James, *English Politics and the Concept of Honour*, p.44. This point about the extremely limited powers of coercion is also made by Wrightson, *English Society, 1580–1680*, pp.130–131.

20. Kamen, *European Society, 1500–1700*, p.302.

21. It is untrue, therefore, to claim that from 1596 'the crown was dominant over the groups which had competed for power in past years'. Donaldson, *James V-VII*, p.212. Clearly the language used to describe crown power at this time needs to be refined.

22. Stevenson, *The Scottish Revolution, 1637–44*, pp.99–101, 127–131 and 137–140.

23. Kamen, *European Society, 1500–1700*, p.303.

24. Sharpe, *Crime in Seventeenth Century England*, pp.95–99.

25. Anderson, *Lineages of the Absolutist State*, p.48.

26. See Stone, *The Crisis of the Aristocracy*, pp.104–105 and 116, on the effects of peace on the Elizabethan nobility in England.

27. The pull of the court had had similar effects in England, Stone, *The Crisis of the Aristocracy*, p.129, and was occurring in contemporary France, Harding, *Anatomy of a Power Elite*, pp.171–179.

28. W. Makey, 'Presbyterian and Canterburian in the Scottish Revolution', in N. Macdougall (ed.), *Church, Politics and Society, Scotland 1408–1929*, Edinburgh, 1983, pp.156–159.

29. D. Stevenson, *Alasdair MacColla and the Highland Problem in the 17th Century*, Edinburgh, 1980. There are some comparisons between the highlands and Catalonia where feud was also channelled into banditry, Kiernan, *State and Society, 1560–1660*, p.41.

30. Wormald,, 'Bloodfeud, Kindred and Governmemnt in Early Modern Scotland', pp.92–94, where the 1649 act is discussed.

31. This was especially true in the area of law, see Williamson, *Scottish National Consciousness in the Age of James VI*, p. 49, where he comments that 'The institution of effective law was a central and integral feature of the process of reformation'.

32. See above, p. 205.

33. *R.P.C.*, xii, p.262.

# Appendix 1.
## Feud Statistics

The sample of 365 feuds on which the following analysis is based is certainly not exhaustive. It represents no more than a minimum number of feuds, particularly in regions like the highlands and borders, and among lower status groups. As one can see, there is a large percentage of unknown factors, and the subjective nature of some of the evidence must also be borne in mind. The results, therefore, are less than accurate, but on the whole they are consistent with other historical evidence, and they do provide useful indicators even if precise percentages are doubtful. (See Graph on page 276).

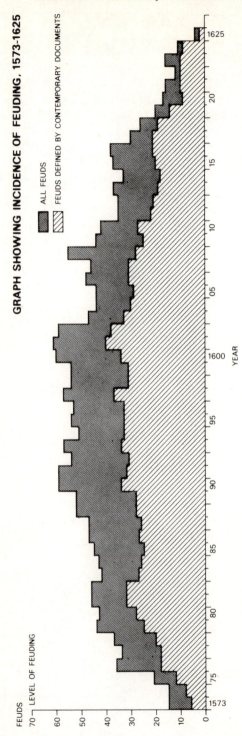

GRAPH SHOWING INCIDENCE OF FEUDING, 1573-1625

*Table 1: The Length of Feuds*

Feuds Identified By:

| Minimum Length in Years | Contemporary | Conduct Process | Conduct | Process | All |
|---|---|---|---|---|---|
| 1 or less | 46 33.6% | 44 50.6% | 52 65.8% | 55 88.7% | 197 54.0% |
| 2–5 | 34 24.8% | 23 26.4% | 13 16.5% | 7 11.3% | 77 21.1% |
| 6–9 | 16 11.7% | 2 2.3% | 2 2.5% | 0 0% | 20 5.5% |
| 10–19 | 21 15.3% | 11 12.7% | 6 7.6% | 0 0% | 38 10.4% |
| 20+ | 20 14.6% | 6 6.9% | 4 5.1% | 0 0% | 30 8.2% |
| Unknown | 0 0% | 1 1.1% | 2 2.5% | 0 0% | 3 0.8% |

(The figures here discriminate in favour of shorter feuds.)

*Table 2: The Distribution of Feuding*

Feuds Identified By:

| | Contemporary | Conduct Process | Conduct | Process | All |
|---|---|---|---|---|---|
| Highlands | 16 12.8% | 15 20.8% | 13 23.2% | 4 8.5% | 48 16% |
| Borders | 31 24.8% | 21 29.2% | 10 17.9% | 7 14.9% | 69 23% |
| Lowlands S. of Tay | 46 36.8% | 25 34.7% | 21 37.5% | 28 59.6% | 120 40% |
| Lowlands N. of Tay | 32 25.6% | 11 15.3% | 12 21.4% | 8 17.0% | 63 21% |
| Unlocated or Personal | 12 | 15 | 23 | 15 | |

The percentage figures given are calculated only from those feuds which have been located and were not personal affairs.)

*Table 3: The Significance of Feuding*

Feuds Identified By:

| | Contemporary | Conduct Process | Conduct | Process | All |
|---|---|---|---|---|---|
| Personal | 8 5.9% | 16 18.4% | 22 27.8% | 13 21.0% | 59 16.1% |
| Local | 124 90.5% | 70 80.5% | 56 70.9% | 49 79.0% | 299 82.0% |
| Regional | 5 3.6% | 1 1.1% | 1 1.3% | 0 0% | 7 1.9% |
| (Also at Court) | (14 10.2%) | (9 10.3%) | (3 3.8%) | (0 0%) | (26 7.1%) |
| (Also in burghs) | (24 17.5%) | (6 6.9%) | (6 7.6%) | (1 0%) | (37 10.1%) |

(Those at court only include feuds of major importance to court politics, not those which simply sought some form of court patronage.)

Table 4: Status of Parties at Feud

Feuds Identified By:

| | Contemporary | Conduct Process | Conduct | Process | All |
|---|---|---|---|---|---|
| Peer v Peer | 21 15.3% | 17 19.5% | 8 10.1% | 2 3.2% | 48 13.2% |
| Peer v Baron/Laird | 23 16.8% | 24 27.6% | 17 21.5% | 10 16.2% | 74 20.3% |
| Peer v Burgess | 0 0% | 1 1.5% | 1 1.3% | 0 0% | 2 0.5% |
| Baron/Laird v Baron/Laird | 79 57.7% | 37 42.5% | 36 45.6% | 33 53.2% | 185 50.7% |
| Baron/Laird v Burgess | 2 1.4% | 2 2.3% | 3 3.8% | 1 1.6% | 8 2.2% |
| Burgess v Burgess | 3 2.2% | 1 1.2% | 1 1.3% | 1 1.6% | 6 1.6% |
| Others | 9 6.6% | 5 5.7% | 13 16.4% | 15 24.2% | 42 11.5% |
| (Infra-Kindred) | (23 16.8%) | (10 11.5%) | (14 17.7%) | (4 6.5%) | (51 14.0%) |

Table 5: Violence and Feuding

Feuds Identified By:

| | Contemporary | Conduct Process | Conduct | Process | All |
|---|---|---|---|---|---|
| Non-violent | 5 3.7% | 15 17.3% | 5 6.3% | 6 9.7% | 31 8.5% |
| Challenge sent | 0 0% | 6 6.9% | 15 19.0% | 0 0% | 21 5.8% |
| Property only | 4 2.9% | 7 8.0% | 5 6.3% | 0 05% | 16 4.4% |
| Bodily assault | 21 15.3% | 20 23.0% | 16 20.3% | 0 0% | 57 15.6% |
| Selective killing | 29 21.2% | 14 16.0% | 17 21.5% | 0 0% | 60 16.4% |
| Indiscriminate killing | 35 25.5% | 16 18.4% | 15 19.0% | 2 3.2% | 68 18.6% |
| (Property also) | (28 32.9%) | (15 30.1%) | (14 29.2%) | (2 100.0%) | (59 32.0%) |
| Unknown | 43 31.4% | 9 10.3% | 6 7.6% | 54 87.1% | 112 30.7% |

(The figures here show the maximum level of violence only, i.e. a case of selective killing may also have included the sending of a challenge and an assault, but these are not recorded. The percentage shown alongside property also is a percentage of those cases where a form of inter-personal violence took place.)

*Table 6: Feud Settlements*

Feuds Identified By:

| | Contemporary | Conduct Process | Conduct | Process | All |
|---|---|---|---|---|---|
| Victory | 4 2.9% | 4 4.6% | 13 16.5% | 0 0% | 21 5.8% |
| Private | 11 8.0% | 19 21.6% | 3 3.8% | 21 33.9% | 54 14.8% |
| Crown Initiative but Private | 38 27.7% | 26 30.0% | 2 2.5% | 7 11.3% | 73 20.0% |
| Crown Enforced | 12 8.8% | 3 3.4% | 9 11.4% | 2 3.2% | 26 7.1% |
| Unknown and Unsettled | 72 52.6% | 35 40.2% | 52 65.8% | 32 51.6% | 191 52.3% |

(As one would expect, the majority of entirely private settlements date from before the 1590s.)

*Table 7: Origins of Feuds*

Feuds Identified By:

| | Contemporary | Conduct Process | Conduct | Process | All |
|---|---|---|---|---|---|
| Blood | 18 13.1% | 11 12.6% | 5 6.3% | 20 32.2% | 54 14.9% |
| Honour | 4 2.9% | 7 8.0% | 5 6.3% | 0 0% | 16 4.4% |
| Politics | 4 2.9% | 2 2.3% | 3 3.8% | 0 0% | 9 2.4% |
| Jurisdictions | 15 11.0% | 9 10.4% | 8 10.1% | 0 0% | 32 8.8% |
| Lands/Teinds | 25 18.3% | 13 15.0% | 14 17.7% | 1 1.6% | 53 14.5% |
| Other Natural Resources | 7 5.1% | 7 8.0% | 4 5.1% | 4 6.5% | 22 6.0% |
| Unknown | 64 46.7% | 38 43.7% | 40 50.7% | 37 59.7% | 179 49.0% |

# Appendix 2. Genealogies

*Select Genealogy of the House of Glencairn*

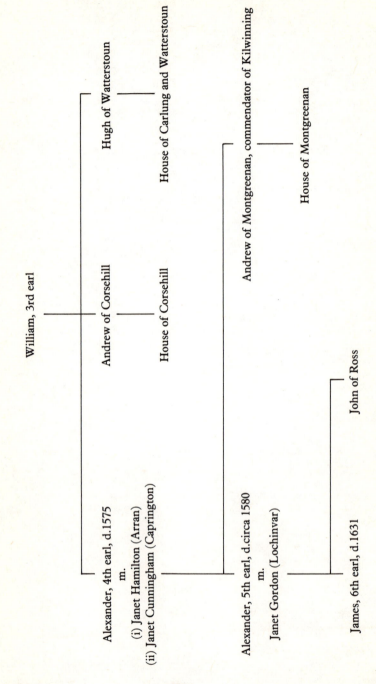

William, 3rd earl

Alexander, 4th earl, d.1575
m.
(i) Janet Hamilton (Arran)
(ii) Janet Cunningham (Caprington)

Andrew of Corsehill

House of Corsehill

Hugh of Watterstoun

House of Carlung and Watterstoun

Alexander, 5th earl, d.circa 1580
m.
Janet Gordon (Lochinvar)

Andrew of Montgreenan, commendator of Kilwinning

House of Montgreenan

John of Ross

James, 6th earl, d.1631

*Select Genealogy of the House of Eglinton*

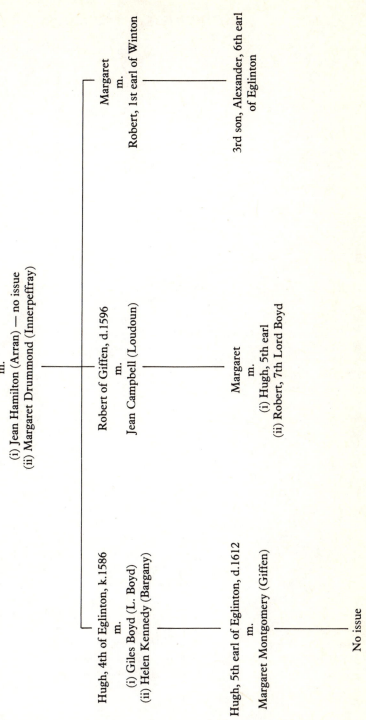

*Select Genealogy of the Houses of Moray and Bothwell*

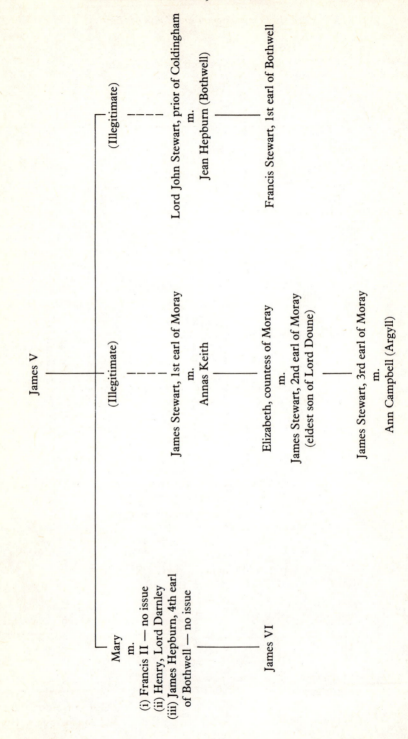

James V

(Illegitimate)

James Stewart, 1st earl of Moray
m.
Annas Keith

Elizabeth, countess of Moray
m.
James Stewart, 2nd earl of Moray
(eldest son of Lord Doune)

James Stewart, 3rd earl of Moray
m.
Ann Campbell (Argyll)

(Illegitimate)

Lord John Stewart, prior of Coldingham
m.
Jean Hepburn (Bothwell)

Francis Stewart, 1st earl of Bothwell

Mary
m.
(i) Francis II — no issue
(ii) Henry, Lord Darnley
(iii) James Hepburn, 4th earl
of Bothwell — no issue

James VI

*Select Genealogy of the House of Huntly*

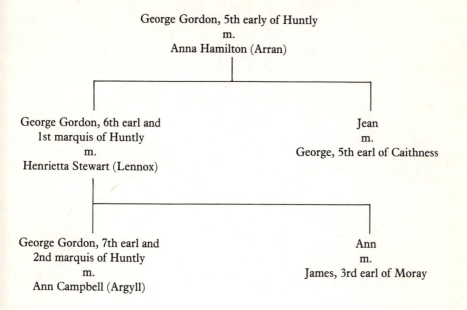

George Gordon, 5th early of Huntly
m.
Anna Hamilton (Arran)

George Gordon, 6th earl and
1st marquis of Huntly
m.
Henrietta Stewart (Lennox)

Jean
m.
George, 5th earl of Caithness

George Gordon, 7th earl and
2nd marquis of Huntly
m.
Ann Campbell (Argyll)

Ann
m.
James, 3rd earl of Moray

*Select Genealogy of the House of Argyll*

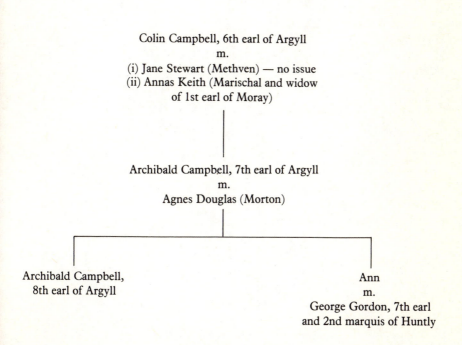

Colin Campbell, 6th earl of Argyll
m.
(i) Jane Stewart (Methven) — no issue
(ii) Annas Keith (Marischal and widow
of 1st earl of Moray)

Archibald Campbell, 7th earl of Argyll
m.
Agnes Douglas (Morton)

Archibald Campbell,
8th earl of Argyll

Ann
m.
George Gordon, 7th earl
and 2nd marquis of Huntly

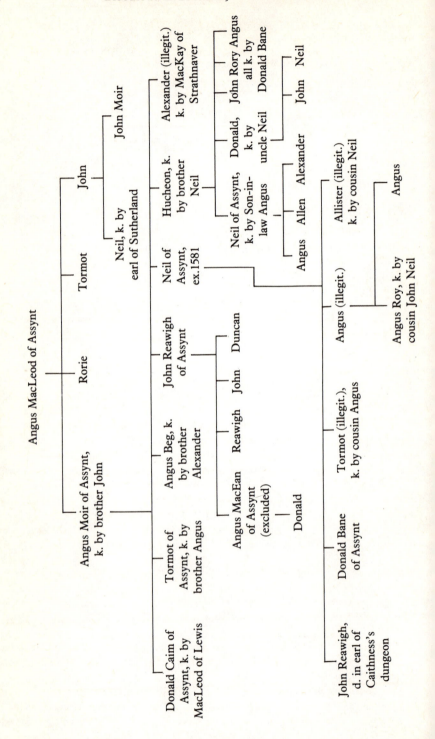

*Genealogy of the MacLeods of Assynt*

# Bibliography

*MANUSCRIPT SOURCES*
*Scottish Record Office*
Airlie Muniments, G.D. 16.
Bruce of Earlshall M.S., G.D. 247.
Breadalbane Muniments, G.D. 112.
Buccleuch Muniments, G.D. 224.
Craigend Writs, G.D. 148.
Eglinton Muniments, G.D. 3.
Elibank Papers, G.D. 32.
Forbes Collection, G.D. 52.
Fraser-Mackintosh Collection, G.D. 128.
Glencairn Muniments, G.D. 39.
Gordon Castle Muniments, G.D. 44.
Livingston of Dunipace M.S., G.D. 1.
Mackintosh Muniments, G.D. 176.
Mar and Kellie Muniments, G.D. 124.

Register of Acts and Decreets, R.D. 1.

*National Register of Archives*
Atholl Manuscripts, N.R.A. 224.
Inventory of Scottish Muniments at Haigh, N.R.A. 237.
Lauderdale Muniments, N.R.A. 832.
Moray Muniments, N.R.A. 217.


*PRINTED PRIMARY WORKS*
*Aberdeen Council Letters, Vol. 1, 1552-1639*, (ed.) L. B. Taylor, Oxford, 1942.
*Accounts of the Lord High Treasurer of Scotland*, (eds.) T. Dickson and Sir J. Balfour Paul, Edinburgh, 1877-1916.
*The Acts of the Parliaments of Scotland*, (eds.) T. Thomson and C. Innes, Edinburgh, 1814-75.
*Analecta Scotica*, (ed.) J. Maidment, Edinburgh, 1834-37.
Balfour, Sir J., *The Historical Works of Sir James Balfour*, (ed.) J. Haig, Edinburgh, 1824-25.
Balfour, Sir J., *Practicks*, (ed.) P. McNeill, Stair Society, 21-2, Edinburgh, 1962-63.
*The Bannatyne Manuscript*, Hunterian Club, 1846.
*The Bannatyne Miscellany*, Bannatyne Club, 1827-55.
Birrel, R., 'The Diary of Robert Birrel', in *Fragments of Scottish History*, (ed.) J. G. Dalyell, Edinburgh, 1798.
*The Booke of the Universall Kirk of Scotland: Acts and Proceedings of the General Assemblies of the Kirk of Scotland from the Year MDLX*, (ed.) J. Bain, Edinburgh, 1894-96.
Calderwood, D., *The History of the Kirk of Scotland*, Edinburgh, 1842.
*Calendar of Letters and Papers relating to the Affairs of the Borders of England and Scotland*, (ed.) J. Bain, Edinburgh, 1894-96.

*Calendar of Letters and State Papers, Spanish, Elizabeth,* (ed.) M. A. S. Hume, London, 1892–99.

*Calendar of the State Papers relating to Scotland and Mary, Queen of Scots, 1547–1603,* (ed.) J. Bain and others, Edinburgh, 1898–1969.

Calvin, J., *Institutes of the Christian Religion,* (tr.) H. Beveridge, Edinburgh, 1863.

Calvin, J., *Commentaries on the Book of Genesis,* (tr.) J. King, Edinburgh, 1847.

Calvin, J., *Commentaries on the Epistle of Paul the Apostle to the Romans,* (tr.) J. Owen, Edinburgh, 1849.

Chambers, R., *Domestic Annals of Scotland,* Edinburgh, 1859.

*Correspondence of Sir Patrick Waus,* (ed.) R. Vans Agnew, Edinburgh, 1887.

Craig, Sir T., *Jus Feudale,* (tr.) J. A. Clyde, Edinburgh, 1894.

*Criminal Trials in Scotland from 1488 to 1624,* (ed.) R. Pitcairn, Edinburgh, 1833.

*Extracts from the Records of the Burgh of Edinburgh, 1573–89,* Scottish Burgh Records Society, Edinburgh, 1882.

*Estimate of the Scottish Nobility During the Minority of James the Sixth,* (ed.) C. Rodgers, London, 1873.

Ferme, C., *Logical Analysis of the Epistle of Paul to the Romans,* Wodrow Society, Edinburgh, 1850.

Fraser, W., *The Annandale Family Book of the Johnstones,* Edinburgh, 1894.

Fraser, W., *The Book of Carlaverock,* Edinburgh, 1873.

Fraser, W., *The Chiefs of Colquhoun and their Country,* Edinburgh, 1869.

Fraser, W., *The Chiefs of Grant,* Edinburgh, 1883.

Fraser, W., *The Douglas Book: Memoirs of the House of Douglas and Angus,* Edinburgh, 1885.

Fraser, W., *The Elphinstone Family Book,* Edinburgh, 1897.

Fraser, W., *Memoirs of the Maxwells of Pollok,* Edinburgh, 1863.

Fraser, W., *Memorials of the Montgomeries Earls of Eglinton,* Edinburgh, 1859.

Gordon, Sir R., *A Genealogical History of the Earldom of Sutherland,* Edinburgh, 1813.

*Highland Papers,* S.H.S., Second Series, 5, Edinburgh, 1914.

*Historical Account of the Principal Families of the Name of Kennedy,* R. Pitcairn, Edinburgh, 1830.

*The Historie and Life of King James the Sext,* (ed.) T. Thomson, Bannatyne Club, Edinburgh, 1825.

Hope, Sir T., *Major Practicks,* (ed.) J. A. Clyde, Stair Society, 3–4, Edinburgh, 1937–38.

Hume, D., *A General History of Scotland from the Year 767 to the Death of King James,* London, 1657.

Knox, J., *The Works of John Knox,* (ed.) D. Laing, Edinburgh, 1846–64.

Leslie, J., *The Historie of Scotland,* (ed.) E. G. Cody, Scottish Text Society, Edinburgh, 1884–85.

*The Maitland Quarto Manuscript,* (ed.) W. A. Craigie, Scottish Text Society, New Series, 9, Edinburgh, 1920.

Melville, J., *The Diary of Mr James Melvill, 1556–1561,* Bannatyne Club, 34, Edinburgh, 1829.

Melville, Sir J., *Memoirs Of His Own Life, 1549–93,* Bannatyne and Maitland Clubs, 1827.

*Miscellany of the Maitland Club,* Maitland Club, Edinburgh, 1840.

*Miscellany of the Spalding Club,* Spalding Club, Aberdeen, 1841–52.

Moysie, D., *Memoirs of the Affairs of Scotland from 1577 to 1603,* Bannatyne and Maitland Clubs, Edinburgh, 1830.

Napier, J., *A Plaine Discovery of the Whole Revelation,* Edinburgh, 1593.

*The Poems of Alexander Hume*, (ed.) A. Lawson, Scottish Text Society, 48, Edinburgh, 1902.

*The Poems of Alexander Montgomerie*, (ed.) J. Cranstoun, Scottish Text Society, 9–11, Edinburgh, 1855–57.

*Poems of Sir John Stewart of Baldynneis*, (ed.) T. Crockett, Scottish Text Society, New Series, 5, Edinburgh, 1913.

*The Political Works of James I*, (ed.) C. H. McIlwain, New York, 1965.

*Regiam Majestatem*, Stair Society, 11, Edinburgh, 1947.

*The Register of the Privy Council of Scotland*, (ed.) J. H. Burton and others, Edinburgh, 1877–98.

*Registrum Magni Sigilli Regum Scotorum*, (ed.) J. M. Thomson, Edinburgh, 1882–1914.

*Registrum Secreti Sigilli Regum Scotorum*, (ed.) M. Livingston and others, Edinburgh, 1908– .

*Report of the Royal Commission on Historical Manuscripts*, London, 1870– .

*Report of the Historical Manuscripts Commission, Various Collections*, Hereford, 1901–13.

*Report of the Historical Manuscripts Commission on the Manuscripts of the Earl of Mar and Kellie*, London, 1904.

*Report of the Historical Manuscripts Commission on the Laing Manuscripts preserved in Edinburgh University*, London, 1914, 1925.

Rollock, R., *Select Works*, (ed.) W. Gunn, Wodrow Society, Edinburgh, 1844–49.

*Satirical Poems Of The Time Of The Reformation*, (ed.) J. Cranstoun, Scottish Text Society, 20, 24, 28, 30, Edinburgh, 1889–93.

Scot, W., *An Apologetical Narration of the State and Government of the Kirk of Scotland Since the Reformation*, Wodrow Society, Edinburgh, 1846.

*Selected Justiciary Cases, 1624–50*, (eds.) G. A. Gillon and J. I. Smith, Stair Society, 16, 27, Edinburgh, 1953, 1974.

*Sermons of the Rev. Robert Bruce*, (ed.) W. Cunningham, Wodrow Society, Edinburgh, 1841.

Spottiswoode, J., *History of the Church of Scotland*, Edinburgh, 1820.

*The Spottiswoode Miscellany*, Spottiswoode Society, Edinburgh, 1844–45.

*State Papers and Miscellaneous Correspondence of Thomas, Earl of Melrose*, Abbotsford Club, Edinburgh, 1837.

*Stewart Royal Proclamations, James I*, (eds.) J. F. Larkin and P. L. Hughes, Oxford, 1973.

*Stirling Presbytery Records, 1581–87*, (ed.) J. Kirk, Edinburgh, 1981.

*Warrender Papers*, S.H.S., Third Series, 19, Edinburgh, 1932.

*The Works of William Fowler*, (eds.) H. W. Meikle, J. Craigie and J. Purves, Scottish Text Society, New Series, 6, Third Series, 7, 13, Edinburgh, 1914, 1936, 1939.


SECONDARY WORKS

Anderson, P., *Lineages of the Absolutist State*, London, 1979.

Anon., *Beowulf*, Penguin, 1980.

Anon., *Eigil's Saga*, Penguin, 1980.

Anon., *Njal's Saga*, Penguin, 1980.

Anon., *The Nibelungenlied*, Penguin, 1979.

Ardrey, R., *The Territorial Imperative*, London, 1970.

Ashton, R. (ed.), *James I By His Contemporaries*, London, 1969.

Aston, T. (ed.), *Crisis in Europe, 1560–1660*, London, 1965.

Baker, D., *Sanctity and Secularity: The Church and the World*, The Ecclesiastical History Society, 10, Oxford, 1973.

Balfour Paul, Sir J. (ed.), *The Scots Peerage*, Edinburgh, 1904–14.

Bindoff, S. T., Hurtsfield, J. and Williamson, C. H. (eds.), *Elizabethan Government and Society*, London, 1961.

Black-Michaud, J., *Cohesive Force: Feud in the Mediterranean and the Middle East*, Oxford, 1975.

Bloch, M., *Feudal Society*, London, 1978.

Bohannen, P. (ed.), *Law and Warfare*, New York, 1967.

Bossy, J., *Disputes and Settlements*, Cambridge, 1983.

Braudel, F., *The Mediterranean and the Mediterranean World in the Age of Philip II*, London, 1973.

Brown, J. M. (ed.), *Scottish Society in the Fifteenth Century*, London, 1977.

Brunton, G. and Haig, D., *An Historical Account of the Senators of the College of Justice from its Institution in MDXXXII*, Edinburgh, 1832.

Bryson, F. R., *The Point of Honour in Sixteenth Century Italy*, New York, 1935.

Bryson, F. R., *The Sixteenth Century Italian Duel: A Study in Renaissance Social History*, Chicago, 1938.

Caldwell, D. (ed.), *Scottish Weapons and Fortifications, 1100–1800*, Edinburgh, 1981.

Campbell, J. K., *Honour, Family and Patronage: A Study of Institutions and Moral Values in a Greek Mountain Community*, Oxford, 1979.

Cannon, J., *Aristocratic Century: The peerage of eighteenth century England*, Cambridge, 1984.

Caudill, B. D., *Pioneers of Eastern Kentucky, their Feuds and Settlements*, Cincinnati, 1969.

Clark, P., *The European Crisis of the 1590s*, London, 1985.

Cockburn, J. (ed.), *Crime in England, 1550–1800*, London, 1977.

Cooper, J. (ed.), *The New Cambridge Modern History, Vol iii, The Decline of Spain and the Thirty Years War*, Cambridge, 1971.

Coveney, P. J. (ed.), *France in Crisis, 1620–75*, London, 1977.

Cowan, I. B. and Shaw, D. (eds.), *Renaissance and Reformation in Scotland*, Edinburgh, 1983.

Davies, N., *God's Playground, A History of Poland*, Oxford, 1981.

Dewald, J., *The Formation of a Provincial Nobility, The Magistrates of the Parlement of Rouen, 1499–1610*, Princeton, 1980.

*Dictionary of National Biography*, (ed.) L. Stephen and others, London, 1855–1912.

Donaldson, G., *Scotland, James V–VII*, Edinburgh, 1971.

Donaldson, G., *All the Queen's Men, Power and Politics in Mary Stewart's Scotland*, London, 1983.

Duby, G., *The Chivalrous Society*, London, 1977.

Elias, N., *The Civilising Process, Volume 2, State Formation and Civilisation*, Oxford, 1982.

Elliot, J. H., *Europe Divided, 1559–1598*, London, 1977.

Endleman, J., *Violence in the Streets*, London, 1969.

Evans-Pritchard, E. E., *Anthropology and History*, Manchester, 1971.

Evans-Pritchard, E. E., *The Nuer*, Oxford, 1979.

Eyre-Todd, J. (ed.), *Scottish Poetry in the Sixteenth Century*, Glasgow, 1982.

Flandrin, S. L., *Families in Former Times: Kinship, Household and Sexuality*, Cambridge, 1979.

Forster, R. and Ranum, O., *Family and Society*, Baltimore, 1976.

Fraser, G. M., *The Steel Bonnets*, London, 1971.

Gatrell, V. A. C., Lenman, B. and Parker, G. (eds.), *Crime and the Law: the social history of crime in western Europe from 1500*, London, 1980.

Gluckman, M., *Custom and Conflict in Africa*, Oxford, 1982.

Goody, J., Thirsk, J. and Thomson, E. P., *Family and Inheritance in Western Europe, 1220-1800*, Cambridge, 1976.

Goody, J., *The development of the family and marriage in western Europe*, Cambridge, 1983.

Grant, A., *Independence and Nationhood, Scotland 1306-1469*, London, 1984.

Greengrass, M., *France in the Age of Henri IV, The Struggle for Stability*, New York, 1984.

Gregory, D., *History of the Western Highlands and Isles*, Edinburgh, 1975.

Haigh, C., *Reformation and Resistance in Tudor Lancashire*, Cambridge, 1975.

Hale, J. R., *Renaissance Venice*, London, 1972.

*Handlist Of Records For The Study of Crime In Early Modern Scotland (to 1747)*, compiled by Rayner, P., Lenman, B. and Parker, G., List and Index Society, 16, 1982.

Harding, J. H., *Anatomy of a Power Elite: the Provincial Governors of Early Modern France*, Yale, 1978.

Hardy, M. J. L., *Blood Feuds and the Payment of Blood Money in the Middle East*, Leiden, 1963.

Hasluck, M., *The Unwritten Law in Albania*, Cambridge, 1954.

Hewitt, G., *Scotland Under Morton*, Edinburgh, 1982.

Hobsbawm, E. J., *Bandits*, London, 1969.

Houlbrooke, R. A., *The English Family, 1450-1700*, London, 1984.

Hurstfield, J., *Freedom, Corruption and Government in Elizabethan England*, London, 1973.

Ianni, F. A. J. and Reussi-Ianni, E., *A Family Business: Kinship and Social Control in Organised Crime*, New York, 1972.

Inciardi, J. A., Block, A. A. and Hallowell, L. A., *A Historical Approach to crime*, Beverly Hills, 1977.

*Introduction to Scottish Legal History*, Stair Society, 20, Edinburgh, 1957.

Ives, E. W., *Faction in Tudor England*, Historical Association, 1979.

James, M. E., *Change and Continuity in the Tudor North: the Rise of Thomas, first Lord Wharton*, York, 1965.

James, M. E., *A Tudor Magnate and the Tudor State*, University of York, Borthwick Papers, 30, 1966.

James, M. E., *Family, Lineage and Society*, Oxford, 1974.

James, M. E., *English Politics and the Concept of Honour, 1485-1642*, Past and Present Supplement, 3, 1978.

Kaiser, D. H., *The Growth of Law in Medieval Russia*, Princeton, 1980.

Kamen, H., *European Society 1500-1700*, London, 1984.

Kamen, H., *Spain 1469-1714: A Society in Conflict*, London, 1983.

Kelley, D. R., *The Beginnings of Ideology, Consciousness and Society in the French Reformation*, Cambridge, 1981.

Kieffer, T. M., *The Tausug: Violence and Law in a Philippine Moslem Society*, Holt, Rinehart and Winston, 1972.

Kiernan, V. G., *State and Society in Europe, 1550-1650*, Oxford, 1980.

Koenigsberger, H. G. and Mosse, G. L., *Europe in the Sixteenth Century*, London, 1979.

Laslett, P. (ed.), *Household and Family in Past Times*, Cambridge, 1972.

Lea, H. C., *The Duel and the Oath*, Philadelphia, 1974.

Leach, E., *Custom, Law and Terrorist Violence*, Edinburgh, 1977.

Lee, M., *John Maitland of Thirlestane and the Foundation of Stewart Despotism in Scotland*, Princeton, 1959.

Lee, M., *Government by Pen, Scotland under James VI and I*, Illinois University Press, 1980.

Lewis, I. M. (ed.), *History and Anthropology*, London, 1968.

Lloyd, H. A., *The State, France, and the Sixteenth Century*, London, 1983.

Lockyer, R., *Buckingham*, New York, 1980.

Lynch, J., *Spain Under the Hapsburgs*, Oxford, 1981.

Lynch, M., *The Early Modern Town in Scotland*, forthcoming.

Macdougall, N. (ed.), *Church, Politics and Society, Scotland 1408–1929*, Edinburgh, 1983.

MacDowell, W., *History of the Burgh of Dumfries with notices of Nithsdale, Annandale and the Western Border*, Edinburgh, 1872.

MacFarlane, A., *The Origins of English Individualism*, Oxford, 1978.

MacFarlane, A., *The Justice and the Mare's Ale: Law and Disorder in Seventeenth Century England*, Oxford, 1981.

MacFarlane, K. B., *The Nobility of Later Medieval England*, Oxford, 1973.

Mair, L., *Primitive Government*, London, 1970.

Malament, B. C., *After the Reformation, Essays in Honour of J. H. Hexter*, Manchester, 1980.

Malinowski, B., *Crime and Custom in Savage Society*, London, 1978.

Marshall, R., *Virgins and Viragos, A History of Women in Scotland From 1080–1980*, London, 1983.

Martines, L. (ed.), *Violence and Civil Disorder in Italian Cities 1200–1500*, London, 1972.

Mason, R. (ed.), *Scotland and England*, forthcoming.

Menzies, G. (ed.), *The Scottish Nation*, B.B.C., 1972.

Mitchison, R., *Lordship to Patronage, Scotland 1603–1745*, London, 1983.

Murray, J. A. H. (ed.), *A New English Dictionary*, London, 1901.

Neilson, J., *Trial By Combat*, Glasgow, 1980.

Nicholls, K., *Gaelic and Gaelicised Ireland in the Middle Ages*, Dublin, 1972.

Parker, G. and Smith, L. M. (eds.), *The General Crisis of the Seventeenth Century*, London, 1978.

Parker, G., *Spain and the Netherlands*, Glasgow, 1979.

Paterson, W., *History of the County of Ayr*, Paisley, 1947–52.

Paterson, W., *From Ayrshire's Story*, Midlothian, 1977.

Peck, L. L., *Northampton, Patronage and Policy at the Court of James I*, London, 1982.

Pennington, D. H., *Seventeenth Century Europe*, Singapore, 1980.

Philpotts, B. S., *Kindred and Clan in the Middle Ages and After*, New York, 1974.

Powis, J., *Aristocracy*, Oxford, 1984.

Preston, H. G., *Poine: A Study in Ancient Greek Blood-Vengeance*, London,. 1923.

Prodi, P., *Il Cardinale Gabreli Poleotti*, Rome, 1959, 1967.

Rabb, T. K., *The Struggle for Stability in Early Modern Europe*, New York, 1975.

Renwick, R., *The Burgh of Peebles*, Peebles, 1911.

Robertson, G., *A Genealogical Account of the Principal Families in Ayrshire*, Irvine, 1825.

Sabean, D. W., *Power In The Blood, Popular culture and village discourse in early modern Germany*, Cambridge, 1984.

Salmon, J. M. H., *Society in Crisis, France in the Sixteenth Century*, London, 1975.

Samaha, J., *Law and Order in Historical Perspective: The Case of Elizabethan Essex*, London, 1974.

Sanderson, M. H. B., *Scottish Rural Society in the Sixteenth Century*, Edinburgh, 1982.

Scott, T. (ed.), *The Penguin Book of Scottish Verse*, Penguin, 1970.

Sellar, D. (ed.), *Stair Society Miscellany*, ii, Stair Society, 35, Edinburgh, 1984.

Sharpe, J. A., *Crime in Seventeenth Century England, A County Study*, Cambridge, 1983.

Sharpe, K. (ed.), *Faction and Parliament*, Oxford, 1978.

Smith, A. G. R., *The Emergence of a Nation State, The Commonwealth of England, 1529–1660*, London, 1984.

Smith, A. G. R. (ed.), *The Reign of James VI and I*, London, 1973.

Smith, R. B., *Land and Politics in the Reign of Henry VIII*, Oxford, 1970.

Smout, T. C., *A History of the Scottish People, 1560–1830*, London, 1980.

Spradley, J. P. and McCurdy, D. W., *Conformity and Conflict*, Boston, 1980.

Stevenson, D., *The Scottish Revolution, 1637–44*, Newton Abbot, 1975.

Stevenson, D., *Alasdair MacColla and the Highland Problem in the Seventeenth Century*, Edinburgh, 1980.

Stewart, D., *The First Bourbon*, London, 1970.

*Stirling Castle*, H.M.S.O., 1948.

Stone, L., *The Crisis of the Aristocracy, 1558–1641*, Oxford, 1977.

Stone, L., *The Family, Sex and Marriage in England, 1500–1800*, Pelican, 1979.

Stone, L. and Stone, J. C. F., *An Open Elite? England 1540–1840*, Oxford, 1984.

Strayer, J., *On the Medieval Origins of the Modern State*, Princeton, 1970.

Syme, R., *The Roman Revolution*, Oxford, 1974.

Tweedie, W. K. (ed.), *Select Biographies*, Wodrow Society, Edinburgh, 1845.

von Greyerz, K. (ed.), *Religion and Society in Early Modern Europe 1500–1800*, London, 1984.

Wallace-Hadrill, J. M., *The Long-Haired Kings and other studies in Frankish History*, Oxford, 1971.

Watts, S. J., *From Border to Middle Shire: Northumberland, 1586–1625*, Leicester, 1975.

Wayne-Baker, J., *Heinrich Bullinger and the Covenant: the other Reformed Tradition*, Ohio University Press, 1980.

Wernham, R. B., *The New Cambridge Modern History, Vol iii, The Counter Reformation and the Price Revolution, 1559–1610*, Cambridge, 1971.

Whyte, I., *Agriculture and Society in Seventeenth Century Scotland*, Edinburgh, 1979.

Williams, P., *The Tudor Regime*, Oxford, 1979.

Williamson, A. H., *Scottish National Consciousness in the Age of James VI*, Edinburgh, 1979.

Willock, I. D., *The Origins and Development of the Jury in Scotland*, Stair Society, 23, Edinburgh, 1966.

Willson, D. H., *King James VI and I*, London, 1956.

Wormald, J. M., *Court, Kirk and Community*, London, 1981.

Wormald, J. M., *Lords and Men in Scotland: Bonds of Manrent, 1442–1603*, Edinburgh, 1985.

Wrightson, K., *English Society, 1580–1680*, London, 1982.

## ARTICLES AND THESES

Adams, S., 'Faction, Clientage and Party, English Politics, 1550–1608', in *History Today*, Dec., 1982.

Bossy, J., 'The Counter Reformation and the People of Catholic Europe', in *Past and Present*, 47, 1970.

Bossy, J., 'Holiness and Society', in *Past and Present*, 75, 1977.

Broude, R., 'Revenge and Revenge Tragedy in Renaissance England', in *Renaissance Quarterly*, 28, 1975.

Brown, J. M., Bonds of Manrent in Scotland before 1603, University of Glasgow Ph.D., 1974.

Brown, K. M., The Extent and Nature of Feuding in Scotland, 1573-1625, University of Glasgow Ph.D., 1983.

Cohen, B. S., Adams, J. W., Ginzburg, C. and Davies, N. A., 'Anthropology and History in the 1980s', in *Journal of Interdisciplinary History*, xii, 2, 1981.

Cowan, E. J., 'Clanship, kinship and the Campbell acquisition of Islay', in *Scottish Historical Review*, 66, 1979.

Cowan, E. J., 'The Angus-Campbells and the Origin of the Campbell-Ogilvy Feud', in *The Journal of the School of Scottish Studies, University of Edinburgh*, 25, 1981.

Coward, B., 'Disputed Inheritances: Some Difficulties of the Nobility in the Late Sixteenth and Early Seventeenth Centuries', in *Bulletin of the Institute of Historical Research*, 53, 1980.

Davies, R. R., 'The Survival of the Bloodfeud in Medieval Wales', in *History*, 63, 1978.

Davies, R. R., 'The Law of the March', in *Welsh Historical Review*, 5, 1970-71.

Donaldson, G., 'The Legal Profession in Scottish Society in the Sixteenth and Seventeenth Centuries', in *Juridical Review*, 1976.

Du Boulay, F. R. H., 'Law Enforcement in Medieval Germany', in *History*, 63, 1978.

Gane, C. H. W., 'The Effect of a Pardon in Scots Law', in *Juridical Review*, 1980.

Hale, J. R., 'Sixteenth Century Explanations of War and Violence', in *Past and Present*, 50, 1971.

Holt, M. P., 'Patterns of *Clientele* and Economic Opportunity at Court during the Wars of Religion; the Household of Francois, Duke of Anjou', in *French Historical Studies*, xiii, 1984.

Ives, E. W., 'Faction at the Court of Henry VIII: The Fall of Anne Boleyn', in *History*, 57, 1972.

James, M. E., 'The First Earl of Cumberland and the Decline of English Feudalism', in *Northern History*, i, 1966.

Kent, D. V. and Kent, F. W., 'A Self Disciplining Pact Made by the Peruzzi Family of Florence, June, 1433', in *Renaissance Quarterly*, 34, 1981.

Kiernan, V. G., 'State and Nation in Western Europe', in *Past and Present*, 31, 1965.

Lee, M., 'James VI and the aristocracy', in *Scotia*, 2, 1978.

Lee, M., 'Scotland and the 'General Crisis' of the Seventeenth Century', in *Scottish Historical Review*, 63, 1984.

Leyser, K., 'The German Aristocracy from the Ninth to the Early Twelfth Century. A Historical and Cultural Sketch', in *Past and Present*, 41, 1968.

Lyall, R., 'Politics and Poetry in Fifteenth and Sixteenth Century Scotland', in *Scottish Literary Journal*, iii, 1976.

MacTaggart, R. A., 'Assault in the Later Baron Courts', in *Juridical Review*, 7, 1962.

Mason, R., Kingship and Commonweal: Political Thought and Ideology in Reformation Scotland, University of Edinburgh Ph.D., 1983.

Peters, E. L., 'Some structural aspects of feud among the camel-herding Bedouin of Cyrenaica', in *Africa*, xxxviii, 3, 1967.

Powell, E., 'Arbitration and the Law in England in the Late Middle Ages', in *Transactions of the Royal Historical Society*, 33, 1983.

Rowney, I., 'Arbitration in Gentry Disputes of the Later Middle Ages', in *History*, 67, 1982.

Russel-Major, J., 'The Crown and the Aristocracy in Renaissance France', in *American Historical Review*, 69, 1963–64.

Sharpe, J. A., 'Domestic Homicide in Early Modern England', in *The Historical Journal*, 24, 1, 1981.

Smith, T. B., 'Master and Servant', in *Juridical Review*, New Series, 3, 1958.

Starkey, D., 'From Feud to Faction, English Politics circa 1450–1550', in *History Today*, Nov., 1982.

Stein, P., 'The Influence of Roman Law on the Law of Scotland', in *Juridical Review*, New Series, 8, 1963.

Stocker, C., 'Office as Maintenance in Renaissance France', in *Canadian Journal of History*, vi, 1971.

Stone, L., 'Interpersonal Violence in English Society, 1300–1900', in *Past and Present*, 101, 1983.

Thomas, K., 'History and Anthropology', in *Past and Present*, 24, 1963.

Westman, B. H., 'The Peasant Family and Crime in Fourteenth Century England', in *The Journal of British Studies*, 1974.

Williams, P., 'The Welsh Borderland Under Queen Elizabeth', in *Welsh Historical Review*, i, 1960.

Wormald, J. M., 'Bloodfeud, Kindred and Government in Early Modern Scotland', in *Past and Present*, 87, 1980.

Wormald, J. M., 'James VI and I: Two Kings or One?', in *History*, 68, 1983.

Wright, A. D., 'Venetian Law and Order: A Myth?', in *Bulletin of the Institute of Historical Research*, 53, 1980.

Wyntjes, S. M., 'Family Allegiance and Religious Persuasion: the Lesser Nobility and the Revolt of the Netherlands', in *The Sixteenth Century Journal*, xii, 2, 1981.

Young, J. C. B., Scottish Political Parties, 1573–1603, University of Edinburgh Ph.D., 1976.

# Index

294